For
My Good Friend
Betty Nix
in memory of a long promise

Milton Quy

Dallas 1985

The Complete Book of the
Quarter Horse

Outstanding Modern Quarter Horse Sires
Champions of the Quarter Tracks
Your Western Horse

Novels

Death Valley Slim
Hideout Mountain
Rafe
Not Grass Alone
The Last Bullet
Gunfight at the OK Corral
The Wolf That Rode
Horses, Women and Guns
Long Run *
The Overlanders
Maverick Marshal
Bandido
The Parson of Gunbarrel Basin
The Lonely Grass
The Red Sombrero
Wide Loop
Hired Hand

Come A-Smokin'
Desert of the Damned
Born to Trouble
Thief River
Caliban's Colt (*juvenile*)
Riders by Night
Gunman Gunman
The Barber of Tubac
Blood of Kings
Wild Horse Shorty
Cartridge-Case Law
Gunfighter Breed
Salt River Ranny
A Bullet for Billy the Kid
Bancroft's Banco
The Weeping Widow Mine

* Spur Award, Best Western Novel, 1959

The Complete Book of the
QUARTER HORSE

A BREEDER'S GUIDE AND TURFMAN'S REFERENCE

Nelson C. Nye

New York: A. S. Barnes and Co., Inc.
London: Thomas Yoseloff Ltd

© 1964 by Nelson C. Nye
Library of Congress Catalogue Card Number: 64-21353

A. S. Barnes and Co., Inc.
8 East 36th Street
New York 16, N. Y.

Thomas Yoseloff Ltd
18 Charing Cross Road
London W.C.2, England

6100
Printed in the United States of America

For
OTT ADAMS—
the Little Man from Alice

Acknowledgments

MANY CARLOADS OF THANKS ARE DUE THE BREEDERS AND TRACKMEN, STUDENTS and historians, trainers, owners, and jockeys, and all those others, who gave of their time and knowledge to make this volume the most comprehensive of its kind ever attempted in the history of the breed. Appreciation is also due all the guys and gals in the Performance Department of the American Quarter Horse Association who ruggedly labored at checking the data the author thankfully dumped in their laps. Several hundreds of people had a hand in the creation of the volume. To single any of them out for special mention would certainly be unfair to those omitted. Hence, to all of you—SALUD!

NELSON C. NYE

TUCSON, JUNE, 1963

Contents

Part I: Background

The Quarter Horse Defined

People connected with this breed are frequently asked, "What is a Quarter Horse? Why is he called that? Where does he come from and what is his purpose?"

Well, to answer the last question first, he is a multipurpose horse, bred in the main for all-around utility—he's a *doer*. A lot of the more discerning breeders have in the past few years become specialists, attempting to produce a horse fitted by temperament and ingrained capacity to do one thing superlatively well. Many breed cow horses for ranch and range use. Some train their efforts on the market for rodeo contest horses. A large number of establishments find their greatest satisfaction in the production of blue ribbon winners—show stock. An ever increasing number of our more affluent colleagues appear to be concentrating on track-performance horses, speed horses, sprinters. The ideal Quarter Horse, with proper training, can fill each of these roles in turn, and fill them remarkably well.

This may seem to be a pretty sweeping statement. It is not. Times without number I have personally seen it demonstrated. One mare I bred could do it all, and she was far from being an exception. Her name was Whistling Cat and she was started as a race horse. Bert Wood and I did enough with her to prove her versatility. Tremendous versatility is the foundation stone of this "using" breed. They are all good for something, and the better individuals are good at whatever you put them to, once they understand what is expected of them. There is no other breed as agile and willing, or one that is faster at a quarter of a mile.

And this brings us to the second question—Why is he called a Quarter Horse? He is called that because, properly mated, he is bred to excel all other breeds at that distance. It is a contraction of the name under which the breed was known as far back as colonial times.

Mr. Robert M. Denhardt, first Secretary of the American Quarter Horse Association, recently said to me: "Until I was drawing up the Constitution and Bylaws, no name had been selected. Jack Casement had been writing articles in several magazines advocating a Steel Dust registry—he called his and his dad's horses 'Steeldusts.' George Clegg and Ott Adams called their horses 'Billys.' I had written an article for *Western Horseman* in the late 1930's in which I showed that most of these horses sired by Billy, Rondo, Peter McCue and others were all related, and all gained their fame on quarter tracks. I suggested the name 'Quarter Horse' and afterward called all short-distance horses by that name. I did not like the designation, Jack Casement and Jack Hutchins did not like it; but where was there a better? Hutchins wanted them called Billy Horses—but not Casement; he wanted Steeldusts. So we unwillingly compromised on the term 'Quarter Horse' to designate short-distance horses, who were all related anyway."

This is the oldest breed-type of horse known to have been bred on the North American Continent. In the 1600's he was called a Colonial Quarter of a Mile Running Horse. When Sir Patrick Nisbett Edgar, of Granville County, North Carolina, produced *The American Race-Turf Register, Sportsman's Herald & General Stud Book*, in 1833, they were called "famous and celebrated American Quarter Running Horses." Now, without any fuss or feathers, we call them simply Quarter Horses.

As for the first question asked—What *is* a Quarter Horse?—Rex Cauble, one of our breeders over at Crockett, Texas, has attempted to answer it in several of his advertisements in the following words:

He's half a ton of poised and controlled energy, held on an easy rein and a hair trigger.
He's a workin' man who can earn his keep on the range all week—and be a handsome dandy at the track on Sunday afternoon.
He's proud when he stands; looks lazy when he walks—
But when he runs he can whip the tears from the corners of your eyes and plaster your hat brim against the crown.
He's big in the haunches, supple in the withers, stout in the neck and wide across the chest . . . to hold his great heart.
He's cow-smart and brave—though sometimes a clown—and to the man with sky in his eye and mud on his boots the Quarter Horse is a faithful hand. . . .
And a friend!

The Quarter Horse has been described as being many things to many men. Garford Wilkinson, of the American Quarter Horse Association, once wrote: "He is the world's fastest horse up to and including 440 yards. He is the best all-around horse that ever stood outdoors. He has no equal as a cutting horse, roping horse, ranch horse or general purpose horse for western-type riding. He is rugged and an ideal mount for children. He is intelligent, usually gentle, and easy to keep."

He was the horse that pulled the wagons, plows, and buggies of our westward migrating pioneers. He was the gambler's horse, the mount of rustlers, sheriffs, and the Texas Ranger. Sam Houston was probably the first to import his kind into Texas. Sam Bass and the notorious train robber, Black Jack Ketchum, had a particular fondness for this breed of horse. Strong infusions of his blood are presently employed to popularize the Appaloosa.

Most kinds of livestock, including horses, were developed for utility purposes, and the Quarter Horse is no exception. He might with truth be described as the greatest all-purpose horse ever devised, with God's grace, by the contriving minds of animal husbandrymen. But it is also true a great many persons had a part in the breed's development who could lay no claim to being animal husbandrymen.

Where He Came From

The Moors brought the Quarter Horse's ancestors with them when, under Tarik, they overran Spain. The Mohammedan conquest was begun in 634. The Moslems, by 696, had completed domination of most of North Africa, entering Spain in 710. Their cavalry was composed largely of Berbers, whose horses had come from Syria, Egypt, Nubia, Zeneta, Barbary, and Arabia. The great preponderance of these were Barbs, a race of desert-bred Oriental horses noted for their speed and endurance. Of Tarik's twelve thousand horsemen, only twelve were Arabs, and, everything considered, it seems unlikely that many others were mounted on purebred Arabian horses.

In the years intervening between 710 and the colonization of Spanish Guale (Florida), begun in 1565 by Admiral Pedro Menendez de Aviles, who fetched the horses there in the first place, this Oriental stock was crossed and recrossed on whatever horses Tarik's hordes found in Spain, and had produced the world-famous Spanish Horse before Menendez ever set sail. The hundred horses he fetched to America were of this breeding, *i.e.* Spanish Barbs. How, indeed, could they have been anything else?

By 1650 Spanish Guale had 79 missions, eight towns, and two royal ranches. These ranches were perpetuating the blood of Menendez's hundred horses and, although other horses of similar breeding were doubtless from time to time imported by these colonies, when the Chickasaw Indians began trafficking in horses with the Carolina planters Spanish Guale must have been line-breeding Barbs on a rather impressive scale.

These Chickasaw horses, to give them the name generally in use among the planters who bought and traded for them, were an agile, blocky type, easily recognized and seldom exceeding fourteen hands in height when the Indians began bringing them north out of Florida. How the Indians acquired them is not certainly known; it does not seem too farfetched to believe they were lured or stolen from the royal ranches.

It was at one time taken for granted that our Colonial forebears got their "wild Spanish ponies" from strays and runaways escaped or abandoned during the travels of De Soto. Others have supposed Cortez responsible. They came, however, from Spanish Guale via the Chickasaw Indians. So the horses which were raced with such zest of a sunny afternoon down the village streets and cowpaths of the Carolinas and Virginia in the 1600's were not the scrub Indian ponies which some writers have called them but, in fact, line-bred Barbs.

Here, in my opinion, was the far-back basic ingredient—the cornerstone, so to speak—of the present-day American Quarter Horse.

The second ingredient, or infusion, was added when some of our wealthier planters, having returned from extensive trips to England, began, as far back as 1619, extolling the marvels of the four-mile heat.

The first serious importers of so-called English horses, for instance, were Messrs. Wood, Sandys, and Gookin, who brought a number of their kind into Virginia as early as 1620. Although such horses were generally described as thorough-breds, England had no Thoroughbred breed until much later. It was not until 1793 that Volume One of their *General Stud Book* was issued, although an *Introduction* was published by James Weatherby, Jr. two years earlier.

But the rank and file of our Colonial planters were, by and large, pretty well satisfied with the sport of breeding and match racing their Chickasaw ponies, frequently wagering quite fantastic stakes on the outcome of such competition. This was a horse they could and did *use*; he was the best all-purpose horse of his day, very maneuverable and willing, and, moreover, he was *rugged* and enduring—a virtue much admired by the people of that time.

So it was not until the middle of the eighteenth century that distance racing and the four-mile heat really took hold of the imagination over here. In the early 1630's Governor Nicholson had legalized horse racing in Virginia. By 1690 purses of considerable magnitude were being offered the owners of breeding establishments whose progeny could show a clean set of heels to the field. Almost all these were match races—we had no circle tracks at that time—usually started by the crack of a pistol or the flutter of a dropped cloth. Somewhat later the favorite means of starting such sprints was lap-and-tap or ask-and-answer, and these are still in much favor where there are no starting gates. It was by lap-and-tap that Peter McCue was run, in the 1890s.

In 1746 the "English" stallion *Jolly Roger,† a chestnut foaled in 1741 by Roundhead out of a daughter of Croft's Partner, was fetched into Virginia. The following year Nathaniel Harrison imported Monkey, sired by Lonsdale's Bay Arabian from a daughter of Curwen's Bay Barb. Of Monkey, Sir Patrick N. Edgar, in the aforementioned *American Race-Turf Register, Sportsman's Herald & General Stud Book*, had this to say: "Was formerly the property of Lord Lonsdale, and imported (we have been informed) by the late Nathaniel Harrison, Esq. of Brandon, Va., at 22 years of age, in the year 1747; foaled in the year 1725—Got by the Lonsdale Bay Arabian—Curwen's Bay Barb—Byerly Turk, out of a natural Arabian Mare. Monkey got an excellent stock of horses in America, and upwards of 250 colts were produced by him. He died in 1754, as we learn."

Of *Jolly Roger, the same source tells us: "(Alias 'Roger of the Vale,') a chestnut horse, bred by Mr. Craddock; foaled in 1741—Got by Roundhead —his dam by Croft's Partner—Woodcock—Croft's Bay Barb—Makeless— Brimmer—Dickey Pearson (son of Old Dodsworth)—Burton Barb Mare. Jolly Roger died at the stable of Mr. James Belford, in Grenville County, Va., in 1772, aged 31 years. He produced most excellent bottomed stock in Virginia. —signed John Goodrum."

From which it may be seen that these, like most of the subsequent importations prior to 1800, were purely Orientals, many of whom, by bloodline, were predominately Barb.

It might be well, here, to examine one of the pages in the front matter of Sir Patrick's 1833 *Stud Book*, a copy of which I have before me. Immediately following several pages of testimonials, captioned "To The Public," there appears the following declaration:

"The English Blood Horse was known in Virginia long before any Stud Book ever made its appearance in England; and pedigrees were only communicated by the certificates of private gentlemen and persons of honor and integrity, which were often lost; hence the great uncertainty of many of the recorded pedigrees of the present day. Many English horses' names never appeared on the foregoing book; hence a very great difficulty arises in tracing many of them, whose stock are valuable at this time, and trace directly back to their loins. Dabster and Bulle Rock (we have been informed) were the first horses imported from England, and they were, in Virginia, what a Barb or an Arabian is in England. Jolly Roger was so distinguished a horse, in Virginia, that he was considered to be a horse of

† Asterisks preceding names of horses denote importation.

the purest blood; and that his pedigree was perfect, from the very high standing of his progeny, which is anxiously sought after by the judicious breeders of the present day. His progeny were of the very first order. In his day, also that of Fearnought, Old Janus (1222), Monkey, Othello, Silver Eye, and Moreton's Traveller, the pedigrees of Virginia horses, when they reached the Godolphin and Darley Arabians, generally stop there; but when they terminated with the above horses' names, they were very deservedly held in the highest estimation.

"It has been said of Fearnought that he was called the 'Goldolphin Arabian' of America, and particularly of Virginia; but Jolly Roger may very justly vie with him, for distinction, at least a very great share of it, as he was anterior, and there never was a horse in Virginia at whose name, and Old Janus, so many *thorough bred* pedigrees terminate—as they were the very first founders of the Virginia Race Horse. In ancient days quarter racing was much in fashion, and generally kept up, in Virginia, until the importation of Fearnought; after that, distance racers were sought after, which have been held in the greatest estimation until the present time."

Now let's see what Sir Patrick had to say about *Janus: "A chestnut horse, 'sui generis,' of low stature, about 14 hands, ¾ of an inch high, bred by Mr. Swymmer, imported into Virginia about the year 1752; foaled in 1746—'The stock of Old Janus in Virginia and the Southern States has been distinctly marked for the last fifty years as if he had been of a different species. For power, swiftness and durability, they have been equalled by no other breed of horses.' Janus had great bone and muscle, round, very compact, large quarters, and very swift; all of which desirable qualities he imparted so perfectly to his progeny that many of them remain in the stock at this remote period, and great speed and muscular form are still found in many horses whose pedigrees reach him, if accurately traced through different branches; or when, as it is sometimes called, there is a 'double Janus cross.' Nearly all his immediate descendants were 'swift quarter Nags'; they never could run far. He was the sire of an immense number of short distance Racers, brood mares and stallions. Indeed, a remote cross of him in the most superior race horses of the present day is generally sought after, as an extract from a letter, lately received, will show:—'A remote cross of Janus is indispensably necessary, at this day, in a distance race horse; indeed, there is no other at this time which can be said to be more desirable; as, to use the slang of a Jockey, *Speed always will help out bottom.*'

"He was the property of the late Mr. John Goode, Sen. of Mecklenburgh County, Va., who agreed to give 150 pounds, Va. currency, for him, provided he was safely delivered at his stable in the winter of 1779 or 1780, being in the 34th year of his age. Janus started for the stable of his new proprietor, Mr. Goode, as aforesaid, and progressed as far as the stable of Col. Haynes, where he died in 1780. He was got by Old Janus (son of the Godolphin Arabian out of the Little Hartley Mare)—his dam by Fox—his grand dam by the Bald Galloway." These remarks of Sir Patrick on the subject of *Janus were attested by (1757) Mordecai Boothe, (1780) John Goode, Sen., (1781) John Bilbo, (1782) Allan Young and Samuel Young, and, in 1783, by Samuel Goode.

Imported Janus was, for my money, the No. 1 progenitor of the modern Quarter Horse—the first great sire of the kind of horses we have today. Sir Patrick's book is generously sprinkled with famous and celebrated American Quarter Running sons and daughters of this eighteenth-century paragon who was bred almost entirely, as were most of those other imported stallions, to Chickasaw mares, and the daughters and granddaughters of Chickasaw mares. Many of his progeny were listed by Sanders D. Bruce in the first three or four volumes of the *American Stud Book*, before it was decided by Thoroughbred breeders to forget their debt to the American Quarter Running Horse.

According to Skinner's *The American Farmer*, *Janus was considered "the most perfectly formed horse ever seen in Virginia by the most skillful connoisseurs" and as "remarkable for roundness of contour, strength of articulation" and generally great power. His get and progeny "partook of these qualities in an eminent degree," exhibiting even in the third and fourth generations "the same compactness of form, strength and power."

With the joining of Janus 1222 with the Chickasaw (Barb) mares the Indians had introduced into Virginia and the Carolinas, the foundation of our present breed was laid and given impetus; the progeny of such unions became the fastest horses at the quarter the world has ever seen. Those of his get which could do four miles or better have come down to posterity through the *American Stud Book* as Thoroughbreds (notable examples are Meade's Celer and Buie); those that could not were called American Quarter Running Horses. The same yardstick appears to have been applied to the get and progeny of Flimnap, Florizel, Oroonoko, and Saltram. For their blood, too, is found in both breeds. What you might call the long and the short of it.

Sol Torey, in the July-August, 1942, issue of *The Western Horseman*, described it this way: "During the years of the first importation, before the 'gentlemen breeders' became more enamored with racing for its own sake than as a proving ground for breeding horses, a large number of

1. Lady of the Lake, by Little Joe out of Silver Queen, by Warrior. Bred by Ott Adams.

2. Imported Bonnie Scotland, 1857.

3. Imported Glencoe.

4. American Eclipse, 1823. From an old print.

Chickasaw mares, and other fast mares which could not be called Chickasaws, were crossed with the line-bred Orientals such as Janus. We must
remember that there was no Thoroughbred breed at that time; the blood
animals were simply animals carrying a high percentage of Arabian and
Oriental blood. A number of the produce of such crosses were accepted
by the racing clique as suitable breeding animals from which to get colts.
This was a matter of necessity, for only relatively few original importations
were possible."

Thus, it is apparent that the same identical blood *originally* went into
both the American Thoroughbred and the American Quarter Horse. The
race track became the determining factor. This is not theory. The proof is
self-apparent in the first three volumes of the *American Stud Book*.

Important as *Janus was to the founding and improvement of the American Thoroughbred, his worth was immeasurably greater in what he did
for the American Quarter Horse. One of the greatest complaints of the
hard-boot brethren was that the bulk of his get were not stayers. The
owner of Janus appears to have worked up considerable sweat over this,
because in the *American Turf Register* he wrote with some acerbity:
"Among the vulgar errors, perhaps the most absurd is that the stock of
Old Janus wanted bottom. This arose from his getting the speediest quarter
horses out of ordinary mares. The FASTEST were out of half-bred or
three parts bred Jolly Roger of Fearnought mares. Whenever he had blood
mares, he got horses that ran any distance."

There is no question but that he got an amazing number of extraordi-
narily fast Quarter Horses, many of them out of straight Chickasaw mares.
And why not? These were Barbs, and it has been said with much authority
that, if the truth were known, the Godolphin Arabian was pretty obviously
a Barb in everything but name. In Sir Patrick's book one may find more
than one hundred head of horses and mares carrying the blood of *Janus.
Sir Patrick, who had a deep love for horses, identified their extreme speed
with the letters F.A.Q.R., meaning Famous American Quarter Racer.

Mr. A. J. Davis, commenting on imported Janus in the *American Turf
Register*, declared: "He was the sire of many distinguished quarter or short
distance horses. His stock were handy, handsome, small-boned, with heavy
but short muscles." Unquestionably *Janus put more muscle and heavier
quarters on his progeny than any other sire of that time, and I suspect
they must, at least in the aggregate, have appeared not greatly unlike the
horse we have today.

Certainly the greatest fame of this Janus stock has been for blinding
speed and their remarkable ability in the stud to consistently pass it—

along with most of those other marked qualities—into the performance of subsequent generations. They were fast and prepotent.

That's a pretty good phrase to hang up in your tack room. It is one of the things that should be firmly kept in mind.

Some Early Beginnings

Garford Wilkinson has said, writing in the *Quarter Horse Journal* of 1960: "In the early days of his existence the Quarter Horse was the darling of those who were determined to produce an animal that could run a quarter mile faster than any other large, solid-footed, man-carrying mammal."

In his remarkable book, *The Horse of America*, Mr. J. F. D. Smith wrote before the American Revolution: "In the southern part of the Colony [Virginia] and in North Carolina they are much attached to quarter racing, which is always a match between two horses to run one quarter of a mile, straight out, being merely an exertion of speed; and they have a breed that performs it with astonishing velocity, beating every other with great ease, but they have no bottom. However, I am confident that there is not a horse in England, nor perhaps in the whole world, that can excell them in rapid speed; and these likewise make excellent saddle horses for the road."

Declared Dr. John B. Irving (*The Turf in South Carolina*): "Before the year 1754, the horses most regarded in South Carolina for the draft or the saddle were known as Chickasaw breed. This was a stock of horses originally introduced into Florida by the early Spanish. They were in general well formed, active and easily kept, but small. The mares seldom exceeded thirteen and a half hands, but being remarkable for their muscular development and great endurance; when crossed with the imported Thoroughbred they produced animals of great beauty, strength, and fleetness, improving thereby the stock of the country in a very great degree."

The Thoroughbred, as we have learned, was not in 1754 a "breed." Substitute "line-bred Oriental" for Dr. Irving's "imported Thoroughbred," and you will have the picture as it really was. Because of breeding practices which still are being continued—perhaps more so now than in some while, and certainly on a more sweeping scale—I think this difference should be carefully noted.

One of those above-cited "imported Thoroughbreds" was Flimnap, a bay horse foaled in 1765 by South (a grandson of the Godolphin Arabian) out of a mare by Cygnet (a son of the Godolphin Arabian). I believe most authorities would agree that by most of the yardsticks we have for measuring him, Flimnap in fact must have been pretty nearly pure Barb. He was one of the most popular stallions in South Carolina in the 1700s. We are informed that during the Revolution several brisk skirmishes were fought to hold or gain possession of him. He sired such excellent stayers as Hampton's Paragon and Betsey Baker; also superior Quarter stock (out of Chickasaw mares and their daughters).

Another great horse of that time was Fallower, who stood, also, in South Carolina during the prominence of quarter racing. It has been suggested that he sired the dam of Timoleon, one of the more famous sons of the celebrated Sir Archy. It has been said that Timoleon sired the dam of Harry Bluff, who has been called the father of Steel Dust, one of the greatest short horses in the history of Texas.

Sir Archy (imported *in utero* and subsequently described as the Godolphin Arabian of America) was by *Diomed, son of Florizel by Herod, and foaled in 1805; dam was *Castianira by Rockingham, son of Highflyer, by Herod. Sir Archy, like Fallower, Oroonoko, Saltram, Flimnap, and others frequently described as Thoroughbreds, was by blood and background an obvious Oriental. There were no Thoroughbreds yet; there were Chickasaws and American Quarter Running Horses and imported Orientals. The Thoroughbred was on the way but was not, *per se*, established as yet.

As the Thoroughbred became more firmly intrenched the Quarter Running Horse increasingly sped toward eclipse. He never quite disappeared completely from the eastern seaboard; even at the height of the popularity of the four-mile heat his blood still could be found. But he certainly lost his running room and came within an ace of losing breed identity. He was shoved back into the mill-pond country and went with hardier persons, the pioneers, adventurers, and gamblers, into Illinois and Kentucky and down into Louisiana and Texas, and was, in this manner, removed from the beaten tracks and from the haunts of fashion and beauty.

Once again he was harnessed to wagons and plows, but he came into his own with the fly-by-night gentry, who loved a fast horse as they did their own lives. Then the cow crowd took hold of him and crowned him king. In the West he was used for a multiplicity of purposes. He was crossed on Mustangs to build up remudas. Out in the brush he became a race horse again, helping money change hands in lap-and-tap matches. He did tasks no Thoroughbred could possibly have stood up to; and the cow crowd finally built a registry for him.

He has always been a *hot blood*, and is today, breeding true consistently when given so much as a halfway chance. Quarter Horse bloodlines have proved sufficiently prepotent to withstand outcrossing for nearly three hundred years.

It has been observed that his best outside nick has invariably been achieved when mated with his close cousin, the American Thoroughbred. All down through the years, since his original cross with the imported Orientals, he has absorbed continuing infusions of Thoroughbred blood; still a knowledgeable person can spot a real Quarter Horse without much trouble. He has that certain way of going, those telltale quarters, wide chest, a close-coupled topline, long underneath, powerful throughout, legs set well under him. A good rustler, an eager doer, he can hit full speed in from two to three strides.

In *Champions of the Quarter Tracks* I wrote: "For well over one hundred years without benefit of registry the worth of the Quarter Running Horse was measured solely by the yardstick of track and stud performance. His kind were bred to excel all others at distances up to and including one quarter of a mile, and those who did best by that yardstick were rebred, the majority of all others being swiftly forgotten—which explains why most of the better present-day stock goes back on one side or the other to little more than a handful of very great horses. They go back to those that could pass it all on."

For many years the Quarter Horse and the Thoroughbred had many things in common, their greatest differences being discernible in the way they ran when put on a track. "Since the first period of racing in America," wrote Sanders Bruce in his introduction to Volume II of the *American Stud Book*, "the annals of the turf are graced with the names of many horses and mares, the pedigrees of which do not come up to the standard. These of themselves, and their progeny after them, from their creditable performances on the turf, have made distinguished records. The reputations they acquired gave them importance in the sporting world. Though not up to standard, these were bought and sold, and even run, as Thoroughbreds."

I would guess that these were Quarter Horses.

In a time when only Thoroughbreds were allowed to compete on recognized tracks, more than just a handful of Quarterbred stock, and others not "cleanly" bred, were registered as Thoroughbreds, to get them running room and a greater dollar value. It is, for instance, pretty apparent that Peter McCue, though registered as a Thoroughbred and raced as one, belonged on the Quarter Horse side of the fence. The stated aim and earnest desire of the hard-boot brethren was to propagate "distance" horses, but, in actual fact, they got a great many sprinters. Some of these must have had Quarter Horse genes.

Not a few Quarter Horses over the years have demonstrably been able to "run all out" for much greater distances than commonly supposed. Some, too, tend to run shorter with each generation without continued infusions of Thoroughbred blood. I doubt that this proves anything more significant than lack of discernment on the part of the breeder.

The current tendency, particularly in the establishments of those presently breeding for track performance, is to infuse into each mating more Thoroughbred blood. This has had a great deal of precedent; some of our more successful operators have always done this. Nor have all of these gentlemen been out to get sprinters. There has been some gnashing of teeth about this on the part of some breeders not dedicated to the turf, but I do not think we need be greatly alarmed.

Legendary Sires; Formation of Early Families

It seems rather unlikely the race horse boys, through continuing use of Thoroughbred blood, will noticeably damage the future of the breed either in appearance or performance.

Less than a tenth of all horses registered by the AQHA in 1962 were bred primarily for track competition. Of those that were, very few indeed carried Thoroughbred blood in excess of 50 per cent. In 1961 the Association registered 50,820 Quarter Horses; as of January 1, 1963, a grand total of 252,138 horses had been registered since the *Stud Book* was opened in 1941.

Breeders still are permitted to outcross to the Thoroughbred. As much as for any other purpose, this is allowed to make sure no stallion of extraordinary merit will be left with his goodies on the outside looking in. Persons going outside the breed in this fashion are compelled, however, to take a considerable gamble. One of the parents must be a registered Quarter Horse. Before the foal from such a mating is eligible for registration he or she must qualify, through track competition, for the Register of Merit, and must then be passed by a bleach-eyed inspector for Quarter Horse conformation and action. Failure to pass either of these requirements will render the foal permanently unregisterable. And, in addition to all the time, red tape, and trouble, the breeder, owner, or whoever is taking this gamble, will be out of pocket about $2500, because it takes, these days, about that much of an expenditure to campaign a young horse sufficiently to get it qualified—even granting the capacity and ability.

In the good old days now too far removed to recall the extent and pinch of their hardships—back, say, about the turn of the century—a number of stallions rose to sufficient prominence and popularity to establish what have commonly been referred to as "families"—individual strains within the breed.

Following *Janus there were several lesser strains which have now been all but forgotten, though their worth may be found far back in the blood of horses prominent at the present time. Much of this blood was lost during the hiatus of interest following the rise of the American Thoroughbred. There were Tigers and Whips, and others whose names I cannot offhand recall. Then the Billy horses appeared, and the Steeldusts, Cold Decks, and Rondos.

About 1900, give or take a few years in either direction, the breed was treated to a number of paragons whose legends are still with us. Most prominent of these, when measured by present importance and current usefulness of progeny, are:

Traveler, unmatchable in his own right and his shining place in Quarter Horse history more securely settled by two great sons, Little Joe and Possum, themselves full brothers and unshakable monuments to the demonstrable worth of Traveler's astonishing prepotence through their own remarkable progeny such as Ace of Diamonds, Zantanon, Dutch, Joe Moore, Grano de Oro, Little King, Guinea Pig, Red Cloud, Miss Panama, Skidoo, Miss South St. Mary's, King, San Siemon, Hill Country, Stella Moore, Hobo, Red Joe, Billy Van, Joe Bailey of Gonzales, Will Wright, Little Joe Jr., Joker Joe, Bacchus, Hoddy, Buster Brown, Tony, Mark, No Butt, and others too numerous to mention.

Peter McCue another "boss hoss" whose performance and progeny have assured him an unassailable place in the annals of breed accomplishment, and whose name will live on through such outstanding sons as John Wilkens, Harmon Baker, Hickory Bill, Badger, Jack McCue, Billy Sunday, Buck Thomas, Chief, A. D. Reed, Duck Hunter, Cotton-Eyed Joe, Shiek; and such daughters as Carrie Nation, Old Squaw, Mary McCue, the Houseparty Mare, Cheyenne Maid, Old Allie, Belle McCue, Hattie Jackson, Emma Hill, Betty Watkins, Dollie Spokes, Juanita Armstrong, Kate Bender, Miss Cornet, Oakford Queen; and such illustrious later individuals as Joe Hancock (himself a sire of considerable magnitude), Red Man, Roan Wolf, Nettie Hill, Grey Badger II, Buck Hancock, Buddy Waggoner, Lady Lux, Badger's Grey Lady, Moca Burnett, War Chief, Chubby, Bill Thomas (who was, according to J. B. Ferguson, one of the greatest sires in the United States during the early '40s), Joe Tom, Little Joe the Wrangler, Midnight,

Young Midnight, Midnight Jr., One-Eyed Waggoner, Revenue, Harmon Baker's Star, J. B. King, Mr. Juniper Bar, Little Meow and She Kitty.

There was Himyar (TB), who, through his Thoroughbred sons Domino and Plaudit, got us Question Mark and his illustrious progeny, Miss Bank and Band Play, Tidy Step, Kansas Kate, Jap, Little Red Raffles, Blackout, Brown Deacon, B'ar Hunter, B'ar Hunter II, Barbra B, Miss Beach, Beau Bob, Rumpus, Duke, and others.

Lock's Rondo gave us Yellow Jacket through Little Rondo. Yellow Jacket sired Cowboy (P-12), who gave us Shue Fly, Hard Twist and all his get, Billy Likes, and Mug. Yellow Jacket also got Yellow Boy and Nettie Jacket, dam of Lone Star, who sired Rainy Day, the daddy of Ben Hur, father of Waggoner's Rainy Day (P-13), who gave us Raindrop and Dan Waggoner, among others.

Undoubtedly I am missing quite a few in tackling this subject, some of them greater perhaps than some of those being listed; I am including only those which come most easily to mind.

*Chicle (TB), sired Chicaro who got Flying Bob, sire of Queenie, Dee Dee, Bay Anne, Lucky, Punkin, Effie, Danger Boy H, Sug, May Flower, Dona Dee, Baby Shot, Bob KK and his whole slue of good ones, Shu Shu Baby, Diamond Bob and his get, Senator Bob and the good ones he's given us, Flying Bob Jr., Babe Ruth (Lady Lee, Magnolia), Jimmy, Bob Randle; Chicaro also sired Chicaro Bill who put into the breed such sterling performers as Senor Bill, Arizona Girl, Bill Doolin and Parker's Chicaro.

From *Leamington we got Bonnie Joe and his son Joe Blair, who gave a deal of their blood to the modern Quarter Horse through Uncle Jimmy Gray and Joe Reed (P-3) father of that great speed strain which, implemented by sprint blood from Himyar and further enriched by early foot from Traveler, produced Joe Reed II, the father of many, including, with help from the running Ashwells, the prepotent Leo, perhaps the very greatest sire in modern sprint history, certainly the greatest brood-mare sire ever to have graced this breed. As of 1961, available figures (through 1949) indicate Leo as the sire of 272 starters, of which 170 were winners; his father, Joe Reed II, got 146 starters, of which 88 were winners. (We'd like to be able to show the total number of registered get for each of the stallions in this group of great sires, and follow up with like figures for each grandson and granddaughter.)

Just as an example of how greatly things can change in a remarkably short space of time, the 1958 list of Leading Sires of Racing Register of Merit Qualifiers showed (through July 31st) the following scores:

5. Rocky Mountain Tom.

6. Tomb of Sir Archy. Foaled on Ben Lomond Estate near Rock Castle, Virginia in 1805, Sir Archy was the first Thoroughbred and sire of note which could truly be called "American."

7. The Mystery Horse, Traveler.

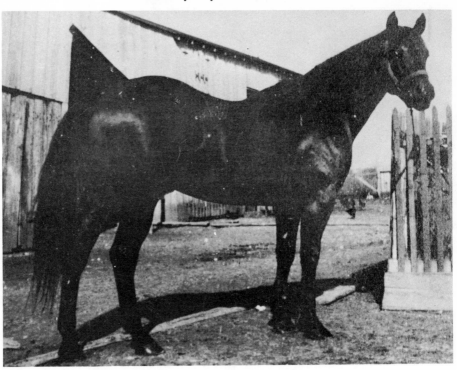

8. Peter McCue in the days when he raced.

9. Domino, by Himyar.

10. Cowboy, by Yellow Jacket.

11. Flying Bob.

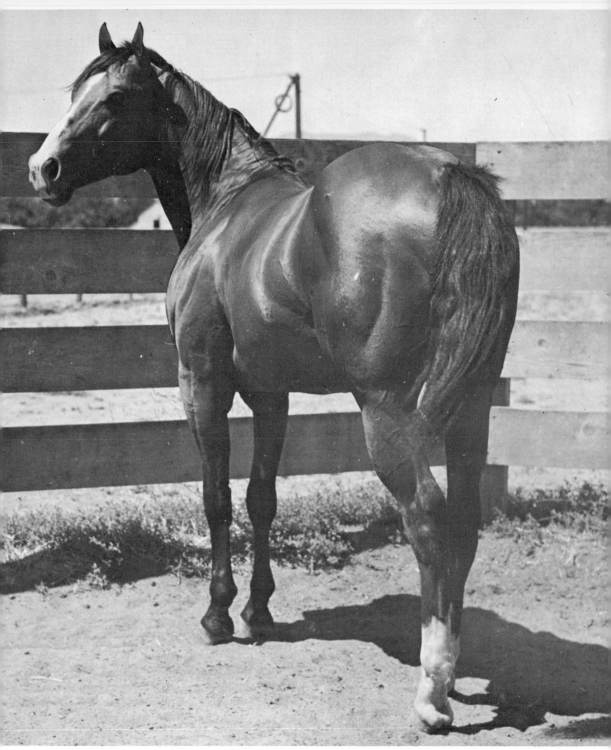

12. Dee Dee, champion quarter running stallion, 1944-45.

13. Squaw H, an old-time Quarter mare who also ran a little.

14. The original Ben Hur, famous sire of several celebrated horses. He once ran a full mile against a sprinting Thoroughbred and was only defeated in the last 100 yards.

Sire	AAA	AA	A	Total
LEO	35	49	28	112
Three Bars (TB)	55	35	15	105
JOE REED II	7	29	26	62
PIGGIN STRING (TB)	15	19	16	50
Top Deck (TB)	19	20	1	40
TEXAS DANDY	10	16	13	39
VANDY	17	17	5	39
Flying Bob	6	10	21	37
HARD TWIST	10	18	8	36
My Texas Dandy	4	5	25	34

Horses in capital letters are Register of Merit qualifiers. The same is true of other tables in this book.

We must include, too, among remarkable sires since the turn of the century, the imported French Thoroughbred Porte Drapeau, celebrated in short horse circles for what one son, his get and progeny, have put into this breed. From My Texas Dandy (one-half TB) have come the "Iron Horse" Clabber, Texas Jr, Texas Star, Colonel Clyde, Texas Dandy, and Captain White Socks. Some Clabber get which will be remembered for a couple of more decades at least are Tonta Gal, Jeep B, Buster, Clabber II, Clabbertown G, Clabber's Lady V, Clabber's Flossie V, Little Bit, Wagon N, and others. Through 1961 Clabber II is credited with 12 winners from 26 starters; back to 1945 he has had 131 foals registered, of which 72 have started, 37 qualifying, of which 17 have run in AAA time. Clabber is shown to have 81 registered foals, of which 59 have started, 26 qualifying for ROM. My Texas Dandy, himself, has had 127 registered foals, of which 68 started and 23 qualified. Texas Dandy (the Finley Horse) has had 159 registered foals, 87 starters, of which 44 made Register of Merit.

In 1959 the official Leading Sires of Register of Merit Qualifiers list reads, for the top ten:

Sires of 18 or more qualifiers	Total	AAA & AA	Sires with 13 or more AAA & AA get	AAA & AA	Total
Three Bars (TB)	125	110	Three Bars (TB)	110	125
LEO	124	97	LEO	97	124
JOE REED II	64	39	Top Deck (TB)	47	48
PIGGIN STRING (TB)	51	35	VANDY	45	50
VANDY	50	45	JOE REED II	39	64
Top Deck (TB)	48	47	PIGGIN STRING (TB)	35	51
TEXAS DANDY	40	27	HARD TWIST	31	39
HARD TWIST	39	31	TEXAS DANDY	27	40
Flying Bob	37	16	CLABBER II	25	29
My Texas Dandy	34	9	War Bam (TB)	22	29

In 1961 this list, for the same ten places, shaped up like this:

Sires of 20 or more qualifiers	Reg. foals	Start-ers	ROM	Sires of 9 or more AAA get			AAA
Three Bars (TB)	316	220	159	Three Bars (TB)			96
LEO	445	272	146	LEO			54
Top Deck (TB)	140	112	70	Top Deck (TB)			40
VANDY	198	109	67	VANDY			32
JOE REED II	276	146	66	Depth Charge (TB)	74	68	24
PIGGIN STRING	83	83	51	LIGHTNING BAR	141	45	22
Depth Charge	74	68	46	Direct Win (TB)	114	56	20
TEXAS DANDY	159	87	44	SPOTTED BULL (TB)	69	46	20
HARD TWIST	152	79	40	Little Request (TB)	58	33	18
CLABBER II	131	72	37	CLABBER II	131	72	17

Twentieth on this list is Question Mark with 205 registered foals, and 59 starters, of which 25 made Register of Merit. This horse was truly one of the finest sires the breed has produced in a good many years. I don't think he ever had a single top mare, yet latest figures from the Performance Division of the AQHA assign him 64 starters, of which five have made AAA, 10 AA, and 10 straight A. At the time of his death, early in December of 1962, he left 15 mares safely in foal.

Question Mark was a grand-looking horse of almost faultless conformation, tremendous speed, and great stamina; unfortunately—it was the curse of his life—he was a golden palomino, a color that was anathema to the men who had the top mares he so richly deserved but never got.

He was foaled in the spring of 1937, bred by Waite Phillips at Cimarron, New Mexico, who had leased the sensational race mare Pepito (she once held the three-eighths record at Tanforan) for the plainly expressed purpose of producing a truly great horse. She was by Kenward (TB) out of Phyllis F by Withers. Phillips bred her to his celebrated Quarter Horse stallion Plaudit (1657), a palomino bred by Tom Mills of Meeker, Colorado. This Plaudit was by King Plaudit by Plaudit (TB), famed winner of the Kentucky Derby of 1898, in which he defeated the previously invincible Lieber Karl by a full length. Plaudit, the Thoroughbred, was one of the two best sons of the speed sire Himyar, Domino being the other.

Practically everyone laughed when it was decided to ready Question Mark for track competition. Yellow Jacket had been up against this color barrier a number of years earlier and, after cutting a swath across Texas pocketbooks, had been dismissed as a freak. Folks from the working ranches never could work up any real interest in what they dismissed as "duded-up hides."

Frankie Burns got Question Mark ready. Old-timers at the short tracks will tell you this horse had a very distinctive way of going, running close to the ground with his head straight out like a chaparral cock. They will tell you, now that he's gone, that he never gave a whisker less than his best, and that Question Mark's best was something to tie to; but in his racing days ranchers just wouldn't believe a "picture horse" could run.

When he stormed his way across the tracks of New Mexico and Colorado, smashing records and strewing reputations in the wake of his flying hoofs, people who had good mares refused to admit that his tremendous reach and win after win could be tangible evidence of bred-in ability. He would move like greased lightning and, to those of us who watched that white forelock flying between laid-back ears, he appeared always completely in control of himself. Time and again I have heard such disgruntled exclamations as "You just can't beat that hide for luck!"

The only luck that horse ever had was hard luck.

He was the victim of pride and prejudice, a casualty of the color barrier. In all his life I doubt if he was bred to a single top mare. Yet he got some running horses—five AAA's. He got good ranch and show stock beyond counting, and out of the sorriest kind of mares. Guy Purinton, a long-time breeder and campaigner of track stock, once said to me: "Question Mark is one of the greatly underrated studs of our time; he's had great runners out of unknown mares. If he had been bred to top mares he could have been the best."

He was the kind of horse that never let you down. His last time out indisputably demonstrates not only his capability but the kind of courage and heart he had. This was a three-horse field, a real test for giants— Question Mark pitted against the best of his day, the celebrated Joe Lewis (named after the fighter) and the Hepler brothers' sensational Shue Fly.

It was a half-mile go, with a judge at each eighth pole. Question Mark, coming away from the score, showed less than his usual verve, but, going into the second eighth after appearing to falter, that gleaming yellow hide drove into the lead. He seemed, just past the quarter, to stagger and it became plain that he was in trouble. The incredible thing is that he not only managed to last the full course, but that he overhauled and passed that track-burning Hepler mare on a broken pastern joint.

The applause was tremendous and burst like toppled thunder when that Trinidad crowd was told what he had done. He had to be helped into the winner's circle; when the announcement was made that he had run his last race more than one pair of eyes shed unashamed tears. This was a *great* horse; he had blinding speed (clocked several times in :21.8 for the quarter, :33.2 for three-eighths), tremendous heart, and as fine a disposition as any stallion in my experience. He died in December of 1962, a lonely old horse, ignored to the last by those who sought the very things he had in such incalculable abundance—scorned for the curse of a golden hide.

The Cold Hard Facts

A number of years ago Helen Michaelis, then Secretary of the American Quarter Horse Association, presented breeders and public with a bill of particulars to what she described as "Leading Quarter Horse Families," which was incorporated into the first two or three editions of the AQHA *Stud Book*. An indefatigable researcher, the ideas she developed about these "families" were largely substantiated by earlier writings.

Here are her findings:

JANUS, 1752	Established by *Janus, 1746–80 by Old Janus—Mare by Fox
PEACOCK, 1764	Established by Old Peacock, 1760–86 by *Janus–*Old Spain
MARK ANTONY, 1767	Establisled by Lee's Mark Anthony, 1763–78
BABRAM, 1770	Established by Goode's Babram, 1766–81 by *Janus–Mare by *Janus
BACCHUS, 1778	Established by Old Bacchus, 1774–89 by Goode's Babram—Mare by *Janus
CELER, 1780	Established by Meade's Celer, 1776–1804 by *Janus–Brandon—Mare by *Aristotle
TWIGG, 1782	Established by Old Twigg, 1778–? by *Janus–Switch—Mare by *Janus
BRIMMER, 1787	Established by Goode's Brimmer, 1766–86, by Harris' Eclipse—Poll Glaxen
PRINTER, 1804	Established by Printer, 1780–1828 by *Janus
WHIP, 1809	Established by Blackburn's Whip, 1805–28 by *Whip–Soeckleback, Randolph's Celer
TIGER, 1816	Established by Tiger, 1812–32 by Blackburn's Whip—Jane Hunt
COPPERBOTTOM, 1832	Established by Copperbottom, 1828–60 by Sir Archy—Mare by Buzzard
SHILOH, 1848	Established by Shiloh, 1844–69 by Union Shiloh
STEEL DUST, 1849	Established by Steel Dust, 1845–74 by Harry Bluff (?)—Mare unknown
BILLY, 1866	Established by Old Billy, 1860–86 by Shiloh—Ram Cat by Steel Dust

COLD DECK, 1872	Established by Old Cold Deck, 1879–1901 by Old Billy—Maudy
ROAN DICK, 1883	Established by Roan Dick, 1879–1901 by Black Nick —Mare by Greenstreet's Boanerges
RONDO, 1884	Established by Old Rondo, 1880–97 by Whalebone —Mittie Stephens
TRAVELER	Established by Traveler, 1885–1910; Pedigree untraced
SYKES, 1891	Established by Sykes Rondo, 1887–1907 by McCoy Billy—Grasshopper
FRED, 1897	Established by Old Fred, 1893–1915 by Black Ball —Mare by John Crowder
PETER McCUE, 1899	Established by Peter McCue, 1895–1923 by Dan Tucker—Nora M
BLAKE, 1900	Established on Steel Dust, Shiloh, and Brimmer lines
JOE BAILEY, 1911	Established by Old Joe Bailey, 1907–34 by Eureka— Susie McQuirter

Assuming all her hypotheses to be more or less accurate and her information to be founded on fact, this data still would not appear to be a great deal of use to breeders. Obviously these strains—if all their founders were as prepotent as we have ample assurance and documented evidence to accept without question where Traveler and Peter McCue are concerned— must have exhibited certain singular traits or other characteristics which would have made them, like the earlier Januses, easily identifiable. No such marks exist today. They have been, in the intervening years, so crossed with each other—and *out*crossed—as to have lost all family identity.

Even later sires, of proven prepotence, such as Joe Reed (P–3), Joe Reed II, Clabber, My Texas Dandy, Leo, Cowboy (P–12), Flying Bob, Three Bars, Hard Twist or even such sires as Top Deck, Tonto Bars Gill, Depth Charge, Vandy, and Moon Deck, have had their get so crossed and recrossed in the continuing hunt for early foot as to have lost not only strain identity but also, in some cases, *breed* identity. Some of them look like Thoroughbreds.

Unpalatable as some may find them, these are the facts.

One cannot, in all honesty, always know a Quarter Horse without greater aid than the human eye—and the same may be said of many a Thoroughbred. They are not confined to one shape or size. We defy anyone to say indisputably that Peter McCue—or Traveler, either—was Thoroughbred or Quarter Horse. We all have our notions, but notions aren't facts. Both

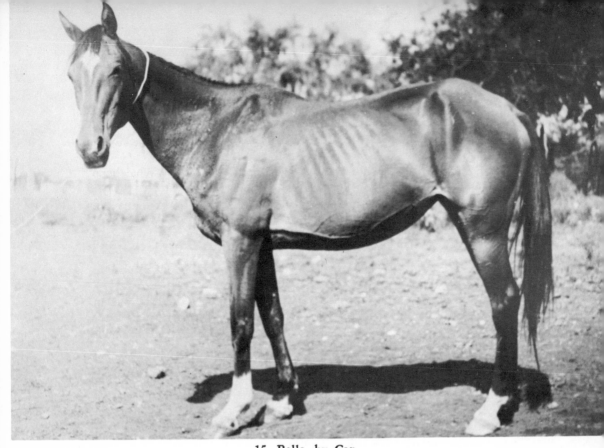

15. Belle, by Cap.

16. Jap, 1944, by Raffles, TB, out of Lady H., by Red Bug.

Photo by Ray Thurman

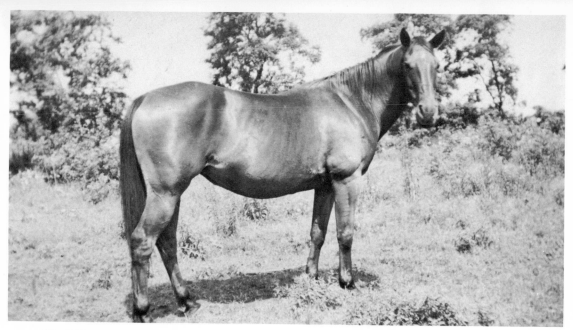

17. Old Bay Mare, by Waggoner's Rainy Day out of a Waggoner Quarter mare. Bred by the Waggoner Ranch, she was foaled in 1933, and is the dam of Barbra B, Little Brown Jug, Coon Dog II, Phoebe Snow, Merry Legs, and Bert's Bonnie. Photo made in 1947.

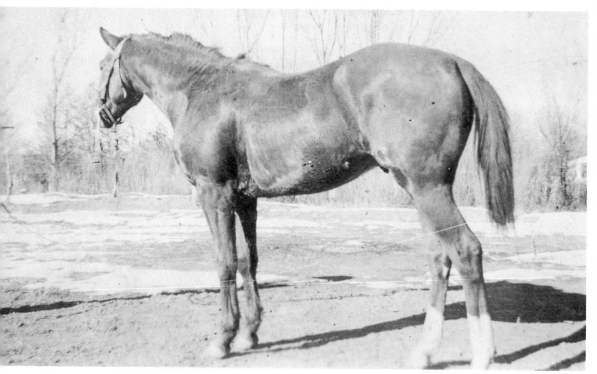

18. An early running horse, Red Shoemaker.

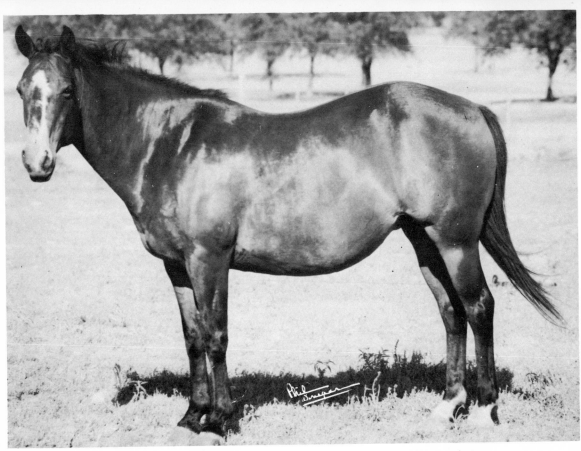

19. Nita Joe, by Little Joe. Dam of Bacchus and daughter of Belle.

Photo by Phil Winegar

20. Lady Edgells, by Ben Hur. Foaled 1932.

21. Saladin, by Ding Bob.

22. A great match race horse, Waggoner's Rainy Day, P-13.

Photo by Dudley Young

24. Celebrated Hard Twist, champion quarter running stallion 1946-7, and co-stallion champion in 1951.

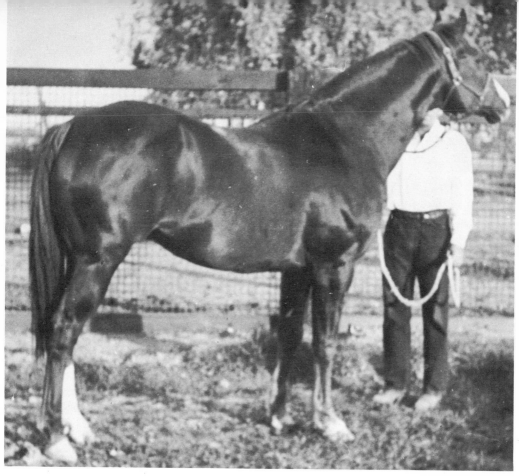

23. Joe Reed II in a photo taken by the author in 1947.

25. My Texas Dandy, by *Porte Drapeau, TB.

26. The "Iron Horse," Clabber.

27. Texas Star, by Lone Star.
Foaled 1935. Bred by George Clegg.

28. Texas Dandy, the "Finley" horse.

29. Question Mark, by Plaudit.
Photo by Robert Pik

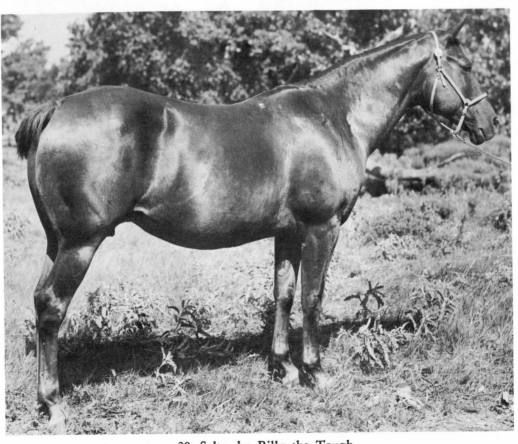

30. Salty, by Billy the Tough.
Photo by Dudley Young

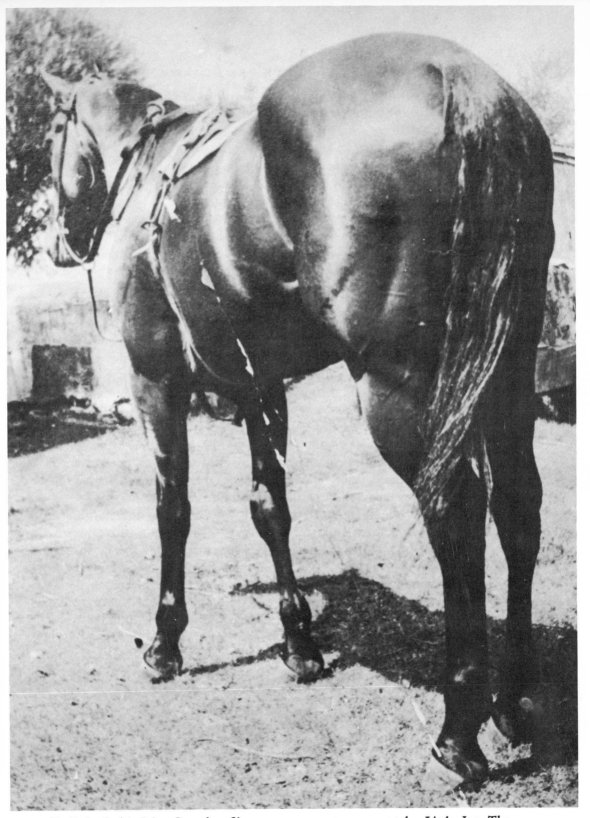

31. Lady S, by John Crowder. She was never outrun except by Little Joe. The Shelys say she was their top mare.

Photo by Tommy Thompson

breeds have been used for a multiplicity of purposes and this variety precludes compressing either group into one all-encompassing mold.

The Quarter Horse, first of all, was a race horse. He was built to be triggered into all-out effort in from one to three jumps from a flat-footed start. This gave him the maneuverability that has made him the world's finest cutting horse, roping horse, rodeo horse, and all-purpose ranch horse. He *is* these things—you can't get around it.

He is likewise a first-rate saddler or road horse, top-drawer for Western pleasures, unmatched for pole bending, barrel or cutter racing. He is usually gentle and a thrifty keeper—a good "rustler" the cowboys tell you. And he has more guts than you can hang on a fencepost. But the best of his kind—and this will bear repeating—are famous first and always for making the trek between stall gate and wire faster, quarter for quarter, than any other breed that has yet been developed.

So perhaps we shouldn't worry too much about our patent inability to fit him into a single mold. Regardless of type—of what specific capability one's plans are geared toward—the knowledgeable breeder has a tried and proved yardstick for guidance, for keeping production within the desired groove. Do what our colonial forebears did and, in the words of that South Texas sage Ott Adams, breed best to best.

Dewey G. Steele of Lexington, Kentucky, long recognized as one of the topmost authorities on horse genetics, once said to me on the subject of ancestors: "The problem of breeding Quarter Horses is not a simple one, because there are at least three powerful influences affecting the breed—racing, utility, and the show ring. Racing tests stamina, and no Quarter Horse dare lack that essential trait. Utility may require a somewhat different manner of going than is necessary for racing, and the horse must have cow sense. Unfortunately a halter show may attract horses that are unable to compete successfully in vigorous competition elsewhere. Whether such shows will favor the breeding of an exhibition type is as yet uncertain. It has, however, happened before in animal breeding. People love to see horses in the show ring, and now with the rapid decline in other breeds which formerly satisfied this demand, it is altogether possible that Quarter Horses may take their place." These remarks were made in 1949.

Mr. Steel said further:

The tremendous influence of ancestors may be observed at an auction of Thoroughbred yearlings. Prospective buyers really study pedigrees and reflect seriously upon them. What is the reason for this almost fanatical interest and respect for ancestors? It is abundantly clear that it is pretty close to the pocketbook.

Pedigrees are abused. Too frequently they are only names arranged in a conventional order. They may even contain irrelevant filler purposely designed to create interest in a particular animal or a particular bloodline. *Pedigrees mean something only when they represent selective breeding.* Where there has been mere propagation rather than selective breeding in the immediate ancestry there is little significance to a pedigree.

In the development of breeds it is interesting to observe that certain individuals wield a disproportionate influence upon the structure of their respective breeds. Perhaps no horse is more outstanding in this regard than Hambletonian 10 in the Standardbred, which is today largely a Hambletonian family. The influence of Anxiety 4th on the Hereford is another well-known example. Curiously enough, some few individuals that have influenced a breed to a marked extent were females.

Families in Thoroughbreds are of two types: paternal families tracing by top male line to Herod, Matchem, or Eclipse, and maternal families tracing by bottom female line to one of fifty so-called taproot mares. These latter are numbered according to the Bruce Lowe system, whereby each family was assigned a number on the basis of its relative standing as a classic winner (Derby, Oaks, and St. Leger in England). Certain of these, such as 1, 2, 3, 4, and 5, have been identified as running families; others have been designated as sire-producing families, and so forth. The scheme lacks scientific validity and critical studies have shown there is nothing to it. In the Quarter Horse there is no excuse whatever to build up any such colossal farce.

It was Steele's conclusion that there is no evidence to indicate that a male will inherit more from a paternal grandsire than from his dam's sire. Or, conversely, a female more from the maternal grandsire than she is likely to find in whatever comes down from her daddy's sire.

Another of his remarks would seem rather appropriate to this discussion.

If a sire in any breed demonstrates his transmitting capacity by the progeny test, then one may well ask: "Why should his pedigree be considered any longer?"

The pull of tradition, however, is so strong that breeders invariably discriminate against an animal that is not fashionably bred. The recent sire [1949] Wise Counsellor lacked fashionable breeding and never attracted the patronage he so eminently deserved.

Racing records loom large these days when one looks about for a prospective sire; but these, like pedigree, recede in importance as progeny reveals the true breeding-worth of parents. Steele noted, also, the unfortunate fact that performance records and breeding do not, of necessity, always jibe. "Zev," said Steele, "failed to get progeny in his own class; Bull Lea, on the other hand, got progeny that exceeded his racing performance."

In our own time this phenomenon may be noted in the case of Three Bars, who was pretty far down as a Thoroughbred race horse yet is currently unmatched as a begetter of stakes-winning quarter-milers.

Mr. Steele further stated: "Individual cases of this nature cause some vociferous persons to make unwarranted assumptions which might lead one to think it is all a matter of chance, that breeding plays a rather minor part. Nothing could be farther from the truth. Until an animal demonstrates his or her transmitting ability, performance will remain the most important index of potential worth."

Steele conducted a series of studies designed to determine whether significant ancestral differences existed between good performing Thorobreds and poor ones, and came up with this electrifying answer: "Evidence indicates that pedigrees should be judged primarily upon the basis of the first and second generations, and that ancestors beyond the third generation may, for all practical purposes, be ignored."

Persons hunting short cuts should take a long look at this.

Speed Is the Cornerstone

Half the possible results in any horse-breeding program stem directly from the mare—potentially, at least—and some of these inherited tendencies come down to us from *her* dam. One should never minimize the importance of obtaining a first-rate sire, but it is the importance of also having an outstanding dam that most of us are all too frequently inclined to overlook. On the basis of genetics, this is likely the big half of our troubles. No sire can do it all. Three Bars for several years has been extremely popular—and deservedly so; but how many of his winners do you imagine have come from cart mares?

In the past ten years (in the last five even more so) the breeding of short horses has displayed remarkable advances. When the American Quarter Horse Association, the National Quarter Horse Breeders Association, and the American Quarter Racing Association ironed out their differences and finally got together, the stage was set for progress. An astonishing improvement became swiftly apparent, particularly in breed and track performance. Records have been toppled with an almost incredible continuity. Shue Fly's world mark of :22.6 for the quarter on a track labeled *fast* has now been duplicated by several carloads of horses; and Woven Web's time (February, 1948) of :22.0—thought by many to have been unbeatable—has been several times lowered. The great record established in 1960 by Vandy's Flash (:21.7) has been equaled by two mares, No Butt and She Kitty, and lowered one-tenth—if accepted—by the fireball stallion Pokey Bar.

I can almost hear the cries from the boondocks. "Sheer velocity! What does that prove?"

To me it proves quite a bit, and I don't think, as some carping critics have rather raucously contended, that this gain in speed is necessarily dependent on infusions of 50 per cent Thoroughbred blood with each mating.

Down in the South Texas brush country, where the hoot owls frequently bed down with us chickens, there lived for many years a man recognized as dean of the short horse breeders. Ott Adams was small, forthright, and, if he liked you, quite articulate. He spent his whole life, all his energies, with bangtails and could just about tell you what they thought.

Uncle Ott once said to me: "I have never been at all interested in raising ranch or cow ponies. I have never entertained an idea of raising anything but the very best in bloodlines that would produce speedy colts."

This is not so harsh as might be thought at first glance. Mr. Adams realized a fact which most of us appear never to have heard of—that outstanding speed and early foot is the key to Quarter Horse performance. He produced a long line of great performance horses with this formula— such individuals as Zantanon, called the Mexican Man O' War, Plain Jane, Old Grey, Lady of the Lake, Rialto, John Gardner, Paul Ell, Billy Sunday, Pancho Villa, Bumps, Hobo, Ada Jones, Joe Moore, and Stella Moore. And it wasn't just chance. Not by a jugful.

Adams said: "The show ring has contaminated the breeding of the Quarter Horse and is definitely detrimental to the production of first-class horses. No better performance can be expected from an individual than is known to have sprung from the blood behind it."

In 1949, when he was eighty-one years old, Uncle Ott declared with some asperity: "Thousands of persons have gone into the horse business but only a few have been truly successful. The trouble with most who try to breed horses can be told in two words—no program. They did not understand, even those who had some kind of a program, that to raise an improved stock of horses you have to have speed on both sides of the family. Speed is the one prime requisite of any properly bred Quarter Horse. The other things for which this breed is famous depend for their existence entirely on this matter of speed. Speed on one side is not enough; both sire and dam must be bred in speed if you would raise the kind that can get the job done. Any horse that is not a producer of speed is merely a horse, and should be properly valued at so much per pound."

32. Joe Blair, TB, jockey Lee Burke at halter.

33. Della Moore, dam of Joe Reed, Joe Moore, and Grano De Oro.

34. Old Joe Reed, by Joe Blair, TB, at Elk City in 1944.

35. A rare photo of Joe Moore taken in 1949 at Alfred, Texas.

36. The incomparable Zantanon, the Mexican Man O' War, a few days after defeating the famous mare Conesa. Zantanon was bred by Ott Adams.

37. Hobo, by Joe Moore out of Paulita, by Paul Ell. Bred by Ott Adams.

38. B-Seven, by Balmy L out of Loma. Foaled 1942. Bred by O. W. Cardwell.

39. B Day, by Balmy L out of Misty Day. Bred by O. W. Cardwell.

40. Randle's Lady, sometimes known as "Little Breeze," "Rosalita," or "Doll." She was foaled in 1938. By Doc Horn, TB.

Photo by Reggie Russell

41. Silver King, P-183.

If this blows your house down, just remember it comes from a veteran who has bred many a horse of the highest value, horses good in themselves and occasionally far better in their ability to pass along the traits and characteristics most knowledgeable horsemen hold in highest esteem.

Some people will tell you they don't care to raise race horses. These are probably their convictions, honestly stated. They have a right to breed any kind they wish. But when anyone tells you that his horses, which demonstrably have no speed, are some of the finest Quarter stock being raised today you should realize you are listening to an ignorant man.

It is performance that counts when you call in the experts, and performance, always remember, will seldom surpass the blood from which it springs. Mr. J. W. House, the man who bred, among other notables, Joe Reed II, Little Fanny, and Leo, put this thought another way when he said: "You can breed it out faster than you can put it in."

Place in America Today

The real Quarter Horse, as we have seen, must be a hot blood. His kind are not just another breed. In performance and endurance they have never been excelled; in bloodlines they have proved sufficiently prepotent to withstand continual outcrossing and hold their own for nearly three hundred years. Nothing but a true hot blood could have survived.

You can frequently recognize a Quarter Horse by his cat-footed stance, his whole-bodied way of going; but the best way to tell is by what he can do. If he can do it all, you've got one!

He has three gaits, each of them natural; the walk, trot, and gallop. The short gallop, or lope, is unequaled for pleasurable riding. He is ridden with a loose rein and responds to signals given with the rider's knees or posture. If he's been raised by a rancher he'll be neck reined. The properly trained Quarter Horse will shape his mood to that of his rider; they are bred to a quicker response than you can get from other breeds. Quickness is his stock in trade.

In 1961 the American Quarter Horse Association registered 50,820 individuals. The highest price paid for a Quarter Horse through 1960 was $125,000. This was paid for the running stallion Go Man Go. A couple of horses have fetched more since, one bringing $150,000. Not a few have sold through public auction for the better part of $100,000.

Proven Quarter Horse brood mares and highly bred or successfully raced stallions bring high prices because this is an expanding industry and breeders are hard put to supply the demand. It is natural that more stallions are produced than can be economically used in the breeding pens. When gelded these become valuable as performance horses for use on the track, in the arena, and on ranch and range; many thus altered find their niche in Western pleasure events—pole bending, barrel racing, cutter racing, polo, parade, and pleasure riding. For the average person a gelding is generally superior to either a mare or stallion if purchased to fulfill some particular need. The remudas of working cow outfits are traditionally composed entirely of geldings.

Fortunately for the ordinary horse enthusiast, geldings are not nearly so costly as good mares or stallions. Geldings generally range in price from two or three hundred dollars up into the thousands, for show and racing stock.

Let a horse be your new hobby. There are few that you'll find more rewarding. As the old axiom has it, the outside of a horse is powerful good medicine for the insides of man. There is no exercise that can do more for you than riding, and there are few finer people than those who share an interest in horses. As Wild Horse Shorty (a character I once pushed through two books) used to fondly remark: "Horses is fine people!"

At Ruidoso, Labor Day, 1961, Quarter Horses ran the richest horse race in history, dollar for distance, when the purse for the All-American Futurity came to $202,425. That year the ten top purses were:

Race	Gross Value
1. Arlington Futurity	$211,750
2. All-American Futurity	202,425
3. Preakness Stakes	178,700
4. Santa Anita Maturity	167,370
5. Kentucky Derby	163,000
6. Hollywood Gold Cup	162,100
7. Delaware Handicap	159,687
8. Belmont Stakes	148,650
9. Hollywood Juvenile Stakes	147,800
10. Santa Anita Derby	145,100

In 1962 the purse for the All-American went to $222,850; the televised winner was Hustling Man, bred and owned by J. B. Ferguson of Wharton, Texas. This same season saw the inaugural running of the Los Alamitos Futurity for Quarter Horses, purse $207,750, the J. B. Chambers' sensational Jet Deck taking home the lion's share of this amount. In 1963, the fifth running of the All-American Futurity carried a purse of $285,000.

Annual yearling sales were launched at Ruidoso in 1962 to coincide with the All-American, and similar sales will in 1963 no doubt make their debut at Los Alamitos.

The Quarter Horse today is Big Business.

Part II: The "Using" Horse

Some Factual Generalities

Horses, as any old-timer will tell you, are real people. Like earlier Americans, they are, for the most part, rugged individualists with quirks and idiosyncrasies as diverse and queerly personal as the foibles found in human beings. No pair are ever quite alike, although the genus, when lumped, presents to the casual eye, no matter the breed, so many things in common it could never be mistaken for anything but horse.

Horses and children have a great deal in common and react very much alike. As you turn these pages it is hoped that, as a kind of dividend to your quest for knowledge, some respite may be found from current cares in this wonderful world of Quarter Horses.

The Quarter Horse, as has been pointed out, is the oldest American family of horses, antedating by many generations the introduction of the Thoroughbred. His tribe strongly flourished in Colonial times, and it has lately been suggested that Paul Revere rode a Quarter Horse. He possessed in those days the same characteristics he exhibits now—which may in some measure explain the remarkable prepotency still displayed in his often marked ability to stamp his get with peculiarities seldom discovered in any other branch of the equine family.

Perhaps the most notable characteristic of the true Quarter Horse is and always has been his astonishing versatility. From earliest times he's been a "using" horse—good at whatever he is put to, be it pulling a wagon or plowing a field. He did those things in Colonial times, and gave the planters relaxation by running for them on weekends. He was marvelously adapted to pioneer pursuits.

Old Fred, owned most of his life by Coke Roberds of Hayden, Colorado, first came to public attention while hitched to a wagon. He and his full sister, Maud, as seen in the enclosed photograph (Old Fred nearest the camera), pulled this wagon all the way from Jim Freeman's farm in Missouri to Pueblo, Colorado, where this picture was taken. The photo was given me by Freeman's grandson, Mr. A. C. Haeberle, currently a realtor at Wheatland, Wyoming. Old Fred was a palomino horse foaled, it is believed, about

1893. He is said to have been sired by Black Ball, and he by Missouri Rondo out of a mare by John Crowder—this, at least, is the breeding attributed to Old Fred by Bob Denhardt, first secretary of the American Quarter Horse Association. However he was bred, he was obviously a Quarter Horse and became, with Peter McCue, a foundation sire of the famous Coke Roberds horses.

In a book titled *The Quarter Horse*, published by the AQHA at Amarillo in 1950, Bob Denhardt says: "The Spanish horse was a horse whose heritage had from the first been nomadic. All his masters for a thousand years had used him to drive their livestock from pasture to pasture. Spain and America proved no exception. Even when he was with Cortes and De Soto, he always had at least a drove of pigs along to keep in line and on which to practice his trade. Later, when he was with our copper-hued natives, he must follow a buffalo and put his rider up next to the galloping brute so that a well placed lance thrust might pierce the vital organ just behind the extended shoulder. Spanish settlements, whether military, civil or religious, depended on livestock and the horse who made their care possible. The Indian lived on and by the horse, once he was adopted into the tribe."

Cow savvy was built into this breed of horses and has always been evident. For several hundreds of years "use" has been the determining economic factor of his propagation. This in no way nullified his need for early foot. Speed is the prime essential of any multipurpose horse. It is the irreplaceable cornerstone from which he was geared to his many endeavors. Ott Adams and his mentor Dow Shely understood this better than most. Naturally, Quarter Horses fit into the scheme of things on a ranch.

Once again let us hark to Bob Denhardt: "Since the modern Quarter Horse has largely been bred on the range alongside cattle, since he has generally received his breaking and usually earned his oats between races at cow work, it is only natural that he should be a master of two trades —cattle and short races. Centuries of specialization for quick speed make him today a thing of beauty mighty pleasing to the cowman. Every contour of his conformation reflects the purpose for which he was bred, and they make him the superior of all other breeds in pure feet-per-second movement. . . . The unusual conformation of the Quarter Horse is his greatest asset in working cattle, as most cowmen agree. They make him the stoutest on the end of a rope, the handiest to cut on in a herd and the fastest and safest when heading a wild one. As long as our West possesses fabulous wealth in natural forage, just so long will this horse be an economic necessity, for to date no visionary has drawn a blueprint of a mechanical

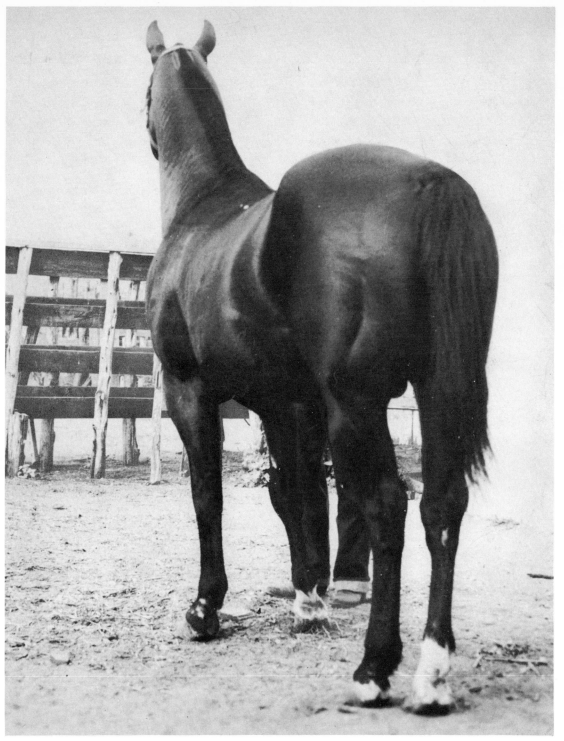

42. Joe Moore, the sire of many famous horses, at 21 years. Bred and owned by Ott Adams of Alice, Texas. Joe Moore was by the original Little Joe, South Texas' greatest race horse.

43. Old Fred and full sister as they appeared after hauling a covered wagon into Pueblo, Colorado, all the way from Jim Freeman's farm in Missouri. Nearest horse is Old Fred. Sister was called Maud.

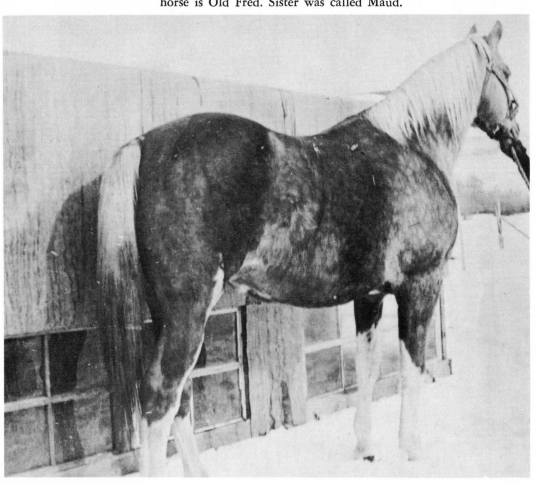

44. Old Fred as he looked on Coke Roberds' ranch.

contrivance cheaper or easier to operate in the rough range country than the Quarter Horse. In many respects this makes him the only horse with a strictly economic future in America."

The Quarter Horse is the world's best cow horse; he is also the finest sporting horse to be found in North America. In addition to early foot, most horseback sports require handiness, an ingredient for which he stands second to none. He has proved by test to be the best in arena competition today and will be found, I believe, to give tremendous satisfaction—with proper schooling—in any area of sport to which he is introduced.

Pole Bending

The American Quarter Horse Association inaugurated Pole Bending (a form of race which has been proving quite popular) as a competitive performance sport in 1961 and added it to the other facets of arena performance for which points are given and an Honor Roll established. High-point horses in this field, thus far, are:

Year	Horse	Points *
1961	BUCK'S LOU, Pal. m. 56 by Buckskin Hank	2½
1961	DAWSON NOWATA, S. g. 54 by Wimpy II	2½
1961	G-FERN SCAT CAT, Ch. h. 50 by Catechu	2½
1961	MIDNIGHT BAR, Ch. g. 51 by BARRED	2½

* Pole Bending classes receive half points.

Rules

264. No horse shall be allowed to show in more than one registered pole bending contest per show.
265. The pole bending pattern is to be run around five poles. Each pole is to be 21 feet apart and the first pole is to be 21 feet from the starting line.
266. A horse may start either to the right or to the left of the first pole and then run the remainder of the pattern accordingly (see pattern).
267. Knocking over a pole, touching the pole with the rider's hand, or failure to follow the course shall cause disqualification.
268. Pole bending is a timed event. Each contestant will begin from a running start. A clearly visible starting line shall be provided. At least two watches shall be used with the average time of the watches used by the official timers to be the official time.
269. In the event of a tie, the horse declared the winner in the runoff must run the pattern within two seconds of its original time or the runoff must be held again.
270. Western type equipment must be used. Use of a hackamore or other

POLE BENDING PATTERN

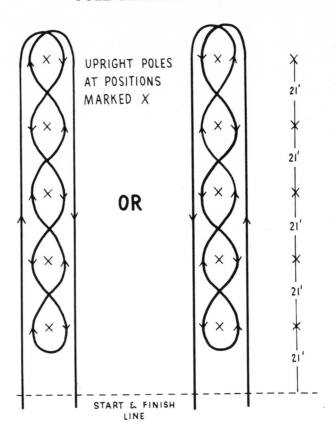

UPRIGHT POLES
AT POSITIONS
MARKED X

OR

START & FINISH
LINE

types of bridles is the optional choice of the contestant; however, the timer or judge may prohibit the use of bits or equipment that he may consider severe.

271. Only horses registered with the American Quarter Horse Association in the Permanent, Tentative, National, New Appendix, or Appendix, are eligible to participate. Any show that denies or restricts entries of any one of the categories above will not have their pole bending results recognized.

Barrel Racing

An Honor Roll was established, with points for barrel racing, in 1957. This exciting sport caught on like wildfire and is now a featured event at many horse shows and rodeos throughout the nation.

Rules

227. No horse shall be allowed to show in more than one registered barrel race per show.

228. Knocking over barrels or failure to follow the prescribed course shall be cause for disqualification. If a rider touches a barrel with his hand, the horse will be disqualified.

229. The course must be measured exactly. If the course is too large for the available space, then the pattern should be reduced five yards at a time until the pattern fits the arena.

230. REMEMBER TO LEAVE adequate space between barrels and any obstacles. The distance from barrel number 3 to the finish line need not be reduced five yards at a time if there is sufficient room for the horse to stop.

231. Western type equipment must be used. Use of hackamore or other types of bridles is the optional choice of the contestant; however, the timer or judge may prohibit the use of bits or equipment that he may consider severe.

232. A clearly visible starting line shall be provided, either through the use of a rope buried in the ground or one marked by lime. At least two watches shall be used with the average time of the watches used by the official timers to be the official time. The barrel race contest is strictly a timed event.

233. In the event of a tie, the horse declared the winner in the runoff must run the pattern within two seconds of its original time or the runoff must be held again.

234. Only horses registered with the American Quarter Horse Association in the Permanent, Tentative, National or Appendix are eligible to participate. Any show that denies or restricts entries of any one of the categories above will not have their Barrel Racing results recognized.

235. REMEMBER TO SET YOUR COURSE SO THAT A HORSE MAY HAVE AMPLE ROOM TO TURN AND STOP.

236. The contestant is allowed a running start. Timing shall begin as soon as the horse's nose reaches the starting line and will be stopped when the horse's nose passes over the finish line.

237. At a signal from the starter or timer, such as the word "go," the contestant will go to barrel number 1 passing to the left of this barrel, complete a 360-degree turn, then on to barrel number 2, this time passing to the right with another 360-degree turn. At barrel number 3 the same passage to the right and 360-degree turn is accomplished.

238. As soon as the turn is completed around barrel 3, the contestant sprints the horse to the finish line where the timers stop their watches as soon as the horse's nose reaches the finish line.

239. This barrel course may also be run to the left. For example, the contestant will start to barrel number 2, turning to left around this barrel, then

BARREL RACING CONTEST

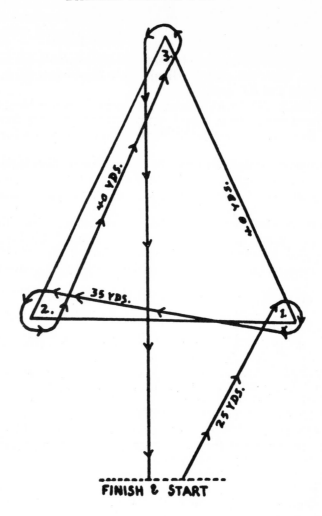

to number 1 barrel, turning to the right, then to barrel number 3, turning again to the right, followed by the final sprint to the finish line.

240. This cloverleaf pattern is designed to test the speed and maneuverability of the horse. When measuring the area for the barrel course, remember to leave ample room for the horse and rider to complete their turns and also to pull to a stop at the finish.

Honor Roll horses in this competition have been:

Year	Horse	Points
1957	LADY J. BAILEY, Ch. m. 52 by Tiger Joe Bailey	5
1958	JACKY'S BABY, Br. m. by JACK IRELAN	12
1959	V'S JOE BLAKE, B. g. 49 by Little Jodie	11
1960	ANADORNO PEPPY, Ch. h. 53 by Peppy Bueno	17
1961	#PAT DAWSON, Pal. g. 54 by GOLD KING BAILEY	25
1962	#PAT DAWSON, Pal. g. 54 by GOLD KING BAILEY	40

Horses preceded by symbol # are AQHA champions.

Reining

An Honor Roll for reining horses was established by the AQHA in 1952.

Rules

200. No horse shall be allowed to show in more than one registered reining class per show.
201. All contestants concerned will gather at the arena at the proper time. Upon call, each contestant will perform the required pattern individually and separately.
202. The arena or plot should be approximately 50 X 150 feet in size.
203. Each horse will be judged on the neatness, dispatch, ease, calmness and speed with which it performs the pattern. Excessive jawing, open mouth or head raising on stop, lack of smooth sliding stop on haunches, breaking gaits, refusing to change lead, anticipating signals, stumbling or falling, wringing tail, backing sideways, knocking over stakes or kegs, changing hands on reins, or losing stirrup, or holding on, or two hands on reins, or any unnecessary aid given by the rider to the horse (such as unnecessary talking, petting, spurring, quirting, jerking of reins, etc.), to induce the horse to perform will be considered a fault and scored accordingly. Horse shall rein and handle easily, fluently, effortlessly, and with reasonable speed throughout the pattern.
204. Any horse not following exact pattern will be disqualified.
205. Scoring will be on the basis of 60-80 with 70 denoting an average performance.
206. In case of doubt, a judge may require any contestant to repeat his performance of any or all the various parts of the pattern. A judge, also, shall have the authority to require the removal or alteration of any piece of equipment or accoutrement which, in his opinion, would tend to give a horse an unfair advantage. Any inhumane equipment will be scored accordingly.

207. A show may have up to three approved reining classes. If three reining classes are to be held at a show, they should be the following:

(a) Senior Reining (five year olds and older, all horses must be shown with bit).

(b) Junior Bit Reining (four year olds and younger, all horses to be shown with bit).

(c) Hackaware Reigning (four year olds and younger, all horses to be shown with hackamore).

If two reining classes are to be held at a show, they should be the following: (a) Senior Reining, and (b) Junior Reining (four year olds and younger, horses may be shown with either bit or hackamore at the discretion of the exhibitor). If only one reining class is to be held at a show it should be: Reining (all ages—horses five years old and older must be shown in bit; horses four years old and younger may be shown in either bit or hackamore at the discretion of the exhibitor).

208. In straight hackamore classes, two hands may be used. In combined bit and hackamore classes, only one hand on the reins of bit or hackamore.

209. For HACKAMORE REINING, horses will be ridden ONLY with a rawhide braided or leather braided or rope bosal. Absolutely no iron will be permitted under the jaws regardless of how padded or taped.

210. For BIT REINING, horses will be ridden with grazing, snaffle, curb, half-breed, bar or spade bit. However, no wire curbs, regardless of how padded or taped, or no chin strap narrower than one-half inch, or no nose band or tiedowns will be permitted.

211. Chain curbs are permissible but must be of the standard flat variety and must meet the approval of the judge.

212. Horses, five years old and older, must perform in the bit reining class.

213. A rider may ride ONLY one horse per reining division.

Any horse not following exact pattern will be disqualified. Ride pattern as follows:

1 to 2—Run at full speed (should be run at least 20 feet from any existing fence or wall).

2—Stop and back.

3—Settle horse for 10 seconds.

4 and 5—Ride small figure 8 at slow canter.

6 and 7—Ride large figure 8 fast.

8—Left roll back over hocks. Upright markers are mandatory at points marked X on pattern.

9—Right roll back over hocks.

10—Stop.

11—Pivot left.

12—Pivot right.

13—Walk to judge and stop for inspection until dismissed.

The following will be judged as faults against the horse: Opening mouth excessively in bit reining, breaking gaits, refusing to change leads, anticipating signals, stumbling and falling, wringing tail, bouncing or side-

214. REINING PATTERN

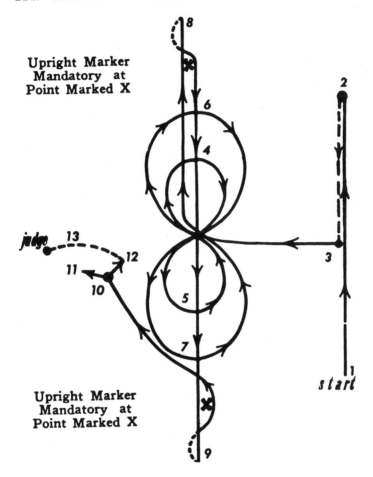

Upright Marker
Mandatory at
Point Marked X

Upright Marker
Mandatory at
Point Marked X

ways stop, backing sideways. And the following faults will be charged against the rider: Changing hands on reins, losing stirrup, two hands on reins at any time, any unnecessary aid given by the rider to the horse (such as unnecessary talking, petting, spurring, quirting, jerking of reins, etc.), to induce the horse to perform.

217. Only horses registered with the American Quarter Horse Association in the Permanent, Tentative, National, New Appendix, or Appendix, are eligible to participate. Any show that denies or restricts entries of any one of the categories above shall not have their reining results recognized.

Horses awarded the Honor Roll for Reining are:

Year	Horse	Points
1952	SOBRE'S SWEETIE, Ch. m. 49 by Sobre	6
1953	#GRAY LADY BURK, Gr. m. 48 by Waggoner	10
1954	PHOEBE CHESS, Ch. m. 48 by Eddie	12
1955	#DEE GEE, B. m. 45 by Bartender	26
1956	#KNOCKY, Ch. g. 48 by King Raffles (TB)	61
1957	OUTER'S STUBBY, Pal. g. 52 by Baker's Oklahoma Star	32
1958	RONDO'S KING, Ch. h. 54 by Saltillo	27
1959	#SONORA MONKEY, Ch. g. 50 by Lauro	50
1960	SHORT SPARK, Pal. h. 56 by SHORTCUT	49
1961	#MAGNOLIA DUNNY, Dn. h. 53 by Sunup H	41
1962	COWBOY JIM, B. g. 55 by VENTURE BILL	62

Roping

A point system Honor Roll for roping contests was set up by the Association in 1952.

Rules

218. No horse shall be allowed to show in more than one registered roping class per show.

219. A roping contest will be held under the usual common rodeo standards and conditions. Horse must start from behind a barrier.

220. Scoring will be done on the basis of 60-80 with 70 denoting an average performance.

221. Only the performance of the horse is to count. Time of the roper will not count for or against the horse. A time limit of two minutes for each contestant will be allowed.

222. The roper may throw as many loops in this two minutes as necessary to effectively show his horse. If more than one loop is thrown, however, the roper must carry a second rope tied to saddle which is to be used for the second loop. Should roper desire to throw a third, or more loops, he may recoil either rope.

223. If roper carries only one rope and misses on first loop, he must retire from arena with no score (this provision is necessary to show that horse will work trailing a rope).

224. The horse will be judged on manners behind the barrier, scoring speed to calf, rating calf, the stop, working the rope and his manners while roper is returning to horse after tie has been made.

225. Unnecessary spurring, quirting with rope, jerking reins, talking or any noise making, slapping or jerking rope, or any unnecessary action to

induce the horse to perform better will be considered a fault and scored accordingly.

226. Only horses registered with the American Quarter Horse Association in the Permanent, Tentative, National, New Appendix or Appendix, are eligible to participate. Any show that denies or restricts entries of any one of the above categories will not have their roping results recognized.

Horses nominated for Honor Roll in this class have been:

Year	Horse	Points
1952	#STAR JACK, JR., B. g. 48 by Scroggins' Little Star	11
1953	BAR V. JO B., Ch. m. 45 by Buck Hancock	6
1954	#PRETTY BOY POKEY, Dn. g. 48 by #POCO BUENO	12
1955	JEANNE'S PATSY, B. m. 50 by Bert	13
1956	#KNOCKY, Ch. g. 48 by King Raffles (TB)	15
1957	#GEORGE DUN, Dn. g. 53 by HOLLYWOOD GEORGE	12
1958	#GEORGE DUN, Dn. g. 53 by HOLLYWOOD GEORGE	18
1959	#HONORA MONKEY, Ch. g. 50 by Lauro	20
1960	#RONDO BILL, Blk. g. 55 by BALDY C	13
1961	#TENDER BOY, S. h. 55 by Bartender	19
1962	#REX DEL RANCHO, Ch. h. 56 by Rey Del Rancho	27

Western Riding

An Honor Roll, with accompanying points, was set up for this class in 1952. The class receives half points.

Rules

282. No horse shall be allowed to show in more than one registered Western riding horse contest per show.

283. This contest is neither a stunt nor a race. It is a competition in the performance and characteristics of a good, sensible, well-mannered, free and easy moving ranch horse which can get man around on the usual ranch chores, over the trails, or give a quiet, comfortable and pleasant ride in open country through and over obstacles. Any Western equipment of the exhibitor's choice may be used; but the kind of equipment apparently necessary for the control of the animal, such as severe bit, spurs, tiedown and the like, may be considered by the judge making the awards. Extra credit will not be given for expensive, fancy or parade equipment of the animal or dress of the rider.

284. All animals entered in a class to be judged must be assembled at the entrance to the arena in ample time for the judging to start promptly and to continue without delay, and shall remain there (except while com-

45. Baldy Buzz, P-43,890. Cutting, 1961.

Photo by Shirley M. Dickerson

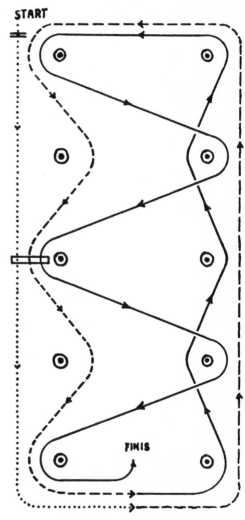

START

FINIS

Western Riding Horse
Contest Course

...... WALK   ⚏ GATE

----- TROT   ▭ OBSTACLE

——— LOPE   ◉ MARKERS

46. Baldy Buzz in 1963.

Chris' Studio of Photography

peting) until dismissed by the judge, unless the judge shall otherwise direct. A tardy contestant may be denied competition.

285. The contesting animals will be judged on riding qualities of gaits (walk, trot, and lope) and movement; response to the rider; manners; disposition; and intelligence. Conformation will not be judged.

286. No more than two classes divided by age are permitted at any one contest.

287. The Association from time to time will prescribe a pattern and routine according to which the animals shall be worked, and, until changed, the accompanying pattern and routine are prescribed. In order to make possible fair competition of animals it is essential that exhibitors and judge adhere.

288. On the pattern the short single line marked "G" represents a swinging gate which the animal on entering the arena must put the rider in a position to open, pass through and close without dismounting. The gate may be located in any convenient part of the arena where it will not interfere with the balance of the routine. The ten small circles represent markers (barrels, kegs or standards recommended). These should be separated by uniform distance of not less than 30 or more than 50 feet. The two short crossed double lines represent obstacles (small logs recommended) just high enough to break the animal's stride in going over. The long and sometimes twisting line indicates the direction of travel and the gaits at which the animal must move. The dotted line indicates the walk; the dashed line the trot; and the solid line the lope. On entering the arena the exhibitor will put his animal through the gate and then proceed on the routine as indicated by the pattern. On completion he will ride to the judge and back his animal as indicated by the judge. The judge may require an exhibitor to repeat or reverse any part of the routine.

Horses which have thus far achieved the Honor Roll in this competition are:

Year	Horse	Points
1952	BROWN JO TUFF, Br. m. 49 by Tuffy Jo Jo	2
1953	#WHITCOMB'S FROGETTE, Ch. m. 50 by FROG W	5
1954	#BETH B, Ch. m. 47 by Little King George	4
1955	#BETH B, Ch. m. 47 by Little King George	6
	#FANCY BRANCH, B. m. 51 by Wimpy III	6
	#FAY KING, Dn. m. by King Gotch	6
	LITTLE ONE, B. m. 51 by Bob Steel	6
1956	#FIGA HANCOCK, Ro. m. 51 by GREY BADGER II	13
1957	#KATY SCARLET, Ch. m. 52 by Snip Reed	24
1958	#KING VAQUERO, Blk. g. 53 by #KING'S JOE BOY	26
1959	DUZER RONDO, B. g. 54 by Billy Rondo	8
1960	ABNEY'S GINGER, Pal. m. 51 by Rattler	7½
1961	DUZER RONDO, B. g. 54 by Billy Rondo	14½
1962	BALDY BUZZ, Ch. h. 52 by Buzz Bomb	7½

Biographical Sketch

Baldy Buzz

"I first came in contact with Baldy Buzz in Rogue River, 1959," said Lucky Warren, a professional horse trainer of twenty-two years experience. "He was at a ranch for breeding purposes. I was impressed. His small ears, intelligent eyes, good withers, deep chest, and good hind quarters made him a picture to look at. Coming back two weeks later with his owner, Vard Miller, I saw the horse out of his stall while he was being led around. His movements were free and easy, hind legs up under him. I thought he was the most perfectly balanced horse I had ever seen. If he had the heart and determination to work, here was a great show horse. Two weeks later Baldy Buzz was in my stables at Roseburg in training."

A chestnut sorrel, 14.2, 1125, Baldy Buzz was bred by Harry Frost and foaled on his Diamond F Ranch near Reno, Nevada, May 16, 1952. Mr. Frost sold him to Charles "Curly" Southern, who brought him to the Grants Pass area of Oregon in September of 1954, Southern placing him in training with Leo Thorn. He changed hands again, November 3, 1954, when he was purchased by Vard Miller, a logging contractor, who left him with Thorn for several more months. "After this," declares present owner S. E. Comfort (Idleyld Park, Oregon), "he was just used as a saddle horse until November, 1956, when he was taken to Bob Mettler to be trained for cutting. He was left with Mettler until February 12, 1957."

Mr. Miller showed the horse some in 1957, riding himself. The period 1957 to 1960 was another inactive one. About then Lucky Warren took hold of him and had a very successful season, as the records show.

Vard Miller died of a heart attack in October of 1960 and the horse was again put on pasture. Says Mr. Comfort: "He remained there until September 10, 1961 when he was purchased by my wife and given to me as an anniversary present. We sent him back to Lucky Warren, who has handled and shown him since then."

In his second show at the Portland International in the fall of 1961, with only one month of training after all that inaction, Baldy Buzz came up with a very outstanding performance. Two months later at the Northwest Quarter Horse winter show he was named Grand Champion Working Horse. This show is one of the really big ones, drawing horses from many states.

During 1962 he earned 37 AQHA working points. In August, at the Clackamus County Fair Quarter Horse Show (Candby, Oregon), Baldy

Buzz was shown with a full brother (Pee Wee Bomb) and a son (Buzzy Risk) in the reining classes. These three horses all corraled firsts—Baldy first in Senior Bit Reining, Pee Wee first in Junior Bit, and Buzzy first in Hackamore Reining. They demonstrated, with Warren up, some pretty clear-cut ability.

The following is a list of the wins within his short period of ownership which, Mr. Comfort feels, is most impressive:

Portland International—October, 1961
  1st Working Cow Horse
  8th in Sweepstakes (only Oregon horse to place)
Oregon Cutting Horse Show—May, 1961
  Champion High-Point Horse
Northwest Quarter Horse Winter Show—Walla Walla, December 7, 1961
  Grand Champion Working Horse—Trophy Saddle
Furnace Creek Show—Death Valley, January, 1962
  Reserve Champion Working Horse
State of Jefferson Quarter Horse Show—Grants Pass, April, 1962
  Reserve Champion Working Horse
Clackamus County Fair Show—Candby, August, 1962
  Grand Champion Working Horse

When one sees what Baldy had to do to attain these honors they are very impressive indeed. He is very alert, a wide-awake horse, missing nothing that happens within his vicinity. In shows he appears to enjoy his work.

Lucky Warren tells me:

Baldy and I hit it off extremely well. I guess we just understood each other. He wasn't a horse who liked a lot of petting and fussing over; he was extremely independent, which suited me fine.

He was quick and easy to make understand what was expected of him—very easy to manage. He seemed to enjoy his work and appeared to get pleasure out of doing it well. He had a good mouth with a lot of feel. He was the kind of horse a trainer dreams about getting. Color, style, and ability. At the Eugene show he stole the hearts of the English riders—they came out of the grandstands to congratulate him, and he seemed to understand he'd done a bang-up job. At Portland I knew he was a champ and one of the proudest horses I was ever on. In 1961 two of Baldy's sons came to me for training; they were extremely easy to work, well balanced, showing a lot of cow sense and working ability. Both made good bridle horses and won at shows. I received another son, Buzzy Risk, and went on to win a Register of Merit with him at AQHA shows as a hackamore horse.

Baldy is now in training for cutting. He has been shown three times this year [1963], winning one first, a fourth, and a second. He is now eleven years old and is sound. He has no bad habits. My son (eleven) can ride him at home or at shows around other horses and he is quiet and well behaved. Baldy, to me, is a horse among horses.

We haven't said much about Baldy's bloodlines. He was sired by Buzz Bomb (P–4, 362) by Show Boy (P–263), by W. D. Wear's great old Tony (P–776), written up by me for the *Texas Livestock Journal* many years ago. Tony was by Guinea Pig, a very good son of Possum. Buzz Bomb's dam, Miss Muffet (P–557), was sired by Mark DuBois' Pee Wee (a top-string son of Red Cloud, sired by the Possum brought out of Texas by DuBois, along with Blue Eyes, for Jim Kennedy of the MK Ranch near Bonita, Arizona, about 1914 or 1915 he thinks).

Baldy's dam, Momie (P–5,554) was the highly regarded mother of eleven (Lucky Pick, by Lucky Fellow; Mike Sam, by Lucky Fellow; Lucky Joe Pick, by Lucky Fellow; Look Down Joe, by Skeeter H; and Sunny Skeeter, by Skeeter H; and, by Buzz Bomb, these topflight five—Baldy Buzz, Bay Momie, Pee Wee Momie, Pee Wee Bomb, and Tinky Frosty). Momie was by the Casement-bred Frosty (P–3610, by Balleymooney). She was out of the Estes Mare by Strawberry (by Guinea Pig). Mr. Comfort tells me: "Baldy Buzz goes to Traveler four times, three by way of Possum, and once by Jim Kennedy's Bulger. He also traces 16 times to Steel Dust—six through Jenny (dam of Possum), six through Cold Deck, and once each by Jack Traveler, Pancho (by Old Billy), and twice by John Crowder. One of Baldy's best qualities is his ability to do many jobs well."

Harry Frost says: "Buzz Bomb is still alive and I'm still using him. He won a lot of purple and blue ribbons at halter and was an excellent 220- and 330-yard horse on the straightaways. He was also used as a rope horse and established quite a reputation. He has proved a mighty good sire and not a few of his get have distinguished themselves in many different ways."

As a matter of fact, Baldy, had he been trained for it sooner, would doubtless have made his mark on the short tracks. At the Furnace Creek show, January 27, 1963, Baldy was first in the working Stock Horse competition (receiving trophy), second in Western Riding, second in Senior Bit Reining, second in his halter class (first time shown at halter); and then was entered in a cross-country half-mile race—this from a standing start. Baldy broke so fast and led the field so far that Lucky Warren (up) thought they must have got off before the signal, so pulled up, allowing six horses to pass him before he got his thoughts unsnarled. In the process he got off the course into sage and rough ground. Even so, back on the course, Baldy overtook two of them to come in fourth.

He was on the list of AQHA Show and Contest Leaders for 1962 in Working Cow Horse for six months, ending the year in a tie for second place.

While the Millers owned him, Baldy Buzz (Lucky Warren training) loped off with a total of 17 trophies; made the AQHA Register of Merit in Reining and as Working Cow Horse; was named Champion Horse, State of Oregon, for 1960; was the High-Point Quarter Horse of the Oregon Horsemen's Association; and was elected High Point Horse by the Western Horsemen of Oregon.

Results of the Baldy Buzz family of Quarter Horses at the third Annual Spring Show of the State of Jefferson Quarter Horse Association, Roseburg, Oregon, April 27–28, 1963:

1. Baldy Buzz (shown only in one class) won 2nd in Registered Cutting
2. Rogue Martin (119,864), by Baldy Buzz, named Senior Champion Stallion of the show, placing over 17
3. Siskyu Star (P–129,815), a grandson of Baldy Buzz, won his class (Foals of 1960) to become Reserve Champion Stallion
4. Buzzy Risk (P–137,309), by Baldy Buzz, named Grand Champion Gelding
5. Pee Wee Bomb (P–134,235), full brother to Baldy, shown in three classes, won:
   Senior Bit Reigning (7 entries)
   Western Riding (13 entries)
   5th in Working Cow Horse (10 entries)

   This was Pee Wee's first senior show (Class A); he placed fourth in number of working points for Grand Champion Working Horse.

"There are very few grown horses by Baldy Buzz in this country," says Mr. Comfort, "but those we have located are doing real well and, I am told, were easy to train. The breeding program for Baldy is just getting under way. We set his fee at $300."

According to the AQHA performance report spread before me, Baldy has appeared in 39 shows, accumulating 18.5 points in Western Riding, 43 in Reining, 1.5 in Western Pleasure, and 14 in Working Cow Horse classes. He was high-point horse in Western Pleasure on the 1962 AQHA Honor Roll.

Western Pleasure

A Western Pleasure Horse Contest was set up by the American Quarter Horse Association, with a system of points and an Honor Roll, in 1959.

Rules

272. No horse shall be allowed to show in more than one registered western pleasure class per show; this class shall receive half points.
273. Open to registered Quarter Horses listed in the Permanent, Tentative, NQHBA, Appendix or New Appendix, normally used for pleasure.
274. Horses are to be shown at a walk, trot and lope on a reasonably loose rein without undue restraint. Horses must work both ways of the ring at all three gaits to demonstrate their ability with different leads. The judge shall have the right to ask for additional work from any horse.
275. Entries shall be penalized for being on wrong leads. Excessive speed is to be penalized.
286. No more than two classes divided by age are permitted at any one contest.

Honor Roll Horses in this class are:

Year	Horse	Points
1959	MOHAWK BUCK, Bkn. g. 50 by Yellow Buck	15
1960	#LETITIA, Ch. m. 52 by Texas Tom	23
1961	#DELL TOMMY, Br. h. 58 by #POCO DELL	31½
1962	#DELL TOMMY, Br. h. 58 by #POCO DELL	33½

Biographical Sketch

Dell Tommy

Says Jimmy Randals of Montoya, New Mexico: "I was the one who bred Dell Tommy and raised and owned him until I sold him to Mr. Moore at the Chicago International Quarter Horse Show when the colt was still a yearling. He was foaled in 1958, is seal brown in color and was sired by my stallion Poco Dell (P–33,075) which was by Poco Bueno (P–3044). Dell Tommy was out of Bonnie Benear, by Dusty Benear, a son of Tom Benear out of Pet Troutman (P–667). Bonnie Benear was out of Bonnie Clegg (by Billy Clegg out of Elena Baca). Poco Dell was out of Shady Dell by Pep-Up.

"The Chicago International was the first show I had put Dell Tommy in. He won his class. Tommy was the first foal from Poco Dell and Bonnie Benear, a brown mare of about 14.2 and weighing around 1100 pounds."

Dell Tommy's present owner, Mr. Jimmy Moore of Tipton, Michigan, says: "I went to the Chicago International looking to buy a good brood mare. Falling in love with Tommy on sight I knew straightaway I was going to have to have him and, forgetting the brood mare, bought him then and there."

What Mr. Moore didn't mention is that when he went to that show he had just enough money with him to pick up the brood mare he'd gone there to purchase. Since this amount lacked considerable of covering the price asked for the colt, he phoned home and had his wife (three hundred miles away) bring another check to make up the difference.

During the winter months Mr. Moore considered having Tommy broke and trained. He presently got in touch with Buster Lowther and arranged for Mr. Lowther to do the job. The colt was sent to Lowther at Union Lake, Michigan, the following spring.

Mr. Lowther states: "As a green colt Tommy showed interest in pleasure. He had won his blue ribbon at the International from a class of 28 yearlings. His first performance class was at the Michigan State Fair. From a class of 37 Junior horses, Tommy came out with the blue again. He went on to win one more first and a second before the end of that show season, at which time he was accredited with a Register of Merit."

Inasmuch as Mr. Lowther had other horses demanding his attention and was therefore unable to make as many shows as he thought he should, his daughter Judy, sixteen, took over the showing of Dell Tommy and handled most of his campaigning, at least through 1961.

Lowther says the colt took to Pleasure Classes "as a fish takes to water." He began to place consistently and, by the middle of June, his name was known throughout Michigan and Ohio. By the end of 1961 Dell Tommy had accumulated 31.5 points and was presented with an AQHA certificate and a Roll of Honor certificate and was named the Nation's Top Pleasure Horse in Junior and Open classes for 1961!

During the spring of 1962, Mr. Lowther decided to show Tommy to a few cows. "From the first he showed an avid interest," Lowther declares. "With only six weeks of training Tommy placed second in a novice cutting." But with the show season beginning, this training was discontinued.

As in 1961, the try for top pleasure horse was not really planned, but, since he was already on top, they campaigned him in 1962. Dell Tommy not only commanded respect as a good pleasure horse, but was conceded one of the best-mannered stallions around. Once, at a show, Tommy got untied and went to playing out in a field. Just one call of "Tommy!" from Lowther brought him up short. There he stood, still as a statue, until Lowther walked up to him.

He has been used to pony mares and geldings and, occasionally, stallions. Being used so extensively for showing and performance, he has had very little time for stud service and has bred a very limited number of mares.

In addition to other training, Mr. Lowther has reined him and now is working to make a cutting horse of him. Tommy has been shown in reining classes three times, placing twice; he has even been entered in barrel racing when a horse was needed to fill a class. He is versatile, agreeable, and willing.

Leading again in the race for top honors and with one show to go, Dell Tommy was returned to the Chicago International. The class was introduced as the largest pleasure class ever recorded, containing 90 of the country's best pleasure horses.

Tommy won, was awarded Roll of Honor again and named the Nation's Top Pleasure Horse for 1962.

During the winters of 1961 and 1962 Tommy's cutting education was furthered by trainer L. V. "Pee Wee" Clemnt who says: "I have ridden and trained some of the better cutting horses around and about and, in my opinion, Dell Tommy is the most versatile horse I have ridden. He is surely an outstanding horse."

Dell Tommy has accumulated a total of 70.5 points, 17 of which were earned at halter.

Halter Classes

City and State	Judge	Class		Placing
Chicago, Illinois	Finley	1959	Stud	1
Kalamazoo, Michigan	Ruetenik	1960	Stud	1
Kalamazoo, Michigan	Ruetenik	1960	Stud	Reserve
Canton, Ohio	Woodard	1960	Stud	1
Canton, Ohio	Woodard	1961	Stud	Champion
Pontiac, Michigan	Fuller	1960	Stud	1
Pontiac, Michigan	Fuller	1960	Stud	Reserve
South Lyon, Michigan	Davis	1960	Stud	1
Belleville, Michigan	Bentley	1960	Stud	Reserve
Saginaw, Michigan	Bradley	1960	Stud	1
North Randall, Ohio	Howe	1960	Stud	1
Lowell, Michigan	Blumenfel	1961	Stud	1
Lowell, Michigan	Dillman	1961	Stud	1
Montpelier, Ohio	Bechtol	1961	Stud	1
Columbus, Ohio	Dee Burk	1961	Stud	1
Dayton, Ohio	Bradley	1961	Stud	1
Dayton, Ohio	Bradley	1961	Stud	Reserve
Howel, Michigan	Jackson	1961	Stud	1
		Total points in Halter		17

Pleasure Classes Class

City and State	Judge	Class	No. of Horses	Place
Bristol, Indiana	Alderson	Pleasure	16	1
Ashland, Ohio	Call	Pleasure	23	1
Jenison, Michigan	Mick	Pleasure	24	1
Midland, Michigan	Survant	Pleasure	12	1
Montpelier, Ohio	Bechtol	Pleasure	14	1
Columbus, Ohio	Dee Burk	Pleasure	36	1
Ann Arbor, Michigan	Decker	Pleasure	22	1
Morrice, Michigan	Vanloozen	Pleasure	12	1
Belleville, Michigan	Fuller	Pleasure	11	1
Detroit, Michigan	Roper	Pleasure	37	1
Centreville, Michigan	Sharp	Pleasure	15	1
Detroit, Michigan	Ruetenik	Pleasure	25	1
Columbus, Ohio	Bentley	Pleasure	60	1
Ashland, Ohio	Holihan	Pleasure	41	1
Kokomo, Indiana	Leech	Pleasure	19	1
Battle Creek, Michigan	Hannagan	Pleasure	22	1
Grand Rapids, Michigan	Hannagan	Pleasure	20	1
Grand Blanc, Michigan	Warren	Pleasure	14	1
Sandusky, Michigan	Leech	Pleasure	11	1
Deleware, Ohio	Snider	Pleasure	15	1
Sparta, Michigan	Williams	Pleasure	30	1
Chicago, Illinois	Milligan	Pleasure	90	1

Total points in Pleasure 70.5

(Above are listed only the shows Dell Tommy won first in.)

In concluding his remarks Buster Lowther says: "Each Christmas Tommy has a Christmas stocking hung on his door and Santa never forgets him. Sometimes I think he is more human than some of the folks I run into. He is fond of music and always expects to get a kiss on his nose when he does well at the shows. He can be away for a week or more and Judy will not let any other horse be put in his stall. We have 25 box stalls in our barn and we could leave all the doors open and he would not enter any stall but his own. Folks from all over the States can tell you about Dell Tommy. He's real folks and his manners and disposition just naturally make him popular."

He has been featured on a cover of the *Quarter Horse Digest*, and appears in the booklet *How To Ride A Quarter Horse*.

Working Cowhorse

Points and an Honor Roll were set up for this rugged class in 1952.

Rules

241. No show may offer this working cowhorse class as an approved class for which points will be awarded unless the show also offers an approved Reining class with the AQHA reining pattern.

242. No horse shall be allowed to show in more than one registered Working Cowhorse class per show.

243. The approved pattern will be used and each contestant will cause his horse to travel at the gait indicated for each part of the pattern.

244. Horses will enter the ring at a walk, taking a jog-trot and slow lope upon request. They then shall line up or retire from the ring at the judge's direction. Horses shall then be worked individually.

245. Rider shall start his workout with a figure eight, executed at a lope two times and of sufficient size to avoid short, choppy turns. Failure of horse to change both front and hind leads shall be faulted. The smoother and more even the gait, the more credit to the horse.

246. The entry shall then go to the end of the arena, turn and run full length of the arena, make a straight sliding stop, turn away from the rail, run to the other end of the arena, make a straight sliding stop, turn away from the rail, run to the center of the arena, and make a straight sliding stop.

247. After allowing the horse to gather itself, back the horse in exactly the opposite direction in a straight line for 10 to 15 feet.

248. Horse shall then be brought up to the judge, stopped and, with weight on the hindquarters and with hind legs in one position, make a quarter turn to the right, half turn to the left, and half turn to the right. The entry shall then retire from the arena.

249. The judge may request additional work at his option.

250. In the event that cattle are to be worked, it shall be so stated in the premium list and the working procedure will be as follows:

251. One animal shall be turned into the arena and the contestant shall hold the animal at one end of the arena long enough to indicate to the judge that the horse is watching the cow.

252. The cow shall then be allowed to run down the side of the arena and the contestant shall turn the animal twice each way against the fence. The cow shall then be taken to the center of the arena and circled once each way.

253. Scoring will be on the basis of 60 to 80, with 70 denoting an average performance. The same basis of scoring shall apply to both the reined work and cow work.

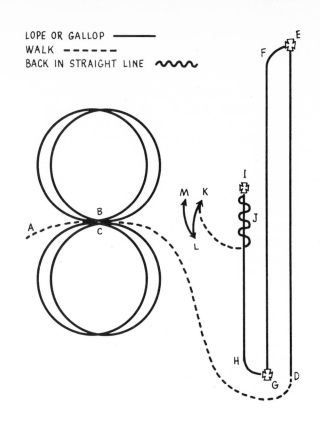

LOPE OR GALLOP ——————
WALK ― ― ― ― ―
BACK IN STRAIGHT LINE ∿∿∿

47. Dell Tommy, Judy Lowther up.

Don and Pearl Stickney

254. Fall of horse and/or rider while being shown either in cow work or reined work shall not eliminate the entry.

255. The following characteristics are considered as faults: Switching tail, exaggerated opening of mouth, hard or heavy mouth, nervous throwing of head, lugging on bridle, halting or hesitation while being shown—particularly when being run out—indicating anticipation of being set up, which is characteristic of an overtrained horse.

256. The characteristics of a good working horse are: Good manners; horse should be shifty, smooth and have his feet under him at all times; when stopping hind feet should be well under him; horse should have a soft mouth and should respond to a light rein, especially when turning; head should be maintained in its natural position; horse should be able to work at reasonable speed and still be under control of the rider.

257. Entries shall be shown with stock saddle, without tapaderos. When a bit is used in this class, horses will be ridden with grazing, snaffle, curb, half-breed, bar or spade bit. No wire curbs regardless of how padded or taped, no chin strap narrower than one-half inch; no nose bands or tie-downs will be permitted. Chain curbs are permissible but must be of the standard flat variety and must meet the approval of the judge.

258. Rider shall wear Western hat, chaps (shotgun chaps or chinks), cowboy boots, and carry rope or reata. Spurs are optional.

259. The use of shoes other than standard horseshoes is to be discouraged and may be penalized by the judge.

260. Only one hand may be used on reins and hands must not be changed. Hand to be around reins. Fingers between reins not permitted. Spurs or romal shall not be used forward of the cinch. While horse is in motion, rider's hands shall be clear of horse and saddle.

261. Judge should instruct exhibitors to keep hands clear of saddle except when it is necessary to use them to prevent a fall. Riders may be disqualified for not following judge's instructions. Judges should pay particular attention to the hands of juniors, as a light hand is paramount to becoming a good showman of stock horses.

262. A hackamore horse is not more than four years old and must never have been ridden in a bridle other than a snaffle bit. Rider may use both hands. Horses shall enter arena and work in the same manner as prescribed for bridle classes. Horses will be ridden only with a rawhide braided or leather braided or rope bosal. Absolutely no iron will be permitted under jaws regardless of how padded or taped.

263. Ride pattern as follows:

    (a) begin work
    (b) first figure eight
    (c) second figure eight
    (d) begin run
    (e) sliding stop
    (f) turn away from rail and begin second run
    (g) sliding stop
    (h) turn away from rail and make short run

(i) sliding stop
(j) back up
(k) quarter turn to right
(l) half turn to left
(m) half turn to right

Honor roll horses in this class have been:

Year	Horse	Points
1952	ANGUS JOE, Ch. g. 45 by Joe Traveler, Jr.	2
1953	ANGUS JOE, Ch. g. 45 by Joe Traveler, Jr.	2
	BUTTERSCOTCH PARKE, B. m. 48 by General Ike	2
	K4 BISK, Ch. g. 49 by Johnny Boy	2
	SHOEMAKER'S PAY DAY, B. h. 49 by NUGGET McCUE	2
1954	#FAME MOUNTY, Pal. g. 50 by Cripple Mount	2
1955	#L. M. SHE'LL DO, Pal. m. 51 by Brush Mount	6
1956	#SQUATTY, Br. g. 51 by Tony L.	5
1957	#SKIPITY SCOOT, Pal. h. 52 by SCOOTER W.	9
1958	MELODY MOUNT, Bkn. m. 48 by MUSIC MOUNT	6
1959	JOE LAURO, S. h. 50 by Lauro	2
1960	#BALDY C., Ch. h. 45 by King Clegg	2½
	MESCAL BROWNIE, Br. g. 55 by Driftwood	2½
	PRETTY POKEY, Dn. h. 48 by #POCO BUENO	2½
1961	#TENDER BOY, S. h. 55 by Bartender	3½
1962	BLACK LAGOON, Blk. g. 58 by Alumnus (TB)	9
	BOB BRITCHES, B. h. 56 by #BAY BREEZY BOB	9

Biographical Sketches

Black Lagoon

Bred by Roddy Anderson of Las Vegas, Nevada, this fine gelding is out of Bunkie by the good running and cow-working stallion Red Man (by Joe Hancock), and is jointly owned by Paul Hayward and Tex Gates of the same city. Working throughout the year in Utah, Nevada, and California, Black Lagoon earned a total of nine points in this event. This was extremely good when set up against the records of previously honored contenders; it is even more impressive when we learn this was his first point-earning season in the arena. Not only did he earn these nine points, he also garnered a point in Western Riding, nine points at halter, 18 points in Reining, and 12 points in Western Pleasure. This four-year-old won five of his six classes in which he earned the points which put him into this roster. In the remaining class he was third of 13 entries.

Some of his more impressive wins were at Las Vegas with a first in five and a first in nine, and at Salt Lake City with a first in 12, and a first in nine at Heber, Utah.

Bob Britches

Co-winner of the 1962 Honor Roll Working Cowhorse award was the veteran Bob Britches, a grandson of King. Bred by J.M. Frost III (Houston, Texas), he is out of the mare Fiesty Britches by that grand old match-racing pappy of top cowhorses Chubby—twenty times a winner. Chubby was one of the last surviving sons of old Midnight. Owned by Ralph Cook (Springfield, Oregon), Bob Britches, working primarily in the far Northwest, earned nine points in this event, picking up additionally seven Western Riding points, one halter point, eight Reining points, and 11 Western Pleasure points; these pushed this campaigning show horse's total counts to 11 Western Riding, eight at Halter, 13 in Reining, 10½ in Working Cowhorse, and 19½ in Western Pleasure. His more notable wins came from Eugene, Oregon, where he was first in ten, Canby where he was first in 11, Salem with a first in 12, and at North Portland where he was first in 19.

Halter

An Honor Roll for Halter Horses was set up in 1952 and the following horses, by scoring highest, achieved inclusion:

Year	Horse	Points
1952	Bill Cody, Ch. h. 44 by Wimpy	19
1953	MONSIEUR JOE, Br. h. 48 by Red Star Joe	68
1954	Pretty Pam, Gru. m. 49 by Buckskin Joe	59
1955	#DEE GEE, B. m. 45 by Bartender	69
1956	Barbara Star, Ch. m. 48 by Star Duster	62
1957	Hank's Sue, Ch. m. 53 by HANK H.	68
1958	#POCO LYNN, Dn. m. 54 by #POCO BUENO	72
1959	Pandarita Hill, Ch. m. 54 by Showdown	99
1960	#MISS JAZEBEL, B. m. 58 by #PUDDEN HEAD	129
1961	Wimpy Leo San, S. h. 59 by Leo San	77
1962	Poco Margaret, S. m. 58 by #POCO PINE	177

Biographical Sketch

Poco Margaret

Foaled by Charlotte Ann, a granddaughter of Peppy, Poco Margaret was bred by B. D. Wheelis (Jacksboro, Texas) and is owned by Mike Rutherford of Buda. Competition for the 1962 Honor Roll award at halter proved extremely spirited and was characterized by a continuing seesaw battle for supremacy which necessitated careful tabulation and a constant rechecking of points before the final winner stood revealed. The four-year-old Poco Margaret was campaigned in 83 approved shows ranging from northern Illinois to west Texas. Her winning count of 177 points plainly represents the highest number of halter points ever piled up in a single year since the Honor Roll was established; and the defeated runner-up (the high point stallion, Jim Harlan) with 170 points was way out ahead of any previous winner.

The 1962 show season pushed Poco Margaret's lifetime total halter points to an astonishing 415. Her best scores this year came from Fort Worth where she won in a class of 22, and Houston where she was second of 26.

Chariots and Cutters

The world's maddest, most spectacular horse competition is currently sweeping all before it as a spectator sport in Idaho's Boise Basin. As Robert M. Hyatt said in a *Quarter Horse Journal* article on the subject, "With the possible exception of occasional movies, this is the first time America—if not the rest of the world—has witnessed charioteering. These latter-day Ben Hurs exhibit a brand of dare-deviltry that makes you grip the edge of your seat as they pound around the track at breakneck speed. Their pre-Bible contemporaries never went so fast. Anything can happen— and does time after time—in these thunderous quarter-mile heats. Real danger lurks at the last turn when the drivers, cracking whips and yelling like fiends, coax the last ounce of speed out of their teams as they near the finish line. A chariot flips over, spilling its driver, or a couple of chariots lock wheels in close contention, causing a terrific mixup."

Alfred L. Hahn, one of the AQHA Directors for Idaho and an official of the Spring Fever Quarter Horse Association, had this to say when I questioned him: "This is mainly a winter event. They run on cutters when we have enough snow, and when we don't they put on wheels. Some Associations use a turn; around here they run a quarter of a mile straight

48. Dead heat in chariot races sponsored by the Upper Snake Valley Racing Association, Rigby, Idaho, June 30, 1962. Elvin Palmer and Ferra Young are the drivers.

out, two teams at a time. The way it is worked, these cutter people form an association, generally having 22 to 24 teams. There are about twelve associations currently engaged in this sport throughout Idaho, Utah, Wyoming, and Montana. Most of them operate, I believe, on a 12 to 13 week schedule, usually starting the latter part of January and finishing about the middle of March.

"They start the first race by drawing; afterward winners compete against winners and losers against losers; in each association the end of their season leaves one team on top. Ivan L. Ashment of Idaho Falls was winner this past year of the local cutter association; he is also president of this association and could probably give you further information."

A letter from Mr. Ashment states:

I was real pleased to end up as the 1963 Champion of the National Cutter Association. I was beat twice during the year, which included meeting Rocky Mountain, All American, Magic Valley and other fine associations of the area. I had a return race a week later with the one team, defeating him; the other team and mine were never re-matched.

This has become quite a winter pastime in this area, and they are getting some very fine teams. In our meets with other associations we were only defeated once in the entire year. Many of the teams and drivers are veterans of many years' experience but year after year a few new teams join up.

The trend has always been toward the use of Quarter Horses for this kind of competition; we do have a number of teams that are Thoroughbred and they have done well in competition, depending on the track. Keeping in mind these races are run 440 yards and on a different track each week, a given team will not always perform consistent with past experience. Sometimes a track will be six inches deep in mud and the following week will be covered with snow—so you can see why I lean toward the Quarter Horse. He is more versatile. The fact that we don't have photo-finishes leaves me without any picture, but I will try to find some. The team referred to in the photo Mr. Hahn sent was sired by Hayer (by Piggin String) and Rukin String (by Piggin String); the other team was by Fiddler—some of Hank Weiscamp's good breeding.

During the past year there were some AAA-rated horses in competition. The one horse I had, Star Bypass (by Leo Joe and Glen Bypass) was AAA, and the filly was also by Leo Joe (never had a rating); she was injured the year before and unable to compete on the track. This team sold in the later part of the season to Hyle Taylor of Aberdeen for $15,000, to give you some idea of values up here. They were just one of the many good teams in the Association. In my estimation I was real lucky. There were eight teams in the Association and any one of them could have won.

It would take a good bit of research to get all the names and breeding, but I will give you some of the top bloodlines we are drawing from—Leo, Vandy, Palleo Pete, Tonto Bars Gill, Hayer, Rukin String; and the coming year will find Go Man Go, Triple Chick, Palleo Pete, Joe Less, Breeze Bar, Clabber's Win, Barred, Direct Win (TB). There are many more good ones I may have forgotten.

I would say the All American Cutter Association was one of the first to get going, probably twenty years ago. Since that time there are a number that have started in Idaho and Utah. Our particular Association is one of the largest, with 22 to 24 teams in competition. They usually run on Saturday of each week for a total of about 16 or 17 meetings a year.

Racing

An Honor Roll, with points, was set up for straightaway Racing in 1952. High-point horses in this field (with AQHA Champions marked #) are:

Year	Horse	Points
1952	#LITTLE EGYPT, Ch. m. 49 by TEXAS DANDY	39
1953	MISS MEYERS, Ch. m. 49 by LEO	32
1954	GOLD BARS, Ch. m. 49 by Three Bars (TB)	29
1955	SECO JIMMIE, B. h. 52 by Seco Joe	26
1956	EASTER ROSE, Pal. m. 53 by Monterrey	30
1957	MR. BAR NONE, Ch. h. 55 by Three Bars (TB)	24
	VANNEVAR, S. g. 53 by VANDY	24
1958	MISS LOUTON, S. m. 56 by TONTO BARS GILL	23
1959	MISS LOUTON, S. m. 56 by TONTO BARS GILL	30
1960	ARIZONAN, Ch. g. 53 by SPOTTED BULL (TB)	21
1961	CONNIE REBA, S. m. 59 by SUGAR BARS	23
1962	THAT'S FRANCIS, Br. f. 60 by THAT'S MY BOY	24

Biographical Sketch

That's Francis

Breeder-owner is N. W. Gates (Batesville, Texas). This stylish filly won the 1962 Honor Roll award in racing, having a very successful freshman year. From 11 starts, she won five, grabbed place money three times, and earned $8065.50. Eight of her starts were run in AAA time. Carrying heavy weights her best times were: 330 yards at Sonora in :17.4; 300 yards at Junction in :16.0; 400 yards at Sunland Park in :20.4; and 440 yards at Sunland in :22.3, while outlasting such sprinters as Goodwin Girl (by Lapara Joe), Miss Bar Leo (by Three Bars, TB), Lady Venture (by Johnny Dial), My Bar None (by Mr. Bar None), Miss Bo Bars (by Sandy Bar),

Running J. Bar (by Mr. Bar None), and Marooned (by Bob's Folly). In the first four of her 1963 starts That's Francis placed in the money.

Jumpers

On page 7 of *The Quarter Horse* (February, 1949) there was a photo captioned "Is There Anything A Quarter Horse Can't Do?" It showed Mrs. Beverly Young going over a hurdle on the Quarter Horse stallion Charlie Horse (NQHBA 12559). This jumper was sired by Center Fire (by Lucky Strike by Old Sorrel) out of Beauty by Grano de Oro (by Little Joe). Cut lines read: "Charlie Horse is said to be the only jumping Quarter Horse in the world. It is also possible he enjoys the distinction of being the only stallion ever successfully trained for jumping. Charlie Horse is owned by Mrs. Young and her husband, Jack C. Young, but a transaction now pending may soon send him to Guatamala to breed jumping horses for use in the 1952 Olympics."

Page 5 of the April issue of the same periodical carried a photograph of another Quarter Horse going over a hurdle. Cut lines here read: "Wayne Dennis of Windfall, Indiana, promptly corrected us with the above photograph of his stallion Tiger Joe Bailey (NQHBA 49) easily clearing a 4'2" hurdle with Joe Bird of Ozark, Missouri, more or less in the saddle. Tiger Joe Bailey is by Joe Bailey (Gonzales) by King (Possum), and is out of Pamilia by Lion d'Or. Any more jumpin' stallions?"

Nothing more was heard on jumpers, at least around here, until an article by Frank Newsom appeared on page 274 of the *Quarter Horse Journal* (December, 1962), titled "Quarter Horse Wins Renown As Jumper." The story concerns Fire One, a registered Quarter Horse lent to the United States Equestrian Team to "join the best jumping horse flesh in the nation after a brilliant first season in the Green and Open Jumper divisions." This is a very engrossing article concerned with Fire One's subsequent exploits, and just goes to prove that, with a Quarter Horse, anything is certainly possible.

Next, on page 120 of the *Quarter Horse Journal* for February, 1963, an article by Linda McKay discusses "Oregon Quarter Horses Trained for Jumping." We know of no reason why a Quarter Horse, or any number of Quarter Horses, could not compete with the best in this field.

Part III: Cutting Horse Country

General Information

During the 1890s, when the branding chute first came into use, it was thought that great cowhorses would soon be following the buffalo into limbo. And they might indeed have become less numerous (as my good friend Bob Denhardt has somewhere pointed out) if rodeo contests, or the commercial beginnings of what are now called rodeos, hadn't started at about the same time. Rodeo today, like Quarter Horse racing, has become big business; in fact, everything about the Quarter Horse is big business. Rodeo has become a proving ground for bold men and quick horses. Because of the tense and often dangerous competition offered by modern rodeo contests, greater speed and all-around ability is now demanded of all who expect to wind up in the money. It takes a lot better horse than the one we had on the ranches before the turn of the century. It takes a lot better horse than the one we had ten years ago.

The cowhorse achieves considerable prestige from this sport, earning for his riders many thousands of dollars each year. Without a top-flight mount no rider can hope to find himself in the money. Co-operation and co-ordination are extremely important. Both horse and rider must do their very best for the whole duration of their time in the arena or success will pass them by. It is no place for amateurs.

Various horse-using sequences in rodeo today are roping, bulldogging, wild cow milking, bronc riding, and cutting. Because the popularity of cutting horse contests, both as a spectator sport and as a sport for participants, has increased enormously since the NCHA got into the picture, we're devoting this section entirely to cutting horses.

In 1952 the American Quarter Horse Association devised an Honor Roll and a point system for registered competition involving cutting horses.

Rules

188. The management of any contest shall determine whether or not an elimination is necessary, the number of Go-Rounds to be held, and the number of horses to be shown at each performance.

189. Scores made in an elimination shall not be carried over into a Go-Round or Final. However, the score of each horse for each Go-Round will be added to determine placings in contests having no Finals; and, in contests having Finals, the score of each horse for each Go-Round will be added to get the top horses for the Finals.

190. The score of each horse in the Finals plus his score in the Go-Rounds will determine the final placings, consistency of performance being recognized as a major factor.

191. NO CONTEST IS COMPLETE UNTIL ALL TIES TO SIXTH PLACE HAVE BEEN WORKED OFF, TIME PERMITTING.

192. An exhibitor may enter one or more horses in a class, but a rider may ride only one horse in each class, except that in Junior working classes a rider may show as many as two horses, but no more than two. Each horse may have only one rider per class.

193. If there is an elimination the same rider must ride the same horse in the elimination and the class.

194. No horse shall be allowed to show in more than one registered cutting class per show.

195. The American Quarter Horse Association strongly recommends that Registered Cutting Contests be held whenever possible. In this contest only registered horses (Permanent, Tentative, National, New Appendix and Appendix) can compete. NCHA rules will be used.

196. If a show holds both open and registered cutting classes, separate works must be held for each event. The scores earned in an open cutting may not also be used as the scores for a registered cutting at that same show.

197. Numbered, Appendix, or New Appendix horses participating in contests sponsored by the National Cutting Horse Association or the Canadian Cutting Horse Association are eligible for points on the final placings of such contests except for novice contests, which are not recognized by the American Quarter Horse Association.

198. The pertinent rules of the National Cutting Horse Association are available in printed form upon request from the National Cutting Horse Association. Address: P. O. Box 9006, Fort Worth, Texas.

Honor Roll horses through 1962 are:

Year	Horse	Points
1952	MISS NANCY BAILEY, B. m. 46 by ROYAL KING	31
1953	MISS NANCY BAILEY, B. m. 46 by ROYAL KING	57
1954	MISS TEXAS CRAFT, Blk. m. 49 by Double Star	115
1955	TRINKET BENNETT (Snooky), Pal. m. 48 by SAND BOWL	21
1956	TRINKET BENNETT (Snooky), Pal. m. 48 by SAND BOWL	33
1957	#POCO STAMPEDE, Dn. h. 52 by #POCO BUENO	32
1958	#POCO STAMPEDE, Dn. h. 52 by #POCO BUENO	32
1959	#POCO LENA, B. m. 49 by #POCO BUENO	130

1960   #POCO LENA, B. m. 49 by #POCO BUENO   147
1961   #POCO LENA, B. m. 49 by #POCO BUENO   162
1962   #CUTTER BILL, Pal. h. 55 by Buddy Dexter   156

Open Cutting Horse Contests

The National Cutting Horse Association is dedicated to the cause of the Cutting Horse, whether on the ranch or in the show arena. From its small beginning at the Southwestern Exposition & Fat Stock Show, Fort Worth, in the spring of 1946, when a group of interested ranchmen and cowboys got together, it has rapidly developed into a nation-wide organization. The first objective of the Association was the development of a standard method under which all cutting horse contests could be conducted in an equitable manner.

The cutting horse has always been and will continue to be a ranch necessity. On the ranch no rules are needed since all a horse has to do is to cut out a particular head of stock from a herd of cattle. However, in the contest arena the absolute necessity of having a uniform means of judging horses caused the second objective of NCHA—namely, to standardize rules for judging. In other words, to give contestants as well as spectators a better understanding of what a cutting horse must do and must not do when in the show arena. This also provides the means by which contests are judged, as it gives definite penalties and provides a fair basis for judging cutting horses and determining their good work and occasional faults.

As more and more contests are held each year, with increased prize money, a greater amount of time is given to the training of cutting horses. This results in making competition more intense and each year it becomes necessary for the National Cutting Horse Association to add more stringent penalties to the judging rules, to enable a judge to draw a finer point between horses. The NCHA Director must be constantly alert.

Encouragement of fair play among contestants and the performance of good horses have always been high on the agenda of this Association; this is as true in 1963 as it was in 1946. Credit for the success of the Association goes to its members. The affiliates of the National Cutting Horse Association also play an important part in the presentation of cutting horse contests.

At present the NCHA has 63 affiliates and 1800 members in 48 states, the District of Columbia, Canada, Mexico, and Arabia. This organization has grown from 54 members in 1946. Membership numbers ranchers as well as businessmen who either own cutting horses for competitive sport or have a very great interest in cutting horses.

One of the important functions of the NCHA is the approval of championship cutting horse contests and the keeping of complete records of these contests. In addition a record is kept of points won by member-owned horses at approved contests. At the end of each point year the NCHA top ten cutting horses are designated, which of course include the world's champion and reserve champion and the recognition of the champion stallion, mare, and gelding.

The NCHA Rules

Instead of quoting from the Rules Book I have decided to present a summary of an *interpretation* of the rules which was published several years ago in the NCHA magazine, *Cuttin' Hoss Chatter*, by a committee of past Presidents—Tom Saunders, Ray Smyth and H. Calhoun—at the request of the Executive Committee.

It must be remembered by the layman that when the NCHA was organized the cutting horse had already been an institution on the ranches of Texas for at least a hundred years. The service this great horse performed was an integral part of the early development and growth of the Southwest's vast livestock industry, a service to man which is still of essential importance on the ranches of today.

The advent of the cutting horse into the contest arena came only recently, as compared to its long history, and this inevitable introduction was due in part to the demand of the show-going public to see this horse of fabulous performance and legend in action.

As the cutting horse grew in popularity as a contest and exhibition horse, and shows other than Fort Worth sought their talents, the NCHA established and constantly improved rules by which these horses could best be judged on their actions in competition under standard conditions provided by a show arena, as compared to the essentials that determined a top cutting horse in actual ranch work.

In order for the novice to assimilate this reasoning more easily it must be stated that the men who formulated the rules were cattle ranchers intent on stressing the fundamentals of the job a cutting horse is supposed to do, whether in a show arena or on the range. Even with the addition of turn-back men and other factors totally foreign to ranch conditions but provided to increase the action and entertainment from a spectator's point of view, the rules and their descriptive terms never deviated from the objective that the horse judged to place must first, last, and always be a true cutting horse. Therefore the reining horse, the schooled or circus horse has never found a place for long in an NCHA approved cow-cutting arena.

With this background in mind it can be readily understood why the stage set for the contest is a facsimile of that encountered in ranch work, with the rules constituting a fair basis for a qualified judge to determine the best, next best, and so on, by observing and scoring the good or bad points of the horses competing. This tie-in with actual ranch work and ranch cutting horse ability, which is the foundation of all rules, enables the qualified observer to form an opinion the minute a horse travels toward the herd as to whether or not it has the makings of a cutting horse.

Thus Rule 1 is the essential first step in judging a contest. This rule states in effect that "a horse will be given credit for the way he enters and acts in a herd, also credited for the manner in which he cuts one out and penalized if he (or his rider) creates unnecessary disturbance."

This rule, to all cowmen and cowboys who have participated in a ranch roundup and held herd in an open pasture, is of major importance. A nervous, high-headed, high-stepping horse or careless rider approaching, entering, or working in a skittish herd just thrown together on a roundup ground can mean but one thing—trouble, causing unnecessary chousing and possibly a stampede, with hours of additional work for men and shrinkage and damage to cattle.

A jittery, dancing, prancing counterfeit of a would-be cutting horse is the worst economic hazard a cow outfit can own, and by the same token its counterpart in the contest arena should be severely penalized. Therefore the horse that carries its head low, travels cautiously toward the herd, stepping with a quiet cushion-like jog, holds ears alert, exhibits anticipation and know-how of the job about to begin, and continues this display of cow sense while in the herd—that is the horse deserving credit. A horse and rider relaxed, with the confidence that comes from knowledge and experience in working cattle, is a picture long to be remembered by the spectator and an important cue to the judge to be on the alert for the action and ability that will probably follow.

In actual ranch work, when an animal is cut from the herd it is driven past the herd holders and thrown on toward the cuts. A horse to have any value as a cutting horse on the ranch must have the ability to drive an animal away from the herd and in the general direction of the cuts.

In a contest, when an animal is cut from the herd and a horse tries to drive it toward the center of the arena, the horse pretty well duplicates the act of driving one past the herd holders and letting it go to the cuts. Instead of going to the cuts, of course, the animal is turned by the turnback men in order to provide more play and demonstrate the horse's ability to keep it from returning to the herd.

Rule 2 states: "When an animal is cut from the herd, it must be taken toward the center of the arena. If it goes down the arena fence, that is alright, but the horse should never get ahead of the animal and duck it back toward the herd to get more play but should let the turnback men turn it back to him."

When this rule was put into effect it was to help correct some horses that were working cattle on the arena fence. Sometimes the back fence behind the herd was used. This fence usually was curved or had a slight angle in it where a horse could hem a yearling in and give it a good chousing by ducking ahead of it and turning it back, regardless of the direction it had started.

This was being criticized by the spectators and show managements. It did not in any way resemble cutting cattle on the ranch, or give the judges a chance to see what the horse was capable of doing about heading an animal when there was no fence to turn it against.

This rule has worked well, especially in eliminating the working of cattle on a fence. Some improvement may be needed at times in driving cattle away from the herd toward the center section of the arena. This was not intended to mean the geographical center of the arena but a cross section of the arena far enough away from the herd to represent driving toward the cuts.

The previous rules discussed were two of the carry-overs which, in the 1946 to 1949 *Handbooks*, were labeled "Suggestions for judges to consider." There were no set rules of judging at that time; only these suggestions which a judge might follow in penalizing horses that had faulted, according to his judgment.

Published in these early booklets was a statement which gives food for thought even in this day when perfection in contest rules is being sought. The old paragraph stated: "It is almost impossible to make an ironclad set of rules for judging cutting horses since no two performances are going to be alike; neither are any two cattle cut from the herd going to act alike." This verified the fact known then in cow country—now known everywhere —that it takes a true cutting horse to perform a cutting horse's job, and a qualified judge to determine which particular job was the best.

During the early days of the Association it was presumed that all cutting horse judges would be men engaged in the livestock business and duly qualified to pass judgment on the training and natural ability of a cutting horse. It was also presumed that those entering contests were folks well versed in this same knowledge of ranch work.

This presumption, however, was short-lived as cutting horse contests spread like wildfire throughout the nation. The amazing part of this transition was that these horses never lost their traditional instinct for accomplishment and performance, even in the hands of new owners and trainers far removed from the cattle ranges of the West, and that these widespread contests and their judges progressed exceedingly well in this fascinating entertainment originally derived from ranch work.

However, in order to further this wide spread of interest and to assist to some extent those judges without the experience gained from actual ranch work to eliminate human errors of judgment, some of the suggestions for judging were changed, penalties were fixed, and the whole was incorporated into a set of rules.

Typifying this farsightedness and progress, rules committees consisting of a cross section of the membership were appointed by the President to recommend these various changes and set penalties. From these recommendations, duly approved by the Executive Committee, came the present rules, some of which are designed to relieve judges, especially where set penalties are concerned, of the responsibility of making a decision based on their personal judgment.

For instance, Rule 3 provides a penalty of two points for using the back fence for turn-back purposes. Regardless of the location of the herd, the action or circumstances involved, a horse and animal reaching the section of the back fence designated by the judges automatically receives a two-point penalty, irrespective of the ability the horse has shown up to this time. This rule was intended to encourage the driving of cattle away from the herd (as was Rule 2) in order to portray ranch cutting, but the return penalty past an artificial point does not tie in with ranch work.

It was not requested or intended that the committee of past Presidents discuss or question the practicability of any rule, but these rules are closely scrutinized in an effort to explain them, and in our unbiased opinion some are found conflicting and a cause for controversy. This opinion is substantiated by information from committee member H. Calhoun, who at the present is actively engaged in judging some of the major shows. He explains that under set-penalty rules, such as Rules 3 and 8, a judge cannot differentiate between the horse of natural ability and the horse of lesser experience, training, or desire, nor can a judge take into consideration the causes of losing an animal.

Some rules were originated for the purpose of serving as a descriptive guide for the layman, as well as for penalty effect, such as Rule 4, which states: "If a horse runs into, scatters the herd, lanes or circles the herd against the arena fence while trying to head an animal, he will be penalized heavily." The predicament described in this sentence does not happen to the horse and rider experienced in handling cattle. Such a display of carelessness on the part of the rider is unpardonable and deserves a severe penalty.

A rider, circling the herd and landing and holding an animal against the fence, after missing an attempt to head him, keeps the animal out of the herd all right but does not exhibit any judgment in cutting. In reality Rule 4, with its suggested heavy penalty, if administered literally could lead to the brink of disqualification. With the penalty of this rule plus those of other rules provide for this predicament—plus Rule 8, which simultaneously assesses 5 points for letting the animal get back—the horse and his rider could well be sent to Siberia for life. The rule (4) describes thoroughly what a horse and rider should *not* do in order to be considered wise in the ways of handling cattle.

One of the first suggestions or rules to remain in their original descriptive form is Rule 5, which states: "If a horse turns the wrong way with tail toward animal he will be disqualified for that go-round with no score." This was a straight reminder that a horse engaged in such a practice was not a Cutting Horse. Nowadays this "goose egg" is rarely ever seen on a judge's card, because the rider promptly takes control and prevents this unnatural twist before it can occur. The rule originated from the simple fact that a horse which does not face or eye at all times the animal being maneuvered has no resemblance to a Cutting Horse and is therefore deserving of no score.

The natural ability, the inherent or cultivated desire, of a true cutting horse is a thing admired by all. To observe the performance of a horse cutting cattle on a ranch or in an arena, requiring very little help from its rider, is a joy to behold. The experienced horse, displaying cow sense in the highest degree, will generally need less man assistance than will the horse of lesser experience, willingness, or training.

Hence Rule 6, which states in effect: "A horse will be penalized one point each time he is reined or cued to the left or right. Penalized each time this occurs during the performance, penalized heavier for having to be picked up hard, plowlined, spurred in the shoulder, etc." The purpose of these penalties is simply to enable the horse possessing an abundance of natural cutting ability to place ahead of the horse needing rider assistance.

Rule 7 states: "For riding with a tight rein through a performance a penalty will be given; for part of the time, less penalty." This is to encourage a loose rein in arena contests and discourage those accustomed to riding ranch horses without slack, for safety while cutting on rough ground or in arenas dangerously undermined with prairie dog holes.

As mentioned already, Rule 8 definitely declares, "If a horse lets an animal get back in the herd he will be penalized five points." This differs considerably from the original ruling, for in those days "a horse that went thataway while the yearling went thisaway" was penalized considerably more.

The statement that a cutting horse is made, not born, is a true one. But he must be born with an inherent desire to work cattle or you're wasting your time. In the early ranching days a cutting horse usually more or less made himself. A cowhorse that, after years of constant work and experience in the routine handling of cattle, began to show astonishing evidence of "thinking cow," outmaneuvering and besting a dodging cow at his own game, was usually soon relieved of regular range work and elevated to the enchanting title of "Cutter."

These early-day self-made horses reached well up in years before gaining such perfection as evidenced by the twenty-two-year-old that won the first recorded money-posted cutting contest, held during the Cowboy Reunion of July 29, 1898 at Haskell, Texas; the fourteen-year-old that was acclaimed the Best Cutting Horse during the first exhibition ever held indoors at Fort Worth in 1919; and the ten horses averaging twelve years of age entering the first contest ever held in connection with a rodeo, inaugurated by the Southwestern Exposition & Fat Stock Show on March 6, 1920, also at Fort Worth.

With such traits embedded in the better-blooded horse of today it is little cause for wonder that this same stage of perfection can be attained at half the age by persistent, wise training and plenty of actual cow-work experience.

One of the first noticeable characteristics of the early-day cowhorse in the process of becoming a cutting horse—a quality to look for in the beginner of today—was the ability to head an animal and turn back simultaneously, without lost motion or without going too far past to keep command of the situation. This ability is necessary for any good ranch using horse and a definite "must" for the cutting horse.

Thus Rule 9 provides: "When a horse heads an animal and goes past it to the degree that he loses his working advantage, he will be penalized each time he does so. If a horse goes past as much as his length he will be assessed a heavier penalty. Unnecessary roughness—such as a horse using its working position to paw or bite cattle—will be penalized."

The first part of this rule is intended to penalize the horse that steps too far beyond or deliberately runs by an animal headed. It is understood that any horse, in order to head an animal, has to step past to a certain degree, largely depending upon the speed of both. The severe penalty is for the horse that does not know how to do his job or is indifferent, and is past the animal before he wakes up to the fact.

As in open-pasture cutting, a horse with a knack or ability to maintain its working advantage after heading an animal is in a position to stop and hover the animal, staying head to head with the dodging critter until it gives up and heads toward the cuts. A display of this kind of knowledge and action is what has made a cutting horse and the cutting contest so highly entertaining and popular.

In the latter half of Rule 9, the part dealing with unnecessary roughness was not intended to penalize the horse that refuses to let an animal go past him, but to penalize the horse that wants to play and create a disturbance or the ill-tempered horse that wants to bite or paw. Such horses cannot do a good job; therefore they deserve the penalty.

Rule 10 reads: "If a contestant quits an animal he is working when the horse is out of position, or the animal has undue advantage of the horse, he will be penalized three points." This is to discourage a contestant from quitting an animal felt to be too rank to handle. In ranch work it is time consuming and foolish to cut an animal out of the herd unless it is intended to be driven and thrown with the cuts. By the same token, a contestant in the arena should make a determined effort to work the animal chosen to the best of the horse's ability. Quitting or changing over before the animal is completely out of the herd or before the animal cut out is stopped, under control, or turned away from the horse automatically incurs a three-point penalty.

Although these rules pretty well cover about every fault a horse or rider might conceivably make, they do not in each instance point up what a true cutting horse is supposed to do; it is taken for granted that the judge and contestants will be qualified and understanding. Each year the NCHA publishes a revised *Rule Book*, which persons desiring more detailed information might consult.

No other horse in history has served man in industry to such advantage economically. By continuing to keep the contest and the rules as free of artificiality as possible in the portrayal of this ranch work, and by continuing to raise and train the horse born with the conformation and desire to work stock, the showmen and breeders will have little cause to fear that any "ballet of show horses" will ever take over these contests.

World's Champion Cutting Horses

In the open competitions approved by the National Cutting Horse Association each season the following horses through outstanding nation-wide performance have earned the necessary points to be declared and crowned World's Champion Cutting Horses, a title each has borne with great distinction:

Horse	Year
NIGGER	1946–47–48
HOUSEKEEPER	1949
SKEETER	1950–51
LITTLE TOM W	1952
SNIPPER W	1953
MARION'S GIRL	1954
SNOOKY (Trinket Bennett)	1955
MARION'S GIRL	1956
KING'S PISTOL	1957
SLATS DAWSON	1958
POCO STAMPEDE	1959
BOOGER RED	1960
SENIOR GEORGE	1961
CUTTER BILL	1962

Biographical Sketches

Nigger

Solid black, gelded, 15 hands and 1000 pounds, Nigger was not a registered Quarter Horse, but, as countless old-timers will gladly affirm, he

49. Rukin String, by Piggin String, TB.

Photo by Karl Johnson

VANNEVAR   3RD. RUNNING   JOCKEY LLOYD BALLOU, UP.
PACIFIC COAST QUARTER HORSE RACING ASSN. DERBY PURSE $ 20,000.
Winner Eighth Race April 21, 1956.   Los Alamitos Race Course
    Dolly's Ace (2nd)   (440 yds.-22.2)   Arizonan (3rd)

OWNER: DEE GARRETT   TRAINER: WILLIE KELLEY

50. Vannevar wins the third renewal of the PCQHRA Derby.

50a. Vannevar, Lloyd Balou up.

Photo by Jack Stribling

51. George Glascock on Nigger.

Photo by E. J. (Buck) Bryan

51a. Nigger with George Glascock up.

52. Skeeter, Phil Williams up.

Photo by E. J. (Buck) Bryan

was a lot of horse and thoroughly knew his business. His dam, raised on the Binion ranch in Montana, was a Spanish mare. Old Nigger, as George Glascock calls him, was the result of breeding this mare to the Thoroughbred Band Time (by Band Play). Mr. Glascock says: "Band Time was the sire of a lot of good horses—cow horses and race horses. He was one of the foundation sires of the Binion string, and Benny has always said he would have kept him if he hadn't gone blind. He used to pasture breed all his mares. Benny sold him to Bus Whitesides at Sipe Springs, Texas, where he died last year at the ripe old age of thirty-two."

Mr. Binion declares: "I owned both sire and dam. I don't know who bred Band Time but he was foaled in the spring of 1939 on the X Bar T in New Mexico. An old colored man known as Gold Dollar gave Nigger his name. Nigger's dam was a brown wild Spanish mare raised in the Guadalupe Mountains by some people name of Ward. Band Time has a racing record. Nigger won the national open cutting horse competition three years in a row, 1946, 1947, and 1948. I don't think any other horse has equaled his record yet."

George Glascock explains:

Nigger was never trained for anything but cutting. I was his trainer and rider. I bought 800 cows and calves on the Stewart ranch at Strawn, Texas. Times being not so good about then I was forced to sell them a few at a time. This is where Nigger was started on what turned out to be a quite profitable career. No one but myself ever cut a cow on him until after I sent him back to Benny. When I sent him home, Benny's daughter Brenda showed him some and got along with him good—she was only ten years old at this time. Nigger is the only horse ever to hold the title World's Champion Cutting Horse three times, and he held that record three years hand-running. He took on all comers, regardless of breed or color—they all looked alike to him.

I won every big show there was at that time; Omaha, Tulsa, Houston, Fort Worth and Las Vegas, just to mention a few. I guess the biggest thrill of any was 1948, the year I won Forth Worth.

I don't think there ever was or will be another horse as good as old Nigger. He was always thinking two jumps ahead of the cow. He was smart enough to make her go where he wanted. The ranker the cows were the better old Nigger looked and liked it.

Housekeeper

Mr. R. H. Corbett bought the brown mare Housekeeper when she was five years old, 15.1 and 1175 pounds of whang-tough, quick-moving horse-flesh. Her sire, Westy Jr., a registered Thoroughbred, was foaled in Kentucky. R. L. McNeil owned the dam when, on April 15, 1940, our heroine was dropped. The dam's breeding is untraced.

V. O. Hildreth named her Housekeeper because he thought that she, as a cutting horse, kept house pretty well. McNeil says he raised six foals from her dam (five before Housekeeper), and all of them made first-class cow and roping horses, though none of them, in his opinion, was better than their mother during the time he rode her—one suspects she was a Quarter mare.

It was Silas Hill who brought Westy Jr. into the Breckenridge area for the purpose of raising horses that could get out and go. A number of his colts have made excellent long-distance sprinters.

Housekeeper is a trained cutting horse and has never been used for anything else. R. L. McNeil broke and rode her until she was nearly five; he got her to working cattle very well, and sold her to Mr. Hildreth in March of 1946. Mr. Corbett purchased her from Hildreth in August of that year and used her only as a cutting horse. She has won open contests at such tough shows as the World's Championship Rodeo (Dublin, Texas), Ak-Sar-Ben (Omaha), Colorado Springs, Fort Worth, and the Kansas City Royal.

During her competition she has seldom failed to be close to the top, and has finished below second or third very infrequently. She was started in rodeo at the Southwestern Exhibition & Fat Stock Show when she was three years old. The greatest contest she ever won was at Fort Worth in 1949.

There were 52 horses entered, including practically every top horse in the country. Eliminations cut the entries down to 24. The show lasted ten days and during that time, two shows a day, they had three go-rounds for the 24 contestants. Housekeeper won the first go-round by three points, was second by two in the next go-round, and, winning the third, went into the finals with three other horses, nine points in the lead, and finished 11 points ahead, over Poco Bueno, Cricket and Bitsy H.

Skeeter

Reserve Champion Cutting Horse, 1949
World's Champion Cutting Horse, 1950
World's Champion Cutting Horse, 1951
Died January 3, 1963

Philip Williams, who trained, rode, and owned Skeeter, told me: "I never raced him; I only used him for roping and cutting, and mostly cutting. He was one of the greatest cutting horses in the field. In his time, I don't think there were more than three or four shows in which he entered where he didn't win some part of the money. At Caldwell, Idaho, July 5, 1951, he was badly injured and was out of competition four months, then came on to win the World's Championship. He died in January of 1963 and would have been twenty-six in May. He was a sorrel gelding with a white streak on his face. He weighed 1060 and stood 15 hands. He was sired by Side Car, a Remount stallion, out of Hazel by Fighting Joe, also a Remount."

Mrs. Williams tells his story. Beginning, "I will do what I can to give you the information on Skeeter which you wanted for your book on great horses." She goes on to write:

Skeeter has a wonderful career behind him. Philip and Skeeter were so alike as to never expect any honors for their wonderful work together. Skeeter just seemed to know what Philip wanted of him. As for roping, Philip never did much roping on Skeeter, just a few small shows around in the country in his early training, just for fun.

As a baby colt Skeeter was frail and always getting hurt or sick, which seemed to make the two closer. Before very much training we noticed Skeeter holding chickens in a corner of his stall. He would get a calf or a cow on a fence and hold them there, and took very good care of all the baby colts in the pasture.

In 1948 Philip was going full speed roping [not with Skeeter]. That year he got sick. The doctors advised him to stop roping and stay inside. About the beginning of 1949 they could see this wouldn't work. About ten days before the Fat Stock Show at Fort Worth his doctor said, "Why not show your cutting horse?" So Philip got Skeeter in, rode him a few times and took off to Fort Worth. That was Skeeter's first time to be in a colosseum. I can't remember where he placed. Not very high, I guess, but it sure meant a lot to us.

So on and on he went, all through that year. The only reason he wasn't World's Champion in 1949 was that we made a lot of shows in Colorado, and, because they were not consolidated with the NCHA, these contests were not counted. Housekeeper made Champion, Skeeter was made Reserve.

In 1950 Philip and Skeeter set out to be World's Champions—and were. The road was long and rugged, with Red Boy and Bill Elliott so close behind. The shows weren't putting up as much money as they are now; you had to make quite a lot of shows to get anywhere. The competition became greater and more strenuous, too. We traveled in 1949 a little over 37,000 miles and in 1950 closer to 50,000. In 1949 we made $5995.77, each dollar counting for one point. We also gathered a lot of buckles, ribbons, and trophies. Skeeter entered and showed 19 times in that year.

The year 1950 got off to a good start until July 5th when the most disastrous accident happened. We had been making shows along the West Coast and sight-seeing a lot. From July 1st through the 4th we made the show at St. Paul, Oregon, leaving St. Paul on the 5th.

We drove until 7:30 P.M., at which time we got to Caldwell, Idaho, where we decided to spend the night. We drove out to the Rodeo Grounds. A club was roping. Asked about a stall for Skeeter. One fellow spoke up. "Sure I have stalls." He took us over to a long string of stalls, said, "Take your pick," and left. A small pasture enclosed these sheds. We drove inside to unload.

Just as Skeeter was backing out of the trailer a spotted mule trotted up behind him. Going up on his hind legs Skeeter took off. He circled the pasture two or three times going full speed, jumped a barbed wire fence, landing in a pile of tin and snarled wire, being cut badly in several places.

When we got him loose from that junk he took off toward town. Running back to the car we got in and followed him. But pretty soon we could not see him anywhere. A little boy standing beside the street as we came up cried: "Hey! that horse went that way!" So we did, too.

About two blocks from the main part of town Skeeter fell in the street. A service station attendant ran out and got him off the street and was holding him when we drove up. We loaded him again and took off for the hospital. It took three and a half hours to sew him up, and it was four weeks before we could bring him home. He was kept under the care of a veterinary until October.

The first show we made after that was Omaha. Skeeter came out on top and won $1104.67. We then went to Kansas City, Missouri, again winning, and collecting $1011.00, a buckle, hat, and saddle blanket.

Leaving K. C. en route to the Cow Palace at San Francisco which was where they were holding that year's Finals. We traveled across deserts, over mountains, in almost every kind of weather, having no real knowledge of his actual standing, by points and dollars, in the contest for top honors. The Dallas show had been run off at the same time we were working K. C., and Skeeter's closest competition had been contesting in the Dallas show.

Anyway, Philip and Skeeter won the big doings at the Cow Palace, taking $884 in prize money. San Francisco was one of our happiest memories because Skeeter was awarded the World's Champion Cutting Horse title.

I guess the most amusing or exciting event in Skeeter's career happened in 1950 at the Fort Worth show. Philip and Skeeter had won both go-rounds, but out at the corrals and off on the sidelines rumors were flying twenty-six to the dozen. So on the night of the Finals, never saying a word, Philip, when their names were called, reached down and slipped off Skeeter's bridle and pitched it off to one side as they rode into the herd— of course, this is strictly forbidden. Skeeter picked his cow and brought her out, and I must say he did a fine job of it. He cut three head and worked every one of them perfect. There were about 6000 people watching and it took at least ten hollering minutes to quiet them down enough to go on with the show. As you know, Philip and Skeeter were disqualified for the performance; but the crowd, tickled pink, supposed he had won and there was considerable criticism when they found out he hadn't. But Skeeter finished the year as World's Champion anyway, winning $7334.65 in cash money, the same amount in points, of course, and trophies of all kinds.

The following year, 1951, we went over the same route. The closest competition was the Jesse James horse, owned by Mr. Fussell and ridden by Matlock Rose. Jesse was a good horse and Matlock a fine rider; and a close race it was. But Philip and Matlock, being good friends, traveled together, turning back for each other throughout the year. Until about the last three shows. It was a tossup which would win. But Skeeter only had one boss and old Jesse had two and didn't quite make it, Skeeter going into the lead at the K. C. show.

Finishing up that season of 1951 his winnings were $10,268.57 prize money, and once more we had the pleasure of having Skeeter awarded the World's Championship.

During 1950 and 1951 Skeeter won 39 belt buckles, seven saddles, 365 ribbons, besides plaques, trophies, silver trays, cups, blankets, bridles, Levi's, Lee Riders, hats, boots, bits, spurs, gloves, and so forth.

What training Philip gave Skeeter was just natural talent and love for horses. Today he turns away people wanting him to train horses. P. M. Williams, Sr. bred the horse; he was by a Government Remount.

Snipper W

Owned by E. Paul Waggoner, Snipper W was first shown to third place win at the Parker County Sheriff's Posse Frontier Days Celebration, Rodeo and Quarter Horse Show, July 26–29, 1950. It was the beginning of an eight-year career in the annals of the National Cutting Horse Association.

This dun Quarter Horse gelding (P–15,435) was declared winner of the Open Cutting Horse Contest at the Southwest Exposition & Fat Stock Show in January, 1951, and went on from there to finish the year with the rank of ninth in the NCHA Top Ten. Holder of NCHA Certificate of Ability No. 119, he was awarded Certificate of Annual Achievement No. 9 in 1951. Pine Johnson, long associated with Waggoner Quarter Horses, was Snipper W's rider throughout these early days.

Don Dodge was making frequent trips from Texas to California about this time and seemed to have an uncanny knack for acquiring top cutting horses. NCHA records indicate that Don bought Snipper W early in 1952 and they immediately became a tough pair to beat. Snipper W placed second in the Top Ten for 1952.

There was only one place to go for this pair, if they were to improve in 1953, and they were successful in doing this, Snipper W becoming

53. Phil Williams up. Can you identify the horse?

Photo by L. H. Launspach

54. Marion's Girl,
Buster Welch up.
Photo by Matt Culley

55. Jim Calhoun on King's Pistol in a cutting contest. This picture is world famous. It has been engraved on the Life Membership Plaque of the National Cutting Horse Association and also appears on the NCHA sticker.

56. King's Pistol, painted in his seventh year by Orren Mixer.

World's Champion Cutting Horse for that year, receiving all customary emoluments.

During the Houston Livestock Show and Rodeo of 1954 Don Dodge sold Snipper W to Clyde Bauer of Victoria, Texas. Although not campaigned extensively, he ranked twelfth among NCHA Top Cutting Horses of 1954.

Absent from National ranking in 1955, Snipper W again appeared in the NCHA Top Ten of 1956. Now ridden by Stanley Bush, he placed eighth and was presented with a Certificate. Stanley and Snipper W remained together in 1957 and made a battle for Horse of the Year honors to the end, Snipper again becoming Reserve World's Champion Cutting Horse and at this time being named World's Champion Cutting Horse Gelding, in recognition of which honor an additional Certificate was added to his kudos.

The *Cuttin' Hoss Chatter* of March, 1958, records the sale of Snipper W by Clyde Bauer to D. H. Braman, which brought to a close his career as a contestant for national cutting horse recognition. No further winnings are recorded.

In his eight years as a campaigner against all who challenged, Snipper W won a total of $44,815.47 in contests approved by the NCHA. In fitting recognition of this great lifetime performance he was awarded NCHA Hall of Fame Certificate No. 4 and a plaque attesting to this honor has been hung in the Association's home office.

Marion's Girl

When the Hall of Fame award was launched by the National Cutting Horse Association a series of covers were devoted by *Cuttin' Hoss Chatter* to pictures of cutting horses eligible for this new honor, with vignettes of their careers. Each of these superb performers must have won in excess of $35,000 in cutting competition approved by the NCHA in order to become eligible for consideration for Hall of Fame honors.

It was thought fitting that the cover series be started with the only two-time World Champion Cutting Horse to receive this award, Marion's Girl. Since I was unable to unearth at this late date sufficient performance information about some of these champs, the Association has kindly given me access to information assembled by its staff. Of Marion's Girl the magazine reported:

A bay registered Quarter Horse mare by Silver Wimpy out of the mare Joan Scharbauer, Marion's Girl was owned by Marion Flynt, Midland, Texas, and ridden throughout her career by Buster Welch of Roscoe, Texas.

Marion's Girl had one of the most brilliant records ever recorded in the history of this Association. Holder of NCHA Certificate of Ability No. 196, she was awarded NCHA Certificate of Merit No. 9 and Certificate of Annual Achievement No. 1 in 1954, her first year to be World's Champion Cutting Horse. In 1955 she received NCHA Certificate of Annual Achievement No. 4. To crown her outstanding performance of past years Marion's Girl was again World's Champion Cutting Horse in 1956. In recognition of this accomplishment she was awarded NCHA Certificate of Merit No. 11 and NCHA Certificate of Annual Achievement No. 1–1956.

Marion's Girl was retired by Mr. Flynt in 1957 with the expectation of her spending many years in his band of broodmares. However fate intervened and Marion's Girl died suddenly in the summer of 1958.

In these brief years as a campaigner in the arena against all challengers Marion's Girl won a total of $36,020.81 in NCHA Approved Cutting Horse contests. She is being awarded NCHA Hall of Fame Certificate No. 8 and a plaque attesting this honor will be hung in the office of the National Cutting Horse Association.

Says Marion Flynt: "She won every major show in the United States. She is a holder of the gold certificate, the bronze certificate and the silver certificate, which put her in the cutting horse Hall of Fame. She was as near human as it is possible for a dumb brute to be. There was no quit to her. She worked the same every day. On several occasions she worked in contests while crippled and it was a real effort for her to walk. However, once in the herd it was impossible for anyone to imagine there was anything wrong with her. She worked just as good as if she were well. She won more than $50,000 in her career, and a roomful of trophies. She was not the hit-and-miss type of cutting horse but true and sincere every time she worked, making her almost impossible to beat. She is buried now in the front yard of our North Ranch."

King's Pistol

A mahogany bay stallion foaled April 15, 1950 and bred by Bud Warren at Perry, Oklahoma, King's Pistol stands 14.2 and weighs right at 1250. He has a few white hairs in the forehead and a white left hind pastern. His dam is Flit (P–9697) by Leo out of Julie W (P–9796) by Joe Hancock. A bay, she was foaled in the spring of 1945 on the Ed Simpkins' place just out of Pawhuska, Oklahoma, and stood 14.3 and weighed approximately 1175. Mr. Warren ran her as a four-year-old, racing her at Garfield Downs, Enid, Oklahoma. In a matched race at 250 yards against Black Polly, Flit came in the victor by a length and a quarter to set a new track record of :13.8 which still stands. At this time Flit was carrying her first foal, King's

Pistol. Listed herself in the Register of Merit, Flit has produced four ROM foals and one AQHA Champion. It seems hardly necessary to dwell here on the merits and many accomplishments of the great King, which can be found in the pages devoted to Poco Bueno. Flit was bred to King in 1949 to produce King's Pistol, World's Champion Cutting Horse of 1957.

Jim Calhoun of Cresson, Texas, says:

While attending Oklahoma State University I saw King's Pistol and bought him, at that time a coming two-year-old. In the summer of 1952, after I had graduated, King's Pistol began to earn his keep in regular ranch work, showing unmistakable evidence of speed and action. He had an alert eye and an intelligent looking head. By the time he had been ridden half a dozen saddles, he had evidenced a natural ability to co-ordinate these basic essentials for the making of a cutting horse. And he did it in a graceful and easy manner.

He had more than his share of cow sense and handiness, but I brought him along slowly and did not work him in a cutting pen until Pistol fully realized what it meant to separate a yearling from a pasture herd and drive the cowbrute across the pasture and away from the other cattle. Nothing can replace the wealth of experience and understanding a horse learns in good everyday ranch work.

About the third time I had him in a pen with cattle he showed an interest and would try to follow one particular animal. Of course he did not know all that would soon be expected of him, but he did learn fast. I did not have to correct him many times about any one thing, and he soon was doing his best to perform. He had some ideas of his own, naturally enough, but was never stubborn about working cattle the way I wanted it done.

Within a short time I had him on a regular training schedule. I never worked King's Pistol until he was tired; this kept him from forming a dislike for his work. I used patience rather than punishment while training him. And I used Pistol enough in other ranch work to give him plenty of exercise, and saw that he was properly fed.

Because of his quick and powerful action while in the cutting arena I have often been asked if he was hard to ride. My answer to this was "Yes and no." I explain that he is quick, fast and powerful. If I was careful and would watch what was going on I seldom had any trouble while riding him, but if I got careless when he 'turned it on' I was apt to think something hit me and hit me hard. I recall that Pistol has been scared a few times because of some unexpected something, but if I could get to him and get my hands on him and talk to him, he would quiet down promptly.

He seemed to have confidence in me, and I know I had a lot of confidence in him. The only time I ever failed to talk him out of something was when I tried to carry home a live game rooster while riding him. I soon decided I had rather turn that rooster loose than to get bucked off.

I had used King's Pistol for roping and dragging calves to the fire during branding time, and cutting on him during general ranch work. Because of his natural cow sense I began to contest him some. I won halter, reining and cutting on him, and he soon became an AQHA Champion at the early age of four the first year I contested him. At that time, 1954, there were very few horses that achieved this honor at such a tender age.

Many people thought I should have run King's Pistol because of his speed background. Early foot I knew he had but an honest, consistent cutting horse had always been my only thought. I needed him in my way of life. I felt that if he would breed true, which he has, his offspring would be desirable and also be able to perform any task for which they might be called upon. The cutting horse has gained prominence because of the fascinating and entertaining prowess of his fabulous kind in action. The factual and legendary exploits of the cutter in actual ranch work and arena performance has been a feature of the cattle spreads in Texas for mighty near a century.

In the early days of ranching a cowhorse that had earned the always-well-deserved title of *cuttin' hoss*, was to the ranch folks—as it is today—a symbol of pride, service, action, intelligence, and fascinating entertainment unequaled.

In selecting a cutting prospect I look for a horse with "cowsense," blood-lines along with action, speed, disposition, and all the other qualities that go to make up an alert, sound young horse. In starting such a prospect we begin with actual ranch work. After the colt has been gentled and green broken, I like to ride him in the pasture driving cattle and doing general ranch work. This teaches the prospect how to travel, and the work is usually slow enough that you can start to develop and bring out his cowsense.

In a while he will be traveling quiet and moving with cattle. In working cattle out of a herd you get the chance to teach a horse 'herd work.' By this I mean being quiet and working one animal out without disturbing the rest of the critters. The time spent on this phase of training depends entirely upon the horse's eagerness to learn. In some cases the horse, within a few times, will catch on to what is expected. Others take more repetition.

By now the prospect is far enough along to go to actually cutting cattle in a pen. It is important that a young horse isn't rushed. Give him a chance to figure out what you are trying to show him. If a horse is shown the right way to do something, by repeating this process he does not pick up wrong ways.

I try to keep him feeling good and liking his work. I feel there are more young horses overworked than underworked. There is plenty of time to really get down to work after the colt has matured some. As it is with any other kind of performance horse, condition is important to a cutting horse. He needs to be ridden or ponied enough that he is hard and "legged up."

When working the young prospect, care should be taken not to let him get to moving just because the turn-back horse moves. Therefore I cut a few cattle from time to time without using a turn-back man. I ease a calf out of the herd and wait until he moves. This impresses upon the horse to move only when the calf moves. I practice this occasionally after the horse is considered a finished product.

An intelligent prospect, sound and able, combined with enough use and patience on your part, will give you a cutting horse you can use on the ranch, enjoy at a neighborly gathering or in the show ring, with success.

After King's Pistol had become an AQHA Champion in 1954, Calhoun hauled him to an occasional show. Jim says:

It was at Odessa, Texas, where I was judging in 1957, that I decided to carry Pistol down the road in a try for Championship honors. I realized it would be an extra long year as the first show starting the new year had been put on at the Cow Palace, in San Francisco, and I would not be through before reaching Odessa again in 1958. The cutting horse that won the Odessa show was several thousand dollars in the lead and there I was "afoot" with my horse back home on pasture.

Soon as I got gack to the ranch I began to work Pistol on tough cattle and even a few goats that I borrowed to "help tune him up." When I felt he was ready for tough competition we took off. We won the two week-end shows held on January 21st and 22nd, but the big one coming up would be Fort Worth's Southwestern Exposition & Fat Stock Show, January 26–February 3, 1957. King's Pistol won the cutting and was Reserve Champion at halter.

King's Pistol and I traveled to shows that were weeks and, sometimes, only days apart, from one end of the United States to the other, winning and placing in cutting and halter contests. We began to feel like gypsies, moving around so much, but the satisfaction we had we shared; we both liked stiff competition and it gave us the will to win. King's Pistol never once went off his feed, and only once had a cough, which I had developed also. We both took the cough medicine a doctor had prescribed for me, and this cured us both.

While at the Tucson Livestock Show on April 6th and 7th, King's Pistol was working his heart out tearing up Mother Earth when, astonishingly, he let a calf get back into the herd. The crowd and myself were bug-eyed. I couldn't imagine why he'd lost that calf, thus losing our contest. As I piled off I found his right eye had swelled shut. He had gotten particles of hay in it and couldn't see when the calf got on his blind side—the injury, fortunately, healed fast.

We had 42 shows through January 4th. King's Pistol won 20, tied and placed in 22 others. His total earnings for the year were $16,217.16.

At Odessa, that January 4th of 1958 King's Pistol was named Grand Champion Stallion, Grand Champion of the Registered Cutting contest, and won the NCHA Open Cutting Contest, open to the world. King's Pistol was the first stallion in history to become World's Champion Cutting Horse. He had broken a new record in winnings, earning more money in one year of competition than any other cutting horse before him, and this distinction he held for several years.

"It was a cold, snowy night when King's Pistol, my wife Jane Venita, our small daughter Virginia Jane, Jim Jr. and I," Calhoun says, "loaded 13 trophies we had received and move out toward the ranch, back to the everyday life we had started together not so long ago."

Everything King's Pistol has gotten he has earned—his AQHA Championship at four years of age in his first season of campaigning, his Register of Merit, Certificate of Ability, Certificate of Annual Achievement, the gold and silver awards presented by the National Cutting Horse Association. The sticker the NCHA uses depicts King's Pistol cutting. The Life Membership plaque of the NCHA bears an engraved cutting picture of King's Pistol at work. Ending the 1962 season, King's Pistol at the age of 13 tied with Hollywood Gold, age twenty-three, for second place in number of Cutting Horse winners, second to that other great son of King, Poco Bueno (age nineteen), only six points in the lead.

There have possibly been more articles written about King's Pistol than about any other working sire. He makes good copy, and provides something to write about. His fine career has won our breed a great many friendly admirers in the course of his travels. His get with performance points to their credit have averaged 17.6 points per winner as compared with 7.4 points per winner for the next sire of performance horses.

"At this writing," says Jim Calhoun, "probably King's Michelle (P–75878) is Pistol's most famous get. Her dam, Brown Shorty, was in the Calhoun broodband and was bred to King's Pistol. Brown Shorty was sold and King's Michelle thus came to be foaled on the Jewel Russell place at King, Texas. Dr. and Mrs. E. F. Meredith of Olney, Texas, purchased both Brown Shorty and King's Michelle. Michelle was trained and ridden exclusively by Glenn McWhorter of Throckmorton, Texas. She started winning cutting horse contests not long after the unheard-of age of 30 months. She was the talk of the town, and no mistake. With the highest points won for 1962, King's Michelle was awarded 'Horse of the Year' in the West-Central Texas Cutting Horse Association. In the lead for World's Champion Cutting Horse of 1962, King's Michelle had just won her last Championship show in Oklahoma and was being hauled toward home on August 13th when she died from an acute case of peritonitis at the age of eight years."

Even after death took her away she held the World's Championship lead to within a few weeks of the finals, and was posthumously awarded Reserve Champion Cutting Horse of the World and World Champion Cutting Mare titles. On the AQHA's 1962 Honor Roll for Cutting she was named high-point mare with 128 points. During her short career she accumulated 352 cutting points, earned her Register of Merit, Certificate of Ability, and the gold, silver, and bronze awards presented by the NCHA. Among the hundreds of letters, wires, and telephone calls which the Merediths received as the word of their tragic loss got around, the following excerpts will give some indication of the very real esteem in which she was held:

To compete against her when she was alive was a real challenge, and you always knew you had been in a contest whether you lost or won.

She will be remembered by all horsemen and Cutting Horse enthusiasts as one of the truly great mares of our time. King's Michelle showed the big heart she had by the tough jobs she fulfilled. Her style and beauty thrilled the audiences.

To me she was the perfect example of a truly great Cutting Horse—her record speaks for itself. There was no doubt in my mind that King's Michelle would have been the 1962 World Champion Cutting Horse as well as the largest money-winner of all time for a single year.

Another famous daughter of King's Pistol is Janie Cal (P–57827). Her dam was Caesar's Bonnie (P-21750) by Brown Caesar, the well-known roping horse. Caesar's Bonnie was in the Calhoun broodband until her death. Bred to King's Pistol she produced Janie Cal (owned by Charles Coats of Chappel Hill, Texas), trained and ridden by Jim Daniels. Janie Cal is an AQHA Champion with points gained in cutting and halter contests. She has at this time some 60 points in this field of endeavor.

King's Pistol was bred to Ken Ada Jane (P–33825), an extremely fine mare owned by T. F. and Matt Larkin of Dallas, and produced King's Pistola (P–61522), now owned by Ed Porath of Watercress Farms, Northville, Michigan. King's Pistola is an AQHA Champion, winning her points at halter, reining, and cutting.

One of the best-known sons of King's Pistol is Pistol's Man, out of Jim Calhoun's good mare Jazz Band, and bred and raised on the Calhoun ranch. As a coming four-year-old he was sold to Roland Stacy of Natchez, Mississippi. He sired the famous Pistol Bit, winner of many grand championships at the age of two, with a total of 48 halter points. Pistol's Man also sired the AAA Huts Pistol and AA+ Cop's Pistol. Pistol's Man himself won many halter and cutting contests before being retired to the stud.

Rock Pistol, out of Zantanon Babe, is another respected son of King's Pistol. Residing at Perry, Oklahoma, the property of T. M. Jones, Rock Pistol has thus far earned 19 cutting points and is one of his sire's not uncommon get which are rated Register of Merit.

Slats Dawson

Slats Dawson's winning history as a cutting horse begins in Neosho, Missouri, on June 21, 1952. Owned at that time by Roy Hyatt and ridden by Chester Minton, this sorrel gelding sired by Chico Dawson out of the mare Dawson Fan was destined to compile an enviable record in the annals of the NCHA for the next eight years.

Shown successfully throughout the Midwest by both Chester Minton and Jim Gideon, Slats, as he was more commonly known, then became the property of Jack Denio, Bakersfield, California. Slats and his rider, Karl Taylor, appeared frequently in the results from California throughout 1955 and early 1956. Slats was purchased by George Pardi, who kept him until his unfortunate death. At the time of Pardi's purchase Jim Gideon was training for Mr. Pardi and the reunited pair exhibited such teamwork that Slats became champion of the Florida Quarter Horse Association and received the NCHA Affiliate Trophy for 1956. Before leaving Florida for Texas, Slats was also shown by Willard Davis, Jr.

January, 1958, saw the beginning of a partnership that will long be remembered by all cutting horse enthusiasts—that of Slats Dawson and Minor Johnson. This team's first win was the "big one," the Southwestern Exposition & Fat Stock Show at Fort Worth. A prelude of things to come, Slats continued to pull down big money and was declared World's Champion Cutting Horse for 1958 at the State Fair of Texas (Dallas). Here he was awarded a certificate of Merit and one of Annual Achievement.

In 1959 the title of World's Champion Cutting Horse Gelding was won by Slats. Standing third in the Top Ten he received another Annual Achievement certificate.

From February to August of 1960 the No. 1 cutting horse in the nation was Slats Dawson. Then, on page 1 of the September *Cuttin' Hoss Chatter*, the stark announcement of Slats Dawson's death was blazoned. A great competitive career was ended. Although missing from the arenas during the final five months of the point year, his great early record stood up so well that he was posthumously awarded, for his fifth place among the Top Ten, a 1960 Certificate of Annual Achievement. During his six active years in the arena of cutting horse competition Slats Dawson won a total of $38,374.90 in contests approved by the NCHA. In recognition of this outstanding performance he will be awarded NCHA Hall of Fame Certificate No. 6, and a plaque attesting to this honor will be hung in the home office of the Association.

Poco Stampede

A new name, Poco Stampede, appeared in the contest results received by the National Cutting Horse Association during 1956. Owned by Mrs. G. F. Rhodes of Abilene, Texas, this dun son of Poco Bueno out of the mare Pretty Rosalie was destined to have a far-reaching impact on both the Quarter and Cutting Horse worlds.

His first recorded win in open competition was a second-place finish in the Abilene Range Riders Fourth Annual Cutting Contest, December 31, 1955. Ridden by trainer Jack Newton, who was to continue as his rider through the peak of his career, Poco Stampede finished twenty-first in the NCHA Top Cutting Horses for 1956.

In 1957 NCHA Certificate of Ability No. 258 was awarded Poco Stampede. This also marked his first entry into the NCHA Top Ten Cutting Horses of the Year. Placing in 31 approved open contests, he ranked eighth and was presented with a Certificate of Annual Achievement. In so doing he was awarded the title World's Champion Cutting Horse Stallion for 1958, along with another certificate of Annual Achievement.

The partnership of the owner, Poco Stampede, and his rider, Jack Newton, reached its climax in 1959 at the Southwestern Exposition & Fat Stock Show, Fort Worth, the site that year of the World's Championship Cutting Horse finals. Here, in the midst of spotlights and packed stands, Poco Stampede was crowned World's Champion Cutting Horse of 1959, picking up a Certificate of Merit and another of Annual Achievement.

Shown only to a very limited degree in 1960, another crown must be added to the laurels he accumulated. On the night of November 16, 1960, he was declared Champion of Champions at the Tournament of Champions, Sweetwater, Texas. He continued his semiretirement during 1961. His championship ability was still evident, however; he completed the season with the rank of seventeenth in the Top Twenty.

In any summary of Poco Stampede's career it should be pointed out that he was the first horse to wear both the title of World's Champion Cutting Horse and that of NCHA Champion of Champions. It is perhaps worthy of note that he is also the only stallion thus far to qualify for enrollment in the National Cutting Horse Association Hall of Fame.

In recognition of his outstanding performance and his total earnings of $39,640.16 in competition approved by the NCHA, Poco Stampede has been awarded Hall of Fame Certificate No. 5 and a plaque attesting this honor will be hung in the office of the National Cutting Horse Association.

Booger Red

Booger Red first appeared in the records of the NCHA as a fourth-place contestant in the finals at the Westland Volunteer Fire Department Rodeo, Forth Worth, June 1, 1952. Owned and ridden by L. E. Shawver (Millsap, Texas), this sorrel Quarter Horse gelding (registered as Wardlo's Rusty) by Wardlo out of a Ferguson mare, is still contesting actively in the cutting arena today.

In 1953 Booger Red became the property of Roy Barnes (Denver) and in 1954 was owned by Young Gamblin, also of Denver. During these two years he was shown mainly in the area represented by the Western States Cutting Horse Association.

National prominence for this fine performer was launched in 1956 when Shawver repurchased him and took the cutting horse trail in earnest. Beginning with a third-place win at the Southwestern Exposition & Fat Stock Show, Booger Red went on to place seventh in the NCHA Top Ten and was presented with a Certificate of Annual Achievement, also garnering a testimonial to his ability.

Campaigned only to a limited extent in 1957, he missed the Top Ten, but in 1958 he really got rolling. Placing in 54 NCHA approved open contests he was awarded a new Annual Achievement Certificate in recognition of his placing third among the Top Ten of that year. The 1958 World's Championship Cutting Horse finals were held in Dallas during the State Fair of Texas in mid-October. Shortly thereafter, at the LSU National Quarter Horse Show in Baton Rouge, Booger Red was sold to Manuel Kulwin of Chicago. Mr. Kulwin still owns him.

Ridden now by Delbert Eskew, Booger continued his winning ways by placing in both go-rounds of the first contest entered. He contested well throughout the year, but Manny Kulwin's desire was to have a World's Champion. To this end he and L. E. Shawver reached an agreement, and as a result L. E. climbed back in the saddle They finished the 1959 point year in fifth position and picked up another Certificate of Achievement.

In 1960 Mr. Kulwin, Booger Red, and Shawver combined their talents with but one goal in mind and, on the night of January 7, 1961, at Odessa, Texas, Booger Red was declared World's Champion Cutting Horse of 1960. Placing in a total of 78 NCHA approved open contests, he was additionally awarded the title of World's Champion Cutting Horse Gelding for the same period, picking up certificates both for achievement and merit.

Since winning the foremost yearly award in the cutting horse world Booger Red has campaigned less strenuously. In 1961 he placed in 21 approved shows and ranked eighth among the Top Ten, adding another certificate to his collection.

In 1962, with John Carter in the saddle, Booger Red split first and second at the Southwestern Exposition & Fat Stock Show, going on to place at some of the nation's larger contests, including NCHA World's Championship Cutting Horse finals at Las Vegas, Nevada. Here, ridden by Bob Killion, he won sixth in one of the fastest, finest cutting contests ever seen. Booger Red ranked fourteenth among Top Cutting Horses of 1962.

In recognition of this performance—in addition to total earnings of $47,885.82—he has been awarded NCHA Hall of Fame Certificate No. 3 and a plaque attesting this honor will be hung in the office of the National Cutting Horse Association.

Señor George

By Claude (P–26,156) out of Miss Bartender (P–12,530) by Bartender, Señor George was bred by George Gilham at Claude, Texas, and was purchased by Gene George of Amarillo. "The first time I saw Miss Bartender," the *Quarter Horse Journal* reports Mr. George as saying, "I decided she was the best mare I had ever seen and I was anxious to view the results of this mating. I did not arrive at Mr. Gilham's place until three days after Señor George was foaled but the moment I saw the colt I knew I had to have him." And he did buy the colt that very same day, arranging to take mare and foal until the colt could be weaned. "My confidence in this foal," he says, "proved correct, for he has turned out to be the best horse I have owned in the 38 years I have been raising horses."

Until April 20, 1958, Señor George had competed in but six open cuttings and had won money in each. His all-time record as of May 1958 showed 18 points at halter, 13 in performance; 19 firsts, nine seconds, five Grand Championships, and five Reserve Grand Championships. This, plus 1087 points approved by the NCHA and a National Cutting Horse Association Certificate of Ability before he was twenty-six months old, lends him something of the aura of a prodigy. He was among the first horses in 1958 to receive the AQHA Register of Merit rating in cutting, and is the first horse to receive an AQHA Championship under the 30-point system which became effective January 1, 1958.

He received his first training from Jerre Roach of Olney, Texas, and was not worked between May, 1957, and January 10, 1958. He was then put into training by Sonny Perry, who tells me he found Señor George easy to work but needing further control. "I rode him five times before the Amarillo

Fat Stock Show during the last of January," Sonny says, "then put him up against 38 of the top horses that were competing. He came through in a way that did me proud, scoring 77."

Mr. Perry thinks George has got a head on his shoulders. "This," he says, "makes him more, rather than less, difficult to train, because he's usually thinking at least one jump ahead of his rider. He responds to kind though firm direction, is quite alert, showing more interest in his cattle than any horse his age I've seen; he's got an awful lot of action."

Said to be, from the spectators' view, one of the finest cutting horse exhibitions ever put on, the Tournament of Champions, held November 10–12, 1961 at the Horse Lovers Club, Phoenix, Arizona, saw Señor George crowned Champion. One short week before, this lightning-quick little bay stallion had been named World's Champion Cutting Horse by the NCHA at San Francisco's Cow Palace. In the Tournament he compiled an astonishing 882 points in six go-rounds, an average of 147 points per performance. He is owned currently by Jernigan, Tully, and Langford of Goldthwaite, Texas, and was ridden, as always, by Sonny Perry.

Judges for the Tournament were Marion Flynt, Frank Daws, Novis Rodgers, Slim Trent, Cliff Magers, J. T. Fisher, Don Carr, Casey Darnell, H. L. Aken, Tom Finley, Jack Elliott, and Earl Albin.

"Señor George," said Mr. Perry in a long-distance call from Texas, "was foaled in 1954. Gene George bought him at three days old and showed him successfully at halter through three years old. I commenced riding him in 1958. He was sold to the syndicate in the fall of 1958. I got on him again in 1960 and wound up fourth among the Top Ten with only a half-year of performance. During 1961 I had him under lease. He made World's Champion and was then retired to the stud. He won more money than any previous Champion in that one-year period. This was topped in 1962 by Cutter Bill, but Señor George was the first Cutting Horse in open competition to win the Tournament of Champions the same year he made World's Champ."

Cutter Bill

Rex Cauble, in enumerating for me the many exploits of the mighty Cutter Bill, said: "He's a golden palomino, 14.3, 1180. Mr. R. L. Underwood owned and bred the sire, Buddy Dexter, and he owned Billie Silvertone, the dam, when they were crossed in the mating which produced my stallion. As you know, he had his own ideas about what to breed to what. The mare had already produced by Buddy Dexter two previous AQHA Champions,

Buddy Bill and Smutty Bill, both of which are full brothers to my horse. All were foaled on the Underwood Ranch at Wichita Falls, Cutter Bill on May 8, 1955."

Buddy Dexter was a blood bay by Dexter (P–193) by Golden Chief (194), a copper horse foaled in 1918. Golden Chief's dam was an unnamed Quarter-type mare. Dexter's dam was Miss Tommie by Tom (Scooter) by Midnight. Buddy Dexter's dam was Little March by March (361) by Mustard Seed, TB.

Cutter Bill's dam, Billie Silvertone, was a smutty palomino-colored mare that Pine Johnson and several other cutting horse trainers claim to have been one of the best at the business. Cauble, when he bought Cutter Bill, knew nothing of this and very little about the dam's pedigree. Rex says: "I imagine the color of Cutter's sire and dam has something to do with the way he breeds. He gets more sorrels out of sorrel mares than he does palominos; he gets duns and palominos primarily out of bay mares."

Billie Silvertone, standing 14.3 would weigh perhaps 1150. She was sired by Silvertone (190, a palomino) by Dunny Boy (by Jud). Silvertone's dam was a bay Cardwell Quarter mare. Billie Silvertone's dam was Star Light (P–236, a sorrel) by Golden Chief out of a Y Ranch Quarter mare by Tom by Rainy Day. Which gives Cutter Bill Golden Chief for a great grandsire on both sides of the family tree.

Asked how he happened to acquire Cutter Bill, Mr. Cauble had this to say: "My wife, Josephine, insisted that I buy this colt at the Underwood breeder sale of 1956. She fell in love with him when she discovered him standing tied to a fence before the sale began. Even then, as a yearling, he was the color of new gold. I said reluctantly I would buy him if he didn't go over $1000. He went over that quick; on her insistence I did, too. I bid him in for $2500. I did not like his conformation as a two- or even as a three-year-old, and consequently did not breed him until well into his fourth year, using him for a teaser until that time. After the breeding season when he was three (in May) we started him on cattle. I knew then he was a 'natural.' Will not comment on the many riders I put on him, save only to say Willis Bennett made him a world champion junior registered cutting horse in 1959."

Cutter Bill is probably the only horse to achieve this distinction and go on to become the "open" World's Champion Cutting Horse (1962). He also won the Tournament of Champions (65 entries) at Little Rock, Arkansas (December 4th to 6th), after his coronation at Las Vegas.

"Incidentally," says Rex Cauble, "after discovering what we had in Bill we sent to California and bought Billie Silvertone with a stud colt on her

57. Booger Red.

58. Senor George, Sonny Perry up.

Photo by Beverly Savage

59. Cutter Bill at Prescott. Sonny Perry is the rider.

Photo by Matt Culley

60. Cutter Bill.

61. Cuttin': Austin Beebe on Holey Sox.

Photo by Sierra Studio

62. In the winner's circle: Holey Sox at Centennial.

Photo by Ralph Morgan

by Starduster. This was three years ago. The colt has since been gelded; he also is a palomino, and we are now putting a rein on him. We bought also a filly yearling (by Bosun and out of Billie Silvertone) at the same time. The filly, now four, has been bred to a son of Hard Twist that we raised. Billie Silvertone died last winter at the age of twenty-four years. She was in foal to Hard Twist and her death was a cruel blow. As you know, we lost Hard Twist last June 26th."

Buddy Dexter was a pretty good halter horse and beat Poco Bueno at both the Fort Worth and San Antonio shows. Mr. Cauble says: "We don't know anything about Buddy Dexter's performance or ability in that field, but it appears pretty obvious Billie Silvertone made up for anything performancewise that Buddy might have lacked.

"I personally broke Cutter Bill as a two-year-old. It was really easy as he just looked back at me on both sides and then walked off. That's all there was to it."

Other persons later taking a hand with Cutter Bill are Connie Wills, Roy Huffaker, Willis Bennett, Milt Bennett, John Carter, and Sonny Perry.

Rex Cauble tells me: "I owned stallions that I thought were more capable of producing outstanding horses than Cutter Bill and did not breed him to any mares until he was four years old. I only bred him to four mares that year as Willis Bennett kept him on the road and we only got two of the mares in foal. We have these two three-year-olds in training now and they are really responding nicely. Both foals—one a gelding, the other a mare—are out of granddaughters of Old Sorrel and are both entered in the NCHA Cutting Horse Futurity for three-year-olds."

Cutter Bill, as mentioned earlier, was World's Champion Cutting Horse for 1962, and set a new all-time record in earnings by one horse in one year. Sonny Perry campaigned him. During 1962 he was flown from Phoenix, Arizona, to Washington, D.C., where he made the Washington International Horse Show along with Arthur Godfrey. He was then flown, with three other horses, to San Francisco's Cow Palace, which show he won handily. From there he went to Las Vegas where he was crowned Champion.

Starting off the 1963 season with top money at the Tournament of Champions (Little Rock), he continued to win or place high in all major shows through the Tucson show (March 17th–19th), and was officially retired on March 21st, still in front both in open cutting and registered cutting for the year 1963—several hundred ahead of his nearest competition in open cutting, Woodey Searle's hard-knocking Holey Sox (a son of Leo and full brother of Palleo Pete).

During 1962 Cutter Bill also became an AQHA Champion, acquiring his final halter points at the Dallas Fair. The American Quarter Horse Association presented him with an award as the outstanding registered Quarter Horse as well as Open Champion (NCHA) of 1962.

It was agreed in Cauble advertisements to book ten outside mares to Cutter Bill, at $1000 each, for the 1963 breeding season. As it turned out, they actually took twelve. One mare, Linda Lou Coty, came all the way from Potomac, Maryland. The famous Nancy Bailey, owned by Bob Burton, was one of those bred this year to Cutter Bill.

Rex Cauble says: "Cutter Bill is the most natural cutting horse I ever saw in action. He appears to love every minute of it; works his cow from the back fence right on through the herd and straight on out to wherever you want to stop him. His golden color and white mane and tail give him, of course, an edge on most of the competition as he looks so good and seems to be really enjoying what he is doing."

The Mayor of Crockett, Texas, proclaimed April 12th as "Rex Cauble–Cutter Bill Day" and gave a testimonial dinner at which 120 persons, including visiting dignitaries, sat down. The Governor of Louisiana was among those present. "Cutter Bill Day" was instituted to show appreciation on the part of the town and its citizens for all the good and widespread publicity Cutter Bill's campaigning had brought them. They even closed the schools and had one of the largest parades ever held in the town of Crockett, which Cutter Bill led—Rex Cauble up—and in which Sonny Perry rode Cutter Bill's first colt, now three. These big doings were advertised in a hundred newspapers, 34 radio stations, and 23 television hookups.

Properly mated to selected mares, it appears altogether possible that Cutter Bill may become the most sought-after sire of performance horses in the history of the breed.

Poco Lena

In a way, the inclusion here of Poco Lena is a tribute to her owner, trainer, and rider, B. A. Skipper, Jr., affectionately known as "Barney." During recent years Barney and his great mare Poco Lena have become synonymous with cutting, and, in fact, cutting was at the very core of Barney's life, the interest around which his time, thoughts, and activities revolved and a pursuit to which he was completely dedicated. A lifelong horseman and a recognized authority in many other fields of horsemanship, it was nevertheless in cutting that Barney's talents came to fullest fruition. No other man and no other horse have been more prominent in the public eye in this sport than B. A. Skipper and Poco Lena.

In presenting this account we have drawn heavily, with permission, from

material originally presented by Dean Sage and others in issues of *Cuttin'*
Hoss Chatter. Barney Skipper was killed in the early hours of Monday
morning, October 1, 1962, while flying his own plane home from Douglas,
Arizona, where he had competed in what proved to be his last cutting
horse contest. Shortly before 3 A.M. on Monday his plane was picked up
by radar some nineteen miles east of Dallas. When he failed to reach Longview a search was instituted, but it was not until Friday afternoon of
October 5th that the wreckage of his plane was found near Winnsboro,
east and somewhat to the north of Dallas.

But Poco Lena deserves a place in this book in her own right. Though
never a World's Champion by crown and points, she has many times been
the runner-up that pushed another horse into those coveted honors. A
master of showmanship with an encyclopedic knowledge of cattle, Barney
Skipper took this mare to five Reserve World Championships and won
more money than any other cutting horse has ever won or is likely to win.
There are few parts of the United States to which Barney and Poco Lena
did not travel, and few devotees of cutting anywhere who have not seen
this great team in action.

Poco Lena for ten consecutive years has been among the NCHA Top
Ten Cutting Horses! She has won well over twice as much money in
approved contests as her nearest competitor. Reserve World's Champion
five times. NCHA World Champion Cutting Horse Mare three times. Co-
champion of an NCHA Tournament of Champions. No other horse has
matched this record.

She was foaled on E. Paul Waggoner's famous Three D's Ranch near
Arlington, Texas, in 1949. Her sire is Poco Bueno; her dam is Sheilwin.
Poco Lena has set more records in the cutting arena than any horse in
history. Mr. Waggoner gave this bay filly to the Three D's manager, Glen
Turpin, and it was under Glen's ownership that she first appeared in the
NCHA files.

She entered the cutting arena as a competitor in the summer of 1952.
Shown only to a limited degree, because of her age, her first approved
contest win was a tie for third and fourth places at the Dallas County
Championship Rodeo on the Josey Ranch, Carrollton, in mid-June. With
Pine Johnson as her rider Poco Lena set her first record the following fall
by winning both the Junior Registered and NCHA Approved Open Cutting (33 entries) at the State Fair of Texas (Dallas) as a three-year-old.

Don Dodge of North Sacramento, California, has much renown for picking and purchasing great horses. He has bought, for instance, Poco Tivio,
Fannie James, and Snipper W. Each of these piled up notable records. Don

now set out to acquire Poco Lena and, buying her, became her owner-rider, this pair being a success from the start. Finishing second in the Fort Worth Show they went on to place in 21 NCHA approved contests, ranking fourth among the Top Ten of 1953.

During 1954 she won the Southern Arizona International Livestock Show at Tucson and, for the first time, the Cow Palace contest in San Francisco, placing in a total of 34 approved contests that season and finishing as Reserve World Champion Cutting Horse, adding several new Certificates to her accumulating collection.

After placing in 38 contests, including wins at the Odessa Sandhills Hereford & Quarter Horse Show and Kansas City's American Royal, during 1955, she was stricken seriously ill following the second go-round at the Cow Palace, taken to Davis, California, where surgery saved her life. She had, however, gained sufficient points prior to this to be named Reserve World Champion Cutting Horse for the second straight year.

In 1956, fully recovered, Poco Lena placed in 27 NCHA approved contests and ranked fourth among the Top Ten. She repeated her triumph at the San Francisco Cow Palace in 1957, placing in 26 approved shows, was fifth among the Top Ten, and repeated this standing in 1958 after placing in 22 shows.

Early in the spring of 1958 Barney Skipper, having sold his good cutting mare Poco Mona, began looking around for a replacement. In 1959 he bought Poco Lena from Don Dodge. She had already won about $50,000 in cutting arenas; during 1959, under Barney's guidance, she won her third Reserve World Champion Cutting Horse title with the additional honor of being named NCHA World Champion Cutting Horse Mare for the first time, having placed that year in 55 approved contests. Still another kudo came her way when she was crowned Co-champion of the 1959 NCHA Tournament of Champions at Mansfield, Texas. Forty-seven top cutting horses had entered and, by weird coincidence, her Co-champion was Poco Mona.

In 1960 she collected such titles as Champion of the Cow Palace Contest, NCHA Reserve World Champion Cutting Horse, and NCHA World Champion Cutting Horse Mare and another paper for her growing pile of NCHA certificates.

In 1961 she placed in 61 NCHA Championship contests, including wins at the big Tucson and Omaha shows, and finished the year with the rank of second among the Top Ten, named for the fifth time Reserve World Champion Cutting Horse, and, for the third time, NCHA World Champion Cutting Horse Mare. Said the *Cuttin' Hoss Chatter* of April, 1963: "Tragedy struck at this winning combination on all sides in 1962. Through September Barney and Poco Lena had placed in 51 NCHA Championhsip Cutting Horse Contests. Fresh from a first place win at Douglas, Arizona, on September 30, Barney Skipper attempted to fly home in his private plane. He did not survive the crash. Poco Lena was believed to be following him home by trailer but was not located until October 5th. When she arrived home her front legs were no longer sound and competent veterinarians say she will never cut again. Her record of winnings stood up well through the remaining month of the 1962 point year and on November 12th at the Thunderbird Arena in Las Vegas, Nevada, Mrs. B. A. Skipper, Jr. accepted what will probably be the last NCHA Certificate of Annual Achievement awarded to the immortal Poco Lena: No. 4–1962."

The Skipper horses have been dispersed at auction. With an overflow crowd, Poco Lena brought $14,200 from J. G. Madden of Minden, Louisiana.

In eleven years Poco Lena placed in 395 cutting horse contests approved by the NCHA, winning a total of $99,782.13 in competition against all who challenged. This amount stands first in the all-time Cutting Horse Money Winners list. In fitting recognition of this tremendous achievement, this great lifetime performance, Poco Lena has been awarded Hall of Fame Certificate No. 1 by the National Cutting Horse Association, and a plaque attesting to this honor will be hung in the home of the Association.

Holey Sox

This chestnut stallion has never been a World's Champion, though he may be. As of late May, 1963, he ranked first among the Top Ten, a couple of snorts ahead of last year's Champ, Cutter Bill.

His owner, Woodey Searle of Vernal, Utah, tells me he first saw Holey Sox in January of 1957, when the horse was being readied for the National Western at Denver. On his way to the sale Woodey had told Mrs. Searle he wasn't going to buy any horses. "But when I saw Holey Sox—all bets were off."

Mrs. Searle, eying her husband, said: "Go ahead and buy him."

Woodey plunged in, scarcely aware that there was anyone else present except as their continued bidding began to irritate the hell out of him. He finally got the horse for $3000, which topped the Denver sale that year. He'd been planning to take the horse home, use him on the Searle mares, and maybe make a calf or steer roper out of him if he showed any savvy. "I heard so much about him being a full brother to Palleo Pete, and how he ought to be running," Woodey told me, "I decided to give him a chance."

Holey Sox was foaled at Ponca City, Oklahoma, in 1955. He was bred by Fred Swalley, sired by Leo and dropped by a daughter of Osage Star. Swalley says: "He was Osage Star Lady's third foal, and being Pete's full brother he had a lot to live up to. He was gentle from the very first and seemed to love people. We named him because the sorrel spots on his legs looked like holes. After mulling it over we decided to consign him to the Denver sale. He was well advertised; a lot of people came there looking for him. There was snow on the ground and it was colder than blazes. We had him broke and he behaved like a little gentleman. You could see right off Mr. Searle was wild to get him."

Mr. and Mrs. B. A. Skipper, Jr. of Longview, Texas—Mrs. Skipper especially—were equally sold on the colt's appearance. She says: "I really did want to take him back to Texas. Then Barney quit bidding; Sox went to Mr. Searle. The next time I saw the colt he had done well on the tracks and they had started him on cattle. I talked with Austin Beebe at the Tournament in Phoenix about purchasing Sox, but Mr. Beebe did not think he could be bought."

Holey Sox was trained by Clarence Kiser, who at the time owned Vanetta Dee. Both at Denver and Ruidoso Mr. Searle's stallion qualified for AA ratings; his disposition and easy charm made him the favorite of all who knew him.

"Betty Kiser," Woodey says, "has told me many times of how quickly she became fond of him." On his way to Los Alamitos Sox caught cold and came down with pneumonia. Woodey had him fetched home. He says, "I hadn't wanted to run him in the first place and was only looking for an excuse to get him off the tracks. I did not realize then what it would have meant to get him rated AAA; if I had let him stick it out I'm pretty certain he'd have made it."

Sox is not a tall horse. After Searle got him home and cured, a number of persons came along with horses they wanted to run at him. "Roy Showalter," Woodey says, "had a Thoroughbred called Bing. After much talk we agreed to run Sox at him for $4000 a side at 440 yards, this match to be run during the Vernal Race Meet. I had a little girl from Hayden, Colorado—Kay Conyers—come down to ride for me. Lawrence Allen of Vernal got Sox ready. There was a lot of money bet in that crowd. This was a circle track and Sox had never seen one before. When they were ready to leave the paddock I told Kay: 'I want to win this race more than I ever wanted anything in my life—but win it fair.' "

Sox broke on top and never was headed. On the backstretch Kay stood

63. Holey Sox with Jim Lee up.

Photo by McNerney-Dompierre

up in her stirrups, looked back, and brought Sox in on an easy run. "After that," Woodey says, "I started to rope calves and steers off him and run barrels during the rest of 1958. In August, Leland McNeil was working for me and had Sox on a rope next the lambing shed. He threw the rope out in front and stepped down to make him work the rope. The horse backed into the corner of a rafter, tore open his left hip until the hide turned inside out and dropped almost down to the gaskin. I gave him a big shot of penicillin and went for my M.D., Dr. R. E. Spendlove.

"Gathering up what he thought we might need, we hurried back to the house and commenced a job that took three hours. We had to make several trips to the hospital; after the first trip Doc said to send someone else, that he hadn't realized how an animal would respond the way Sox did for me as I stood with my arms around his neck and talked to him. The cut was so large it wasn't possible to keep it deadened, but as long as I stood there talking to him Doc could go ahead with the stitches, of which it took 75 on the inside of the hip and 50 on the outside. He never put any medication on the inside of the wound. We gave him 10cc of penicillin every day for a month and had to keep him tied to both sides of his stall, though I took him out and exercised him every day. He has never favored the leg at all."

Woodey kept him home the rest of that year. The summer of 1959 he resumed calf and steer roping and running barrels; in barrel racing Sox never ran out of the money. "It makes no difference what you ask him to do, or how often, he will always try his best every time. I had heard a lot about cutting horses, had watched them work though I'd never owned one. Talking with Austin Beebe at Salem, Utah, a deal was hatched for him to take Holey Sox and train him to be a cutter. I was with cutting just as I'd been with racing—a sight too impatient for anybody's good.

"I waited ten days before calling Austin to find out how he was doing. I was told, 'He's a real nice horse and we're getting along fine.' I waited another week and called again. 'He started to look at cows the first time I tried to work him,' Austin admitted. 'He's doing exceptionally well.' At the end of the third week Austin told me: 'He is the best horse I have ever put a leg over.' It wasn't long after this that Austin's hip went out of joint. This was reported to me over the phone; it was suggested I had better come get the horse as there was no telling how long it might be before any more rides could be put on him. Austin recommended Joe Gray at Denver."

Woodey will never forget the day he went to pick up Sox. The horse spotted him coming and, as Searle got out of his car, rushed across the corral, bucking and playing and shaking his head. Austin, leg in traction on a bed by the front room window, said to his wife: "Look at that horse— Woodey must be out there!"

In January of 1960 a friend of Fred Swalley called Woodey from Oklahoma offering $25,000 for Holey Sox. "By this time," Woodey allowed, "he'd become a member of the family—I'd sooner have cut off my right arm than sell him."

Joe Gray was engaged to take over Sox's training. The horse was taken to Denver and left in a stall—this was on January 10, 1960. Through some kind of mix-up Gray failed to get him. Woodey, unaware of this, a few days later took off for Illinois. "While there," he says, "I was contacted by a reporter who wanted a picture to put in a magazine. I called Joe Gray and, of course, asked how the horse was doing. Gray informed me he had not seen the horse, but would check and call me back. I put in a bad while, waiting for that phone to ring."

A Denver paper, under date of February 5th, ran a two-column head: 'Lost' Horse Heads Home. They gave it eleven paragraphs, the first of which reads: "A high-priced Quarter Horse stallion that was 'lost' for three weeks in a stall at the Denver Stockyards will be on his way home Saturday."

One can imagine Woodey's state of mind when he gave that interview over the telephone. In recounting the story to me, he said, "I never did find out how long he was in that stall. Ed Paul, chief brand inspector for Colorado, took him in charge when no one seemed to know who the horse belonged to. We'd sent him over there by van. Mr. Paul turned Sox over to Dr. Ledbetter, the State Veterinarian, who took the horse to his stables out east of town. Furious, once again—as I had previously done in California—I called the whole deal off and had Sox brought home, my mind made up that he would never leave again."

But Austin Beebe had a long talk with Searle, pointing out how unfair Woodey was being to the horse. "One day," said Beebe, "Sox could be one of the nation's top cutting horses, but not if you take him out of it now."

The upshot of this was that, in March of that year, Beebe came and picked up Sox, and, at St. George, put a month's work on him before fetching him back for the spring breeding season. About the first of July Beebe took Sox again, this time into Nevada, Idaho, Arizona, Colorado, and California, returning him in the spring of 1961 for stud duty. In July, Austin Beebe went to work for Woodey at the Diamond Hills ranch, and took Sox to several shows that summer, using him in team roping and barrel racing.

In January of 1962 Searle and Beebe took Sox to Denver. While at the Denver show Woodey got pretty well acquainted with the B. A. Skippers, who had previously bid against him there when they were each trying to acquire Holey Sox. The Skippers owned Poco Lena (World's Champion Cutting Mare), and again tried to buy Sox. "I told them," says Woodey, "I was just not interested in selling the horse."

Beebe brought Sox home about the first of March. "At this point," Searle remarked, "Mrs. Skipper called, wanting to know what I was going to do with the horse. Frankly, I couldn't honestly make up my mind. I talked to Barney and he once more asked for a price on Sox. 'Barney,' I said, 'you know I have been offered $25,000 for him and wouldn't sell.' He said, 'How about twice that much?' I told him there was no use talking, that nobody was going to own Sox but me. I did, however, finally agree to let Barney borrow him for the rest of that year."

Due to the tragic death of Barney Skipper in the crash of his plane on October 1st, all plans were off. Barney had been returning from a show at Douglas, Arizona. Poco Lena and Holey Sox were en route to the Skipper ranch in a trailer. The handler, on learning of Barney's death, went all to pieces, Woodey says. The two horses consequently were left in the trailer for three or four days. "I flew to Longview to help find Mr. Skipper. After the services the horses were located. Mrs. Skipper recommended Jim Lee, who had previously worked for them and who was then working in Dallas. She told me he was planning to start training horses for himself. I was impressed with him immediately."

Jim Lee tells me:

I had only worked with Sox a very short time when it became obvious he was outstanding cutting horse material. I was thrilled and amazed every time I got on him. He was willing and caught on fast. After some three weeks work I felt he was ready to do a few of the smaller shows. We went to a Quarter Horse clinic at Spanish Fork, Utah, where he was shown and judged, receiving much applause.

He has a very fine disposition. There's not one mean thing about him. He displayed his gentleness to me one day when I had the misfortune to throw my hip out of place. I'd been caught off balance in a mighty swift turn.

I pulled him up. I didn't think I could move. I called for help but no one heard. This was early in the morning. I was afraid I would fall off. I had five stallions and one mare tied to the fence. I was afraid Sox would get away from me and get in with those other horses. At least a half hour passed before I got help and not once did Sox so much as move. I kept talking to him; am sure he knew something was very wrong. When he was surrounded by people trying to get me off he continued to remain calm and motionless—never once showed excitement.

In November I took him to the Tournament of Champions at Phoenix, then back to the Golden Spike show at Ogden; there he tied for first in one go-round. From there we went to Denver, toured down through Texas, Arizona, and back to the Diamond Hills. I have a tender spot in my heart for this horse. He has so much ability, and such a good disposition along with it, that you can't help loving him. In all the time I've spent with him there wasn't once I asked him to do a thing that he did not do his level best. I've seen him get down on his knees trying to turn a calf. I have never used a tiedown or any kind of gimmick on him. What he has done has been on his own and through his own natural ability.

On January 30, 1963, Fred Swalley (breeder) wrote Woodey: "We certainly enjoyed watching Holey Sox work. Know you are very proud of him."

Jack Elliott says:

I first saw Holey Sox at the Utah State Fair in 1960. I was judging the horse show. Sox was entered in the novice cutting horse contest; Austin Beebe was showing him. To my knowledge it was the first time he had been shown in competition. Normally in a novice contest a score of 70 to 72 is considered very good. Sox scored a 74—he was the high-marked horse on my scorecard. I told several bystanders he was the most promising young horse I had ever seen.

Two years later I was in Longview, Texas, at the home of B. A. Skipper, who had owned and shown many good cutters and was continually training young horses. They were working some that afternoon. Mrs. Skipper was riding Holey Sox. I saw, as she worked him on cattle, the same style and manner I had marked before; he was now emerging as the smooth finished product that only time, patience, and training can produce.

With Jim Lee riding I have watched him in the last three big shows of the cutting horse circuit—Las Vegas, Little Rock, and Odessa. Against the toughest horses in the business he has consistently gone to the Finals and been one of the top four winners in each of these shows. So far as Quarter Horses go he is bred in the purple. This is, of course, a great factor —good breeding counts when the chips are down. He is more than just a royally bred horse, however; he possesses that undecipherable quality that elevates him from a good horse to a potentially great horse.

This statement from Mr. Elliott is dated January 18, 1963.

Dean Parker, former Horse Editor of *Western Livestock Journal*, says: "When I was at Las Vegas I had a chance to work on Holey Sox. I can't remember when I have been so thrilled by a horse. He is the quickest, smoothest, most deceptive animal I have ever been on. Believe me, he sure reads cattle."

Back to Jim Lee:

We started out the year of 1963 at Little Rock, placing in the top ten of the nation's 65 toughest horses competing; right after that the spring shows started everywhere. We began at Odessa, placing both go-rounds and winning the second in the Finals (44 horses).

At San Antonio (64 horses) we won a second and a go-round; this is the only spring show we did not go to the Finals. At Houston we split first in two go-rounds and picked up third in the Finals (64 horses). From there we went to Maricopa, Arizona, where we won first (13 horses). At this writing we have split the first go-round at Tucson.

I have been training cutting horses for better than ten years and I think Holey Sox is probably the greatest horse I have ever ridden. He is the only horse I have ever ridden that could work any kind of cattle in any kind of pen, and yet be tough on all occasions. He is just as good with my ten-year-old son up.

Woodey has now been offered $65,000 and still says he won't sell.

Here is a list of the Top Ten Cutting Horses as compiled by the National Cutting Horse Association as of May 25, 1963. Points are computed from NCHA Championship Cutting Horse Contest results received by the Association:

1. HOLEY SOX, Woodey B. Searle, Vernal, Utah; 20 shows, $7389.26; ridden by Jim Lee
2. CUTTER BILL, Rex C. Cauble, Crockett, Texas; 10 shows, $6946.01; ridden by Sonny Perry
3. HOPPEN, Del Jay Associates, Gates Mills, Ohio; 21 shows, $6417.61; ridden by Shorty Freeman
4. ALICE STAR, Houston Clinton & Co., Burnet, Texas; 10 shows, $5065-.31; ridden by Stanley Bush
5. KID FIVE, Westernhook Farm, Southbury, Conn.; 8 shows, $4461.60; ridden by Buck Harris and Buster Welch
6. DOC'S DADDOO, R. E. Palmer, Casa Grande, Arizona; 11 shows, $3911.87; ridden by J. T. Fisher and Leo Thorn
7. SWEN MISS 16, James E. Kemp, Dallas, Texas; 12 shows, $3481.02; ridden by Jack Newton
8. SMOKY SO, Louis M. Pearce, Jr., Houston, Texas; 6 shows, $2737.30; ridden by owner and Charles Habermacher
9. SANDHILL CHARLIE, Slim Trent, Fallon, Nevada; 13 shows, $2595-.53; ridden by owner
10. JILL'S LADY, James A. Cheek, Dallas, Texas; 15 shows, $2322.38; ridden by Leroy Ashcraft

Summation

In wrapping up this section I feel that a few observations from Bob Denhardt, first Secretary and one of the prime movers in the launching of the AQHA, are particularly appropriate. These are taken from his book *The Quarter Horse*, published in 1950 at Amarillo by the American Quarter Horse Association.

Bob writes:

One might wonder why more horses of other breeds are not tops on the ranch and in rodeo. There have been some exceptional horses which were good, but the simple answer lies in the fact that most other breeds do not have what it takes for ranch and rodeo work. . . . Only the Quarter Horse has been bred for that one thing which every cow horse and every rodeo horse must have to be worthy of the name—rapid breaking speed, the ability to stand flatfooted one moment and the next to be running at full speed.

Good rodeo horses must be carefully trained. Steer roping horses are taught to run on after the catch, and when the steer is down to face away from the animal to be tied. The calf horse must be taught to stop when the loop is thrown and to face the calf. All roping horses must be taught to keep a tight rope. The dogging horse must be taught to run beside the steer and, when his rider leaves him, to wait and see if his rider needs to try again. If his rider does want to jump again, he must stand quietly while his owner runs up to him. The horse hazing for the bulldogger must be taught not to run past the steer, to stop when the steer stops, etc. Team roping horses must be taught to work as a team and to work right on either the head or the hind feet. A cutting horse has to learn so much that in the range country they are still arguing whether one is born or trained. There is one quality which the Quarter Horse possesses which each and every one of these horses must have above all others—quick maneuverable speed, the ability to start and gain full speed in a fraction of a second.

There is another Quarter Horse characteristic which is essential, and that is level headedness. Level headedness, quietness even after strenuous action, is a wonderful attribute enjoyed by all good Quarter Horses. It is a factor which is too often ignored. . . . With the single exception of his ability to gain momentum rapidly, probably the Quarter Horse's greatest asset is his level headedness and his quiet temper.

Part IV: The Show Horse

General Information

It should be realized that within the past two decades Quarter Horses have created a breeding, selling, using industry reaching presently into every state in the nation—and beyond. Manufacturers and distributors of bridles, saddles, trailers, blankets, medicines, books and magazines—indeed, a whole complex of gear and clothing and feed, have sprung up to supplement or replace items dropped from general use when horse power began to be replaced by motor power.

It may astonish you to know that more than two hundred Quarter Horse Associations now are functioning in this country, Canada, and Hawaii. Although not tied administratively to the American Quarter Horse Association, the shows and registered activities of each of these groups must, to be approved, comply with AQHA rules and regulations. Members of these organizations are earnest ambassadors of the breed.

Here it seems advisable to inject a note of caution. Keep alert and keep your eyes peeled. Wherever there is Big Business there is likely to be considerable green stuff about, both the folding and the two-legged kinds. *Don't be taken in by glib words and wishful thinking.* The American Quarter Horse Association is the only breed association whose registry and papers have any monetary significance inside the United States. It has the only *recognized Stud Book* and contemplates no merger.

The AQHA is proud of its remarkable progress, and of the numerous Quarter Horse clinics held annually in various parts of the United States and Canada. These clinics, frequently held at state universities, are sponsored by local, regional, or state Quarter Horse associations. The American Quarter Horse Association defrays expenses of one of its representatives to join with college personnel to conduct the clinics. Subject matter is varied, including virtually everything of interest, from health problems to training and performance exhibitions. During 1962 several such clinics were held for the first time along the Eastern Seaboard and drew large numbers of interested persons, many of whom in garb and appearance might have stepped straight out of a Western movie. This is not mentioned so much in a spirit of friendly amusement as to point out the very real enthusiasm which this transplanted descendant of the Spanish Horse seems able to evoke wherever he appears.

The American Quarter Horse registry represents owners in all 50 states of this country, Canada, Mexico, and 21 nations overseas. Owners of these horses annually sponsor hundreds of Association-approved shows. Quarter Horses have become predominant in professional rodeo where championships and thousands of dollars are at stake, and in Western motion pictures and television.

APPROVED SHOWS

	1960	1961	1962
"A" Shows	30	56	70
"B" Shows	67	148	158
"C" Shows	222	397	490
"D" Shows	376	222	157
Horses Shown	18,184	22,822	24,868
Halter Point Earners	* * *	2,420	2,683
Working Point Earners	* * *	2,576	2,942
Total Shows	695	823	875

LARGEST SHOWS—1962

Shows having largest number of entries in halter classes will be found in left-hand column, largest number of classes in performance events in center column, and largest total entries (individual halter classes, group classes, and performance classes) in right-hand column.

Halter	Performance	Total
482 Fort Worth, Tex.	293 Fort Worth, Tex.	795 Fort Worth, Tex.
314 Chicago, Ill.	275 Chicago, Ill.	589 Chicago, Ill.
276 San Francisco. Calif.	243 Dallas, Tex.	530 Dallas, Tex.
260 Dallas, Tex.	228 Houston, Tex.	455 Houston, Tex.
245 Springfield, Ill.	204 Baton Rouge, La.	451 Prescott, Ariz.
239 San Antonio, Tex.	196 Walla Walla, Wash.	447 Walla Walla, Wash.
238 Prescott, Ariz.	191 Walla Walla, Wash.	395 San Francisco, Calif.
229 Walla Walla, Wash.	173 St. Paul, Minn.	395 Ogden, Utah
222 Houston, Tex.	170 Harrisburg, Pa.	391 Walla Walla, Wash.
216 Ogden, Utah	166 Ogden, Utah	389 Baton Rouge, La.
216 Denver, Colo.	166 Gladewater, Tex.	370 St. Paul, Minn.
215 Albuquerque, N. M.	164 Saginaw, Tex.	363 Albuquerque, N. M.
214 Kansas City, Mo.	163 Prescott, Ariz.	353 Baton Rouge, La.

Halter		Performance		Total	
211	Stockton, Calif.	160	Columbus, Ohio	333	Columbus, Ohio
209	Tucson, Ariz.	152	Baton Rouge, La.	325	Detroit, Mich.
205	Omaha, Nebr.	150	Grants Pass, Oreg.	322	Tucson, Ariz.
192	Columbus, Ohio	150	Louisville, Ky.	313	San Antonio, Tex.
192	Los Alamitos, Calif.	148	Indianapolis, Ind.	310	Columbus, Ohio
191	Walla Walla, Wash.	146	Longview, Tex.	307	Ontario, Oreg.
190	Detroit, Mich.	144	Ontario, Oreg.	304	Indianapolis, Ind.
185	St. Paul, Minn.	141	Columbus, Ohio	300	Denver, Colo.
184	Baton Rouge, La.	141	Yreka, Calif.	296	Odessa, Tex.
183	Hutchinson, Kan.	138	Cleburne, Tex.	295	N. Portland, Oreg.
183	Des Moines, Iowa	137	St. Paul, Minn.	293	Springfield, Ill.
174	Norco, Calif.	132	Eugene, Oreg.	292	Grants Pass, Oreg.
172	Stillwater, Okla.	130	N. Portland, Oreg.	288	Stockton, Calif.
168	Baton Rouge, La.	130	Caraway, Ark.	287	Stillwater, Okla.
163	Odessa, Tex.	129	Sweetwater, Tex.	286	Hutchinson, Kan.
156	Salt Lake City, Utah	128	Oshkosh, Neb.	278	Gladewater, Tex.
155	Adel, Iowa	127	College Station, Tex.	276	Harrisburg, Pa.
154	N. Portland, Oreg.	126	Odessa, Tex.	271	Cleburne, Tex.
152	Kalamazoo, Mich.	123	Martinsville, Ill.	270	St. Paul, Minn.
152	San Jose, Calif.	123	Rockdale, Tex.	270	Los Alamitos, Calif.
150	Columbus, Ohio	122	Albuquerque, N. M.	269	Omaha, Nebr.
148	Kansas City, Mo.	120	Montgomery, Ala.	268	Saginaw, Tex.
146	Castaic, Calif.	120	Gordon, Nebr.	266	Kansas City, Mo.
145	Noblesville, Ind.	120	Salem, Oreg.	260	Longview, Tex.
144	Kechi, Kan.	117	Syracuse, N. Y.	260	Eugene, Oreg.
144	Kinsley, Kan.	116	Columbus, Ohio	259	Des Moines, Iowa
140	Paris, Tex.	116	Beatrice, Neb.	257	Yreka, Calif.
138	Indianapolis, Ind.	115	Branchville, N. J.	255	Noblesville, Ind.
138	Yakima, Wash.	113	Marshall, Mich.	254	Kalamazoo, Mich.
137	Lincoln, Neb.	112	New Orleans, La.	252	Norco, Calif.
136	Grants Pass, Oreg.	111	Layton, N. J.	251	Salt Lake City, Utah
136	Spanish Fork, Utah	109	Stillwater, Okla.	250	Paris, Tex.
134	Ontario, Oreg.	109	Littleton, Colo.	248	Columbus, Ohio
134	Palm Springs, Calif.	109	Solon, Ohio	247	Adel, Iowa
134	Kennewick, Wash.	108	Maryville, Mo.	243	Louisville, Ky.
133	St. Paul, Minn.	107	Fort Worth, Tex.	241	Kansas City, Mo.
133	Filer, Idaho	107	N. Terre Haute, Ind.	239	Salem, Oreg.
				239	Lincoln, Nebr.
				239	Beatrice, Nebr.

The AQHA employs more than 215 people, including nine inspectors who traveled a combined total of 572,988 miles during 1961, for instance, in the United States, Canada, and Hawaii to examine horses for possible advancement in the registry. AQHA offices are equipped with the most modern machines and filing systems. Quarter Horse auctions during the first six months of 1962 continued the pattern formed in 1961, when 4949 registered animals sold in 101 reported auctions for $6,736,100, to average $1361. These figures, from what I have seen, have materially improved since 1961.

The *Official Handbook of the American Quarter Horse Association* is kept up to date and available to all. The Association also provides at nominal rentals a variety of Quarter Horse films suitable for group showings. Inquiries should be mailed to P. O. Box 271, Amarillo, Texas.

No other horse-breed registry in the world has come so far so fast as has the American Quarter Horse Association. The American Quarter Running Horse was an established breed as far back as 1665, but it had no registry distinctly its own until the AQHA came into being on March 15, 1940. Helen Michaelis, the Association's first official historian, wrote in Vol. I or Vol. II of the AQHA official *Stud Book and Registry*: "Primarily a short distance race horse, the Quarter Horse was secondarily a stock horse. Before long races became popular, the Quarter Horse spread to all parts of the United States and was accepted as the fastest short distance race horse in the world. After the Thoroughbred was established in the United States and long races became popular, the Quarter Horse moved on to the great Southwest, where he became known as the greatest cow horse in history. He has maintained this title, both on the range and in the arena, and as a race horse, his time has never been lowered, going a quarter of a mile. . . . In performance and endurance the Quarter Horse has never been excelled, and in bloodlines he has held his own well over two hundred and fifty years. There is but one way to preserve the Quarter Horse, and that is to breed Quarter Horses."

The title AQHA Champion is awarded to individual stallions, mares, and geldings registered by the Association which meet the following requirements:

At such time as any horse qualifies on points for the AQHA Championship award, the records of said horse will be submitted to the Secretary for his approval. The title may be awarded to any individual registered in either the Permanent, the Tentative, or the NQHBA Book, or listed in the Appendix Registry or New Appendix Registry of the Association after it has won a total of thirty or more points in competition in official shows and contests recognized by the AQHA, provided:
(a) That the points have been won in two or more shows and two or more contests and under two or more judges.

(b) That at least twelve of the points have been won in halter classes and of these twelve points a minimum of four points must be won in either A or B class shows and that at least twelve of the points have been won in performance classes.

The purpose of the Register of Merit is to establish a record of performance. Horses are advanced to the ROM when they have won at least five points, as outlined in the 'scale of points,' for contests, or four points earned at racing. To qualify for the Register of Merit horses must be entered in approved AQHA shows in one of the approved contests listed below:

A—Working Classes
1. Registered Cutting and NCHA sponsored contests
2. Registered Reining
3. Registered Roping
4. Registered Barrel Racing
5. Registered Working Cowhorse
6. Registered Western Pleasure Horse
7. Registered Western Riding
8. Registered Pole Bending

B—Racing
For racing, points will be awarded at the end of each calendar year toward an AQHA Champion and/or inclusion in the Register of Merit. Using the list of "Best Times" for the year at the various distances, as compiled and attested to by the Secretary of the Association, horses listed in Grade AAA and AA at each distance will be divided into three groups as nearly equal as possible.

Horses in the top group will be awarded six points, horses in the second group five points, and horses in the lowest group four points.

Only races approved and recognized by the AQHA will be considered for the awarding of points for Championships or admission to the Register of Merit.

Such races must be run under the rule book entitled "Rules and Regulations of Quarter Racing" as adopted by the AQRA.

Any organization, club or individual desiring to stage or sponsor a race meeting, or races, will be required to obtain a "Certificate of Recognition" from the Secretary's Office.

Halter Show Classes

The following halter classes are recommended for every show:
    (a) Weanling fillies (foaled in calendar year of show)
    (b) Yearling fillies (foaled calendar year preceding show)
    (c) Two-year-old fillies
    (d) Three-year-old fillies
    (e) Four-year-old and older mares
    (f) Weanling colts (foaled in calendar year of show)
    (g) Yearling colts (calendar year preceding show)
    (h) Two-year-old colts

(i) Three-year-old stallions

(j) Four-year-old and older stallions.

Champion Stallion (chosen from first-place winners).

Reserve Champion Stallion (chosen second-place winner in the Grand Champion Stallion's class and first-place winners in other classes).

Under no circumstances may any of the three gelding classes be combined.

Champion Gelding (chosen from first-place winners).

Reserve Champion Gelding (chosen from second-place winner in the Grand Champion Gelding's class and first-place winners in other classes).

Aged Mare class may be divided into two classes—dry mares and brood mares: brood mares to have had a foal in the current or previous year.

Champion Mare (chosen from first-place winners).

Reserve Champion Mare (chosen from second-place winner in the Grand Champion Mare's class and first-place winners in other classes).

Weanling colts and fillies may not be shown together in the same halter class.

If the show management desires, it is permissible to divide the yearling colt and yearling filly classes into two divisions, senior and junior. Senior division with foaling dates January 1st to May 31st. Junior Division with foaling dates June 1st to December 31st.

MINIMUM REQUIREMENTS

For a show to be approved and points awarded, a minimum of four halter classes for stallions and a minimum of four halter classes for mares must be offered. These to include yearlings, two-year-olds, three-year-olds, and four-year-olds and older, and a minimum of one performance class limited to registered Quarter Horses must be included. Effective April 1, 1961: As one of the minimum requirements for show approval, a show must offer three gelding classes. These classes shall be: one class for two-year-olds and younger, one class for three-year-olds and four-year-olds, and one class for five-year-olds and older.

GROUP HALTER CLASSES

The following are additional classes that are recommended if interest or entries justify, but no points will be awarded for Register of Merit or Championship. Horses shown in a group class must be eligible to show in their individual halter class at that show.

(a) Produce of Dam. Two produce, either sex, can show. Dam need not be shown nor need produce be owned by owner of dam. The entry at the show must be made by the owner of the dam. Horses actually shown as the Produce of Dam will be limited to horses three years old and younger.

(b) Get of Sire. Three get, either sex, can be shown. Sire need not be shown nor need get be owned by owner of sire. The entry at the show must be made by the owner of the sire or by someone with written permission from the owner of sire. Horses actually shown as the Get of Sire will be limited to horses three years old and younger.

(c) Mare and foal. Mare with one foal to be shown. Foal must have been foaled within current calendar year. Mare and foal need not be property of same owner.

(d) Sire and Get. Sire with two get to be shown. Sire and get do not have to be property of same owner. Horses shown as the get in this class will be limited to horses three years old and younger.

(e) Exhibitor's Group. Group of four head, any age or sex, all owned by exhibitor.

AGE REQUIREMENTS

For the purpose of determining eligibility for competition, the age of a horse shall be computed by the calendar year starting January 1st of the year foaled; i.e., it is a *weanling* during the calendar year in which foaled, regardless of time of year foaled; a *yearling* during the first calendar year following foaling date. For example: a horse foaled any time in 1958 will be termed one year old January 1, 1959, two years old January 1, 1960.

All stallions and mares two years old and younger listed in the Old or New Appendix are eligible to participate in *all approved halter classes*.

Stallions and mares three years old and older *must* have a *registration number* to be eligible to participate in approved halter classes.

All weanlings must be eligible to receive a registration number *or* eligible to be listed in the New Appendix.

Geldings may show at any age on an Appendix or New Appendix certificate.

Any horse entered in an approved AQHA show or contest must be listed under his registered name and number, or his Appendix or New Appendix name with the designation of Appendix or New Appendix following his name. To be eligible for AQHA points, a horse must be exhibited under its complete registered name.

Working Classes

In all performance classes where one individual at a time performs, the order of competition shall be determined by drawing lots.

In all working classes, except Western Pleasure, horses are to be judged on performance ability only.

In any approved performance class the judge shall have the authority to require the removal or alteration of any piece of equipment or accouterment which, in his opinion, would tend to give a horse an unfair advantage or which he believes to be inhumane.

In any contest points shall be awarded on the basis of the total number of horses actually judged in each contest, whether or not an elimination is held. Example: If 100 horses are entered and exhibited in an elimination, points will be based on that number even though entry fees were returned on horses which were worked and eliminated.

A stallion, mare, or gelding, any age, may show in any performance contest on a New Appendix or Appendix certificate, or a numbered certificate.

Any horse listed in the Appendix registry prior to January 1, 1962, shall be eligible to compete in approved arena performance and recognized race meetings after that date.

The office of the Secretary will be available for information and guidance in all matters relating to the planning and conducting of official shows and contests.

The results of any approved contest should be forwarded, by the contest management, to the Secretary of the Association within five (5) days after the completion of the contest.

In the event the contest management does not report the contest results to the AQHA Secretary within thirty (30) days, those horses participating shall not receive points.

If the contest management does not report the contest results to the Secretary of the American Quarter Horse Association, any subsequent approval request may be withheld.

Leading Sires of 1962, Performance-Class Winners (Top Five)

Sire	Winners	Wins	Different Events
ROYAL KING, Ch. h. 34 by King	23	76	7
#POCO BUENO, Br. h. 44 by King	20	66	5
KING, B. h. 32 by Zantanon	19	32	4
MAJOR KING, Ch. h. 46 by ROYAL KING	12	19	5
#POCO DELL, B. h. 50 by #POCO BUENO	11	36	5

Leading Sires of 1962, Halter-Class Winners (Top Five)

Sire	Winners	Class Wins	Grand Championships
#POCO DELL, B. h. 50 by #POCO BUENO	43	188	70
#POCO PINE, B. h. 54 by #POCO BUENO	31	169	96
#POCO BUENO, Br. h. 44 by King	28	103	45
Showdown, Ch. h. 51 by Wimpy	23	81	24
Leo San, Ch. h. 49 by LEO	18	171	43

Biographical Sketches

The next part of this section will be given over to several sample vignettes which may discover for the reader the important traits and/or characteristics which have had some part in bringing the stallions discussed the degree of success and popularity shown by their standing on the two foregoing lists. Sires shown on the lists but not mentioned here have been omitted because insufficient data were available.

King & Company

The Ott Adams-bred stallion Zantanon spent most of his life racing south of the border, where he was celebrated both in song and story as the Mexican Man O' War. Most of what we know about him came from M. Benavides Volpe, one of the few surviving old-time Quarter Horse men whose experiences, in the words of one AQHA spokesman, "reach far back into the age dominated by such titans of the industry as Ott Adams, George Clegg, Coke Roberds, Joe Gardner, Milo Burlingame, Tom Martin, W. W. Lock, Crawford Sykes, Dow and William Shely, Billy Anson," and others.

The story of Zantanon reveals how rugged and enduring a properly bred Quarter Horse can be. Mr. Volpe, the Laredo ranchman who fetched Zantanon back into the United States, declared that this great son of Little Joe was starved to death all his life; that when he purchased him at the age of fourteen years the horse was so emaciated and weak he could scarcely walk. Volpe tells us the men who raced him in Mexico were made wealthy by him, yet would unfeelingly walk him over four miles of hard streets to the race track, where they would trot, gallop, and jog him until his sweat disappeared, and then walk him home over those same cobbled streets. Even then, they never bothered to cool him out but tied him under some tree and let him stand there through the heat of the day. At four in the afternoon, when the heat became more bearable, they would again saddle him up and walk him over the hard streets until dark. He was fed at night, I am told, on oats and corn, with a handful of cornstalks and shucks for roughage. "By the day of the race," declared Volpe, "he was so poor you could count every one of his ribs. By that time, of course, he had no pep, but was absolutely dead on his feet. Yet in that condition and with his owner's son, weighing 140 pounds, and a sear singer (we did not know the race saddles at that time down there), he could run 300 yards in fifteen and two-fifths seconds from a walking start."

Zantanon was the sire of King (P–234) whose dam, according to his registered pedigree, was Jabalina by Strait Horse (by Yellow Jacket by Little Rondo by Lock's Rondo). Most people are under the impression that Jess Hankins, King's long-time owner, bred him, and the *Stud Book* lists Burney James of Encinal, Texas, as breeder; but Garford Wilkinson, in an article on Volpe in the *Quarter Horse Journal* of August, 1962, says Volpe bred King. Jess Hankins acquired him in 1937 and built his fame as a breeder around King's get and their accomplishments. The *Stud Book* lists 608 registered foals by King. Seventeen have become AQHA Champions; 67 have qualified for Register of Merit in the show ring; 36 have started on recognized tracks; 11 have qualified for the racing Register of Merit; one of these, Squaw H, achieved AAA. Probably the best-known and unquestionably the most influential of Zantanon's get, King died at twenty-six years of age on March 24, 1958, at the Rocksprings ranch of Jess Hankins.

Volpe ran King a couple of times before selling him as a two-year-old to Byrne James at Raymondsville. James made a roper out of him and used him after cattle, for which he showed a natural aptitude. Winn DuBois bought him as a four-year-old, made a finished roper of him and, with Johnny Stevens, carried him around to most of the southwest Texas rodeos. Though sadly overshadowed by his sire's reputation, King was not without ability. He was a first-rate stock horse of very impressive appearance; it was not his fault that Mr. Hankins bought him just for riding and breeding. The two races we have a record of he won very handily.

Zantanon, by Little Joe (most consistent begetter of all Traveler's sons), had a number of other fairly prominent horse colts—Ed Echols, Chico (out of a daughter of Possum), San Siemon, Quatro de Julio, Zantanon Jr., and El Bandido—but none have held a candle to King's influence in the stud. A controversial stallion, he stimulated much conversation; you either liked him or you didn't, but no one can deny the mark he left upon the breed. His get are strong in the show rings, admired by many ranchers. At the time Mr. Hankins acquired him King was standing at $15; when death overtook him his service was in demand at a fee of $2500.

Any list of his more notable sons must include Royal King, Hank H, Old Taylor, Little Tom B, King Banner, King April, D-Day, Clovis King, Jimmy, Jess Hankins, King Joe, Zantanon H, and Cactus King, and there are many others. But none of those were as popular as the much-publicized Poco Bueno (P–3044), winner of countless awards, both in halter shows and cutting horse contests. Poco Bueno's owner, according to Roy Davis (presently editing the *Quarter Horse Journal*), has several times turned down $50,000 for him.

Garford Wilkinson, writing of him in 1961, said that, through 1960, the following could definitely be chalked up to Poco Bueno's credit: first in Leading Sires of Performance Contest Winners; first in Leading Sires of 1960 Halter Horses; second only to King among Leading Sires of off-track Register of Merit Qualifiers; third to King and to his half-brother Royal King in Leading Sires of Point-Earning Performance Horses; third in Leading 1960 Get of Sire Class Winners; fifth in Leading Sires of Yearling 1960 Halter Class Winners; eighth in Leading Sires of 1960 Arena Register of Merit Qualifiers. In addition to these kudos Poco Bueno, in 1958, made owner E. Paul Waggoner the leading breeder of halter class winners, Register of Merit designees, and Winners of Grand Championships.

Poco Bueno was bred by Jess Hankins. His dam was Miss Taylor by Old Poco Bueno (by Little Joe by Traveler). To those who have never seen the horse he is said to have the same attraction Roger Maris exerts on baseball fans, while to Fagan Miller, boss of the realm in which Poco Bueno currently reigns, the big stallion—notwithstanding his outstanding attributes—is a ham actor. Visitors come from all over the world, clamoring at the Waggoner gates to get a look at him. It is claimed that at the first scent of strangers Poco Bueno will perk up his ears and strike a handsome pose.

Foaled in 1944 he was not early recognized as a potentially great horse. For some time Mr. Hankins was unable to sell him at $1250. As a two-year-old he was exhibited at Stamford, Texas, placing first in his class. Frank Vessels and Channing Peak looked him over with interest and Brother Jess advanced his asking price to $3500. Both prospects left without the horse. Poco Bueno's first bid for fame came at Hankin's first auction, when Paul Waggoner acquired him with a bid of $5700, a rather astonishing price for a Quarter Horse in those days.

Glenn Turpin says:

Soon after we got Poco Bueno to the Three D's Farm at Arlington we put him under the saddle. Bob Burton was then foreman and trainer for the Three D's and the man who first saddled the horse. He also broke him out and started him at working cattle.

Though Bob started roping calves off Poco Bueno, it was not long until he discovered that the horse had an inherent talent for cutting. One evening Bob came riding back to the barn from a roping workout on "Old Pokey" and remarked to me he thought the pony would sure watch a cow. I said, "Well, then, Bob, why don't you just put your rope away and see what sort of a cutting horse you think he will make?" From that time Poco Bueno was a cutting horse. He took to the job the way a duck takes to water.

Not long after the horse had been put in training Burton left the Three D's to start his own business. His job was taken over by Pine Johnson, who gave the horse his best efforts and took him to the kind of shows that had the toughest competition. Poco Bueno gave some brilliant performances.

He first distinguished himself as a boss hoss at Denver's 1947 National

64. Zantanon pictured a short time before his death.

65. Poco Bueno, by King.

66. King, P-234, by Zantanon.

67. Major King, by Royal King.

68. Major King on the M and M Ranch. Milt Bennett up.

69. Poco Dell.

Photo by Harvey Caplin

Western when he walked off with the Grand Champion Stallion award. He went back the following year as a competitor in cutting; he didn't grab off the top, but in placing third he made a mighty good show and attracted the interest of some pretty important horsemen. Mr. Turpin says, "I think it was the first time any of our champion halter horses had been shown getting something done under a saddle."

Poco Bueno and Poco Tivio were the first father-and-son cutting combination to appear in contest arenas. As a matter of fact, they started the fad.

Each breeding season Poco Bueno, according to the Waggoner formula, was put out on pasture with about 35 mares and not picked up until the end of the season; he has seldom been 'hand bred.' He acquired his AQHA Championship after he turned seven and won his points in the Major League of Quarter Horse competition.

He has sired 19 AQHA Champions (at this writing); these are Poco Bay, Poco Bob, Poco Bow, Poco Champ, Poco Dell, Poco Doll, Poco Lena, Poco Lynn, Poco Maria, Poco Mona, Poco Nadine, Poco Pine, Poco Robin, Poco Speedy, Poco Stampede, Poco Tianna, Poco Tivio, Poco Willy, and Pretty Boy Pokey.

Thirty-six head of Quarter Horses featuring the get and service of the then sixteen-year-old Poco Bueno were sold at public auction in Vernon, Texas (June 20, 1960) for $293,725, or an average of $8159.

The stud fee charged for Poco Bueno service during the past several years has been $5000, and has been limited to thoroughly screened outside mares.

In 1962 the Waggoners advertised Poco Bueno with the following credits: Leading Sire of AQHA Champions; sire of 48 horses which have qualified for the Register of Merit by their efforts in approved arena performance events, making him the all-time Leading Sire in this category; his daughter, Poco Lena, was the high-point individual and high-point mare in the 1959 AQHA cutting horse. Standings; his son, Poco Stampede, was high-point stallion in the same standings, same year; Leading Sire of Halter-point Earners during 1961 competition—during which year 32 of his get earned points at halter, 21 were Grand Champions and won 69 Grand Championships; two were in the Top Ten NCHA Cutting Horses of 1961, and one was Top Mare.

To this we might add that he was also Leading Sire of 1956 Halter Winners. That year he was also Leading Sire of New Qualifiers for Performance Register of Merit; was beaten only by King in Leading Sires of Performance Register of Merit Qualifiers (1951 through 1956); topped the 26 Leading Sires of Horses with Halter Points (1951 through 1956). Among Leading Sires of 1962 Performance Class Winners he was topped only by Royal King; was third among Leading Sires of 1962 Halter Class Winners, led only by two sons, Poco Dell and Poco Pine.

A pretty fine record any way you want to cut it.

Poco Dell

Topping the list of Leading Sires of 1962 Halter Class Winners is that great bay of 1950, son of Paul Waggoner's Poco Bueno, Poco Dell, with 43 winners of 188 class wins and 70 Grand Championships—no mean feat in anybody's language. And he is also fifth on the list of Leading Sires of 1962 Performance Class Winners, having in this category 11 winners of 36 wins in five different events.

He stands 14 hands, 2¾ inches tall and weighs, without markings, 1150. He was bred by E. P. Waggoner at Vernon, Texas, and was out of the favorably known Shady Dell (bred also by Mr. Waggoner), Leading Dam of AQHA Champions.

Shady Dell was knocked down in the Waggoner Sale (September, 1952) as a six-year-old, with foal at side and bred back to Poco Bueno, for $310 to Bill Howard of Pleasant Grove, California. Bill McNabb, of Sacramento, paid $5000 for her in 1960; she topped his sale the following year at $11,400. Through 1961 this mare had produced 12 foals by four different stallions; three of her four AQHA Champions had different sires; three of her other foals have Register of Merit ratings.

Poco Dell was this mare's first foal.

He is an AQHA Champion himself and is currently owned by Jimmie Randals of Randals Ranch, Montoya, New Mexico, where he is standing at $300. In addition to his present high standing among halter horse sires, he is the father of 11 Register of Merit get, six of which have captured the much coveted title of AQHA Champion; one of these six, Dell Tommy, was High Point Stallion in Western Pleasure for 1961, repeating himself for the same title in 1962; Madonna Dell won the Three-Year-Old Mare Class and was named Grand Champion Mare of the 1963 Houston Livestock Show and Rodeo.

Poco Dell was also the Leading Sire of Halter Class Winners in 1961. That year he was sixth among Leading Sires of Performance Class Winners. This is an enviable record and one that is eminently deserved.

Jimmie Randals says:

I have always been interested in good ranch-type Quarter Horses, and my Number One interest is in cutting horses. I've always had a love for them. When I got ready to buy one the best source, I figured, was E. Paul

Waggoner's Three D's Ranch, from which I hoped to come away with a Poco Bueno colt.

I went down to Arlington where the horses were being fitted for the big Waggoner sale; I went about two weeks early, wanting to have a good look at all the offerings. Soon as I saw Dell I knew he was the one I wanted; nothing else stirred my interest after I'd looked at him. I went back home still thinking about him. Come sale time I took my trailer and headed for Fort Worth, where the auction was to take place. Dell looked even better this second time I saw him.

The sale got under way. Dell was the second colt to come into the ring. The first to sell had brought considerable money for that day and time. It really let the air out of me. I knew I couldn't afford to pay so much; I felt sure enough sick. I bid a spell, and then dropped out. I figured I'd gone as high as I should. I wanted that colt so bad I could taste it—what the hell, I thought, was a few more dollars on a horse like him! I screwed my nerve up again and got back in the bidding and ended up buying him for $2800.

I have stopped and looked back many and many a time, but I have never regretted bidding in Poco Dell.

On my way home I stopped off in Texas to see the folks and show off my stud. I will never forget the look in my Dad's face when I unloaded Dell and told him how much he had cost me. For the next year or so my folks all acted like I was ready or maybe past due for the nut house. Things eased up a little when we began to win ribbons and a little prize money. The whole picture changed when we started breeding outside mares and selling some of our colts. They get a prideful look when they talk about it now.

When Poco Dell was a three-year-old Jimmie Randals took him down to Phil Williams at Tokio (Texas) and put him in Phil's charge to be trained for a cutting horse. And he surely went to the right man there.

Jimmie remarks:

I left him for some six or eight weeks, then fetched him back to the ranch. Phil showed him in his first novice class at the New Mexico State Fair that fall. From then on, I was the only one to ride him. I was up when he won his AQHA Championship at cutting.

After winning this I let up on Dell and started breeding him. That fall we started showing him again in cutting competition. He hurt a stifle so we let him rest. We started training a few of his colts and were so well pleased with the way they came along I fetched Dell home—after all, he was a Champion. And I sure didn't want him hurt again. He got over that stifle injury in fine shape. He hasn't had a saddle on his back since the fall of 1958. All I do with him is breed booked mares.

It would take more room than can here be spared to give a complete run-down on Poco Dell's outstanding get. He is presently the sire of 15 ROM. His get have been Grand Champions at Fort Worth, Denver, San Antonio, Houston, Odessa, Chicago, Tucson, Albuquerque, San Angelo, Kansas City, to name just a few of the bigger shows.

"One of his most outstanding colts," declared Mr. Randals, "is Poco Dondi, which I am keeping and using for my junior sire. He is proving to be a chip off the old block. His daughter, Lady Dondi, was the second-place mare for the nation in 1962."

Major King

As far back as 1949, while I was Horse Editor of the *Texas Livestock Journal*, it had been in my mind to do a story on this stallion. His owners were approached several times with requests for information, but it wasn't until we ran onto each other at the AQHA's Tulsa Convention that Mike and Millie Leonard actually got around to bestirring themselves; this material, when it finally arrived, looked bulky enough to have been the rough draft of *Gone With The Wind*.

Major King was foaled August 4, 1946, the son of Royal King (P–2392) and the celebrated Moon Harris (P–3215), 15 hands and 1100 pounds of fast and agile roping mare.

Major's sire, Royal King, has long been in the public prints as the father of outstanding performance horses. Before proceeding further with the discussion of Major King, we might glance with profit through the following sire lists.

Leading Sires of Performance ROM Qualifiers—1951 through 1956

Sire, Color, Foal-Date, Sire	Total Qualified	Cut	Rein	Rope	Western Riding	Working Cowhorse
King, B. 32 by Zantanon	35	24	20	1	2	
POCO BUENO, Br. 46 by King	34	24	10	3	3	2
ROYAL KING, Ch. 34 by King	24	16	9	2	4	
Bert, Br. 34 by Tommy Clegg	13	2	6	5	1	1
Bill Cody, Ch. 44 by Wimpy	12	5	4	2	4	1
Hollywood Gold, 40 by Gold Rush	12	10	2			
KING'S JOE BOY, Blk. 46 by King	12	7	9			
Scooter S., B. 43 by Silver King	12	6	8	2	1	
Pretty Buck, Br. 42 by Pretty Boy	9	6	3	1		
Bartender, Ch. 40 by Manitobian	7	5	4	3		
Grey Badger II, 41 by Midnight Jr.	7		3	1	4	
Nowata Star, 40 by Oklahoma Star	7		4	3		2
Old Man, Ch. 35 by Old Sorrel	7	3	5	1	1	

Leading Sires of Horses with Halter Points—1951 through 1956

Sires	No. Get Earning Halter Points
POCO BUENO, Br. 44 by King	58
King, B. 32 by Zantanon	45
Bill Cody, Ch. 44 by Wimpy	30
Pretty Buck, Br. 42 by Pretty Boy	28
Star Deck, B. 40 by Oklahoma Star	24
Bert, Br. 34 by Tommy Clegg	20
Star Duster, Ch. 44 by Nowata Star	16
Little Tom B., B. 45 by King	14
Scooter S., B. 43 by Silver King	14
Scroggins' Little Star, B. 43 by Lone Star	14
Skipper W., Ch. 45 by Nick Shoemaker	14
Wimpy II, Ch. 44 by Wimpy	14
BUZZIE BELL H., Ch. 47 by Daybreak	13
Nowata Star, Br. 40 by Oklahoma Star	13
Oklahoma Star, Jr., Ch. 34 By Oklahoma Star	13
ROYAL KING, Ch. 43 by King	13
Leo, Ch. 40 by Joe Reed II	12
MUSIC MOUNT, Dn. 44 by Gold Mount	12
Stormy Day Moore, Ch. 46 by Waggoner's Rainy Day	12
KING'S JOE BOY, Blk. 46 by King	11
Chubby, B. 44 by Midnight	10
Gold Mount, Dn. 40 by Brush Mount	10
Paul A, Blk. 48 by Star Deck	10
Wimpy, Ch. 35 by Solis	10
Hank H., Ch. 42 by King	9
Little Jodie, B. 38 by Little Joe Springer	9

The following list was published in May, 1957:

Leading Sires of Halter Class Winners

	Winners	Wins
MAJOR KING, Ch. 46 by ROYAL KING	7	8
POCO BUENO, Br. 44 by King	5	7
Scroggins' Little Star, B. 43 by Lone Star	4	4
Bill Cody, Ch. 44 by Wimpy	3	3
Brian H., B. 46 by Y Bar	3	4

As late as 1961 King and his tribe were still in there snatching off the brass rings:

1961 Leading Sires of Performance Contest Winners (First Fifteen)

Sires	*Winners*	*Cut*	*Rein*	*Rope*	*BR*	*WR*	*WC*	*WP*	*PB*
King, B. 32 by Zantanon	26	36	23		2	2		5	
ROYAL KING, Ch. 43 by King	25	43	11	1	1			13	1
POCO BUENO, Br. 44 by King	19	72	6					21	
MAJOR KING, Ch. 46 by ROYAL KING	13	2	10	2	1	1	1	4	
Bartender, Ch. 40 by Manitobian	11	4	12	10	2		3	5	2
POCO DELL, B. 50 by POCO BUENO	11	4	7		1	3		26	1
MUSIC MOUNT, Bkn. 44 by Gold Mount	10	5	6		2	1		1	
Scooter S., by Silver King	10	13	7	12	8		2	3	5
BLACK GOLD KING, Blk. 49 by King	9	10	5			1		1	
KING'S JOE BOY, Blk. 46 by King	9	12	3			1		2	
Leo San, Ch. 49 by LEO	8	32		5	1			2	
MOORE'S ACE, D. 52 by Stormy Day Moore	8		12			2		10	
POCO TIVIO, B. 47 by POCO BUENO	8	8	3				1	2	
Wimpy II, Ch. 44 by Wimpy	8	8	5	1	4	2			5
Bert, Br. 34 by Tommy Clegg	7	6	4	4	5			1	

1961 Leading Sires of Point-Earning Performance Horses (First Fifteen)

First column, total number of point-earning get; second column, total number of performance points earned by foals of each sire

King, B. 32 by Zantanon	36	267
POCO BUENO, Br. 44 by King	29	435½
ROYAL KING, Ch. 43 by King	28	274½
Scooter S., B. 43 by Silver King	17	132
POCO DELL, B. 50 by POCO BUENO	17	111
MAJOR KING, Ch. 46 by ROYAL KING	15	83½
KING'S JOE BOY, Blk. 46 by King	14	71
Wimpy III, Ch. 47 by Wimpy II	14	31½
BLACK GOLD KING, Blk. 49 by King	13	89½
Bill Cody, Ch. 44 by Wimpy	12	31½
Hollywood Gold, Dn. 40 by Gold Rush	11	130
MUSIC MOUNT, Bkn. 44 by Gold Mount	11	41½
Bartender, Ch. 40 by Manitobian	10	81
MOORE'S ACE, D. 52 by Stormy Day Moore	10	54½
Corkey Barnes, B. 50 by HARD TWIST	10	53

In this class Major King stood fourth in 1962; Poco Bueno stood first. But the 1962 lists were not available in time for inclusion in this section.

Leading Sires of 1961 Halter Horses (Top Fifteen)

First column, number of get that earned halter points; second column, number of Grand Champion get; last column, cumulative total of Grand Championships awarded get

POCO DELL, B. 50 by POCO BUENO	35	16	54
POCO BUENO, Br. 44 by King	32	21	69
Leo San, Ch. 49 by LEO	23	13	93
POCO PINE, B. 54 by POCO BUENO	20	15	34
Wimpy II, Ch. 44 by Wimpy	17	10	43
PAUL A., Blk. 48 by Star Deck	17	7	14
MUSIC MOUNT, D. 44 by Gold Mount	16	4	6
MAJOR KING, Ch. 46 by ROYAL KING	15	4	10
King, B. 32 Zantanon	15	4	4
Showdown, Ch. 51 by Wimpy	14	9	15
POCO TIVIO, B. 47 by POCO BUENO	14	5	10
MOORE'S ACE, Dn. 52 by Stormy Day Moore	13	3	34
POCO CHAMP, B. 50 by POCO BUENO	12	8	23
SUGAR BARS, Ch. 51 by Three Bars (TB)	12	7	35
Bill Cody, Ch. 44 by Wimpy	11	8	11

Leading Sires of 1961 Halter Class Winners (Top Ten)

Sires credited with 10 or more get which have won AQHA approved halter classes. Horses in CAPITAL LETTERS (as in all lists) are Register of Merit qualifiers. Those whose names are preceded by the symbol # are AQHA Champions.

Sires	Winners	Class Wins	No. Times Grand Champ.
#POCO DELL, B. 50 by #POCO BUENO	39	154	54
#POCO BUENO, Br. 44 by King	30	133	69
#POCO PINE, B. 54 by #POCO BUENO	25	106	34
MAJOR KING, Ch. 46 by ROYAL KING	24	54	10
Leo San, Ch. 49, by LEO	22	252	93
Showdown, Ch. 51 by Wimpy	22	81	15
#PAUL A., Blk. 48 by Star Deck	19	69	14
Wimpy II, Ch. 44 by Wimpy	18	86	43
Sure Cash, Pal. 54 by Spot Cash	18	62	7
STEEL BARS, Blk. 53 by Three Bars (TB)	15	81	15

While we're neck-deep in statistics we may as well look at the latest ones available:

Leading Sires of 1962 Performance Class Winners (Top Five)

Sire	Winners	Wins	Different Events
ROYAL KING, Ch. 34 by King	23	76	7
POCO BUENO, Br. 44 by King	20	66	5
King, B. 32 by Zantanon	19	32	4
MAJOR KING, Ch. 46 by ROYAL KING	12	19	5
POCO DELL, B. 50 by POCO BUENO	11	36	5

In October, 1953, Major King, with his trainer-rider, went into the registered cutting competition at the State Fair of Texas (Dallas). Six horses went into the finals—Major King one point behind the winner. In the midst of his performance Milt Bennett was left with nothing more substantial than air beneath him; Major, after turning out from under Milt, finished sixth. Bennett said: "I knew he was going to do it—I just couldn't stay on him. This ain't the first time old Major has dumped me on a turn, but I sure hated he had to do it in front of all those people."

Major was contested only at Dallas and Fort Worth. Mrs. Leonard says: "We never did have a rider for him, just had someone ride him who wasn't mounted for the top cutting shows, which wasn't fair either for the rider or the horse. Milt Bennett begged Mike to let him have Major King for one year to make Horse of the Year out of him, but we couldn't neglect our mares. Milt said Major was the best King horse he'd ever ridden."

According to Millie Leonard, who bred and has owned him all his life, Major always paid his way in these contests, at halter as well as in registered cutting. "One time we took him and his half sister Kincie to a cutting at Sulphur Springs and brought home $950 for five minutes' work. On that occasion Milt Bennett rode Kincie and Tex Hensley had Major, though Tex had never been on him until the day before and that was just to see if he could *stay* on. At that time Milt was working for Ervin Glaspy at Ennis. Hensley rode Major King in several big shows for us. Due to the many mares we had booked we could only campaign Major during the winter months. Fetching home $350 in those days for two and a half minutes' work was really something. Major was shown in open and registered cutting at the Fort Worth Exposition & Fat Stock Show on at least three different occasions. It was the practice then to hold eliminations in the open cutting, keeping only the top 24 entries. Major King was never moved out in this fashion. Through 119 entries he stayed in the top 24 horses. He always brought home more than we spent.

"The show worked four horses each rodeo performance, and the night

Major King won the show I don't believe there was a person in the stands who wasn't on his feet and cheering the whole time Major was working. There were 6000 people in the coliseum that night. The noise was really deafening—I don't think the crowds today are nearly as demonstrative. Royal King, Major's sire, won the cutting that year."

Major's first halter show was on the 4th of October in 1946; he was two months old to the day, and placed third in a class of good colts much older than himself. Mrs. Leonard says: "He was always the youngest in his class but never failed to place. On November 9th he was shown again, winning this time. When he was five months of age we took him and his dam to the livestock show at Brownwood, Texas, where he again won his class, his dam winning hers over many aged mares, several of which had won championships in larger shows. Moon Harris was a great show mare; her best and biggest winnings were in 1940, the year the AQHA was organized.

"From Brownwood we took Major and Moon Harris to Fort Worth, where she won the mare class (Racing Division), Major placing second in his. Next in turn came San Angelo, Kerrville, Llano, Coleman, the State Fair at Dallas, Comanche, Fort Worth again, San Angelo, Hamilton, Kerrville, Stamford, Weatherford, the East Texas Quarter Horse show at Gladewater —by this time Major King had won four Grand Championships and was dubbed 'The Grown Horse in Miniature.' He has never placed lower than sixth—never out of the money. The largest halter class he showed in was at San Angelo, with 64 entries; he was the only colt eligible to show in the Champion of Champions class at Fort Worth in 1947. Comanche was where he got one of his Grand Championships, and in this class there were 11 former Grand Champion horses."

Major was ridden for the first time February 20, 1949, with Bob Burton of Arlington, Texas, up. The Leonards moved their M&M Ranch from Junction to Milford in 1950 and not until then was Major's court open to outside mares.

Major's dam, Moon Harris, became a big name in show business. She was foaled in Kentucky in 1937 and was brought to Texas by the wife of her breeder (Eustice Harris). Moon's dam was Millie Jerden (TB) and a very old mare, Mrs. Leonard says, when she saw her in 1940. Moon Harris before her halter career had been a noted roping mare. Her sire was Billy the Kid M (bred by Allen Mayes at Big Lake, Texas) by Elmendorf (TB) out of Ruby by Old Jim (P-10), a grandson of Texas Chief, the terrific sprinter killed in a storm on the Waggoner Ranch; second dam was Nellie (by Possum, another speed-packed son of Traveler).

Major's sire, Royal King, was bred by Felton Smathers at Llano, and was out of Rocket Lanning (P–39,024) by Dolph; second dam, Cricket by Cody.

The Leonards bought Moon Harris in 1945 from Clarence Albin in foal to Royal King for a summer foal. "No one was sure she was in foal but we took the chance and bought Moon along with another mare (Molly Albin); she had a filly at side by Dogie Boy. We named the filly M&M's Libby and still have her. Libby has foaled many blue ribbon winners and is the dam of Major's Maco (P–40,735), by Major King, the great cutting horse owned by Gene and Madlyn Shaw (Bryan, Ohio) who recently [1963] won the cutting competition at Amarillo, scoring 77 points to defeat World Champion Cutter Bill, who piled up 76."

Mike and Millie Leonard got into the breeding end of the Quarter Horse business before the breed had an AQHA registry. Mike had been a Texas ranger along the Rio Grande and Millie had been a sheepman's daughter. Traveler bloodlines predominate in the Leonard horses, with an occasional dash of Peter McCue. Mrs. Leonard says: "Moon Harris goes back through her dam to Ballot (TB) by Voter—Ballot is the great-grandsire of Three Bars. Moon's sire, Billy the Kid M, is a topline grandson of Ballot. We feel that Major King, with two crosses to Ballot, carries all the Thoroughbred blood we need in our Quarter Horses."

Billy the Kid M was a famous running horse, twenty-seven years old when he died.

Major King is a hard horse to fault. And his disposition, if anything, even surpasses his conformation. During the breeding season he is ridden through the various pastures while the mares are checked for readiness. Those found ready for court are halter-led back to the barns behind Major, and there is never any commotion about this.

Some of his best-known get include Major Thunder, Major's Maco, Major's Manana, and Major's Mano, all of whom have commanded much attention both in performance and at halter. Other well-known get include Chubby Waspy, Lady's Man, Kip Mac, Shoemaker's Dude, and Major's Mena.

The last named was foaled in 1958; the dam was Snooty Nina by Nouncer (by King, P–234). She was bred by the M&M and was Snooty Nina's first foal. Her show career started at Tyler, Texas, in September, 1959, where she won the yearling filly class; her most recent show was in October, 1962, at San Francisco's Cow Palace, where she placed fourth in the Aged Mare Class. The judge, Bill Wartchow, called this the greatest aged mare class he had ever seen. Between these shows, under 30 different judges, Major's Mena (owned by Don G. Pabst, Menlo Park, California) has won three Grand Championships, three Reserves, 16 first places, 16 seconds,

70. San Siemon (1950). Charlie T. Lee up.

71. Zantanon, Jr. M. Benavides Volpe is the owner and breeder.

72. Showdown as a foal with dam in back. J. Frank Norfleet is beside them.

73. Western pleasure: Showdown, O. G. Hill, Jr. up.

Photo by Ed Ellinger

four thirds, three fourths, two fifths, and one sixth. In combined halter and performance appearances she was out of the ribbons just once in each division. She tied for the PCQHA 1950–60 Halter Mare Championship. Official records of the AQHA accord her 37 ROM points; 19 of these were received in A and B shows.

Due to an injury her performance career had to be shelved. Despite this, in three shows under saddle she won the Western Pleasure class at the Santa Maria Quarter Horse Show, took second at Anderson, California, and sixth at Sacramento. "These three shows," says owner Pabst, "took place within a period of six weeks and we were hopeful of taking her on into cutting; but because of the injury she will not take hard work even though she is sound when not worked. We have, therefore, put her into our breeding program and she was bred last spring to Don Tivio, 1958 Pacific Coast Cutting Horse Champion."

Because of the current breeding program at M&M there are only two ways of acquiring a Major King foal; by breeding your acceptable mare at the cost of $500 (live foal), or for the same price choosing one of the Leonards' mares and reserving her next available colt.

Showdown

"I put the name 'Showdown' on a gelding, in order to save it for a stallion I might sometime own, which I hoped would be an outstanding show horse and sire," said O. G. Hill, Jr. in discussing with me the merits and history of P–33,178. "When I bought Showdown his name was Robert Kleberg.

"The Mashed O Ranch had a King Ranch stallion named Bob Kleberg, and I felt like it would cause confusion to have two stallions with names so similar. I had started showing in 1950 and the boys beat me pretty regular. Some day a horse would come along that I could have a showdown with against these galoots that had been beating me, and, because I wanted to be prepared, I had saved up this name for just such a horse. So when I got P–33,178 another name was given to the gelding and 'Showdown' was given to Robert Kleberg."

Some years ago the King Ranch gave Mr. J. Frank Norfleet a mare for services he had rendered them when he was a Texas Ranger. Cacuchia (P–22,969), Showdown's dam, was this mare. She was bred and raised on the King Ranch, and in foal to Wimpy (P–1) at the time she was given to Mr. Norfleet. She was a sorrel, 14.3, 1200 pounds, no markings.

Cacuchia was sired by Peppy (P–212) by Little Richard, P–17. She was out of Cuata Numero Uno (P–72) by Solis; second dam was Cuata.

Showdown's sire, Wimpy, was given the first number in the *American Quarter Horse Stud Book*. "To my knowledge," says O. G. Hill, Jr., "when the Association was started it was decided to give the Grand Champion Stallion of the Forth Worth Fat Stock Show that year the first number in the book. Wimpy was Grand Champion Stallion."

He was by Solis, who was by Old Sorrel (P–209) bred by George Clegg from the Lazarus Mare (TB). Wimpy's dam was Panda (P–163) by Old Sorrel out of a daughter of Hickory Bill.

Showdown was broke on the Norfleet ranch and used for all types of ranch work, including roping, cutting, and the moving of cattle. J. Frank Daugherty (named after Mr. Norfleet) later acquired the horse and was the first man to put a saddle on him. Mr. Hill purchased this stallion from Mr. Daugherty in 1953.

Gayle Borland trained Showdown for arena cutting in 1960, but due to a heavy breeding schedule Showdown was never campaigned extensively on the rodeo or cutting circuits.

He was pasture bred as a two- and three-year-old, and was, therefore, at this time never in show shape. As a two-year-old he was pasture bred to 13 of Hill's mares shortly after Mr. Hill acquired him, settling 12 of them. Of these 12 get, nine were stallions and three were fillies. Pandarita Hill, the AQHA high-point halter horse of 1959, was one of these three.

Mr. Hill remarked: "Since acquiring my first registered fillies in 1947 I had tried a number of stud prospects that didn't prove out. I saw Robert Kleberg (Showdown) for the first time to pay any attention to him at the Tri-State Fair in the fall of 1952. I immediately fell in love with him, but he was not for sale. Unable to forget him, I made the trip from Hereford to Olton (where the Daugherty ranch is located) about every two weeks for six months, at which time I succeeded in buying him for $5000—a lot of money for an unproven colt at that time. J. Frank Norfleet was in his nineties when Showdown was foaled and felt he couldn't give him proper care and training, so he had let Frank Daugherty have him. Incidentally I bred a mare to Showdown for Mr. Norfleet in 1962, when the old gentleman was over a hundred years old."

Among Showdown's more outstanding get are the two stallions, Excuse and Showdown Wimpy; these are AQHA Champions. Another, Showdown Nick, is an AQHA Champion gelding; and Show Maid has become an AQHA Champion mare.

The year 1962 marked the initial appearance of Showdown among the Top Five Leading Sires of Halter Horses, but he was well up on this Leading Sires list in 1958, 1959, 1960, and 1961. The four AQHA Champions listed above received most of their performance points in cutting and reining, with a dash of Western Pleasure thrown in.

Halter Futurity

Something new has been added to the show business—new anyway to me —and the view from here looks quite promising. The Arizona Quarter Horse Breeders Association appears to have dreamed up an almost sure-fire way of bolstering horse-show purses, which they call the AQHBA Halter Futurity. It packs a guaranteed purse of $1000 plus entry fees. The one that came off at Tucson in March, 1963, was a remarkable success. The Gross Purse for this 1963 shindig turned out to weigh in at $1952 plus entrance fees of $230. Nominations currently in hand for the 1964 renewal exceed one hundred and ninety colts and fillies.

The facsimile of a handbill clearly points up the pertinent details.

In 1963 there were get of Three Percent, Kibitzer, Dynamite Reed, Black Tide Mac, Traveler Sam, War Chant, Silver Spur, Tamo, Three Bars (TB), Casbar, Echols Dandy, Skipper's Prince, Float Hy, Poquito Mas, Steel Bars, K4 Hickory Skip, and Lew Garcia in the finals. There were two divisions, fillies and colts. The colt class of 1963 was won by an unnamed individual sired by War Chant out of Miss Tivio. The other division was won by a filly sired by Casbar.

To provide a sample biography in the show-horse category we have gone to La Pryor, Texas, to the ranch of Paul Jessee & Sons, Order Buyers of Stocker and Feeder Cattle, who are breeders of Registered Quarter Horses.

Katy Taylor

By Old Taylor (by King, P–234) out of Scat by Waggoner, 14.3½ hands high and weighing 1200 pounds, Katy Taylor has been chosen for description here because, to me at least, she typifies all that is most attractive in the *show mare* category.

She is owned and was bred by Paul Jessee, La Pryor, Texas, who says: "After purchasing her dam, Scat (P–2886), from Joe Elliott, I devoted much time to studying her from the standpoint of conformation. I knew she had raced successfully, and wanted to raise a foal that would be as near the perfect horse as one could find. The stud I thought would make that cross was Old Taylor (P–11,521), by King out of Miss Taylor. Miss Taylor was sired by the old Poco Bueno that was by Little Joe and out

ATTENTION

SHOW HORSE EXHIBITORS

ENTER YOUR BROODMARES NOW!

$5 per head, making their

1962 FOALS ELIGIBLE FOR BIG YEARLING HALTER FUTURITY SHOW IN 1963

OPEN TO ANYONE

TIME & PLACE: TUCSON, ARIZONA — MARCH 1963

CONDITIONS

ELIGIBILITY: 1962 Fillies or Colts, must be AQHA registered.

PURSE: $1,000.00 Purse Plus Entry Fees.

RULES:
1. Nominators or Owners must be or become members of A.Q.H.B.A. Dues $10
2. Nominator must be Owner of mare at time of foaling.
3. No limit to number of nominations.
4. Change of Ownership does not void a nomination, but SELLER must report transfer to secretary within 30 days.
5. 10% of Gross Entry Fees will be deducted for office charges.
6. The A.Q.H.B.A. reserves the right to change these regulations if unforeseen circumstances so necessitates.

FOR ENTRY BLANKS: WRITE

A.Q.H.B.A. HALTER FUTURITY

P. O. DRAWER 950
SANTA RITA HOTEL
TUCSON, ARIZONA

74. Handbill for AQHBA Halter Futurity.

75. Arizona Quarter Horse Breeders Association 1963 Halter Futurity, Tucson.

76. Show mare, Katy Taylor.

of the Eads mare by Hickory Bill. Old Taylor had a lot of muscle as well as a lot of gaskin. My prayers were answered.

"Katy was foaled at my place March 19, 1956. Every Quarter Horse man that came by was unanimous in the opinion she would be a show mare. The first produce of this cross was Kitty Taylor, 1955, whom I sold in the Show Window Sale (Tucson) in 1958—a honey herself. I have two younger full sisters for whom I have considerable hope."

Katy was broke to saddle by Mr. Jessee's son, Johnnie, and under his guidance has shown much ability in the cutting arena, although they have not campaigned her in that field. "Our slate," Mr. Jessee says, "has been too full."

Many times, horsemen looking at Katy as a two-year-old, would tell her owner that he ought to put her on the tracks. Others have told me she was very racy looking at that age—too much so to win in the halter classes of that time.

But her time came. She has been a Halter Champion 69 times under 25 judges, horsemen all: Bob Collins, Dr. Northway, Sig Jernigan, Jack Tourney, Dee Harrison, Dr. Jerry Miller, D. C. Weinert, John Dublin, Sparks Rust, Jr., O. G. Hill, Jr., Earl Albin, Don Wilkins, Huey Long, Wilber Lecklider, Hugh Bennett, Watt Hardin, Percy Turner, H. S. Miller, B. F. Yates, Russell Moore, Ralph Howe, J. B. Bullard, Ray Lewis, Amy Gamblin, and J. A. Meeks.

Katy Taylor has been Champion of Champions at three shows. Major shows at which she was made Grand Champion Mare include those at Houston (1961), Rosenberg (1960), Del Rio (1960 and 1961), Uvalde (1960), Junction (1960), San Angelo (1960), Blanco (1960 and 1961), Alice (1960 and 1962), Sonora (1960), Boerne (1960 and 1961), Edna (1960), Seguin (1960), Angleton (1961), Hemstead (1960 and 1961), Beeville (1961), Breckenridge (1961), Bay City (1961), Mercedes.(1961), Edinberg (1962), Goliad (1961), San Saba (1960 and 1961), Winters (1961), Georgetown (1961), Big Spring (1961), Dumas (1961), Mangum (1961), Robstown (1961 and 1962), Roswell (1962), Childress (1962), Ozona (1962), Burnett (1962), Carthage (1962), Giddings (1962), and Coleman (1962). She was named Champion of Champions at Houston in 1962 and received the same high honor twice at Alice.

Many persons consider Katy Taylor to be one of the best mares of the breed. Many others have stated she was their idea of a typical Quarter mare.

She has now been retired—with 156 halter points—to the stud, and is presently carrying a foal by Johnnie D. Cash (he by Sure Cash out of

Ribbon Sash). Mr. Jessee says: "I have high hopes for another top individual."

Leading Sires of AQHA Champions

Sire	Champions
#POCO BUENO, Br. 44 by King	22
King, B. 32 by Zantanon	17
LEO, S. 40 by JOE REED II	9
Bill Cody, Ch. 44 by Wimpy	7
Skipper W, Ch. 51 by Wimpy	7
#POCO DELL, B. 50 by #POCO BUENO	6
Bartender, Ch. 40 by Manitobian	5
Bay Bob, B. 46 by King	5
Great Chance, P. 50 by Skipper W	5
#KING'S JOE BOY, Blk. 46 by King	5
MUSIC MOUNT, D. 44 by Gold Mount	5
Three Bars, TB, Ch. 40 by Percentage	5
Wimpy II, Ch. 44 by Wimpy	5
Wimpy III, Ch. 47 by Wimpy II	5

Leading Maternal Grandsires of AQHA Champions:

Grandsires	Champions
King, B. 32 by Zantanon	18
Blackburn, D. 27 by Yellow Jacket	14
Bert, Br. 34 by Tommy Clegg	12
Pretty Boy, Br. 28 by Dodger	10
LEO, S. 40 by JOE REED II	7
Barney McCue, S. 40 by Jack McCue	5
Pep Up, S. 41 by Macanudo	5
Revenue, Ch. 42 by Young Midnight	5

Part V: Some Remarks About Tracks and Track Horses

Past and Present

Quarter Horses, traditionally, were developed to run a quarter of a mile and do it with greater swiftness than the best representatives of any other breed. Though used for a multiplicity of purposes they were bred particularly to run, those which did not meet this goal being rapidly forgotten.

The truth of these statements is demonstrable. Extreme velocity, *early foot*, is the true historic basis of the astonishing Quarter Horse versatility, and this same remarkable agility is and always has been the yardstick of its worth.

The horse without some sprinting ability is better kept for halter shows and, in the words of Ott Adams, should be properly valued at so much per pound.

Ott said:

Speed can be bred in horses through the use of the right kind of pedigree, and it can be bred out of horses by using pedigrees which include blood never known to have been associated with speed. You don't have to use mongrel blood to reduce speed in the off-spring; it is as easily reduced through the use of blood from conformation horses whose background shows no speed, or inferior speed, or even speed bred down too short.

Conformation itself, or the matter of pleasing looks, should cause no worry to the breeder versed in these elementary facts, for it comes of itself with the use of proper bloodlines. Consider those horses whose fame rests securely on the solid foundation of known track performance. Almost all of them have excellent conformation.

Speed is the only thing worth while as a goal in the breeding of Quarter stock; it is the only thing that should worry you. You can usually get it if you breed in speed famous bloodlines, mating top performer with top performer.

And there you have it, without frills or frummery.

This is the recipe with which a few breeders in less than twenty-five years have jumped the short horse out of the backlands brush—where the AQHA rounded up the most of its foundation stock—onto the big-type front pages of today's racing news, smashing record after record, putting

Ruidoso's All-American on a television par with the historic Kentucky Derby.

And here is another of Uncle Ott's observations:

You can sell a good horse that has speed, in good times or bad, but during hard times you cannot sell a horse that does not have speed. Back when Cleveland was being inaugurated for his second term horses were selling around here for fifty cents. You could buy lots of good cow horses for fifty cents apiece. I rode one of my good horses into Alice during that time and a group of Texas Rangers were there. One of them came up to me and asked, "Do you want to sell that horse?" I had not planned to, so without much thinking I said it would take fifty dollars to buy him. After a little conversation the Ranger stepped over to his saddlemates, collected the fifty dollars and bought my horse.

I know of course that fifty dollars wouldn't buy much of a horse today. In those days there was a whale of a difference between fifty dollars and fifty cents—about one hundred times the difference. There are lots of cheap horses still stumbling around, but if you have a good one that can win on the tracks there still remains that hundred-to-one difference in price. Unless a horse has speedy bloodlines on both sides, I would not be interested in even looking at him for breeding purposes.

Some of the horses raked out of the brush in the early days of the AQRA had, or soon acquired, track performance records. It was this kind of horse that commanded the most attention and the highest prices. Many of their names have been all but forgotten, yet without their individual and collective efforts I shudder to think what might have happened to the registry. Some of these sprinters never did get a number, but you will find their performance, or at least allusions to it, if you will take the time to go through those early records.

I remember Red Man and Red Cloud and Red Joe of Arizona. Prissy, Cyclone, Red Racer, Colonel Clyde. Pay Dirt and Don Manners, Blueberry Hill, Chicaro, Arizona Girl, Bartender and Sugar Foot, Painted Joe and Cowboy.

Some of those early ones dug from the brush became big names—Mamie Taylor, Little Joe, Jr., Shue Fly, Joe Reed II, and Leo. Some, forgotten or never heard of by our current crop of breeders, include Joe Jimmy, J. B. King, Bull's Eye, Bill Reed, Rosita and Rosalita, Alex the Great (TB), Silver Static, Chain Lay, Noo Music (TB), Jeep, Rumpus, Texas Lad, Punkin, Black Princess, 803 Babe, Chester C, Rocket, Jap, Dusty Hancock, Idleen, Lilly Belle, Lost Toy (TB), Sam's Pride, Idle Tom, Wayward Girl, and a host of other brave runners—some of whom, strangely enough, are still around, gone back to the brush after writing their names across the history of the straightaways.

Out of nowhere came Joe Jimmy to whip Miss Panama at Del Rio; he is still alive and in good shape, settling each year a few Oklahoma mares. Red Man, too, is around somewhere, I believe. Bull's Eye and J. B. King are still available, one in Wyoming and one in south Texas.

Up to but not including 1944 the Top Twenty of the more than one hundred sprinters competing on the old Hacienda Moltacqua track in Tucson, according to the records of the American Quarter Racing Association (since absorbed into the Performance Division of the AQHA), with their officially accepted times, are as follows:

Horse, Color, Sex, Year Foaled	Time:	220 yards	350 yards	660 yards	300 yards	440 yards
SHUE FLY, Ch. m. 1937		:13.0			:22.6	:36
CLABBER, Ch. h. 1937		:12.8		:18.4	:22.8	
JOE REED II, Ch. h. 1936		:13.0			:22.8	
RED MAN, Ro. h. 1935		:12.6		:18.4		
ALEX THE GREAT, Br. h. 1936		:13.0		:19.4	:22.8	
NOBODIES FRIEND, Blk. h. '39		:13.0			:22.8	
PAINTED JOE, Pt. h. 1939		:12.8	:16.2		:22.8	
ARIZONA GIRL, B. m. 1938		:12.8	:16.2	:18.6	:23.0	
BLUEBERRY HILL, Gr. m. '37		:12.8		:19.2	:23.0	
DON MANNERS, Ch. h. 1936		:13.0			:23.0	
CHICARO, Blk. h. 1938		:12.6			:23.2	:36.6
LITTLE JOE, JR., Ch. h. '37		:12.8			:23.2	
CYCLONE, B. g. 1928		:12.8		:18.4	:23.2	
COWBOY, B. g. 1935		:12.8	:16.4	:18.6	:23.2	
RED RACER, B. g. 1936		:12.8			:23.4	:36.0
PAY DIRT, Ch. h. 1939		:13.0			:23.4	:36.6
DOMINO, Ch. h. 1939		:13.0			:23.4	:35.8
BARTENDER, Ch. h. 1937		:12.8			:23.4	
PRISSY, Ch. m. 1940		:13.0			:23.4	
SUGAR FOOT, Ch. m. 1936		:12.8	:16.2		:24.0	

NOTE: Time was taken from instant gates opened, gate set exactly on line, average of three watches. Some of the 220-yard times are not official, but are fractional times taken from longer races. The above Twenty were designated Celebrated American Quarter Running Horses by the AQRA.

To gain some idea of how far Quarter Horses have come in the blinding speed of track competition since those early days, one has only to glance at the table below.

77. Prissy, by Colonel Clyde. Foaled 1940.

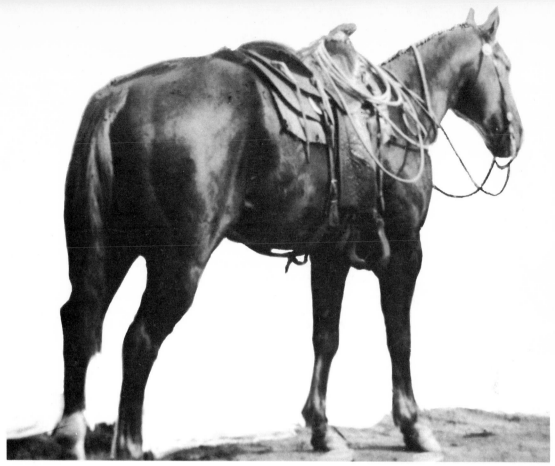

78. Colonel Clyde. He could do it all.

79. Red Man (nearest camera) and Cyclone battle to a dead heat at 350 yards. The time was :18.3. Arizona Girl finished third and Clabber fourth.

Current World Speed Records

440 yards	POKEY BAR 1962 LA 118f :21.6	
400 yards	TONTO BARS HANK 1962 ALB 122f :19.9	
	SHE KITTY 1962 CEN 118f :19.9	
	BREEZE BAR 1961 LA 117f :19.9	
350 yards	VANDY'S FLASH 1960 LA 120f :17.5	
330 yards	KIMALETA 1962 SPG 124f :16.7	
300 yards	CLABBERTOWN G 1951 LA 125f :15.5	
250 yards	MADDON'S BRIGHT EYES 1950 RIL 120f :13.4	
	SUPER CHARGE 1954 PSP 112f :13.4	
	MONITA 1949 DR 107f :13.4	
220 yards	MADDON'S BRIGHT EYES 1950 RIL 125f :12.1	
	TONTA GAL 1946 RIL 120f :12.1	
	MY TEXAS DANDY JR. 1947 EP 115f :12.1	

Leading Money Earners of 1962 Racing (Top Ten)

Horse	Starts	Wins	Place	Show	Earnings
JET DECK, B. c. 60 by MOON DECK	15	11	1	2	$138,341.91
HUSTLING MAN, S. c. 60 by GO MAN GO	17	7	2	3	105,122.33
TINY CHARGER, B. c. 60 by Depth Charge	13	4	5	3	58,561.84
MR. JUNIPER BAR, Br. c. 60 by MR. BAR NONE	11	7	3	0	56,196.91
LIGHTNING BELLE, S. f. 60 by LIGHTNING BAR	12	3	7	0	54,434.37
LITTLE CHLOE, S. f. 60 by Three Bars (TB)	7	5	1	0	$ 53,571.26
BAR DEPTH, Blk. c. 60 by Three Bars (TB)	18	4	4	1	51,540.92
POKEY BAR, S. c. 59 by Three Bars (TB)	8	6	1	1	41,846.53
MISS BAR LEO, S. f. 60 by Three Bars (TB)	17	10	1	1	32,745.84
TOP MOON, Blk. c. 60 by MOON DECK	20	7	7	3	30,698.07

Leading Sires of Money Earners for 1962 Racing (Top Five)

	Starters	Starts	Wins	Earnings
Three Bars (TB), Ch. h. 40 by Percentage	57	489	86	$281,671.01
MOON DECK, Blk. h. 50 by Top Deck (TB)	12	203	41	215,265.07
GO MAN GO, Eo. h. 53 by Top Deck (TB)	11	127	23	154,923.58
LIGHTNING BAR, Ch. h. 51 by Three Bars (TB)	43	348	55	124,050.25
MR. BAR NONE, Ch. h. 55 by Three Bars (TB)	28	183	37	95,691.25

Futurities

During 1962 Quarter Horse futurities were run at:

Burwell, Nebraska (2)
Centennial, Denver (3)
Park Jefferson, Jefferson, South Dakota (2)
Yakima Meadows, Yakima, Washington
Lamesa Park, Raton, New Mexico (2)
Los Alamitos Race Course, Los Alamitos, California (2)
Illinois State Fair, Springfield, Illinois
Ontario Fair Grounds, Ontario, Washington
Rillito, Tucson, Arizona
Sunland Park, New Mexico
La Bahia Downs, Goliad, Texas
Sonora Park, Sonora, Texas
Tropical Park, Miami, Florida
Garfield Downs, Enid, Oklahoma (2)
Colfax, Washington
Elko County Fair, Elko, Nevada
Portland Meadows, Portland, Oregon (2)
Hawthorne Park, Chicago, Illinois
Humboldt County Fair, Ferndale, California
Junction, Texas
Los Angeles County Fair, Pomona, California
Hazel Park, Detroit, Michigan
Beaumont, Montana

Among additional futurities to be run in 1963 will be one at Fayetteville, Arkansas, one at Uranium Downs, Grand Junction, Colorado; and one at Towaoc Race Track, Towaoc, Colorado.

Leading Maternal Grandsires of Register of Merit Qualifiers, 1945 through 1962

Horses listed in capital letters are Register of Merit Qualifiers.

Grandsired 18 or More	Total	With 12 or more daughters producing	Total
LEO by JOE REED II	99	LEO by JOE REED II	60
Flying Bob by Chicaro (TB)	70	Three Bars (TB) by Percentage	36
CLABBER by My Texas Dandy	67	Flying Bob by Chicaro (TB)	35
Chicaro Bill by Chicaro (TB)	58	Chicaro Bill by Chicaro (TB)	30
Three Bars (TB) by Percentage	57	CLABBER by My Texas Dandy	29

BLOODLINE CHART ANALYSIS

Horses Registered in APPENDIX REGISTRY — ONLY

	1962	1961	1960	1959	1958	1957	1956	1955	1954	1953
1. Q. H. ex* Q. H.	67%	65%	63%	66%	51%	56%	60%	60%	70%	68%
2. Q. H. ex T. B.	17%	12%	11%	24%	6%	7%	7%	8%	5%	7%
3. Q. H. ex Appendix	16%	22%	26%	9%	17%	12%	11%	10%	8%	9%
4. Q. H. ex mare by Q. H.		—	0%	1%	3%	4%	4%	4%	3%	4%
5. Q. H. ex mare T. B.		—	0%	1%	2%	2%	2%	3%	2%	3%
6. Q. H. ex unregistered		1%	0%	1%	21%	19%	15%	14%	11%	8%
7. Appendix ex Appendix ⎫		—	0%	0%	0%	0%	1%	1%	1%	1%
8. Appendix ex T. B. .... ⎭										

*Out of

TOTAL HORSES   1962   1961   1960   1959   1958   1957   1956   1955   1954   1953
REGISTERED (APP.) .. 13,506   16,820   18,188   14,844   16,485   11,631   9,674   6,854   6,869   6,923

EXPLANATION

Each month, the pedigree of each horse registered in the Appendix Registry is studied and catalogued. The above percentages show the various categories into which the horses qualify.

TOTAL PARI-MUTUEL HANDLE ON RACES FOR
QUARTER HORSES DURING THE YEARS 1949-1962

Units of One Million Dollars

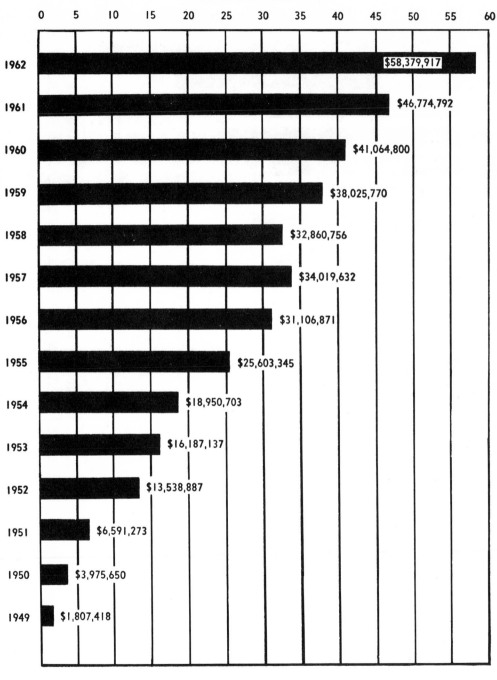

1962	$58,379,917
1961	$46,774,792
1960	$41,064,800
1959	$38,025,770
1958	$32,860,756
1957	$34,019,632
1956	$31,106,871
1955	$25,603,345
1954	$18,950,703
1953	$16,187,137
1952	$13,538,887
1951	$6,591,273
1950	$3,975,650
1949	$1,807,418

Total Handle for 1949-1962 .... $414,058,146
Average Handle per Year .... $ 29,575,571

THE NUMBER OF RECOGNIZED RACES FOR QUARTER HORSES DURING 1945 THROUGH 1962

Units of 100 Races

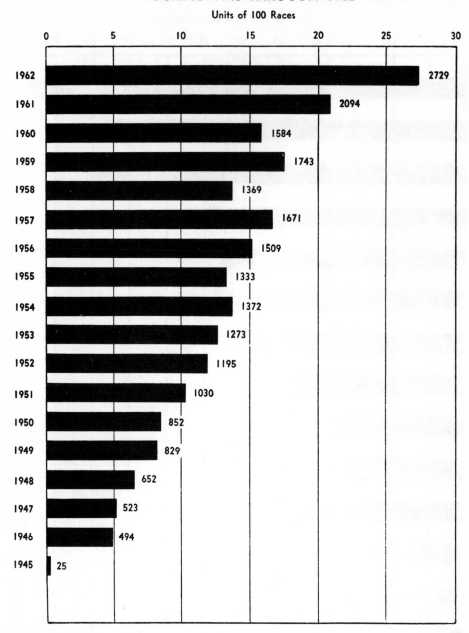

1962 STARTERS ON RECOGNIZED QUARTER HORSE TRACKS

1292 Two-year-olds raced		
848 Three-year-olds raced	1918 Horses made first official starts	
898 Older Horses raced	1120 Horses had raced previously	
3038 Horses raced in Quarter Horse Races	3038 TOTAL	

TOTAL PURSE DISTRIBUTION IN RECOGNIZED RACES FOR QUARTER HORSES DURING 1949-1962

Units of One Hundred Thousand Dollars

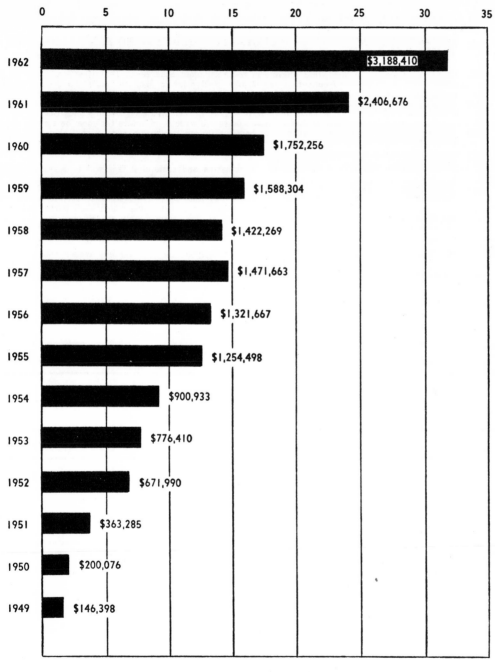

1962	$3,188,410
1961	$2,406,676
1960	$1,752,256
1959	$1,588,304
1958	$1,422,269
1957	$1,471,663
1956	$1,321,667
1955	$1,254,498
1954	$900,933
1953	$776,410
1952	$671,990
1951	$363,285
1950	$200,076
1949	$146,398

Total Purses for 1949-1962 .... $17,464,836
Average Purse per Year .... $ 1,247,488

PURSE $50,000

(ESTIMATE)

ENTRY BLANK FOR 1963 HAWTHORNE FUTURITY
HAWTHORNE RACE COURSE—OCTOBER 12, 1963

RULES AND CONDITIONS FOR THE 1963 QUARTER HORSE FUTURITY

DISTANCE 400 YARDS — STARTING GATE — WEIGHTS 115 POUNDS — NO SEX ALLOWANCE — TO BE RUN AT HAWTHORNE RACE COURSE — CHICAGO — USE OF BAT PERMITTED

NOMINATION & ELIGIBILITY. Open to foals of 1961 eligible in the Permanent Stud Book, Tentative Stud Book or Appendix of American Quarter Horse Association. Nomination fee, $25.00, paid prior to May 15, 1963. To remain eligible $100.00 paid prior to June 15, 1963, $100.00 on or before July 15, 1963, $100.00 on or before August 15, $100.00 on or before September 15th and $75.00 to be paid at entry time of trials. Late entries will be accepted upon payment of the regular fees plus an additional $250.00 only until July 15, 1963. $1000.00 only until August 15, 1963 and $5000.00 only until October 1, 1963. An owner may nominate as many entries as desired. If one or more horses are withdrawn before the race, be sure to specify which one when making payments. There can be no substitution of horses after one has been nominated, but change of ownership will not affect eligibility. Regulation racing equipment and colors must be used. To be eligible to race nominee must be a member of good standing in the M.N.Q.H.A. Dues $25.00.

ELIMINATION TRIALS. Registration papers will be required. Nomination and sustaining fees will be accepted through the mail post marked not later than dates due. Trials will be run under the same conditions as the stake. Each trial not to exceed eight horses. Final eight horses selected for Futurity on time classification of trial heats, however, should variables exist which would prevent this from being feasible, the Stewards may then select the finalists in their order of finish in the trials. If for any reason a tie exists, the horses involved shall draw lots to determine which shall participate in the finals. The decision of the Stewards in all matters shall be final and entries are accepted only on the condition that those persons nominating and/or starting a horse in the trials and/or the Stake agree to abide by their decisions. Horses will be entered at 12'00 o'clock noon on day before race. All horses shall be okayed out of gate before being allowed to start.

Mid-West National Quarter Horse Assn. reserves the right to cancel or postpone the race for any reason which it deems good and sufficient. Nominations or subscriptions to this Stake may be refused or cancelled, without liability, by Board or by the track at which said race is run at any time prior to the actual running thereof, except for the return of any nomination and entry fees paid.

FUTURITY PURSE. Estimated Purse of $50,000 split 50% Winner, 18% Second, 14% Third, 10% Fourth, 8% Fifth.

NOMINATION BLANK

	NAME OF HORSE	REG. NO.	SIRE	DAM	FOALS OF	SEX	BREEDER
1.					1961		
2.					1961		
3.					1961		
4.					1961		

I have read the rules and conditions of the Hawthorne Futurity and agree to abide by them. I will concur in full with any decisions made by the advisory board.

Owner _____ Date _____ 1963

I, the undersigned, hereby release the Management & Racing Assn., their officers, members, agents, employees, representatives, or any of them, of and from all claims, demands, action or causes of action, of any kind or nature whatsoever, whether now known or ascertained, or which may hereafter develop or accrue to me in favor of myself, my heirs, representatives or dependents, on account of or by reason of, any injury, loss or damage, which may be suffered by me or them or any of them, or to any property, animate or inanimate, belonging to me or used by me, because of any matter, thing or condition, negligence or default, whatsoever, and I hereby assume and accept the full risk and danger of any hurt, injury or damage which may occur through or by any reason of any matter, thing or condition, negligence or default, of any person or persons whatsoever.

In witness whereof I hereunto set my hand and seal this _____ day of _____ 19_____

Witness _____ Signature _____ (Seal)

Address _____

The advisory board shall have jurisdiction over all phases of the Hawthorne Futurity. The decision of the board in all matters shall be final and all entries are accepted only on the condition that those persons nominating and/or starting a horse in the trials and/or the stake shall abide by their decisions.

ADDRESS ALL CORRESPONDENCE AND MAKE CHECKS PAYABLE TO:

Mid-West National Quarter Horse Racing Assn., 886 Linden Avenue, Winnetka, Illinois, HIllcrest 6-7444

King by Zantanon	56	Joe Moore by Little Joe	29
JOE REED II by Joe Reed	51	JOE REED II by Joe Reed	25
Joe Moore by Little Joe	41	King by Zantanon	24
Beggar Boy (TB) by Black Tony	40	My Texas Dandy	
My Texas Dandy by Porte Drapeau	37	by *Porte Drapeau	23
Cowboy (P-12) by Yellow Jacket	33	Question Mark by Plaudit	19
Red Joe of Arizona by Joe Reed	32	Bear Hug by Norfleet	18
Joe Reed by Joe Blair (TB)	31	Beggar Boy (TB) by Black Tony	18
Bear Hug by Norfleet	30	Cowboy by Yellow Jacket	18
TEXAS DANDY		Joe Reed by Joe Blair (TB)	18
by My Texas Dandy	30	TEXAS DANDY	
Question Mark by Plaudit	29	by My Texas Dandy	17
Ben Hur by Rainy Day	27	PIGGIN STRING (TB) by Ariel	16
Doc Horn (TB) by Flying Squirrel	25	Red Joe of Arizona by Joe Reed	15
HARD TWIST by Cowboy	25	Ben Hur by Rainy Day	14
Midnight Jr. by Midnight	23	Doc Horn (TB) by Flying Squirrel	14
PIGGIN STRING (TB) by Ariel	23	HARD TWIST by Cowboy	14
Catechu by Joe Reed	22	VANDY by Going Light (TB)	14
BARRED by Three Bars (TB)	21	Bert by Tommy Clegg	13
Jack Dempsey by Big Boy	20	Band Play by Band Time (TB)	12
Little Dick by Sleepy Dick	19	Joe Bailey (P-4) by Little King	12
Oklahoma Star		BARRED by Three Bars (TB)	12
by Dennis Reed (TB)	19	LITTLE JOE, JR. by Joe Bailey	12
Band Play by Band Time (TB)	18	RED MAN by Joe Hancock	12
Billy Van by Cotton Eyed Joe	18		

Holman on Speed

"In the old days," said J. S. "Jap" Holman, "a horse in the cow country was judged on performance alone. Speed is, and always has been, the main requirement of a good Quarter Horse or Thoroughbred. Without

1962 Stakes and Features, with Winning Horses

Horse	Race	Date	Track
ALAMITOS BAR	Autumn Championship	December 22nd	Los Alamitos
ALAMITOS BAR	Hard Twist Stakes	November 24th	Los Alamitos
ALAMITOS BAR	Pomona QH Championship	September 22nd	Pomona
ALAMITOS BAR	Shue Fly Stakes	April 9th	Los Alamitos
BELL DIAL	Minnesota QH Futurity	July 7th	Park Jefferson
BILLY GREENSHAW	Two-Year-Old Championship	August 5th	Prescott Downs
BOBETTE PARKER	Nick Hall Cup	February 25th	Rillito Park
BUCK'S BAR NONE	Nebraska QH Futurity	August 10th	Burwell
BUCK'S BAR NONE	Rocky Mountain QHA Futurity	September 8th	Centennial
BUCK'S BAR NONE	South Dakota QH Futurity	July 28th	Park Jefferson

Horse	Race	Date	Track
CANALES BLACK	Peter McCue Stakes	June 3rd	Ruidoso Downs
CANALES BLACK	Ruidoso QH Championship	July 8th	Ruidoso Downs
CAPRIDECK	Ariz Downs QH Championship	November 11th	Arizona Downs
CAPRIDECK	Gold Bar Handicap	November 4th	Arizona Downs
CAPRIDECK	Go Man Go Stakes	December 8th	Los Alamitos
CAPRIDECK	Inaugural Handicap	October 18th	Arizona Downs
CAPRIDECK	Los Alamitos	March 3rd	Bay Meadows
CARVER'S DOLL	South Dakota QH Derby	August 4th	Park Jefferson
FLY STRAW	Barbra B Stakes	April 21st	Los Alamitos
FLY STRAW	Chicado V	April 28th	Los Alamitos
FLY STRAW	New Mexico Breeders Ass'n. Purse	October 13th	Sunland Park
GUY BAR	Yakima Meadows Futurity	May 20th	Yakima Meadows
HANDY BARGAIN	Tri-State Derby	June 9th	Colfax
HI B. HIND	La Mesa QH Futurity Trial	June 16th	La Mesa Park
HI BUTTONS	LSRVQHA Derby	June 3rd	Ontario
HUSTLING MAN	All-American Futurity	September 3rd	Ruidoso Downs
HUSTLING MAN	Thanksgiving	November 22nd	Los Alamitos
IRON MAIDEN	La Mesa QH Handicap	July 29th	La Mesa Park
JET DECK	Ariz Downs Juvenile Championship	November 4th	Arizona Downs
JET DECK	Juvenile Championship	May 8th	Los Alamitos
JET DECK	Kindergarten Stakes	December 22nd	Los Alamitos
JET DECK	Los Alamitos Futurity	December 15th	Los Alamitos
JET DECK	PCQHRA Futurity	December 1st	Los Alamitos
JODY'S TINKER	Rainier Stake	July 22nd	Rainier Downs
KIMALETA	Illinois State Fair Futurity	August 10th	Springfield
KIMALETA	Two-Year-Old Championship	July 7th	Eureka Downs
LEO TAFFY	LSRVQHA Futurity	June 3rd	Ontario
LITTLE CHLOE	Juvenile QH Championship	July 1st	La Mesa Park
LITTLE CHLOE	La Mesa QH Futurity 2nd Div	June 16th	La Mesa Park
LITTLE CHLOE	Ruidoso QH Futurity	July 22nd	Ruidoso Downs
LOOKIE HERE BOY	South Texas Derby	April 7th	La Bahia Downs
MAGBY'S LASAN	Southeastern QHBA Futurity	March 31st	Hartshorne
MAGNOLIA BAR	Inaugural	April 9th	Los Alamitos
MANOR BORN	Southwestern Futurity	March 11th	Rillito Downs
MAROONED	Golden Spread QHA Futurity	November 23rd	Sunland Park
MAROONED	New Mexico-Bred QH Futurity	September 21st	Albuquerque
MISS BAR LEO	Colorado Lassie QH Stakes	September 22nd	Centennial
MISS BAR LEO	Colorado QH Futurity	October 6th	Centennial
MISS BAR LEO	Texas Futurity	April 8th	La Bahia Downs
MISS DANDY BOB	Eureka Downs Championship	July 8th	Eureka Downs
MISS JET DECK	Freeway	September 29th	Pomona
MISS JET DECK	Gift Horse	March 10th	Bay Meadows
MISS LADY BAR (DH)	Nebraska QHA Derby	August 11th	Burwell
MISS PAY BRACKET	West Texas QH Futurity	May 5th	Sonora Park
MISTY PRIEST	Florida QH Futurity	January 13th	Tropical Park
MONSIEUR'S CHARM	Nebraska QHA Derby	August 11th	Burwell
MOOLAH BAR	Las Ninas	December 5th	Los Alamitos
MR. JUNIPER BAR	Kansas QH Futurity	July 1st	Ruidoso Downs
MR. JUNIPER BAR	Magic Empire QH Futurity	October 14th	Enid
MR. JUNIPER BAR	Oklahoma QHA Futurity	May 26th	Enid
MR. MINNIE BARS	Tri-State Futurity	June 10th	Colfax
MR. SAMBO	Florida QH Championship	April 7th	Gulfstream Park
NO BUTT	Clabbertown G	November 19th	Los Alamitos
NO BUTT	Miss Princess Stakes	April 14th	Los Alamitos

Horse	Race	Date	Track
NO BUTT	Mr. Bar None	May 19th	Ruidoso Downs
NO BUTT	Palo Alto	December 20th	Bay Meadows
NOORELLA	PCQHRA	June 16th	Bay Meadows
NO PAYOLA	Intermountain QH Futurity	September 3rd	Elko County Fair
PACIFIC BARS	Los Ninos	October 28th	Los Alamitos
PASAMONTE PAUL	Juvenile Handicap	September 23rd	Albuquerque
POKEY BAR	Los Alamitos QH Championship	May 5th	Los Alamitos
POKEY BAR	PCQHRA Derby Trial (2nd)	April 14th	Los Alamitos
POKEY BAR	PCQHRA Derby	April 21st	Los Alamitos
POKEY BAR	Ruidoso QH Derby	August 5th	Ruidoso Downs
PRINTER'S DEVIL	Arizona QH Derby	February 4th	Rillito Park
PRINTER'S DEVIL	Cortez Handicap	December 8th	Sunland Park
PRINTER'S DEVIL	Mt. Oyster Club Handicap	December 23rd	Rillito Park
RANIER FROSTY	Tri-State Futurity (Fall)	October 20th	Portland Meadow
RANIER FROSTY	Clark County RQHA Futurity	May 30th	Portland Meadow
RICKETTA	Northern RQHA Derby	May 13th	Yakima Meadows
SADIE FIELDS	Sunland QH Stakes	October 6th	Sunland Park
SANDY BOLO	Michigan QH Futurity	September 14th	Hazel Park
SAVANNAH CATES	Sunland QH Championship	April 15th	Sunland Park
SCHOOL TEACHER	Aztec Handicap	December 15th	Sunland Park
SHE KITTY	Colorado QH Derby	September 29th	Centennial
SHE KITTY	Colorado Wonderland Handicap	October 13th	Centennial
SILENT ARIEL	Magic Empire QH Derby	October 13th	Garfield Downs
SILENT ARIEL	Rocky Mountain QH Futurity	September 1st	Centennial
SKI CAT	Hawthorne QH Futurity	October 13th	Chicago
SKIPPA STRING	Bright Eyes	September 23rd	Albuquerque
SPUNKY CAT	Cow Capitol Derby	June 23rd	Miles City
STAR BY PASS	Beaumont QH Futurity	July 4th	Beaumont Park
STRAW FLIGHT	Arizona QH Derby	October 28th	Arizona Downs
STRAW FLIGHT	City of Pueblo Handicap	June 17th	La Mesa Park
STRAW FLIGHT	Shue Fly	October 21st	Arizona Downs
STRAW FLIGHT	Sunland QH Derby	March 25th	Sunland Park
STRAW FLIGHT	Shu Fly	September 19th	Albuquerque
SUGAR BARS' HANK	Southeastern OQHBA Derby	March 31st	Hartshorne
TERRY RICKY SHAY	Jefferson QHA Futurity	August 18th	Humboldt County Fair
THAT'S FRANCIS	Hill Country Futurity	August 11th	Junction
THREE CHICKS	Josie Bar	December 1st	Los Alamitos
TIME REQUEST	BM Juvenile Championship	June 18th	Bay Meadows
TOMMY SANDS	Nebraska-Bred Futurity	August 11th	Burwell
TONTO BARS HANK	Lightning Bar Memorial Handicap	September 1st	Ruidoso Downs
TONTO DINERO	Montana QH Futurity	August 4th	Great Falls
TOP CAT	Nebraska QH Championship	August 11th	Burwell
TOP CAT	Park Jefferson QH Championship	August 19th	Park Jefferson
TOP MOON	Bardella	November 19th	Los Alamitos
TOP MOON	PCQHRA Futurity	September 27th	Pomona

it he is just a horse that may win a prize in a horse show, and very little else." Mr. Holman continued:

The polo player and the roper, for instance, want horses with early speed; it is found extremely useful in a horse for general ranch work. With these facts in mind I select my own breeding stock from individuals which have pedigrees that carry early speed, for this is the kind of horse I want to raise.

On the tombstone of Himyar are these words: Speed Springs Eternal from His Ashes. This prophecy has been amply fulfilled. Many of the best horses produced in America have traced their ancestry through Domino and others to this great stallion. My own horse Raffles was a direct male-line descendant of Himyar.

Through the years I had gotten together a nice band of mares to breed to Raffles; several of these Red Bug mares I registered with the American Quarter Horse Association. From them I raised many good race, roping, and polo horses, and, true to tradition, his young stallions always got good colts when bred to good mares.

Some of the better-known stock from this Raffles-Red Bug cross are Snip II, Jap, and Little Red.

When it came time [said Mr. Holman] to find a stallion to breed to my Raffles mares I recalled the two great race horses Sir Gallahad III and Epinard. These two horses ran several matched races; both were wonderful individuals and great sires. Being unable to decide which bloodline would provide the best nick with my own stock, I bought grandsons of both. Hyon by Hygro by Epinard, and Pop Quest by High Quest by * Sir Gallahad III.

Now the great grandsons and daughters of these two famous horses make the Holman Ranch their home. Hyon only lived one year after coming here, but he got some nice fillies which I bred to Pop Quest. The resultant colts have shown fine conformation and carry the blood of Himyar, Epinard, and Sir Gallahad III.

I have never gone in for racing in a big way, but do try to have a horse or two in training most of the time. I do this to prove to myself and those interested that I am still raising good horses. Some which I have success-fully raced in the past are Black Jack, Lady H, Amos, Yankee Doodle, and Raffles H (Little Yankee). In addition, Snip, Little Red, Jap, and Boot-legger have good track records; these latter were bred by me, though bought and raced by others.

If the produce of a mare show no signs of speed I do not breed that mare again. I sell her cheap or give her away. I think it a disgrace when a registered Quarter Horse goes on the track to race and throws his tail up before going three hundred yards.

"Don't be afraid to get Thoroughbred blood in your horses—I mean, of course, if they need it," Mr. Holman wrote away back in 1948. "But don't go about this in a haphazard manner; be sure your TB blood is of the right type and will be acceptable to the Quarter Horse stud book. I can't believe the Association would refuse papers on a colt by some good Quarter Horse

80. The only known picture of Mame Taylor. Louis Kirk is holding in this 1940 photograph.

stallion out of, for instance, Miss Princess. Nor do I think they would pass up a colt from a good Quarter Horse mare and Olympia (TB). At any rate, if you breed a better horse than you have had and do not get him registered, there is the satisfaction of knowing you own and have raised good horses."

Biographical Sketches

Himyar

A light bay bred and owned by Major B. G. Thomas of Dixiana Stud (Lexington, Kentucky), Himyar was foaled in 1875 out of Hira by Lexington. He was winner of the Belle Meade Stakes for two-year-olds at Louisville, the Belle Meade Stakes (No. 1) at Nashville, the Phoenix Hotel Stakes at Lexington, the Merchants and Turf Stakes at Louisville, and the January Stakes at St. Louis.

His sire, Alarm, was by * Eclipse, and made his debut as a two-year-old at Saratoga in 1871 in a match race for $5000 a side against Inverary (by * Leamington) at one mile, Alarm winning in 1:47½. This was on the 16th of August. The following day he ran third in the Kentucky Stakes at the same distance—winner's time 1:47¼. He ran second to Joe Daniels in the Nursery Stakes, ran second in the Desert Stakes to Inverary. As a three-year-old he ran five races, winning all. His final race was a club purse at Saratoga in which he defeated Fadladeen and Kingfisher, going the distance in 1:42¾—the fastest mile ever run to that date. He made his first season at the Walnut Hill Stud. A bright bay horse, he stood 15 hands, 3¾ inches; is said to have had a neat, expressive head and great breadth between the eyes, great sweep in his hindquarters, good hocks, sound legs and feet.

Himyar, Alarm's greatest son and the founder of a family still known for blinding speed, was called by Sanders Bruce in 1883 "one of the best race horses ever saddled." He started his career as a two-year-old in Lexington in the five-furlong Colt and Filly Stakes, finishing third to Pomeroy in 1:04¼. He won the three-quarter-mile Colt Stakes in 1:16¾, defeating Leveler, Blue Eyes, and five others. At Louisville he won the Belle Meade Stakes in 1:16¼, beating Leveler and others, and came in behind Blue Eyes and Day Star in the Sanford Mile, running time 1:45.

As a three-year-old Himyar was started in five races, winning three, and grabbing second in two. He won the Belle Meade at Nashville and the Phoenix Hotel Stakes at Lexington on a track deep in mud—time 3:22½ for the one mile and three-quarters. At Louisville he ran second to Day Star in the Kentucky Derby of 1878—at that time one and one-half miles—Day Star covering the distance in 2:37¼, the fastest Derby ever run in Kentucky up to that time. In the privately printed book *History of the Kentucky Derby, 1875–1921*, John L. O'Connor says: "The track was in admirable order, but many thought it was fully two seconds slow. . . . Out of 56 nominations nine splendid colts faced the starter. Himyar was such a big favorite, 3 to 1 over the field, that he was left out of the pools, and Day Star was next in favor, closely pushed by Bergundy and Leveler. The result is easily told. Day Star made all his running and won the race like the first class colt that he is, just as he did the Blue Ribbon at Lexington. Himyar was miserably ridden, and ran fully sixty or seventy-five yards farther in the race than was necessary." Day Star won by two lengths.

At St. Louis on June 4th Himyar won the January Stakes (mile heats) in 1:42½ and 1:43½, defeating Leveler, Kate Claxton, and McHenry. In his four-year-old season he started four times, winning all. At five he started twelve times, meeting and beating the best; four times he was the winner, four times second, twice third, and twice unplaced. Many of these outings were mile heats. He ran once unplaced at six years.

Hira, Himyar's dam, was considered a top race mare; Hegira, his second dam, had no equal for speed in her day. In 1850 at New Orleans she ran two miles in 3:34¼, the fastest time made up to that date. Himyar's great-granddam, Flight, was a very distinguished race mare and, later, the dam of Oliver.

A light bay, Himyar had a long star and white hind feet, a neat though bony head broad between the eyes, splendid shoulders, great depth of girth, good body though with rather short back ribs, which gave him a rather light-appearing flank, broad hips, immense stifle, sound feet and legs. Sanders Bruce proved himself a sound judge by predicting, "If racing lineage and speed is worth anything, Himyar should be a success in the stud."

He was a most remarkable success, and his progeny after him. He sired the mighty Domino and the Kentucky Derby winner Plaudit. From these two sons alone have come a long and able list of top-flight track horses and prepotent sires. From the Plaudit line have come such excellent individuals as Questionnaire, Hash, Requested, and Third Degree. Domino, though but briefly in the stud, gave the racing and breeding world such paragons as Commando, Ultimus, Colin, Peter Pan, High Time, Stimulus, Zacaweista, Black Tony, Bimelech, Balladier, Black Servant, Big Pebble, Blue Larkspur, Best Seller, Blue Swords, Noah, Peter Hastings, Pennant,

81. The winner at Bay Meadows: J. B. King is the winner with Jimmie Dee Garrett second and Little Meow third.

82. Rumpus, by Master Bunting, TB, out of Baby, by Popcorn.

83. Little Joe, Jr. with Steve Riggs up. The photo was taken in 1946 just before his victory in a match race against the mare Mexico. Little Joe, Jr. was then three.

84. The sire of Question Mark: Plaudit, by King Plaudit, TB, son of the Kentucky Derby winner.

85. Snip Raffles, by Raffles out of Chessie E. Bred by H. T. Espy of Sonora, Texas.
Photo by Phil Winegar

86. Gold Mount, foaled 1940, Cimarron, New Mexico. Bred by Waite Phillips, also the breeder of Question Mark. The sire was Brush Mount, by Chimney Sweep, TB. Miss Helen, by Plaudit, was the dam. Second dam was Spotlight, by Rainy Day, by Midnight.

87. Brush Mount, by Chimney Sweep, TB, out of Hula Dancer, by Jiggs.

Photo by Cecil Hellbusch

88. Famous six-mule team that handled the starting gate when Arlington Downs
was in its palmy days.

Equipoise, Attention, Carrier Pigeon, Equestrian, Equifox, Swing and Sway, and others.

Himyar's blood has also embellished the short-horse fraternity with the great sire Plaudit (a Quarter-bred grandson of the Kentucky Derby winner). Among others, this Plaudit (1657) gave us Question Mark, Miss Helen (dam of Gold Mount) and, among others, the 1948 Champion Quarter Running Stallion, Scooter W.

Captains Courageous, a son of Stimulus, gave us the great Miss Bank, also C.B.; and from the same line came Bob Shade. One of High Time's grandsons, Band Play, gave us Band Man and his short-horse progeny; Time Signal gave us Streak W; High Step contributed the good mare Tidy Step; and a son of High Time (Fleeting Time) sired the mare Nellene, who was the halfbred dam of Joe Reed II. One of High Time's grandsons, Etcetera, sired Kansas Kate. Luke McLuke's son Raffles put a number of sprinters on the straightaways; Luke's son, Don Diego, gave us Brown Deacon.

The Leggett Horse, who goes to Ultimus, gave the short tracks Sleepytime Gal. Black Tony's son, Beggar Boy, sired a host of speedsters, including Blackout and several top matrons. Black Servant was the great-grandsire of the celebrated Barbra B, who so soundly whipped the record-holding * Fair Truckle. From the Pennant line came Rumpus and Forever Young gave us Duke.

Fast Travelers

For the past sixty years one rock-ribbed line of old-timey short horses has held its own through good times and bad, continuing to supply a seemingly inexhaustible stream of hard-knocking cowhorse progeny while sending remarkable numbers of spectacular winners to the nation's quarter tracks. This celebrated strain of do-it-all stock comes down to us from the loins of mighty Traveler.

No one today knows for sure how he was bred, nor does it greatly matter. He stamped his own for what they were. He never lost a race, though he ran against the best his day produced. In the stud he sired a line of stand-out horses second to none. Of all the sires ever to found a do-or-die Quarter Horse family, Traveler, with his remarkable speed heritage, some observers feel, is the greatest example of short-horse prepotency since Janus.

Unknown and unhonored, he came into Texas pulling a wagon. On the Texas and Pacific railroad dump in Eastland County, he was hitched to a dirt-moving slip. He belonged to a remuda of work animals owned by a contractor whose name has been forgotten, said to have been an out-of-state man whose work stock was gathered before he bid in the job.

Traveler was an aged horse then, if not already smooth mouthed. Jim Edwards, B. F. Austin, and Bob Perry, all with well-established reputations as cowhands, horsemen, and observers, were pretty well agreed that the horse had never had a saddle on his back before he was eight years old. B. A. Gardner of Willcox, Arizona, told me: "They couldn't ride him with a stock saddle—only with harness or with a jockey saddle. He bucked every time they got near him with a stock saddle." Jim Edwards thought he was ten, or maybe eleven, before he was "rode out." He pitched like a bobcat but (to quote Edwards) showed great savvy and soon quieted down.

He was fetched to Baird by the Self brothers, who subcontracted dirt-removal work. Having finished their job, the Selfs one evening were about to head for home when the boss contractor suggested they might want to swap one of their mules for the light sorrel stallion. It wasn't the first time he'd dropped such hints, but this time Cam looked at his brother, Trigger-foot, and said, "Believe we will." And that same evening the Selfs drove Traveler off between the shafts of their wagon, to the everlasting good of the Quarter Horse breed.

This was in 1880. Traveler, at least three years old at this time, very probably had come from upper New York state and was shipped down to Texas in a carload of horses according to later testimony from the contractor who swapped him for Cam Self's mule. There were still a few good Quarter Horses in the northern part of New York state at that time.

No one today appears to know how long the Selfs kept Traveler. Lee McCameron had a mare he called Mayflower, held to be about as fast as they came, yet Self boldly matched his dirt mover against her for a quarter of a mile. Everybody figured Cam Self was daft. Will Crutchfield rode Mayflower. Declared Bob Perry: "Crutchfield could not have thrown a rock off Mayflower and touched Traveler's dust!"

After several other hopefuls had taken a fall at the Selfs' former work-horse, never managing to do more than join the parade of the vanquished, Cam Self began to feel pretty good. Brown Seay, a shrewd judge of horses, owned a saloon in Baird and kept a stable of fast ones, short as well as distance runners, and had had his eye on the Selfs' dappled stallion for some while. One evening he made Cam a proposition whereby he would run a horse called Froggie against Traveler for $500 a side and, if Traveler beat Froggie, Self was to take an additional $500 off the Seay bankroll—and Froggie to boot—transferring Traveler to the ownership of Seay.

There was a good-sized crowd on hand for the race. They came to

Baird from all over; a thousand dollars being a considerable pile of money. Traveler, of course, won going away and became Seay's property forthwith.

Traveler's fame was now assured. He was blue-forked lightning and everybody knew it. People living around Baird at that time have testified that this dirt-moving sorrel was the "finest looking Quarter Horse any man ever set eyes on." Franklin Reynolds, who wrote Traveler up for the *Quarter Horse Journal* (May, 1957), has said that Mr. C. S. Boyles, who had lived in Baird from 1893 to 1911 and was married to a sister of Brown Seay, thinks Seay got hold of Traveler about 1892.

The men who knew him have declared that Seay's sorrel stallion, Traveler, was a genuine Quarter Horse—no doubt about it. He had a blazed face and gray roanish hairs about the flanks, and there were collar marks on him. They say he had the most powerful quarters they had ever seen on a horse. All have attested to his wonderful disposition—and this he must have had to have been shipped loose, in a carload of horses, all the way from New York. One of the people Franklin Reynolds talked to was Joe Allphin, who groomed and fed and rubbed Traveler down every morning and night during the several years he was owned by Brown Seay. Allphin says: "We took mighty good care of him." He also told Reynolds, "He must have been nine or ten years old when Mr. Seay got him," and, "He was the fastest breaking horse I ever saw in my life. . . . He'd leave the score with a terrific rush; he was a hard horse for a jockey to stay with. He was an easy horse to handle."

All over Texas folks were talking about him. Under Brown Seay's ownership he raced steadily, mostly around Baird but not always, and was used at stud between races. The toughest race of his life, I've been told, was against Bob Wilson, a real weight carrier and rougher than a cob. Austin Merrick, a hard-twisted Calahan County cowhand owned and broke Bob Wilson and is said to have been the only man that could get on him. Merrick and his tack weighed 165 pounds, dry. Here is what Mr. Merrick has to say about that go:

I did not ride Bob Wilson against Traveler. Cheese Jackson, a jockey from Coleman, Texas, rode that day. He weighed 112 pounds. Traveler had a good boy up, too; his name, as I recall, was Ben Estes. The race was very close and was decided as a dead heat, though I'd say Bob Wilson had six inches the best of it. Betting was three to one against Bob, and we split the purse and they paid me the difference between even money and three to one as had been put up. Bob Wilson was as fast as they come. But I always had a jockey. He would not let the jockey ride him more than three times before he would pitch him off; then I would have to train him a few days. The race was carefully timed—440 yards in :22.0. I think

Traveler was the greatest Quarter Horse of all time. He was then fourteen years old and time was against him. Bob Wilson was in his prime, six years old, weighed 928 pounds, stood 14½, and had the nature of a demon.

Traveler was a good-natured horse. He did not show any Steeldust breeding, but I was told he was Shiloah and Argile. He was slim faced and had no big jaw. I raised several of his colts. They were all good. He was a chestnut sorrel with gray hairs. Brown Seay owned Traveler, and when the horse was very old he sold him to Chris Seales, about five miles south of Baird, where he stayed several years. The Trammells bought him, and later let the Gardners have him. He died in that area. His colts were very fast.

Traveler was also a "boss hoss" in the breeding pen. He sired fast "travelers" out of just about anything. For example—

Tump Pace of Baird owned a mare they later called Fanny Pace. At the time of this story she was strictly "breeding unknown" and pulling an ice wagon. Tump bred her to Traveler for three straight seasons, getting Judge Thomas (holder of the World's Record for three and a half furlongs for 25 years), Judge Welch (a horse that ran as well as Judge Thomas but was never campaigned on organized tracks—hence no accurate data regarding his record), and Jack Tolliver (renamed Buster Brown), a running horse in Texas and, according to a breeding publication issued in 1908, "the world's greatest polo pony."

These three were all gelded. A number of good mares were bred to the dirt mover, notably Jenny (with good Tiger blood back of her); good mares were also bred to Possum (King) and Little Joe, but they were few and far between. Short horse men who knew him have never sought to detract from Traveler's reputation or the old horse's accomplishments.

George Clegg described him as "one of the most perfect looking horses I ever saw." Bob Perry and Jim Edwards have declared: "He had the most powerful hind end for sprint running we ever saw on a horse."

Also to be considered, for whatever it may be worth, is the Texas Chief controversy which raged for many years. Chief was by Traveler out of the brown mare known as The Halletsville Mare. Ott Adams, who said he remembered this mare, once told me, "She was a big brown mare, a Percheron-bred mare. The reason I got rid of Texas Chief is that I was and am still raising Quarter Horses and wanted no Percheron blood in my stock."

Bred by Dow Shely to Traveler, this mare produced Texas Chief in 1909. Many years ago, as a result of my inquiries, J. W. House of Cameron, Texas (breeder, among others, of Joe Reed II, Leo, Little Fanny, Red Joe of Arizona, and Bill Reed), wrote me: "I know a Negro who used to ride

Texas Chief and have finally got in touch with him for you. This man farms about fifteen miles from here and is a good substantial person. He tells me Texas Chief was by Traveler and out of Mamie Sykes."

In 1946 Ott Adams told me Texas Chief's mother was purchased by Dow Shely from a German at Halletsville, and suggested Mr. Shely probably hoped to get another horse like Judge Thomas. Texas Chief was indeed Judge Thomas' equal, if one may judge on the basis of Chief's two years of track performance. He whipped all comers and was even alleged to have beaten Ples Walters at Mexico City, winning easily.

Colonel William Warren Sterling, ex-Captain of Texas Rangers, told me: "I knew Texas Chief quite well. He was a large, heavily muscled horse and too big for a small man like Mr. Adams to handle. I went with a shipment of cattle from Alice to Fort Worth on the same train in 1912, when Chief was delivered to the Waggoners."

Mrs. William Shely told me: "My husband's brother, Dow Shely, bought and shipped the brown mare to us; such was our confidence in his judgment, we bred her to Traveler. Texas Chief was her first colt. I will gladly give you a summary of her good qualities; bad ones she had none. She stood well up in height and had a good disposition, slim trim legs, and was never nervous or flighty. Indeed, she was steady as the Rock of Gibraltar, and this invaluable quality she passed on to her foals. Chief was well known as a gentle, kindly and obedient animal with more than average intelligence. We believe the mare had every good quality desired in a breeder."

When I was digging into this, George Clegg declared: "She was a big, fine-looking mare. Adams says Shely told him he bought her in Halletsville, but he told me he bought her in Karnes County and it was my opinion that she was probably by some of the Rondo blood. [Mr. Clegg purchased this mare from the Shelys.] Chief's full sister I bred to Hickory Bill and raised some wonderful colts—the Noelky Horse in San Angelo, a horse I gave to Dr. Strickland, and one the King Ranch finally got that I had sold to W. K. McMaster. All three of these were full brothers and fine breeders. The old mare's filly by Rattler was not much of a breeder. Shely and I trained Chief, Little Joe, and Lady S. They were tops."

A book could be written on the controversial issues raised by Traveler and his sons; but one thing all knowledgeable horsemen agree on—they all had speed and most of them passed it along. Most of Traveler's colts, before these facts were understood or fully appreciated, were gelded, including most of those produced while he was standing at the ranch of Chris Seales (Teller Blakely broke most of these and has called them a great string of ranch horses, fast learners and easy handlers); none were kept for breeding purposes. Seales and Brown Seay presently sold the old horse to the Trammells at Sweetwater.

It is generally believed the Gardners had him next on their ranches at and around Big Lake. B. A. Gardner believes his grandfather got rid of Traveler in the late 1890's. They, the Gardners, raised Rowdy (by Traveler). Rowdy is considered to have been one of the greatest steer-roping horses of all time. He was the favorite of Little Joe Gardner and of Clay McGonigal, who was on him about as much as was his owner. Rowdy was a heavily muscled bay. He had so much endurance that both men sometimes used him the same day. They took him to South America with them and Bill Pickens and two or three others. B. A. Gardner told me: "Alec Gardner was the first Gardner to own Traveler, then John Gardner had him. As I recall, Alec didn't think too highly of him as a sire. The last big race I know about was a matched race with old Skinny. I believe old Skinny outran him. Another great roping horse from that line was Silver, a gelding by Possum; it was Jim Kennedy that changed King's name to Possum."

Not long after this the Shely's acquired Traveler. He must have been at least thirty then. George Clegg declared he never saw "a more beautiful sight" than Traveler's first crop of Shely foals. Among these were Little Joe, Texas Chief, and Joe Shely. Mr. Clegg told me: "I am the only one who raced Little Joe. He was very fast—could run the quarter in :22.0. I ran him as a three-year-old against all ages and the only horse ever to beat him was Ace of Hearts. There were four horses in this race and Joe was beaten by not more than a foot."

In the records compiled by the American Quarter Racing Association (which used to locate sprint horses by families) the leading group in 1946 derived from Sunstar (TB) through * Porte Drapeau, My Texas Dandy, Clabber, * North Star II, * Hand Grenade, and Los Molinos, for a total of 22 ROM. Descendants of * Chicle (TB) were next with 21. Then came the Peter McCues and * Leamingtons with 16 ROM each. The Travelers sent 15 reps to the Register of Merit, and this accounted only for male-line descent, with six lesser groups trailing.

In 1947, with many additional families heard from, the Travelers— through Little Joe, Ace of Diamonds, Zantanon, King, Dutch, Joe Moore, Grano de Oro, Possum, Little King, Joe Bailey of Gonzales, and Guinea Pig—came out on top, beating the Chicles by two, the Sunstars by three, the Leamingtons by five, the McCues by six, with the rest trailing badly.

The Travelers in 1948 were still on top with 24, followed by the Sunstars with 22, the Chicles with 21, the McCues with 19, the Himyars with 16,

89. Traveler. The handlers are Grover Pruitt, Turner Breedlove, and Clay Mann.

90. Possum, when he was owned by James J. Kennedy, in southern Arizona. Mabry Gardner, a mighty tall man, is hanging onto him.

91. Possum as a young horse. Van Hastings is up.

92. Texas Chief, by Traveler. The Shely family believed he was a greater horse than Little Joe and could outrun him. The late Col. William Almond Shely up.

Photo by Tommy Thompson

93. Little Joe, by Traveler.

94. Red Cloud as a yearling with Mabry Gardner holding.

95. Joe Bailey of Gonzales (by Possum).

the Leamingtons with 16, and those from Ben Brush mustering nine. In 1949 the Travelers jumped well in the lead with 36 Register of Merit contenders, through Little Joe, Ace of Diamonds, Zantanon, King, San Siemon, Joe Barrett, Ed Echols, Dutch, Joe Moore, Grano de Oro, Cotton Eyed Joe, Will Wright, Possum, Little King, Joe Bailey, Bacchus, Guinea Pig, and Red Cloud. The Chicles, were again in second place, mainly through the efforts of Flying Bob progeny, with 30. Leamington (through Joe Reed II, Uncle Jimmie Gray, and Doc Horn, most notably) came up with 22; Himyar, through Quarter stock tracing in male line to Domino, Commando, Ultimus, Stimulus, Captains Courageous, High Time, Luke McLuke, Infinite, Peter Pan, Black Toney, Pennant, and Forever Young, also accounted for 22 ROM. No others were close. These were the latest computations from the AQRA and do not, remember, account for blood which produced impressive performance through the distaff side.

Sprint-blood families today have been so intertwined as to have been pretty well lost sight of, but Traveler blood and its incontravertible influence, no matter how outcrossed or bolstered, can be found like threads of gold through the whole exciting tapestry of short-horse competition.

Anyone who will take a bit of time can trace the great individuals which have come from Traveler in the male line direct. What is never so apparent is the astonishing contribution to the Quarter Horse industry and, even more impressive, to straightaway history made by Traveler through the distaff lines in modern pedigree.

The bottom dam line of Joe Reed II, as an illustration, through Little Red Nell (dam of Nellene) goes direct to Texas Chief, considered by Colonel William Almond Shely to have been Traveler's greatest son. Sonny Kimble, a direct main-liner, went also through his dam by Texas Chief to Traveler. Hard Twist carried Traveler blood. Silver King (P–183 by Old Sorrel) has a deal of Traveler blood through his dam, Clegg Mare #3. Colonel Clyde, a do-it-all horse if there ever was one, through his dam, Old Red, carried 50 per cent Traveler blood, though classified by top male line with the Sunstars. And, to jump right into the sprinting present with this delving, No Butt, consistent stakes winner in the highest class company, goes direct in top male line straight to Traveler. She looks like a Traveler and she travels like one. The whole Tonto Bars tribe, from Bar Tonto straight through Tonto Bars Gill and all his get and progeny, carry concentrated Traveler blood through Tonta Gal, big mama of the line; and Tonto Bars Hank (through *his* dam and Hank H, with Queen H by King P–234 close up) gets Traveler blood from both sides of the tree and you will look a long time to find a more enduring group than this.

The Truth About Peter McCue

Peter McCue was both a legend and a controversy even before he died.

Bred by the Watkins brothers at their Little Grove Stud near Petersburg, Illinois, he was foaled, as nearly as can be fixed, on February 23, 1895. His dam was the celebrated race mare Nora M by Voltigeur (by Vandal by * Glencoe). Her favorite lick was the half-mile, which she consistently ran in 49 seconds. She was out of Kitty Clyde by Star Davis (by * Glencoe). The furor concerning the identity of Peter's sire has raged in the horse and livestock journals and among horsemen for better than half a century.

He was registered with the Jockey Club as a son of Duke of the Highlands, then standing at the Watkins farm. As the colt matured, strangely enough he began more and more to resemble the unregistered Dan Tucker, also holding court at the Little Grove Stud.

Elias Watkins' widow in 1949 dug up a pedigree of Dan Tucker filled out in Elias' hand. This shows Dan Tucker to have been out of But Cut by Jack Traveler by Steel Dust; But Cut's dam being given as June Bug by Harry Bluff by Telegraph (by Old Harry Bluff). Students of bloodlines will discover here some considerable departures from the accepted route of old Dan's forebears. He was shown as having foaled April 20, 1887. His sire, as given, was Barney Owens by Cold Deck out of Dollie Overton.

Dan Tucker was a short horse, no two ways about it. He was also a rip-snorting good one. But Samuel Watkins' record book, under "Foals of 1895," has this entry: Nora M—Duke—Feb. 23.

The following is quoted from a June, 1949 article in *The Quarter Horse*: "The men still living who knew the Little Grove horses, including Sam Watkins' sons, flatly state that Dan Tucker was unquestionably the sire of the magnificent Peter. Several explanations exist for the entry in the record book, including one that a hired hand had bred Nora M to Dan Tucker instead of Duke contrary to Sam Watkins' instructions and without his knowledge. Another more logical (and supported by present members of the Watkins family) explanation is based on the fact that almost all racing in the late 1800's, whether long or short, was restricted to registered Thoroughbreds; for this reason it was common practice for breeders with promising colts out of 'cold blooded' horses to record them as being sired by a registered stallion simply for the purpose of registering and running the colt. Although Peter McCue was registered with the Jockey Club as a Duke of the Highlands colt, the Watkins family always represented him as a son of Dan Tucker and he was sold on that basis."

The illustrious Dan was a very fast horse, a *big* horse both in size and

96. Pee Wee, by Red Cloud, by Possum, by Traveler.

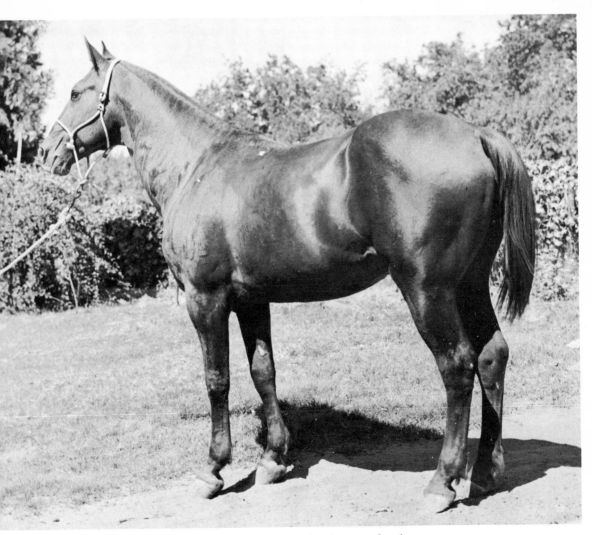

97. Mark, by Red Cloud, sired scads of top rodeo horses.

Photo by Warner Walker Studio

98. Lucky Blanton, by Mark.

99. San Siemon, by Zantanon out of Panita, by Possum. Bred by M. Benavides Volpe. Frank Autry up.

100. Joe Barrett, by San Siemon. Paul Grafe is on the leadshank.
Photo by John A. Stryker

101. Sonny Kimble, by Zantanon. Bred by M. Benavides Volpe.

Photo by John A. Stryker

102. Uncle Jimmy Gray with Henry Pfefferling at halter.

Photo by Harvey Patteson

103. Peter McCue, with Milo Burlingame at the halter in a photo taken at Cheyenne, Oklahoma.

104. John Wilkens, by Peter McCue. Tom Caudill is up in this picture taken just before Milo sold him at 13 months.

performance. At five, while racing in St. Louis, he began to go blind but finished out a highly successful season; he was later, while totally blind, put into a matched race against a speed merchant known as Old Dobbin. This go was run at Ashland, with Russ Watkins up, and Dan's victory was no near thing—blind or not, he ran plumb away from that fraud.

He was bred to run, and that was what he did best. They kept him in a small paddock outside the barn. One night Duke of the Highlands broke out of his stall and attacked the blind stallion. Frightened, unable to cope with his adversary, the frantic Dan ran wildly in circles until he went crashing into a large linn tree and was knocked senseless. The family thought he was dead; but, regaining consciousness, he struggled up, apparently but little damaged. Nothing else that he sired came up to Peter McCue; the same, however, could be said of Duke's get.

The two greatest authorities on Peter McCue, Coke Roberds and Milo Burlingame, have both gone on to better things. I knew both men and, when I was running the Double N, Milo and Minnie (Mrs. Burlingame) always stopped by whenever they came through our country. He said to me once: "Peter McCue was the greatest Quarter Horse of all time. Coke Roberds did not think old Peter was a clean-bred horse. I do not think Peter was ever beaten at the quarter."

Milo said:

I first heard of him in 1893 at the St. Louis Fairgrounds when he was running half a mile to five furlongs. I was just a kid jockey and had been riding other horses. McCue, the Watkins trainer, looked me up one morning and asked if I would ride Peter in a half-mile race. He said, "I see you've got these Eastern boys outclassed in getting away from the post. I think that means a lot in this kind of racing. I've also noticed you won't break a horse unless you've got the best of it."

This was mighty high praise from a man important as the Watkins trainer. I said: "Mister McCue, I'd rather be left standing at the post any time I can't get off in the lead." McCue kind of grinned. "That's what I want," he said. "Any time you're off in the lead with Peter McCue the race is as good as won."

So I rode Peter out onto the track. He was a mighty big horse, at least 16 hands and more than 1400 pounds. I've heard people laugh at Peter's great size but there didn't many laugh when the pay-off came. The competition that day included April Fool, Jeraldine, and Dora Mae. Peter stayed in front from post to wire without the least bit of exertion. I was then engaged to ride him for the balance of the meet; this was 12 to 15 races. When he was shipped back to Chicago I came on West and heard that, shortly after his return to Illinois, Peter fell in a race (they told me later he hit a soft place in the track) and broke his right leg at the pastern.

I kept track of him though. After the first three or four rides I had made up my mind if I ever got hold of the right kind of money I was going to own that horse.

Several years after Peter's accident I heard that John Wilkens, of San Antonio, had gone to Chicago and bought Peter from the Watkins people. I wrote Mr. Wilkens several times and, a few years later, I wrote to ask if Peter could be bought. Mr. Wilkens replied that he had used him about all he could in that country, having got his blood in most of the big outfits, and that he would sell him for $10,000. He told me: "I think Peter McCue is unquestionably one of the most outstanding stallions now at stud. You can't go wrong in buying him."

It was in 1906 or 1907 that I gave Sam Bowman a cashier's check and sent him to take delivery on the horse at San Antonio. I was living at Cheyenne, Oklahoma, and I believe Peter arrived at my place either in May or June of that year. I stood him at public service at $25.

I bought him knowing he was registered as a Thoroughbred. I intended to raise registered colts and bought five top Thoroughbred mares, including one from Dr. McComas and Waldorf Belle from Hix & Harper just before she won the Derby at Elk City. Knowing Peter's extreme early speed I figured that with my son Paul to do the riding, these good mares with Peter's service would produce the kind that would get the job done on the big tracks against the most rugged competition.

Peter McCue was the fastest horse at leaving a barrier I have ever seen. His stride, when he got going, measured 27 feet! He was marvelously cool in his races, never upset or unruly. I think he was the greatest short horse in the history of the world, and also the finest breeder—I have never known another horse like him.

Unfortunately for my plan of breeding outstanding registered horses, about the time I figured to get into production I was taking a flyer in railroads. The one I put my money in was to save the life of Cheyenne, but proved a mighty short horse soon curried. When this Cheyenne Short Line went into the hands of the receivers I, being one of the heaviest stockholders, left Cheyenne for greener pastures, with Peter McCue, a handful of personal belongings, and no brood mares.

Later on I did breed Peter to several Thoroughbred mares and a few good Quarter mares with fair success. While in my ownership, Peter sired John Wilkens out of a Pid Hart mare called Big Alice. She was a first-class Quarter mare out of a C. B. Campbell mare named Big Enough, a fast track mare at the quarter. Big Alice, too, moved pretty sharp at the shorter distances. She stood 15 hands and weighed 1260 in running shape. She was plenty good looking.

I think John Wilkens was possibly the greatest son of Peter McCue. If they could only have kept shoes on him no horse running ever would have caught him. I sold him to Berry Persley at about thirteen months old. He was taken to Chicago, supposedly with a bunch of horses shipped there by the Trammells or Newmans. He was very fast, but the sidewalls of his feet were too thin to hold shoes; he was fetched back into the Panhandle by the Moore brothers, who put him into training but failed to keep him in plates. The next I heard, he was at the JA Ranch in Paloduro Canyon, Texas. While there, a Mr. Mathis of Amarillo, I believe, leased him for two years. One of the best of his get at this period was Peanuts, famous as a racehorse throughout the state.

The Hancocks finally got him, and for them John Wilkens got Joe Hancock out of a fine looking half-Percheron mare; other fast sons were Lindy, Jolly, and Ned Hanger. So far as speed or ability in the stud are concerned, Joe Hancock was his standout son. He ran against Red Nell and the best of that day and, so far as I can determine, never was defeated. His stock were good at any job you gave them; there was power in his blood and it is visible today.

Said Milo: "It was while I was in Magdalena, about 1912, that Si Dawson looked me up and finally purchased Peter McCue to give to his brother-in-law, Coke Roberds of Hayden, Colorado."

In the Editor's Mail Box department of the *Quarter Horse Journal* (June, 1963) this letter, addressed to Albert Mitchell, appeared: "You were a good friend of Mr. Coke Roberds and possibly knew my father, Si Dawson. I saw your name in a copy of the *Journal* and believe you can straighten out a statement in the Quarter Horse records concerning Peter McCue.

"Mr. Willis Goode, manager of the Rancho Lilac, showed me the book on Quarter Horse history in which the statement was made that Mr. Coke Roberds owned Peter McCue. My father bought Peter McCue and left him with Mr. Roberds when he went to manage the Fozueda Marungara in Brazil. My dad left some mares with Mr. Roberds also and after Dad died, December 3, 1919, in Sao Paulo, Brazil, Mother returned to the States and sold the mares. Mr. Roberds kept Peter McCue and I used to visit the Roberds every summer and ride with Coke when old Peter McCue was at his cow camp, the old Jack White homestead—I think that was where Peter McCue died. Mr. Roberds didn't own Peter McCue."

I have no idea how the story got started which names Katie Wawekus as the dam of John Wilkens. Katie was a Thoroughbred mare by Wawekus with six distinct crosses to * Glencoe. Milo Burlingame told me he bred John Wilkens and I believe him. I have seen much evidence in support of this contention. Among other things, I have a photo—a snapshot—of John Wilkens at about seven months with Paul Burlingame up. There is no doubt about this colt being John Wilkens or that the boy is young Paul. My money rides on Milo Burlingame's statement that John Wilkens' dam was Big Alice by Pid Hart. Pid Hart sired some top horses, of which Rocky Mountain Tom was a splendid example. He was the only horse ever credited with having beaten Panzarita (P–747), and he did it twice, according to Slats Helm, whose father was the J. G. Helm who stood Tom at Newark, Texas.

Regardless of the controversies over their parentage, Peter McCue, John Wilkens, and Joe Hancock were all extremely fast, big, fine-looking horses, and they could and did—every one of them—pass all their best qualities along in heaping measure. By the progeny test, their only rival is Traveler.

At siring top horses of the true Quarter mold Peter McCue had no peer. Among others, he sired the following great sons: John Wilkens, Jack McCue, Chief, Buck Thomas, A. D. Reed, Hickory Bill, Badger, Duck Hunter, Sheik, Harmon Baker, and Red Rover; and such great daughters as Old Squaw, the original Carrie Nation, Cheyenne Maid, Lou Trammell, Mary McCue, Old Allie, the Houseparty Mare, Belle McCue, Betty Watkins, Dollie Spokes, Emma Hill, Hattie Jackson, Juanita Armstrong, Kate Bender, Miss Cornet, Oakford Queen, and others.

John Wilkens' greatest son was Joe Hancock; Joe, in turn, sired Red Man, Joe Tom, War Chief, Buck Hancock, Roan Hancock, and a veritable tribe of other top-flight horses.

Chief and Jack McCue sired many great individuals. A whole book might be written on the continuing service and performance of the Peter McCue blood. Badger, for instance, a legend in his time, sired Midnight, the sire of Young Midnight, Chubby, One-Eyed Waggoner, Midnight Jr., and others that will be remembered. Young Midnight got Revenue. Harmon Baker got Harmon Baker's Star, the sire in turn of J. B. King, a sprinter that went up against the country's top speed merchants of the early 1950's. One-Eyed Waggoner got Roan Wolf out of a Harmon Baker Jr. mare.

And, lest it be thought that this blood has quit performing, Murl L by Moca Burnett (he by Texas Jack, a grandson of Peter McCue out of Daybreak 1 by Little Hickory by Hickory Bill) produced Mr. Bar None, the 1957 Champion Two-Year-Old Colt and 1958 World's Champion Quarter Running Horse who, out of Red Juniper (by Red Man), sired Mr. Juniper Bar, the 1962 Champion Quarter Running Two-Year-Old Gelding.

You don't have to wear glasses to see the truth about Peter McCue.

AAA AQHA Champions

As stated in paragraph 123 of the *Official Handbook of the American Quarter Horse Association*, the term AQHA Champion is reserved by the Association for its express use and is awarded to individual stallions, mares, and geldings which meet the requirements herewith set forth:

This title may be awarded any stallion, mare or gelding registered in either the Permanent, the Tentative, or the NQHBA Book, or listed in the Appendix Registry or New Appendix Registry of the Association, *after* it has won a total of 30 or more points in competition in official shows and contests recognized by the American Quarter Horse Association, provided:

(a) That the points have been won in two or more shows and two or more contests and under two or more judges.

(b) That at least 12 of the points have been won in halter classes, and of these 12 points a minimum of 4 points must be won in either A or B class shows, and that at least 12 of the points have been won in performance classes.

In the event this title is awarded, a proper certificate is prepared and forwarded to the owner and, also, a proper notation shall be made in an applicable Stud Book and other records of the Association.

The registration certificate of any horse shall be revoked permanently by the Association if the owner thereof fraudulently advertises, claims or holds forth that this certain horse is entitled to the title "AQHA Champion" prior to the title being officially awarded by the Association.

At the forefront of this group of signally honored horses stand the AAA AQHA Champions, representing as they do superb performance on the straightaway in addition to all the other distinctions above set forth. But eighteen horses have thus far qualified for and been awarded this coveted title. They are as follows:

ALFARETTA
BAR BOB
CACTUS COMET
JAGUAR
LEOLA
LEOLITA
LIGHTNING BAR
LITTLE EGYPT
LEO BINGO
THREE PERCENT
KING LEO BAR
LEO TAG
JAG
MR. THREE BARS
OLD TOM CAT
RICKY TAYLOR
SECO BARS
SUGAREE BARS

105. Joe Hancock, by John Wilkens.
Photo courtesty of Burnett Ranches

106. Jack McCue, by Peter McCue. Photo taken a few days before he died.

107. The great sire Midnight, by Badger, by Peter McCue. The photo was taken with Aubra Bowers, his last owner, in the summer of 1935. Midnight died June 22, 1937.

108. One-Eyed Waggoner, by Midnight out of a mare of Yellow Wolf.

. The noted Bill Thomas, by Buck Thomas,
by Peter McCue.

110. Joe Tom, by Joe Hancock, in Albuquerque at five.
Photo by Ferenz Fedor Studios

111. Goldie McCue. She was by Dr. Blue Eyes, by A. D. Reed, by Peter McCue.
She was out of Naome, by Chief (No. 5), by Peter McCue.

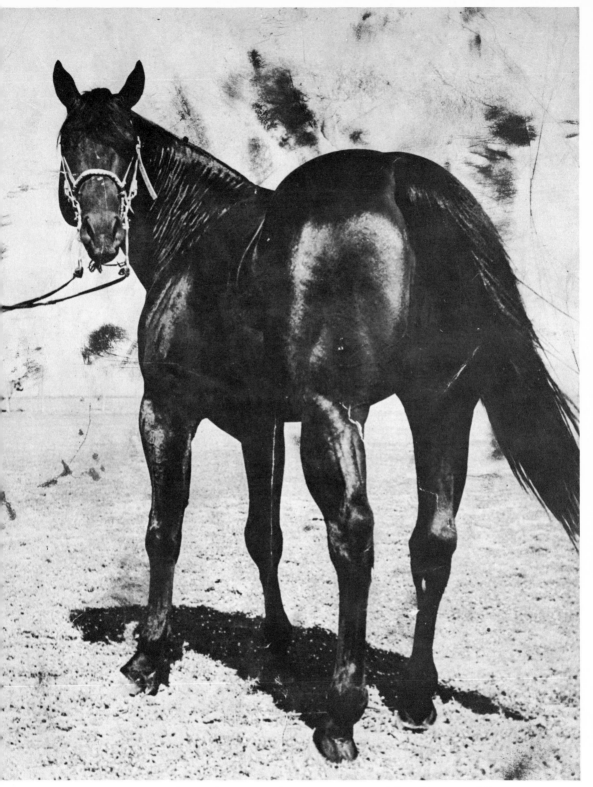

112. Wampus McCue, by Jack McCue, by Peter McCue. The dam was Miss Wampus, by Wampus, TB. The second dam, Black Annie, was by Rodney, by Old D. J. Black Annie was also the dam of Johnny Dial.

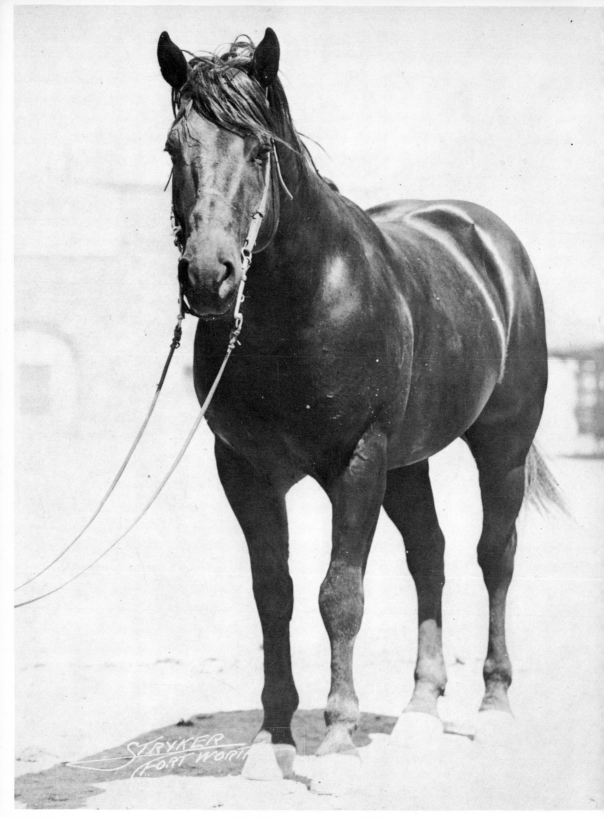

113. Midnight, Jr., by Midnight.

Photo by Stryker-Fort Worth

Grey Badger

114. Grey Badger II, by Midnight, Jr.

Biographical Sketches

Biographical vignettes of some of these AAA Champions will be found in the next several pages.

Alfaretta

A red sorrel roan, and becoming more roan all the time, bald faced and sporting four stockings, branded Triangle Bar on left shoulder, the AAA Running AQHA Champion Alfaretta, bred by Jack Casement at Padroni, Colorado, was foaled in 1953.

Her dam, Cherokee Maiden (P–2008) was rated as one of the finest mares of Casement breeding and as far back as 1951 they were hunting what was hoped would be the ideal mate for her. That summer Bill Welch was running a colt called Robin Reed (a grandson of Joe Reed II by Leo). Welch had been one of the prime movers in the Rocky Mountain Quarter Horse Association and the main promoter of their first pari-mutuel race meet for short horses in Colorado (held at Kremmling). After Welch's colt ran in the Rocky Mountain Futurity at Centennial in the fall of 1951, Jack Casement made overtures relative to breeding a mare. Orville Burtis was at this meet and arranged with Welch to winter Robin Reed for him, ride the colt after cattle, and stand him to a few test mares at his place in Kansas. I am told this plan almost broke the hearts of Mr. and Mrs. John Hazelwood, who had been handling Robin. It was, however, agreed they were to put him back in training the following spring.

Welch knew the Casement mares and said that if Jack would fetch Cherokee Maiden down to Kansas early, he could have a service gratis. So late in April or early May of 1952, having contracted with Bud Warren for a Leo service on another mare, the Casements loaded both, plus Cherokee's eight-day-old foal, and drove the four hundred or so miles to Manhattan. Cherokee was served the next morning and they took the other mare over to Leo. Coming back by way of the Burtis ranch, they had Cherokee served again, just for luck, and brought her and the tiny foal on home. Alfaretta was foaled the following spring, very likely the first of Robin Reed's get to hit the ground.

Cherokee Maiden was sired by Red Dog (P–55). He was by Balleymooney and bred by Dan Casement. Balleymooney was by the Concho Colonel that Dan got from Billy Anson back in 1911. Concho Colonel was by Jim Ned (full brother to Brown Jug, stolen by Pancho Villa). Cherokee Maiden was out of old Papoose, a totally blind mare given Jack Casement by Marshall Peavy. For him she had produced Margie, Champion at Tucson in 1941 or 1942, a real race mare. For the Casements, Papoose dropped Baboon and Cherokee Maiden. Papoose was by the Bob H from Bear River and out of a Bob H mare; according to the way I heard it, Papoose before she went blind won 50 straight short races. Since Cherokee had an Indian name and her dam was called Papoose, Xenia Casement, recalling the lines of an old Pennsylvania song, "Where flowed the waters of the blue Juniata, wild roved an Indian maid, bright Alfaretta," chose the name Alfaretta.

Cherokee Maiden is still with the Casements and will have a Dull Knife foal this spring. A real red sorrel, white marked on face, with two rear stockings and two fore socks, she was foaled on the Casements' Routt County ranch and proved at an early age to have one predominant characteristic—hardheadedness. Also, I am told, she was a "confirmed hypochondriac" and would rather be doctored than eat. She had been almost three before she was broken, did considerable bucking, unloading Jack once, he remembers, when he was working with King Merritt. After she'd also bucked off Jack's older daughter he put her under a pack saddle for a week, and "she gave down like a Jersey." For years she dearly loved to collect wild roses in season and carry them about in her mouth while working cattle. She has had some arthritis in both front knees these past several winters, gets a little more attention, and behaves just about like one of the family.

Robin Reed turned into a good solid AAA track burner and has gotten several exceptionally good colts, some of which have gone to the races. Cherokee had three fillies by him; Alfaretta and Little Moonbeam the Triangle Bar kept, the third topped the 1962 National Western sale at Denver. Jack Casement says: "Our old Cusie mare had three fillies by him, and Little Meow had Old Tom Cat and She Kitty—the former raced AAA by us and made an AQHA Champion by Clarence Roth, his present owner." She Kitty, without much doubt, is the best individual Robin has sired.

Alfaretta was not trained for cow work but was ridden until too heavy with foal. She could spot a cow and was a pleasure to ride, being as catty as they come—so goshblamed quiet you never would have guessed she had made AAA on a race track.

L. R. Pat Thompson (Willard, Colorado) broke and trained her. This was started on the Logan County Fair Grounds at Sterling, then progressed to Centennial, where they were having two Quarter races a day in connection with their Thoroughbred meet.

She was a light runner, handling any kind of track with ease. She was, unfortunately, of the same age as the great colts Bob's Folly and Go Man Go, and was hooked up against them. At Centennial the best she could do was third money in the Rocky Mountain Futurity. She did, however, hold a track record there, equalled a world's record at Albuquerque (not allowed), and beat Go Man Go at Albuquerque. Here is what Van Smelker, then in charge of the *Chartbooks*, had to say of her in the November book for 1956:

As a two-year-old, Pat Thompson's carefully guided Alfaretta made her first start July 22 in a maiden race at Centennial. She outran all but one of the ten-horse field in this 330 yard event, conceding only a neck to the winner, Big Booger. Gaining experience in two subsequent races, she reached the winner's circle August 25 and, to do so, qualified for Grade AA by a handy length and one-half win going 330 yards in :17.6.

In the Rocky Mountain Quarter Horse Futurity trial August 30, she finished a close second to Bob's Folly. On Futurity Day, September 3, she got away quickly and led for a considerable distance only to be overtaken by Bob's Folly and Jayhawker Bar in the final strides.

Alfaretta's freshman year was climaxed at Los Alamitos December 1. Despite a heavy rain, she was clocked in :18.5 over 350 muddy yards, winning by a length and one-half. This easy victory over top juveniles tabbed her as a hot prospect for the 1956 campaign.

Again initiating her season at Centennial, Alfaretta performed profitably with consecutive wins at 350 yards, both in the time of :17.9. These marks, however, did not receive official sanction because of the presence of a tail-wind—an element which confounds many record attempts on the straightaway. Nevertheless, there was no denying her potentiality, for the company she defeated included such AAA performers as Captain Dick, Flicka Hyloah, Ocean Mist, Wall Street, Jaguar, Arrive and Boom Chain. She gained further esteem in the RMQHA Derby June 13. Although Bob's Folly won this quarter-mile feature in :22.3 against a headwind, Alfaretta displaced the rest of the field which included Sure Now, Jayhawker Bar, Bar Three and Cowgirl Star.

After a rest of four months, Alfaretta arrived at the New Mexico State Fair, Albuquerque, to compete in the stake program there. She came very close to victory in her first encounter, beaten a short neck by Bob's Folly at the finish of the 300 yard "Shu Fly," September 30. Nine strong challengers also competed but none got within a length of Bob's Folly and Alfaretta. The seventh annual running of the filly and mare feature, the "Buttons and Bows," gave Alfaretta the chance she had waited for. Breaking on top at the head of the 440 yard chute, she was never headed and was going away by over a length at the finish. Still another record honor was to be denied her, however, for there was difficulty with the electric timer and only hand watches caught her time of :22.1. Fastest official time for this race is held by Maroon, a two-time winner, whose :22.2 stood as a track mark until 1955.

From this same account we learn that Alfaretta's sire, Robin Reed (AAA), held at that time the stallion record of :17.9 for 350 yards; that in four seasons of racing he accumulated 79 Register of Merit points, and was the winner, through disqualification, of the Southwestern Futurity at Tucson in 1951. During his career he started 42 times, garnering 12 wins, nine seconds, and four thirds. His dam, Sue Reed, was declared Grand Champion Mare of the Amarillo Fat Stock Show in 1944; she was by Joe Reed II.

Alfaretta was bred to Bob's Folly early in her fifth year. Her final race was at Brush, Colorado. She had just returned from a trip after halter points to Lincoln, Nebraska, where she was Champion Mare, and was certainly not in racing trim, her pregnancy already obvious; also, the trailer overturned. However, despite all this, she ran the 220 yards in :12.0, but a tailwind caused this record to be disallowed.

In 1959 she dropped Bob's foal, a bay filly imaginatively named Alfie's Folly. This was a hard-luck filly. With a good chance to run second to She Kitty in the Futurity, the horse in the No. 12 slot broke out of the gate, and Alfie's Folly, next to him, flipped and had to be scratched, with She Kitty coming on to win. In the spring of her three-year-old form, Alfie's Folly stifled herself while in training at Raton and had to be retired from track competition. She had started 15 times, for four wins, two seconds, and one third. Six of these outings were labeled officially AAA.

Alfaretta's second foal, Little Chloe (by Three Bars), an almost solid light sorrel, began her track work at Raton, winning her first out. This was in the second division of the Raton Futurity trials. Her second start at Raton was in the Juvenile Quarter Horse Handicap, which she took by one and one-half lengths. Her third outing was at Ruidoso, a win in the Open Futurity trials, and she went on the next week to win the main event; then back to Raton, where she copped an extra–tough feature at 350 in :17.6. At Ruidoso again she was a close second in her division of the All-American Futurity trials, being made favorite for the main dash. It was later discovered, I am told, that she injured herself in this trial; this may have had something to do with her subsequent performance—she did no better than sixth in the big run. X-rays revealed a chipped knuckle in her knee, so she was returned home and put on pasture. All her races were in AAA time; in one of them she beat the sensational Jet Deck. At the 1963 AQHA Convention at Tulsa, Little Chloe was elected Champion Quarter Running Two-Year-Old Filly of 1962.

Alfaretta's third foal, Barbiturate, a full sister to Chloe, is a decided roan like her mama, and more of a down-on-the-ground Quarter type than Little Chloe. She will be broken and readied, and will make her debut on the tracks in 1963.

Pat Thompson, her trainer, has this to say of Alfaretta:

In her maiden year she was a sleepy, good-looking filly. At three, and older, every record she made was denied her, even after setting some of them twice.

She is a great mare any way one measures her, on the track, in the show ring, and in the brood-mare band. One should feel very proud to breed, own, or train such a fine individual. When she was two, Casement asked me if I thought she would make AAA. I told him, "She has not reached her best, but will in her three-year-old form"—and she did! In her second season she would run a good 350 in the spring (:17.9 twice), but didn't care to go on; it has been said she could not run a full quarter. I said that in the fall of the year she might. After three starts in the spring (two firsts and one second) she was turned out and rested at the Casement ranch.

Her fall campaign began at Albuquerque. Her first outing there was a 300-yard stakes. At the gate she broke so hard she fell, or slipped, then got up and ran second, beaten only by a neck. Her next start was the quarter-mile "Buttons and Bows." Breaking fast, she was on top all the way to win by plenty of daylight in :22.1. It equaled the new Track Record just set by Go Man Go. In her next start, the Championship Quarter Mile, she broke, slipped, recovered, and went to the front, leading, when Ridge Butler started laying his shoulder against her hip and crowding her. No attempt was made to take him off. Finally put off balance, she broke stride and finished fifth.

She never was the same. Her back was hurt and continued to bother her the rest of her career even though she ran some good races in this condition. In the fall, at Los Alamitos, she met the best there and beat most of them. Her best race there was when she outran Dividend. She broke on top and opened up daylight, then went to loafing. Dividend took a strong run at her. She turned on again to win a very fast 350 from a mighty tough veteran.

When she was being campaigned, the purses were much lower than they are now. Being good herself, she had to run against the best and proved to be a very honest mare. Our biggest disappointment was when the AQHA Racing Committee sat down at a table and gave the three-year-old filly honors to someone else after she had plainly earned them.

Alfaretta earned 18 points in halter competition and was made an AQHA Champion after her racing career was over.

Bar Bob

In the spring of 1952 Mr. R. W. "Pat" Patterson of Filer, Idaho, a breeder and trainer of Quarter running horses, stopped off at Quincy Farm (Denver) on his way home from delivering several mares to the court of Three Bars (TB). One of those mares was Della Bob (P–13,573), a chestnut mare by Leo out of Sailor Bob (by Flying Bob). During the course of this visit with Ed Honnen, Quincy Farm acquired Della Bob; and on May

115. War Chief, by Joe Hancock, rounding the turn in a quarter mile race at
Albuquerque.

116. Old Squaw, probably Coke Roberds' best mare.

117. Coke Roberds-bred horse, Ute Chief, by Dundee, TB, out of Old Squaw.

118. Top Flight: his dam was a double-bred Peter McCue.

119. Red Man, by Joe Hancock.

120. Chubby, by Midnight. Bred at Vernon, Texas, by the Waggoner Ranch.

121. Harmon Baker, by Peter McCue.

Photo by Tommy Thompson

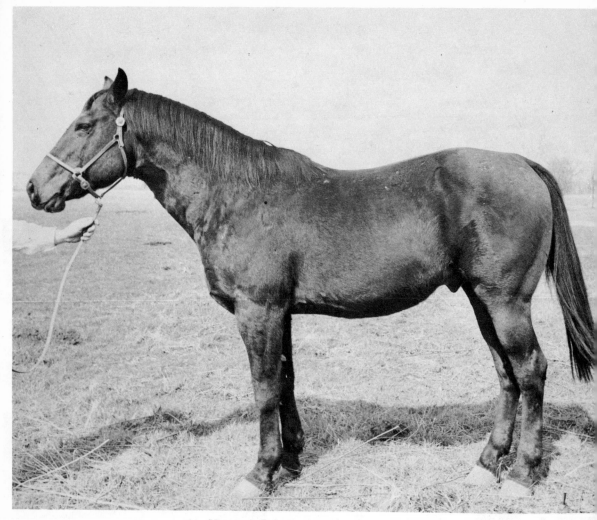

122. Harmon Baker's Star, by Harmon Baker.

123. Alfaretta, after her last race. Leroy Tipton is the rider. Jack Casement lifts hat.

124. Bar Bob.

Photo by W. Pickett

6, 1953, Bar Bob (P–56,698), a dark chestnut, was foaled by this mare on Honnen's farm.

As a yearling Bar Bob was entered by Mr. Honnen in the spring of 1954 in his first halter show, at Denver, where he won his class. At about this time Ralph Bell, of California, purchased the colt from Quincy Farm, Bell keeping the colt until he went to the tracks. Shortly after being put in competition Bar Bob was sold by Bell to C. H. Hall of Casper, Wyoming, who continued to race the colt until May of 1957.

In his three years on the straightaways Bar Bob (AAA) started 71 times for, according to the official record spread before me, 12 firsts, eight seconds, and 16 thirds, earning $11,140.81. In working performance events he corraled 31½ points to be added to his 36 points at racing. It should be mentioned in passing that his earnings were improved considerably by races on unrecognized tracks. One of his trainers, E. R. Beddo, declares he never would let himself be bested getting out of the gates and always ran an honest race.

The Simmons & Wiberg Stables, Inc., purchased Bar Bob from Dr. Hall on July 25, 1958, and fetched him to Layton, Utah, which is still his home, although recently he has been holding court at the stables of Edwin Beauchamp, Phoenix, Arizona, at a fee of $500.

Mrs. Simmons tells me: "At the time of his purchase we had only just become interested in Quarter Horses, having bought our first mare but a few months before. We bought Bar Bob on the strength of his top breeding and racing performance, relying strictly on Dr. Hall's integrity and given evaluation; he has become one of our most valued friends and we have since bought many other horses from him.

"We had no idea Bar Bob was also a halter horse. We had been told that race horses, especially those with Three Bars' blood, were not much good except for running and that not many had much of a record in halter or working classes. As it turned out, the first show we went to—the Davis County Fair—we attended without Bob, convinced he could not be halter shown.

"During the later winter of that year, having acquired some 15 mares, we were fortunate in obtaining the services of Dude Parke (Malta, Idaho) as trainer and stable manager. Dude, with his lovely wife Dee, came to Layton and, in the early spring of 1959—we having arranged with a neighbor to borrow some cattle—started Bar Bob's education in cutting. Five weeks later he went into competition, a jackpot cutting on Easter Sunday at Star, Idaho. The year before Dude had won this event on another horse. To our great joy Bar Bob, Dude up, placed third in the novice, taking first in the open, getting his name on the revolving trophy his first time out."

Bar Bob developed into quite a ham once he got into the swing of things and Dude started packing him around to the shows. His fast action in cutting competitions drew a lot of applause and he became very popular with cutting enthusiasts. Once, at Spokane, Washington, Mrs. Simmons relates, he actually stopped to look around at the stands between cows as though he were waiting for the crowd's approval, going back to work when the applause was forthcoming, never once losing control of his critter.

After five shows he was removed from the novice class. In 1959 he gained his ROM in open cutting and Dude started showing him at halter. In that year he became the third Quarter Horse to receive the coveted AAA AQHA Championship. It was seldom he came home from a show with anything less than blue ribbons; he generally walked off with the purple of either Grand or Reserve Champion. Mrs. Simmons says: "Our records show 72 points as of August, 1961."

In 1960 Bar Bob was retired to stud. Many AQHA judges, inspectors, and breeders have told Simmons & Wiberg that Bar Bob has the most perfect Quarter Horse conformation they have seen. "He has a wonderful disposition, very gentle and kind," I have been told. "While he will tolerate women to the extent of allowing the Simmons' daughter to exercise him daily, he is strictly a man's horse. He likes nothing better than to be saddled up for a good hard ride. He seems to be a horse that will do anything you ask of him, whether it's western pleasure, reining, cutting, racing, or standing at halter." And Mrs. Simmons says: "My eleven-year-old granddaughter rides him beautifully."

A lot of these qualities appear to be cropping up in his get. His books at stud have always been full. "In fact," Mr. Simmons declares, "we have turned down many requests for service."

During 1961 Bar Bob was first in the nation in the Get of Sire classes with 24 credits.

1961 Get of Sire Class Winners—Top Five

Sire	Credits
#BAR BOB, Ch. 53 by Three Bars (TB)	24
Leo San, Ch. 49 by LEO	22
STEEL BARS, Blk. 53 by Three Bars (TB)	22
#POCO DELL, B. 50 by #POCO BUENO	17
#PAUL A., Blk. 48 by Star Deck	15

Says Mrs. Simmons: "We have yet to find a mare he does not cross with. This year (1963) Bar Bob's first foals went to the tracks, and the three we have records of have already received ROM rating. At halter My Dandy Bob, a colt of 1960, appeared in 19 shows as a yearling, taking 14 firsts, one second, one third, two fourths, and one fifth, being named three times Grand Champion Stallion and twice as Junior Reserve Champion Stallion." My Dandy Bob is currently, I am told, competing on the straight-aways.

Bar Bob stuck fast to his last by repeating in 1962 his mark of '61, as may be seen by the list below.

Leading Get of Sire Class Winners—Top Ten (Credits Earned as Follows):

Entries in class	Credits for					
	1st	2nd	3rd	4th	5th	6th
2 – 3	1	0	0	0	0	0
4 – 5	2	1	0	0	0	0
6 – 7	3	2	1	0	0	0
8 – 10	4	3	2	1	0	0
11 – 13	5	4	3	2	1	0
14 & over	6	5	4	3	2	1

Sire	Credits
#BAR BOB, Ch. 53 by Three Bars (TB)	18
#POCO DELL, B. 50 by #POCO BUENO	15
Poco Lad, B. 55 by #POCO CHAMP	15
Leo San, Ch. 49 by LEO	14
#EXCUSE, B. 57 by Showdown	12
#SKIPITY SKIP, S. 53 by Skipper W	11
LEMAC, S. 49 by LEO	10
#SNIPPER REED, D. 56 by LOGAN'S BOBBY REED	10
STEEL BARS, Blk. 53 by Three Bars (TB)	9
Babe Cody, Ch. 54 by Bill Cody	8

And Brenda Sue topped the corresponding list for females, showing Bar Bob's get as produce of dam.

1962 Leading Produce of Dam' Class Winners

Dam	Credits
Brenda Sue, B. 53 by Claude	19
Bertoma, Br. 53 by Bert	16
Dana Wilson, Gr. 47 by Wilson's Smoky Joe	14
Sherry Sue, S. 55 by Jack R.	14

Tallulah, Ch. 49 by King Bob	14
Joe Hildreth H, Br. 45 by Old Man	12
Major Miss, S. 53 by MAJOR KING	12
#G-FERN HARD SAUCE, B. 51 by Joe Bob	10
Miss Red Ant, S. 48 by Little Jodie	10
Judy Mitchell, Br. 54 by Billy Tom	9

Bar Bob has recently been purchased by Louis Dorfman and George M. Underwood, Jr. at a very high figure and is currently standing at the Dorfman ranch at Celina, Texas.

Jag

This bay stallion of 1957 was bred and raised by Quincy Farm and is the pleasing result of breeding best to best, and, as Ed Honnen says, "getting the best." Jag, from the first, showed much promise, being fast, of excellent conformation, and with a determined disposition.

He was sired by the Honnen stallion Jaguar (P–46483) by Custus Rastus (TB), and is out of the good mare Leola (discussed among Outstanding Modern Mares in Part VII), by Leo out of Betty Warren by King, P–234.

Jag was sent to the track as a two-year-old under the able guidance of Tommy Dean. In his first eight races he took five, was second twice, and out of the money but once. He finished a neck back of Table Tennis for all of it in the Pomona Futurity of 1959, run in the graded time of :17.9. This would, at that time, have been a world record except for a ruling that no world records would be acceptable if achieved with any tail wind. There was a four-mile-per-hour tail wind blowing during that race. Jag went on to win the Kansas Futurity. He raced through his fourth year and was retired to stud at Quincy Farm. He won 32 points toward his AAA AQHA Championship on the straightaways.

While at stud Jag was shown at halter, being named Grand Champion at Sweetwater, Texas, at the American Royal at Kansas City, and at Dewey, Oklahoma. In this field of Quarter Horse endeavor Jag won 12 points.

Ed Honnen tells me that Jag is the only AAA AQHA Champion in the world which can boast of both parents having the same distinction. All three are AAA AQHA Champions!

Jag's first crop of colts are now yearlings and they look extremely good. You can see class all over them.

Quincy Farm sold Jag in the fall of 1962 to Dr. M. W. Ickes of Nampa, Idaho, Ivon Maggard, and D. A. Wood, who now have him in public service at Nampa.

125. Jag (P-97,226), by Jaguar out of Leola, by Leo.

126. Jaguar, by Custus Rastus, TB, out of Mame Taylor, by Jack Dempsey.

127. Leola, by Leo out of Betty Warren, by King, and the man who buys her groceries.

128. Leolita, by Leo out of Swamp Angel, by Grano De Oro.

129. Lightning Bar, by Three Bars, TB.

Photo by B. T. "Ben" Maxey

130. Little Egypt, by Texas Dandy out of Jezebel, by Pigeon.

Photo by C. H. and Eva M. Potts

131. Old Tom Cat, by Robin Reed.

Photo by Darol Dickinson

132. Old Tom Cat, just after winning his final race.

Photo by Ralph Morgan

PACIFIC COAST QUARTER HORSE RACING ASSOCIATION FUTURITY
Sept. 22, 1956   350 yds. - 18.1   Purse $15,000.
9th. Race - Los Angeles County Fair

1st.   CUTE TRICK -   Jockey John Orosco   OWNER: R.S. SNEDIGAR
Deadheat for Place
       RICKY TAYLOR   Jockey Richard Beasley   OWNER: HUGH HUNTLEY
       MOBILE'S MITE   Jockey Richard Strauss   OWNER: ERMA MAWSON

133. Ricky Taylor in a dead heat for second in the 1956 renewal of the Pacific
Coast Quarter Horse Racing Association Futurity.

134. Sugaree Bars, by Sugar Bars out of Randle's Lady, by Doc Horn.

Jaguar

Showing considerable speed and much agility as a weanling and a sleek ever-readiness remindful of the cat, this dark stallion was named Jaguar by Lewis Blackwell, his breeder. He was out of Mamie Taylor (spelled Mame, these days, by the *Stud Book*), dam also of AAA Ricky Taylor and the celebrated Hard Twist, a top horse in the middle 1940's, a great broodmare sire and the Stallion Co-champ (with Clabbertown G and Bart B.S.) of 1951 who, for his astonishing record-smashing running proclivities was affectionately dubbed "Come-Back King of the Quarter."

Mamie Taylor (P-6990) was a sprinting daughter of the great Jack Dempsey, a sprinter himself and the sire of several extremely fine matrons, not to mention running horses. I first wrote about Mamie away back when the AQHA was scarcely out of its swaddling clothes. They were spelling the name "Mamie" when I first knew this mare and called attention to her sire's possibilities. Bred in 1934 by Louis Kirk, who was training and running his own string of sprinters by the time he was fourteen (and who in the late 1940's had one of my own raising), Mamie was campaigned from hell to breakfast. Louie gave his wife Mamie Taylor for a wedding present and she thereafter raced in the colors of Vivian Kirk. She cut her swath out in back of beyond before the AQRA came into existence, and she did not have the benefit of the innovations and standards established by organized Quarter Racing. By the system of grading now employed I would say she probably would rate as AA+ (or AAA−). During her time in the sun she was sometimes sensational. (Interested persons may find a write-up by me on the career of Louie Kirk and his horses in the April, 1949, issue of the *Texas Livestock Journal*).

Jaguar's sire was Custus Rastus (TB) by Requested out of Slim Rosie by Tryster. Among other good get, Custus Rastus numbers Ricky Taylor, AAA; Chickadoo, AAA; Gold Note, AAA; and Solid Sada (a chestnut colt of 1960), who was never headed when winning the 13th renewal of the Colorado Breeders' Stakes at Centennial in 1962 by five open lengths.

Jaguar, graded AAA, ran with the best. He was twice second by a short head to Ridge Butler, the Champion Two-Year-Old Colt of 1954. He was a very honest runner, generally taking off with a great burst of speed. In one race at Los Alamitos he tore one hind shoe partly off, cutting the other hind leg as he came out of the gate. Of course this threw him badly off stride, but, gathering himself, he went on and, with a wild burst of determined effort, won the race. He was a pretty popular horse around the tracks, an individual of fine appearance, excellent manners, and demonstrated determination. He became an AQHA Champion, proving that running wasn't all he could do.

He is standing now at Quincy Farm, Denver; and, considering his age, is doing very well. His get have proven themselves both in track work and at halter. One of his good sons, Jag (at the top of AAA and also an AQHA Champion), was Champion of the American Royal, Odessa, Las Vegas, and other prominent shows.

Coys Bananza, a son living in Ohio, has also proven a top halter horse and has run AA his first season.

One of the noticeable characteristics of Jaguar is his extremely good disposition, an asset he passes on to his foals. He produces the type capable of doing whatever they are put into training to do. On the track he has beaten such outstanding sprinters as Palleo Pete, Joe Queen, Rocket Bar, Vanetta Dee, Diamond Mae, La Bar, and Miss Myrna Bar. In the Los Alamitos Derby of 1955, he finished back of the winner by less than a head.

Among others he has sired are Cut Loose, AAA; Lady Jag, AAA; Jag's Jewel, AAA; Miss Hot Heels, AAA; Jagette, AA; Jagalong, AA; and Amber Jag, AA.

Leola

Bred by Bud Warren at Perry, Oklahoma, and sold to John Shuman of Deertrail, Colorado, as a yearling, Leola was sired by Leo (by Joe Reed II) out of Betty Warren by King (P-234, by Zantanon). Through her third year Leola was raced and shown by Shuman, at which time she was purchased by Ed Honnen and taken to Quincy Farm, Denver. Honnen kept her on the track one more year then retired her to the stud. She was foaled in 1948.

As a race mare she won the Colorado, Wyoming, and Kansas Futurities; she also won the Colorado Derby. She was an outstanding performer, graded AAA, and raced also in Arizona and California. Most fans will recall her as a fat little filly that ran with her legs simply flying under her. In many ways she was a masculine-type mare, not easy to beat. She was an ideal type for match racing because no one, eyeing her, would imagine she could run. In this respect her looks were deceitful; she ran with a great deal of heart, never giving up.

At halter she won many points at the big shows in Colorado, being Grand Champion several times. Her toughest competition around Colorado was the beautiful filly April Star, owned by Hugh Bennett, the great roping champion.

Leola's first foal was a filly by Three Bars that looked exceptionally promising; this foal was stolen from a Quincy Farm pasture one night shortly after being weaned. No trace of her was ever found.

It seems altogether possible Leola may become known to posterity as one of the top daughters of Leo, who is one of the truly great brood-mare sires and a top sire of running horses for better than ten years. She is one of the many great Leo mares owned by Quincy Farm.

Under the heading *Triple Crown Quarter Horse* I did a story on Leola back in 1952. At that time I said:

Before Bud Warren became prominent in breeding circles as the owner of the celebrated Leo, he had a mare which had shown quite a bit of early speed. Called Betty Warren, she was by Jess Hankins' horse, King, a grandson of Little Joe (by Traveler). Mr. Warren bred this mare to Leo, knowing she had raced as a two-year-old, finishing second by a nose in the Oklahoma Futurity of 1946. Bud thought Leo might get her a topflight foal, and he sure did.

Named Leola, she was first put under saddle by Gary Marble, helped by his brother Norman. She belonged at this time to John Shuman of the Z Lazy V. Norman Marble wanted to make a dogging horse out of her but Shuman took her home and, about the first of January, turned her over to Elmer "Corky" Keen who readied her for racing. After about a month of Corky's schooling, John, wanting to see how she was coming, suggested running her at Laura Gal, a retired race mare. Leola ran away from her.

The training was continued on Shuman's ranch and a good bit of gate work added to the program. Early in March she was matched at Revenue Barnes, considered then to be the fastest horse in Colorado. Everyone said Shuman ought to have his head looked at but, come race day, John and Corky loaded her and drove the 60 miles to Denver. Arrived, they rested her one hour and then got her ready for the Big Try. The deal was set up for the race to be run at Barnes' ranch and out of his own starting gate with which his horse felt plumb at home.

When they turned them loose Revenue, naturally, broke on top. But a couple of jumps later Leola had him and at 200 yards she had him daylighted.

A short time later some of the hometown boys produced a Thoroughbred mare for her to run at. Leola led the entire distance, finishing five lengths in front; in this 220 one watch made it a cool :12.0; the other watch called it :12.2—Leo Crouse said: "She flew!"

Before selling her, Bud Warren had nominated her for the Southwestern Futurity at Tucson; Shuman decided to pay up and haul her over there, a little matter of some 1200 miles. They departed Deer Trail on April 9, got into Tucson in the evening of the 11th and put her into the Trials on the 15th—no time wasted on change of altitude nor the fact that for the first time in her life she'd be facing a large crowd. She finished second to Little Smoke Echols (the current sensation), that division of the Trials being run in :17.4; because of a tailwind she was officially credited, a length off the winner, with :17.7. Four days later in the main event she broke badly under Joe Hungerford. Little Smoke, coming out on top, ran across her nose and she couldn't regain enough ground to come into the money. At this time she was 22 months old. Had Corky been on her we might have had a different story.

Her next start was at Kremmling where she won a 330 under wraps by three lengths in :17.8. Three days later she ran away with the finals of the Rocky Mountain Futurity in :17.9, still under wraps, by three good lengths. Shuman was sitting on the rail and, as she went past, he jumped back. The photofinish man told us later he would have missed her entirely if he hadn't seen John scrambling for shore.

From Kremmling they hauled her north for the Wyoming Futurity. This was run on the 8th of July. Again she won by three solid lengths under a tight hold, time around a curve being :18.5 with Corky Keen up. From Laramie she went home for a short breather.

By this time you may imagine there was a considerable number of bets being offered that she would not steal the big race at Enid; there'd be some tough stock there and she would get her come-uppance. Shuman paid no attention.

Early in August they loaded her for Enid, arriving August 7. The Trials were run on the night of the 10th. Leola's backers were feeling a mite nervous, what with the lights and all the commotion. She drew in with Bo Peep C, which had just walked away with the Pawhuska Futurity. John put Corky Keen in the irons. Leola drew the rail, Bo Peep right beside her. As on all previous occasions, Shuman told the boy to make 'A' time if he could. This was a 220 and she took the heat by a length and a quarter in :12.7—Bo Peep finishing second.

John Shuman told me, "After she passed this test and was definitely headed for a Triple Crown, we kept her under our eyes day and night. I had already been offered a lot of money to pull her. The Finals of this Oklahoma Futurity were run the night of August 12 and a bushel of dough was bet on this race."

Smart money was split between Leola and Smooth Sailing who had won his division in the same time credited to the Shuman filly. Smooth Sailing drew the outside rail—fastest lane on the track that night. John says: "I was pretty sure we could outrun him because I had been on hand when he won his trial and the boy had been using the bat pretty free. Still, fellows like Walter Merrick and Oscar Cox had bet generously on Smooth Sailing, so I couldn't be sure of anything really. Everyone I knew on the grounds helped me take her to the paddock for saddling. It was quite an event."

Leola broke on top and never was headed. Corky just let her go as she would. She made it by a length and a half in :12.5—just one tenth off the two-year-old record.

It was John Shuman's fault she did not set a new record. He'd instructed Corky he wasn't to touch her so long as she led. The Smooth Sailing contingent got to chewing their toenails because their hero had failed to make it. John offered to run Leola against him for $1000 a side, anywhere and any distance. That ended the conversation.

Turning Leola over to Pete Durfey and Corky, Shuman went back to farming his ranch. The boys fetched Leola to Centennial and on August 30 entered her in a field of 10—mostly aged veterans. This 330 she won in :17.2, paying $10, 4.20 and 3.60. From that day on she was "Denver's Darling"— they even made her the favorite last summer when she ran against Bright Eyes, but she was training off and made a poor showing. Since she had won seven races out of nine starts, including three futurities and a derby, they pulled her shoes and laid her up for the winter.

One of her finest performances was the dash she made in the Rocky Mountain Derby at Centennial after a siege of distemper. Ralph Smith was handling her then and had been in the business for a good many years. It was a 12-horse field, 440 yards, all carrying 120. Leola was practically bet into the ground. She came out like a bolt of blue lightning, daylighted the field on the second or third jump and coasted to an effortless win in :22.7 by electric timer.

She was the first Quarter Horse of either sex to win three futurities.

Leolita

Leolita, chestnut mare, 1949, was bred by Bud Warren of Perry, Oklahoma. She was by Leo out of Swamp Angel (P–1723) by Grano de Oro, who was by Little Joe out of the well-known race mare Della Moore. Della was by Old D. J. (Dedier) out of Belle by Sam Rock; Dedier was by Crazy Cue out of Meon by Carlos. Further back than this things get a little fuzzy, the general assumption being that Crazy Cue was a son of Kantaka (TB), or something which sounds like that. Della Moore, supposedly foaled in 1903, was bred by Ludovic Stemmans of Scott, Louisiana.

Swamp Angel, dam of Leolita, is also the dam (by Leo) of Leota W, winner of the first Oklahoma Futurity, 1947–220 in :12.4. Trained by John Hazelwood, Leota started 16 times, won 14 and placed in both of the others, running against the best of her time. Co-holder of the Two-Year-Old Filly Championship, she went on to be narrowly beaten for three-year-old honors by Stella Moore in 1948.

Leolita was sold by Mr. Warren to Quincy Farm, Denver, as a short three, after being shown and raced through her first track season, winning the Kansas Futurity, and being officially rated AAA. She was class winner at Fort Worth and Reserve Champion at the Chicago International as a yearling. She was raced and shown during her third and fourth years by Quincy Farm, after which Ed Honnen retired her to stud.

She is an AQHA AAA Champion with many Grand Championships to her credit. She won the Kansas Derby and proved to be a very hard-knocking campaigner that would do her best over any kind of track and against any competition. She is one of those that helped in no small fashion to build the reputation of her illustrious sire. She was always one of Bud Warren's favorites and can solidly stand on her demonstrable record of superior performance.

In the stud she is a proven producer of top-quality working and racing offspring. Her oldest foal, Quincy Brand, is an AQHA Champion and one of the two top roping and reining horses in Colorado during 1962; he made the AQHA Honor Roll in roping for 1963, I am told.

Another of Leolita's foals is Good, an AAA race horse that has also been doing a top-performance job in working events in Montana since his retirement from the straightaways. Leolita's other foals, all fillies, have been placed in the brood-mare band at Quincy Farm.

Lightning Bar

Mr. Pollard says: "Anytime discussion revolves around the subject of leading sires of Quarter stock the name of this horse invariably comes into the conversation." Well, sir, it could very well do it. He was only a sire for five short seasons but a lot of his get got onto the tracks, and they have generally been horses that had to be outrun. Through December 31, 1962, he had 155 registered foals. Seventy-nine of these were started, 49 qualified for the Register of Merit and 35 of those achieved AAA. This is a considerable record in anybody's language—nor was he any burro on the racing circuit. In ten starts he had four wins, placed three times and showed once.

At Pomona, on September 20, 1953, he was credited with equaling the Two-Year-Old Colt Record for 330 yards (:17.2), which in that day was also a Track Record. To name a few of his triumphs, he defeated such speedsters as Super Charge, Pokey Vandy, That's My Boy, Miss Myrna Bar, Deep Water, Miss Wonder Bar, Clabber Juan, Cochina, Dandy Time, and Oleo.

He was a son of Three Bars (TB) out of Della P by Doc Horn (TB). Although unraced, Della P has had an enviable record as a matron. The well-remembered Bardella was another of her foals, full sister to Lightning Bar. Della P was also the dam of Tarantula, Intrigue, and Dell Reed. Art Pollard remarks: "Unfortunately for me, she was already an aged mare when I acquired her from Dink Parker."

Not until his fifth and final year at stud did the owners of top producing mares begin to really notice him and commence sending their better matrons to Lightning Bar's court. The performance of his get from generally unproved mares certainly argues that, had he lived, he would have been a sire to reckon with. On the Leading Sires of Register of Merit Qualifiers list, 1945 through 1962, he was ninth with 23 or more qualifiers and fifth with 11 or more AAA get. We find this, in view of his age and short service, rather remarkable.

Among his outstanding get to date are Pana Bar, AAA, Champion Quarter Running Two-Year-Old Colt of 1958, and Lightning Belle, which has banked in excess of $54,000 from three wins and seven seconds out of 12 starts and was very nearly named Champion Quarter Running Filly of 1962. Other good sons and daughters are Cactus Comet, AAA AQHA Champion; Manor Born, AAA winner of the 1962 Southwestern Futurity at Tucson; Dick Killian, AAA record holder at Rillito Park; Heads Or Tails, winner of four straight AAA races in 1962; Silhoubar, in the stud at Wildorado, Texas; Miss Belle Bar, dam of the winner of the 1963 Southwestern Futurity (fifteenth renewal); Explosive, senior sire at an important stud in Seattle; Roan Light, winner of the 1960 Montana Quarter Horse Futurity.

"Someone once said," Mr. Pollard remarked, "that a man deserves one good woman and one good dog in his lifetime. To that quip I would add one good horse. I certainly had one in Lightning Bar."

Little Egypt

Foaled on the Finley Ranch at Gilbert, Arizona, in 1949, Little Egypt, named after the dancing girl whose likeness decorated the back bars of many old-time saloons, was sired by Texas Dandy (P–2112), a son of My Texas Dandy (P–4900) by * Porte Drapeau, (TB). Her dam was Jezebel (P–2760), by Pigeon out of Molly F (by the Parker Dun out of a mare by Ben Hur—the sire of Waggoner's Rainy Day). Pigeon, by Red Joe of Arizona (by Joe Reed, P–3) in 1957 was maternal grandsire of three Register of Merit sprinters.

Texas Dandy, though he qualified for ROM, is better known as a sire of show and running horses. He was frequently well up on the Leading Sires of Register of Merit Qualifiers list during the last half of the 1940's. In 1952 this list (top 12) read as follows:

Sire	ROM	AA
Flying Bob	37	15
JOE REED II	31	15
My Texas Dandy	29	8
LEO	26	11
CLABBER	25	13
PIGGIN STRING (TB)	24	10
LITTLE JOE, JR.	16	9

TEXAS DANDY	16	6
Chicaro Bill	16	3
Three Bars (TB)	14	7
HARD TWIST	14	6
RED MAN	14	5

In 1953 a son of Texas Dandy, Big Dan, was eighth on the list of Leading Money Winning Horses. On the 1955 Sires of Money Winners list Texas Dandy was fifteenth; among leading sires of two-year-old qualifiers that year he stood fourth. Breeders may find it instructive to consider the following tabulation:

Leading Sires of Register of Merit Qualifiers list, 1945 through 1951—Top Ten

Sire	AAA	AA	A
Three Bars (TB) by Percentage	30	12	16
LEO by JOE REED II	18	30	26
PIGGIN STRING (TB) by Ariel	15	18	16
Depth Charge (TB) by Bold Venture	12	7	12
Top Deck (TB) by Equestrian	11	7	4
HARD TWIST by Cowboy	8	16	7
TEXAS DANDY by My Texas Dandy	8	13	13
VANDY by Going Light (TB)	8	6	4
JOE REED II by Joe Reed	6	25	23
Question Mark by Plaudit	5	6	7

Leading Sires of Money Earners (1949 through 1957)—Top Fifteen

Sires	Starters	Winners	Cumulative Earnings
Three Bars (TB) by Percentage	141	100	$528,128
LEO by JOE REED II	195	119	307,312
Top Deck (TB) by Equestrian	49	33	246,204
JOE REED II by Joe Reed	136	85	205,746
VANDY by Going Light (TB)	50	36	198,067
Depth Charge (TB) by Bold Venture	45	31	184,060
PIGGIN STRING (TB) by Ariel	78	57	154,895
HARD TWIST by Cowboy	64	33	129,948
CLABBER II by CLABBER	37	21	127,626
War Bam (TB) by War Glory	28	25	114,737
TEXAS DANDY by My Texas Dandy	69	40	101,957
ED ECHOLS by Zantanon	43	29	101,105
Question Mark by Plaudit	53	30	93,989
Hysition (TB) by Hygro	18	13	86,626
Joe Moore by Little Joe	31	16	82,515

1957 Leading Money Earning Sires—Top Ten

Sires	Start-ers	Starts	1sts	2nds	3rds	Earnings
Three Bars (TB) by Percentage	74	733	127	106	108	$161,932.28
VANDY by Going Light (TB)	32	314	57	59	31	75,718.20
Top Deck (TB) by Equestrian	33	269	34	33	36	59,629.47
LEO by JOE REED II	58	493	72	54	58	50,940.53
Direct Win (TB) by With Regards	16	145	23	10	15	42,888.96
CLABBER II by CLABBER	29	356	36	34	49	39,532.63
Be Sure Now (TB) by War Admiral	5	41	10	3	3	33,657.44
JOE REED II by Joe Reed	19	255	32	30	34	29,967.79
War Bam (TB) by War Glory	18	260	31	27	26	28,795.00
SPOTTED BULL (TB) by *Bull Dog	24	169	25	20	19	24,136.65

The Finley Ranches bred Little Egypt in the hope of getting a race horse with typical Quarter Horse conformation. She started 10 times as a two-year-old in 1951 for three firsts, three seconds, and two thirds. She set a new Two-Year-Old Filly record for 330 yards (Southwest Futurity trials, Tucson) in :17.5 and defeated such horses as Bit, Barjo, Running Iron, Little Sister W, Queen O' Clubs, Robin Reed, Parker's Trouble, and K Hornet.

John Hazelwood, her trainer, says: "She was one of the easiest horses I've ever handled, so honest in putting out all her effort each time she started. She was always sound and retired without a pimple on her."

Paul Jaquez and Manny Figueroa (Sr.) were mostly aboard her, though occasionally Robert Kennedy and J. D. Walker were in the irons. Hazelwood considered her a tough mare to beat. "Besides setting four World's Records, she pushed three other horses to World records in beating her."

As a three-year-old in 1952 she started 26 times for five firsts, five seconds, and eight thirds. Her records (at Rillito) were all Filly records—250 yards in :13.6, defeating K Hornet by one and one-half lengths; 300 yards in :15.9, defeating Barjo by a head; and 220 yards in :12.2 (one-tenth off World Record), defeating Hy Dale by one-half length. The 250- and 220-yard records were Three-Year-Old Filly records and, after eleven years of racing, still stand.

In her third year form she whipped such speedsters as Bart B.S., Miss Tacubaya, Black Easter Bunny, Monita, Tidy Step, Chudej's Black Gold, Miss Ruby, Lorane's Vandy, Grey Question, Dandy Z, J. B. King, I'll Do It, Mr. Prince, Hy Dale, Miss B K, Silhouette, Jady, Barjo, and K Hornet.

Her sire was run mostly as a match race horse though he ran enough purse races to be qualified. Her dam, Jezebel, was unraced.

Shown at halter as a yearling, Little Egypt won many blue ribbons in Arizona and California. She attended halter shows, when not racing, through her fourth year, winning many grand championships while in training for track competition. In 1951 she was Grand Champion Mare of the Tucson show at 11:00 P.M. at the county fairgrounds and the following afternoon set a Two-Year-Old Filly record (Rillito) at 330 yards.

In 1952 she received the AQHA Roll of Honor certificate for racing, having the most Association points of any horse in competition; she accumulated 39 points in track competition, more than any horse has earned in any given year since. That same year she became an AQHA Champion.

Thus far, in the stud Little Egypt has been bred only to Three Bars (TB), producing seven foals. Four have raced—Casbar (AAA), Bank Night (AAA), Bar Flirt (AAA), and Zanzabar (AA). Three—too young to race—met with accidents and died. Bar Flirt and Zanzabar died of a virus, which I am told was contracted at Ruidoso. Her son Casbar (now at stud) also won the Southwest Futurity (1956) making a track record which still stands (330 yards in :17.1). Miss Della Bar (a daughter of Casbar) won the 15th renewal of the Southwest Futurity (1963).

Mr. Three Bars

A AAA+ AQHA Champion, Mr. Three Bars was foaled April 7, 1959, and has matured as a sorrel stallion standing 14.3 and weighing approximately 1100 pounds. His dam is Burke's Gayle (AAA), and E. J. Burke and E. J. Burke, Jr., her owners, bred her to Three Bars (TB) for the one prime purpose of getting a running horse. He was raced by them as a two-year-old in 1961; the trainer involved was H. B. "Tex" Carrell. The colt ran 25 races in his maiden season, winning nine, placing six times, and three times finishing third, while earning $34,746.09. He was sixth on the 1961 Leading Money-Earning Horses list, and 29th on the over-all list going back through 1949. He was fifth in earnings of all two-year-olds through the same period, ran 16 races in AAA time, ten of which were graded AAA+, a record that speaks for itself.

Mr. Three Bars won the Magic Empire Futurity at Garfield Downs (Enid, Oklahoma) picking up $8,000. Out in front he never was headed, winning by one and three-quarters lengths. He carried top weight of 124 pounds and his time was :20.4. He came in fourth in the 1961 running of the All-American, behind Pokey Bar, Bunny's Bar Maid, and Golden Note.

His present owner, Paul B. Ford of Sacramento, has furnished, for comparison, a list of the two-year-olds Mr. Three Bars defeated, and has included their two-year-old records:

Starts	Wins	Place	AAA	Contender and Sire
10	7	2	10	She Kitty by Robin Reed
10	4	2	7	Straw Flight by Jackstraw (TB)
15	7	2	8	Alamitos Bar by Three Bars (TB)
20	7	4	9	Idle Time by Rainy KK
16	5	1	8	Savannah Cates by Everett Jr. (TB)
4	1	—	3	Magnolia Bar by Three Bars (TB)
12	2	2	3	David Cox by Depth Charge (TB)
3	—	—	1	Three Chicks by Three Bars (TB)
9	3	2	5	Leona Dee by Leo
14	3	6	7	Triple Tiny by Triple Chick
9	1	1	—	Tiny Chick by Triple Chick
12	2	—	2	Triple Tet by Triple Chick
10	3	—	2	Mable Chick by Triple Chick
11	3	3	4	Art Bar by Lightning Bar
23	3	5	7	Verna Leo by Leo
19	3	1	4	Gold Seeker by Depth Charge (TB)
8	3	2	6	Little Bits Bull by Spotted Bull (TB)
9	3	2	2	King Bee Leo by Leo
10	5	1	5	Rockin Bar by Royal Bar
10	4	1	4	On I Win by Clabber's Win
7	1	2	4	Top Breeze by Top Deck (TB)
7	5	1	4	Mud Bar by Third Reader (TB)
17	1	4	3	Real Sure by Be Sure Now (TB)
6	1	1	1	Bar Tonto Jr. by Bar Tonto
5	3	2	2	Faila Tabu by Faila (TB)
5	—	1	—	Depth Bars by Depth Charge (TB)
17	4	8	8	Manor Man by Spotted Bull (TB)

Says Mr. Ford:

I bought Mr. Three Bars on January 6, 1962, in partnership with D. H. 'Red' Randall, one of California's leading trainers. Since that time Mr. Three Bars has been at the Randall Ranch, Pleasant Grove, California.

Red Randall and myself had been looking for several years to find a son of Three Bars with Leo or King breeding on the dam's side, a horse that had conformation and working ability in the bloodlines along with speed. We were more than satisfied with his record as a two-year-old in track performance, and, after inspecting him, we were pleased with his appearance.

On the 15th of April, 1962, we started showing the colt in halter classes and by June 30, 1962, Mr. Three Bars had earned enough points in this field which, coupled with his racing points, made him one of the very few AAA rated sprinters to become AQHA Champion as a three-year-old.

During this year of 1963 we will show Mr. Three Bars as a four-year-old in the Hackamore Classes. He is showing remarkable ability and Red Randall feels sure he will make ROM in reining. He will start in the Spring Festival Show at Sacramento. In addition we will breed 30 outside mares—his book is full for 1963. Among mares booked are producers of AAA horses and also producers of conformation and working horses.

Mr. Three Bars has an excellent disposition. We feel that what this stallion offers—AAA+ speed, conformation, working ability, plus disposition—will in time prove him to be one of the greatest sons of Three Bars.

In 13 shows Mr. Three Bars had 13 firsts, 11 Grand Championships, and two Reserve Championships. His dam, Burke's Gayle, is by Leo Tag, who also holds an AAA AQHA Championship.

Old Tom Cat

Jack Casement, his breeder, said of this horse: "Old Tom Cat's dam, Little Meow, was bred to Robin Reed on account of our success with another of his get, Alfaretta. We hauled Little Meow to Denver in the afternoon, breeding her in the evening of her ninth day, breeding her once more the following morning, then fetching her and her ten-day-old foal straight home. Bill Welch, Robin Reed's owner, had purchased his mother right after she was chosen Grand Champion Mare at Amarillo a number of years ago. Her name was Sue Reed; she was by Joe Reed out of Goldie by King O'Neill II. Welch arranged with Art Beall to have her bred to Leo, the result being Robin Reed, a good sprinter which made AAA on the track."

At Bay Meadows in 1953, according to the *Chart Book*, Robin Reed in the 350-yard invitational allowance got up to win in the AAA time of :18.2. "The good sprinter, Miss Ruby, was away on top in this race but faded to fourth in the last 220 yards, giving way to the winner and Question's Gold and War Bar, who finished in that order. The "Fairwell Allowance" for AAA— horses was won by Robin Reed, with a very close finish being provided by the well-balanced nine-horse field. This speedy stallion (who has three crosses of Joe Reed in three generations) equaled the Stallion Record and Track Record in winning the 350-yard Fairwell in :18.1. Co-holder of the Stallion Record is War Bar. Black Easter Bunny co-holds the Track Record mark."

Old Tom Cat stands 15 hands, weighs 1200 pounds, has stockings on left fore and right hind legs. He was foaled April 3, 1958. Old Tom's dam was

Little Meow out of a double Jack McCue mare borrowed from Bill Coy. She was shortly afterward struck by lightning on the Casement ranch—Jackie McCue, that is—so that Little Meow had to be spliced onto another mare. Little Meow matured to be a first-class track contender and show winner and now is well known as the mother of good ones; she is the dam of two AAA AQHA Champions and the Co-Champion Quarter Running Three-Year-Old Filly, She Kitty, in addition to several other ROM foals.

According to trainer L. R. "Pat" Thompson, Old Tom Cat was as honest a horse as ever made AAA time on the straightaways. His first out was at Ruidoso, which he won. From then on most of his tracks were wet and heavy and he handled them with difficulty but invariably did his best, and was generally in the money. He raced also at Raton, Centennial, Los Alamitos, and Bay Meadows. He had on the track—and still has off it—a wonderfully quiet disposition. During 1960, as a two-year-old, he started seven times, won twice, and finished in the money five times, qualifying for a AA rating.

He won his first start by daylight, then caught a virus and became a very sick colt. He ran later on in the summer (though he probably shouldn't have), and won his heat in the Rocky Mountain Futurity trials on a dry track. In the main event he came in third over a very muddy track which he did not even pretend to like.

During 1961, as a three-year-old, he was ridden by Leroy Tipton. Early in the spring he was overturned in a trailer and appeared to be sore all over the ribs. Despite this, however, he was started, and went on to run 11 times (five in AAA), going out of the money but twice in good competition. Through heavy mud he ran third in the Rockey Mountain Quarter Horse Derby. He had two wins, including his last start at Centennial—a 440 which he ran in :22.5.

While at Centennial for the Quarter Horse Meet in the fall of that year Pat and Clarence Roth decided to try to buy Old Tom Cat. Says Mr. Roth:

We had seen him earlier in the summer, had watched him run and also his full sister, She Kitty. We talked with Jack Casement about the possibilities and he agreed to sell him to us. He was entered then in a 440-yard race which he ran in AAA time, after which he was retired from track competition.

We brought him home and got him in show shape, hoping we might make him an AQHA Champion. So few stallions had made AAA and gone on to become Champions. In January [1962] we showed him for the first time at Denver's National Western. There were 27 aged stallions entered in this class and he was only two and a half months off the track. It looked pretty tough. He placed sixth, and we were mighty pleased. In February, at a show in Watertown, South Dakota, he won his class of 11 and was named Reserve Champion. In April we showed him at Glendive, Montana, to place second and again Reserve Champion from a class of 14. Later that month we made up our minds to take him to St. Paul—yep, Minnesota. In their big Spring Show he won his class (16 entries) and was chosen Grand Champion.

This was a great boost to us. We went on showing him as much as we could around through South Dakota, and by June 15th he had acquired enough points to become an AQHA Champion; this was right through the heavy breeding season. He was the eighth stallion to become a AAA AQHA Champion—then, going on to finish out the season, he accumulated nine Grand Championships from 16 times shown, and five Reserve Championships under 13 different judges, and never dropped out of the ribbons. By the end of the year he had a wide margin to win the South Dakota Hi-Point Stallion award. We put him in the National Western again, thinking he might at least be in the top six of the Aged Stallion class. There were 21 entries standing in the ring and the judge took plenty of time looking them over.

Finally he went around and pulled Old Tom Cat out for top horse—it was one of our fondest dreams coming true. We were certainly thrilled. A few nights later they had a parade of champions in the new coliseum between rodeo events, and before a full house Old Tom was presented the American Quarter Horse Association trophy and the Marshall Peavy Award.

He is the only horse in South Dakota to be AAA and an AQHA Champion. Thus far he has 26 racing points and 34 points at halter.

The mares that were bred to Old Tom Cat last year were mostly of fairly high caliber, many being rated and several AQHA Champions. His first colts were on the ground as of March, 1963. Many of these same mares have been rebooked, along with outstanding first-timers from other states. The Casements have earmarked ten for Tom's court, and his big goal now is to become Register of Merit in as many events as can be managed.

Ricky Taylor

Lewis Blackwell, the Trader Horn of the wonderful world of Quarter Horses and, through the 1940's and deep into the 1950's, one of its most discerning patrons and enthusiastic supporters, bred—among other top performers—Ricky Taylor (P–69,475), a chestnut stallion foaled in 1954.

Writes Lucille Blackwell:

Ricky Taylor was foaled by the mother of Hard Twist. We had our mares and a few old cows grazing on wheat pasture in the outskirts of Amarillo in what is presently the city's most exclusive residential addition.

When we went over to feed that morning we found the new baby colt. Mame Taylor always surprised us about her foaling dates. Ann's Daughter, an old gray Thoroughbred mare we owned, had taken Ricky away from his mother and Mame and Ann had run with the little fellow until he was almost exhausted. He was so wet from the rain and so perplexed and wabbly on those long baby legs that our hearts went out to him. When we drove Ann away he came to Lewis as though seeking protection from the cruel wonders into which he had been born.

From the first time we laid eyes on him we felt he was an excellent prospect. As he grew and developed we became more and more proud of him. At Los Alamitos in the fall of 1955 Mr. Don Carse asked Lewis if he had any outstanding prospects for sale. I guess you know Lewis. Although not anxious to part with Ricky, his natural enthusiasm for a trade got the best of him; he has always put a price on anything he owned. For that reason alone we no longer have Miss Panama, Monita, Gold Note, Legal Tender Bee, Custus Rastus (TB), Hard Twist, and the many more good ones we have owned in the past.

Lewis told Mr. Carse about Ricky and priced him. Closing the deal on the spot, Mr. Carse bought the colt, sight unseen.

We owned Mame Taylor when Ricky was foaled and until her death a few years later. We bred her to Custus Rastus, not only because we owned him but because we considered him an exceptional stallion—and we still think the same today. It was Custus Rastus that sired Ricky Taylor.

Mr. Blackwell liked to attend the wrestling matches and at that time there was a young man wrestling who was named Ricky Starr, clean cut, well muscled, and a gentleman in the ring. Lewis wanted to call the colt Ricky Starr, but when we went to register him that name had been taken, so Lewis called him Ricky Taylor.

When the colt was about two months old we moved our mares back to the ranch at Logan, New Mexico, where he was raised until Mr. Carse sent for him—at about eighteen or nineteen months old, I believe—and he was taken to California.

We are always anxious for our horses to please the people who buy them. We never cease to be interested in them and always hope they'll do exceedingly well for their new owners. Needless to say, we are quite proud of this colt's accomplishments; and we are proud of Jaguar, too, for as you may know we raised him and sold him to Mr. Honnen at about the same age we sold Ricky.

Newton Keck, trainer also of Pokey Bar, says:

Hugh Huntley bought Ricky Taylor as a two-year-old from Don Carse. His first qualifying work, at Stockton, was an impressive one. After he had bucked off three different boys that morning, Harold Baker mounted him and stayed aboard. Ed. Burke was heard after this workout to make the remark, "This is a race horse!" I thought so, too, and became more convinced as time went on.

He won his first start at Stockton in :18.6, and bucked the boy off as they went around the turn past the finish line. You'd have to see the Winner's Circle picture of this race to appreciate it, as the expressions on the faces of the horse, the jock, and me all tell the story. I was mad and disgusted with the jockey for allowing this to happen; Ricky's eye was looking back at the jock in distrust, and the boy was mad at me for chewing him out and at the horse for such a display.

Ricky shin bucked at Stockton, but I took him on to Sacramento where he ran a second. He went on to Pomona, where he won his trials for the Pacific Quarter Horse Association Futurity, then dead-heated for second in the finals. After this meet, I had him fired and turned out.

I brought him back to the tracks that fall and he won his only two starts at the Fresno Fair. He came on to Los Alamitos, where he won his first out and where, at the end of the meet, he was sold to Mr. and Mrs. Raymond Guthrie, of the Guthrie Ranch at Prineville, Oregon.

At no time did I ever have this horse just exactly right, but he had a great heart and tried his best, whether he was hurting or not. I think he was one of the gamest horses I ever trained.

In the PCQHA Futurity where Ricky Taylor and Cute Trick dead-heated for second, the winning time was :18.1, and Ricky paid $22.40. From a total of 15 starts he came in first five times, second four times, and third three times, banking $5435.50 and retiring with AAA ratings and 16 Register of Merit points in track performance.

In the February, 1963, issue of the *Quarter Horse Journal* his AQHA Championship was announced:

Raymond and Edna Guthrie were notified on November 19 that their stallion, Ricky Taylor, had been enrolled as an AQHA Champion acquiring 15 points at halter and 16 points in performance. The Guthries began showing Ricky Taylor in the fall of 1959. His first show was at Salem, Oregon, where he stood second in a class of 17 aged stallions to acquire 2 points at halter. In 1961 he received a serious leg injury which kept him out of the show ring for more than a year. His qualifying halter points were completed on October 18, 1962, at North Portland, Oregon, where he took a Grand Championship at the age of eight years. Ricky Taylor is described as quiet, gentle, and easily handled. He has been pasture bred each season and is gaining well deserved fame as a sire. From the first starters on the track he has five AAA get, while two gelding sons showings at halter have accumulated seven Grand and one Reserve Championships.

Austin Beebe has written to say: "I will be very happy to tell you why I placed Ricky Taylor Grand Champion of the Oregon State Fair Quarter Horse Show at Salem. In the first place, he is my kind of a horse. I am a working-horse man. To me he is the type of horse that can get the job done. He shows lots of speed, with power and balance to handle it with good smooth movement. Plus a real good head. Also, he was quiet and easy to handle and very nice looking. It takes all these good qualities to make a Grand Champion. Liking him very much, I was glad to see some of his colts."

Ricky Taylor's final points for AQHA Championship were made on October 18th at the Pacific International Quarter Horse Show (judge, Jack Peak of Longview, Texas), at Portland, Oregon. Placing second in Fillies of 1960 (class of 13) was Snap To It by Ricky Taylor. Colts of 1962 (10 shown) saw Taylor K by Ricky Taylor garnering second place. Ricky Taylor himself took the Stallions of 1958 class (13 shown), and was named Grand Champion Stallion. At this same show his son, Ricky Tim, was named Grand Champion Gelding.

Ricky Taylor's sire is Custus Rastus (JC–482718), a brown horse foaled in 1948, bred and sold at the Keenland Sales by Mrs. Vera S. Bragg, bringing $16,000 as a yearling—a pretty fair price in 1949. W. H. Ingerton bid him in and took him to Hot Springs the following year. He showed, I have been told, exceptional speed but broke a bone in his pastern and had to be taken out of training. Lewis M. Blackwell purchased him from Mr. Ingerton. Lou Tuck, in Colorado, bought him from Mr. Blackwell, and says: "My discovery of Ricky Taylor and Jaguar in their early days convinced me I should buy this stallion as soon as possible, which I did and am very proud of. Although Mr. Blackwell bred him to very few mares, he produced some colts of unusually high class from practically all matings. From the record, his get not only race well but show and work every bit as well."

Some of his get currently showing well are Custus Belle, Capital Gain, Ima Pixie, and Custus Honey. Two Medicine recently won two races and is rated AAA. Baby Rastus is AAA. He has a current total of 27 Register of Merit get, and 15 AAA and 12 AA. Weighing 1350, Custus Rastus stands 16 hands.

Others of Ricky's get, with track-performance records, are Mister Terrific (dam, Legal Tender B by Hard Twist), 10 starts, 7 AAA; Ricketta (dam, Leonella by Leo), winner of Northern Racing Quarter Horse Association Derby, 1962, nine starts, four wins; No Payola (dam, Patricia Dee by Dee Dee), 10 starts, four wins, five AAA; Terry Ricky Shay (dam, Fly Fast by Hobler's Tony), winner of Jefferson Quarter Horse Association Futurity, 1962; Ricktor (dam, Huntley's Shortstop), 37 starts, six wins, five seconds, 8 thirds, 12 AAA; Ricky Echols (dam, Jody Echols by Ed Echols), 14 starts at two, five wins, AAA, never out of the money.

Sugaree Bars

A sorrel, 14.3 and 1050 pounds, blaze and snip and sock on right front,

Sugaree Bars was foaled on the Bud Warren ranch at Perry, Oklahoma, April 15, 1957. She was sired by Sugar Bars (P-42,606) out of Randle's Lady (P–8257) by Doc Horn by Flying Squirrel (TB). Randle's Lady was one of the prominent individuals match raced before standards were adopted by the AQRA. She was once matched against Shue Fly and is said to have been one of the only two sprinters that ever outran Leo. Mr. Warren, after purchasing Leo, located and bought her and for several seasons bred her to Leo, by which she produced Croton Oil, South Pacific, and Rosa Leo.

When weaned, Sugaree Bars was sold to J. T. Walters of Skiatook, Oklahoma, along with the Leonna Leo that later equaled a world's record for two-year-old fillies. Mr. Walters showed Sugaree Bars at halter as a yearling; she won her class seven times out of eight and was Reserve Champion at Tulsa while he had her.

About the time she turned two she was purchased by Rowland Stanfield, of Broken Arrow, and sent to the West Coast to be put into race training. According to present owner T. M. Jones of Perry, after but thirty days of track work she "outworked the greatest colts of that year, and everyone around the track was talking about 'that beautiful Sugar Bars filly' that could run so fast while yet so green."

Well, she shin bucked. Instead of then being given an appropriate rest, she was blistered and kept at the track. When the California meet was over she was sent to Ruidoso.

It has been said she was very good at the gates—the competition had to catch her. The story was told that she would run on top until that front leg began to hurt, when she would begin to drop back and permit the others to catch and pass her. She always ran better on a soft or muddy track. I am told she outran Leonna Leo and all the best of that year (1959) in the mud; and, at Ruidoso where they had plenty of that, she was officially rated AA.

Later that year she was sent to Denver. When she got back to the Stanfield Stallion Station she was put up for sale at their first public offering (fall of 1959), when, on the advice of Bud Warren, she was bid in by Mr. Jones. Jones says: "I brought her home and turned her out for the winter. The following spring I booked her to Leo and put her in race training myself, and this despite the fact I had never previously owned a race horse, much less trained one. Mr. Warren gave me pointers as we went along.

"At Pawhuska's spring race meet I started Sugaree Bars—my first horse at any official track—and she ran and won! I then sent her with Ted Wells to Ruidoso when we were positive she was in foal. Three days after that 650-mile trip he started her (on May 30, 1960) and she won at 350 yards in :18.4."

She made several additional starts during the summer and ran well. By this time, of course, T. M. Jones had his mind pretty much on that foal she was carrying, and on the weekend of August 6th he came down to Ruidoso, determined to take her home. She was at this time about three and a half months along.

She was entered in the ninth race (August 6th). About post time it began to rain, and the jockey, Don Allison, who had always ridden her (even as a two-year-old), was on another horse. E. Garza was up—Don had told him how to get the most out of her.

The track was muddy. Sugaree broke badly. Garza whipped her for about 50 yards, then hand rode. At around 300 yards she began to move, and she went through that field like a bat out of Carlsbad, for a win in solid AAA time. Jones, elated, took her home.

She foaled in the spring of 1961 a fine looking horse colt (by Leo) which Jones named Rip Rip (P–157,299). This colt was subsequently sold to Mr. Charles S. Jones of Los Angeles.

While Rip Rip was a suckling, T. M. Jones began to show mother and son at halter—"She was never defeated in a brood mare class." When the colt was weaned Jones decided to see if he could make an AQHA Champion of her. She had 14 points at racing and needed 16 more at halter. In a short career she made Grand Champion four times, Reserve three times, and won her class many times as a brood mare. He says:

"Sugaree has done everything and has been retired to my small brood-mare band. She is still being bred to Leo."

He doesn't think the accompanying photo does her justice, but it was all he had. He says: 'She was the most controversial mare I ever saw; people either thought she was the greatest or didn't like her at all. She is small but has the best-muscled hind legs ever put on a little race mare. She is the first Sugar Bars get to be rated AAA and AQHA Champion."

As a kind of postscript to this account, further mention might be made of Randle's Lady, better known perhaps as Rosalita or "Little Breeze" to race-track buffs of the early 1940's. She was bred by Tobias Cominer at Welsh, Louisiana. Her next owner of record was Helen Michaelis, who also had another Doc Horn mare called Rosita (or "Big Breeze"). After they were retired from racing both were purchased by V. S. Randle of Richmond, Texas.

The second *Year Book of the American Quarter Racing Association*

(1944) contains several mentions of both these mares. The names of what were then designated "Celebrated American Quarter Running Horses" were printed in boldface type; both mares rated this type. On page 8, Rosalita (Randle's Lady) is shown to have been a chestnut mare foaled in 1939 (the *Stud Book*, however, says 1938 and is probably correct) with a record at 440 of :23.2f under 125 pounds. It also shows (on page 9) that she ran 220 yards, carrying 115, in :12.6, track slow. On page 18 the *Year Book* says: "A very fast mare, probably capable of winning up to three-eights in good company, ROSALITA shows her Thoroughbred blood more strongly than most horses that excel at the shorter distances, and surprisingly runs even 220 in excellent time. Under 125 pounds at the quarter she won her first start at Rillito from Queen (100 lbs.), CHICARO (130), Lost Toy (100) and PAY DIRT (125) in Track Record time. At the Speed Trials she again easily defeated Queen in a special race for mares under catch weights."

Her sire, Doc Horn was by Flying Squirrel (TB), a son of Cesarion, he by Faustus, a son of Enquirer who was by *Leamington. The dam of Randle's Lady is reported as a daughter of D. J. Colt, second dam a mare by Rodney.

In addition to Sugaree Bars, Randle's Lady had produced South Pacific; Bud Warren's Croton Oil, the Leading Sire of Winners at the Oklahoma Quarter Horse Meet (95 races, 675 starters) in 1962; Rosa Leo; and Della Rose (dam of Bar The Door). Rosa Leo made AAA and won the Oklahoma Futurity of 1955. South Pacific (by Leo) produced the following starters through 1961: Gold Pacific (AAA), Sugar Breeze (AAA), and the stakes winning Pacific Bars (AAA), described (*Quarter Running Horse Chart Book*, November, 1962), as one of the bright new stars among the juvenile ranks.

Mr. Warren says:

We bought Randle's Lady when her racing days were over for the express purpose of raising a stud by old Leo. We got five fillies in a row before Croton Oil was foaled. Two of these fillies died. The third one, South Pacific, had delivered three consecutive AAA colts. Then came Sugaree Bars (by Sugar Bars), and Rosa Leo (again by Leo). This mare's last foal is a stallion we call Little Doc Horn—he is now two years old.

Randle's Lady was reported to be a full sister to Della P (dam of Lightning Bar and Bardella). Both Bill Rowe, of Pawhuska, and V. S. Randle (from whom we bought the mare—he also owned and stood Flying Bob) have told me this.

World's Record Holders (as of June, 1963)

World Record:	440 yards,	118f	:21.6	POKEY BAR
World Record:	400 yards,	122f	:19.9	TONTO BARS HANK
		118f	:19.9	SHE KITTY
		117f	:19.9	BREEZE BAR
World Record:	350 yards,	120f	:17.5	VANDY'S FLASH
World Record:	330 yards,	124f	:16.7	KIMALETA
World Record:	300 yards,	125f	:15.5	CLABBERTOWN G
World Record:	250 yards,	120f	:13.4	MADDON'S BRIGHT EYES
		112f	:13.4	SUPER CHARGE
		107f	:13.4	MONITA
World Record:	220 yards,	125f	:12.1	MADDON'S BRIGHT EYES
		120f	:12.1	TONTA GAL
		115f	:12.1	MY TEXAS DANDY

Pokey Bar
(440 yds., 1962 LA 118 :21.6)

Nearly everyone by this time has heard of the Wright Brothers' contraption, and most of the folks in the flat-saddle set have probably caught wind of the latest sensation from Madera, California—the Hugh Huntely flying machine called Pokey Bar. In case you've missed a few of the more spectacular details, a bit of review may help set the record straight.

This ground model of the X–15 was put together at the Huntley Ranch and unveiled on the afternoon of January 7, 1959. There was much enthusiasm floating around on this gala occasion, and brother Hugh—having a bottle of champagne left over from New Year's—slipped into his prophet's robes and, dividing the bubbly among assembled friends and well-wishers, proposed, "To the future champ!" And from here it would seem like he's sure enough got one.

Pokey Bar's mama, Pokey Vandy, raced as a two-year-old and did fairly well, but, due to soreness and illness, kept pretty much away from the tracks in her third year. A Mr. Johnson, who owned her then, held a dispersal at Los Alamitos on November 24, 1955, and Pokey Vandy at four years was in this sale. The Huntleys, having in their stables the Vandy mare Miss Okmulgee, considered Pokey Vandy a worth-while addition and finally bid her in at $2900. Newton Keck, Huntley's trainer, was so dadgummed tickled he had hold of her lead rope almost before the auctioneer could say, "Sold!"

Keck took her to the track and a week later plopped her in a race, which she won without any trouble at all. On December 10th they loaded her into the eighth race at Los Alamitos, The Gold Bar Stakes for three-year-olds and upward, net value to the winner $1375, a 10-horse go at 400 yards —in which Huntley's new mare was up against such veteran campaigners as Monita, Miss Pitapat, Vanetta Dee and Stalking Gal among the more notable. Pokey Vandy reached the wire first by a head, paying $37.00 for a $2.00 ticket, carrying 117 pounds.

Encouraged by two wins, Keck put her into the Autumn Championship the following week, a 440 at fixed weights. This proved to be a record maker right down the line. Pokey Vandy won by half a length over Arizonan and Miss Pitapat, collecting the not negligible sum of $5750.00 and paying $14.70, $6.30 and $4.10. Time was :22.0, equaling the then World and Mare Records jointly held by Monita and Woven Web. Not knocking off there, she went on to Bay Meadows and set a new track record of :17.9 for 350.

A great believer in "best to best," Mr. Huntley bred Pokey Vandy (Champion Running Mare of 1955) to Three Bars (TB) and she dropped the jet-propelled rocket he calls Pokey Bar.

Pockey Bar was broke and gentled on the Huntley ranch. He was strong-willed and it was a trying time for all concerned. Says Newton Keck: "He was a tough nut to crack. He had fire and determination, and during this period I sometimes wondered which was the horse and which the boss. After riding him one day some 45 minutes in deep sand, which should have tired him out if anything would, I was starting to light up when he came plumb apart. The cantle came up and cracked me in the back and while I was gagging he tossed me again. Seemed like I went up so far this time the birds could've built a nest in my britches.

"I've trimmed plenty of horses' feet in my time but this was the roughest one of the lot. With two men to help, we'd tied up a foot and, before you could cuss, he'd throw himself and pull out of it. He just wouldn't give up. It was during one of these attempts to trim his feet—and I had *three* helpers this time—he threw himself hard enough to break his tail. For a long time he couldn't use it. He still handles it like a new hand with a broom, sort of switching it when he runs. But when he finally quit trying to foul up our endeavors he never got ornery or acted up with us again. He's sound-legged, big, and responds well to training. He likes lots of work. He always feels good and comes out of his stall bucking and playing."

Up to the first half of 1962 Pokey Bar had run 13 official races. In the late fall of his yearling year he was sent up to Fresno and schooled with other colts; then on to Los Alamitos, where Newt Keck got him accustomed to the track, Tommie Chavez riding. From Los Alamitos he was taken to Bay Meadows and, with Chavez up, went into his first race. This was on February 3, 1961, a 10-horse go on a muddy track. But first let's hear from his Fresno mentor.

Malcolm Anderson says in a letter to Huntley:

I recall very well your trainer unloading that nice big chestnut colt to leave with us while he went on to race at Los Alamitos. The last thing he said was "Be careful—he can really buck!"

We started him as we did the other 39 yearlings we were schooling for various breeders, riding him in a stall several days until he relaxed and obeyed the boy on his back. When we felt the boy could handle him we rode him inside a large barn along with several other colts. There he learned to walk, trot, and gallop with weight on his back. We also had the colts do figure-eights, learning to change leads. In this manner we developed his mouth as he gained confidence.

Pokey Bar was a suspicious colt, didn't trust us at first, and was quick to defend himself. When we finally felt he had relaxed and was doing his work well in the barn—which took about 12 days—we took him to the track with four other colts to gallop. We started with an even mile and after a few days he was going a mile and a half, and continued to do so for the next 30 days. He did very well those weeks. We galloped them in sets of four, and they would alternate, inside, outside, behind, in front— learning to relax and move with other horses in preparation for days to come.

I recall we had Decidedly here for Mr. Pope at the same time we had Pockey Bar. I got the same report from both boys. Each felt he was riding a colt that had the power and co-ordination to do anything you asked, and that could whirl and unload him easy as pie. The two grooms that took care of them said the same thing—give them time to know what you wanted and they'd do anything for you, but don't rush them or get tough or they'd be all over you. Both horses were quick movers.

Pokey Bar and Decidedly were foaled scarcely eight miles apart. Both took their first track schooling from Malcolm "Andy" Anderson at the Fresno Fairgrounds, training in the same bunch. Both were shod for the first time by the same farrier, Floyd Boss of Fresno. Among the 39 yearlings in Anderson's class were both Thoroughbreds and Quarter Horses. Quite a number were from the El Peco Ranch where Decidedly was foaled. Either this was an unusually talented bunch of youngsters or Anderson was re- markably successful in his methods that fall; out of this class of 39, nine or ten won their first times out and four or five proved to be stakes winners. Both Pokey Bar and Decidedly were ridden by a boy called "Frenchie," who had been exercising prospects for some 30 years. While Pokey was in training he developed a bad cold which might have turned into pneumonia save for the excellent treatment prescribed by the El Peco Ranch vet- erinarian, Dr. William Maderious.

Anderson concludes: "After Pokey Bar was with us for about 40 days we started breezing him slow, always with three others. We started them at an eighth and worked up to a quarter of a mile, this about every fifth day, galloping them the other four. Since Pokey Bar went to Los Alamitos to complete his training, we never got to see him really cut loose. We enjoyed having a small part in developing this great horse."

At the same sale at which the Huntleys obtained Pokey Vandy, a mare called Gold Note was sold to Johnny Longden's Alberta Ranch. In 1959 Pokey Vandy foaled Pokey Bar and Gold Note dropped the great filly Golden Note; both were first foals. Both qualified and ran in the 1961 All-American Futurity, Golden Note finishing third.

In his first official race—Bay Meadows, February 3, 1961, 350 yards of muddy track—Pokey Bar came in third. His second out, one week later on a track labeled "fast," he got there just behind Bobbie Coca, whose time for the 350 was 19-even; and eleven days later, going the same distance, Pokey Vandy's colt hung up his first win—:18.7, defeating nine contenders.

Keck had him entered for another go, but on the morning of the race he came down with a virus infection, a gland in his neck swelling up pretty badly. The track officials came for a look. Keck says he thought they suspected him of using a needle to get Pokey scratched. When they could not find any mark they put a needle into another of Huntley's horses and shaved the spot to see if they could detect the needle mark. Since the puncture was very apparent they finally allowed Pokey Bar to drop out. Pokey's ailment kept Keck at the track several days past the end of the meet. Even after Pokey was brought back to the ranch the gland remained very swollen A flax-seed poultice finally brought it down.

Huntley's son, Sid, all 200 pounds of him on top of a stock saddle, rode Pokey Bar at the ranch to keep him in condition and get him legged-up for Ruidoso where he was nominated for the All-American. Dr. Maderious dropped by one day, took a look at the pair of them, shook his head and remarked: "I believe that's probably the heaviest exercise boy on record!"

The colt's fourth outing, on August 5, 1961, was a 10-horse field at 400 yards which he won handily in :20.5. Then came the Futurity trials, Pokey winning the second division against a four-mile head wind in :20.8 for the 400 yards.

The day of the Big One dawned bright and fair. They hung out the "Fast" sign. A four-mile head wind sprang up as Pokey Vandy's colt lined up with Bunny's Bar Maid, Golden Note, Mr. Three Bars, Three Chicks, Savannah Cates, Magnolia Bar, Leona Dee, Art Bar, and David Cox for the third renewal of the richest purse in Quarter Racing.

This was the race that had everything. As the late Leslie Ernenwein said in his *Western Horseman* column for November (1961): "A dramatic page in racing was written at Ruidoso Downs when ten of the fastest two-year-old Quarter Horses in the country met in a showdown stampede for the third running of the $200,000 All-American." A record crowd was cramming the stands. The purse figured out at nearly $10,000 per second, or $500 per yard, ranking high above the Kentucky Derby's $163,000, the Preakness' $178,000, and the Belmont Stakes' $148,000.

Says Newton Keck:

In my opinion this was Pokey's most colorful race. He went to the post as third favorite, behind Bunny's Bar Maid and Golden Note. He came out of that gate like hell a-whoopin', widening his lead every jump of the way—you should have heard that crowd! I'd had a hunch he had a pretty fair chance from the way he'd worked the previous Saturday. Kenny Chapman, our rider, says: "That's when I got excited about this colt." The trials only made him sharper.

You'd have to know how quiet, soft spoken, and shy acting Kenny is, and that you can scare Pokey Bar by squalling out at him, to really appreciate this; but as I was going to the post with Pokey Bar, ponying him, I glanced up at Kenny and asked if he reckoned he could yell $10,000 worth. He allowed he'd try.

Bunny's Bar Maid, undefeated thus far and odds-on favorite, was in fifth position at the furlong while Pokey Bar had a half-length lead over Mr. Three Bars; Golden Note and Leona Dee were lapped on the Burke colt. Close up to the finish it appeared Bunny's Bar Maid was moving like hell emigrating on cart wheels, but she just couldn't catch that fast-flying Pokey. Chapman hand-rode him, coming in first by a length and a half, with Bar Maid second and Golden Note third, beaten by a nose. Coming into the winner's circle Kenny Chapman asked, grinning, "Did I holler $10,000 worth?"

Huntley's flying machine next took The Thanksgiving Stakes—350 in :17.7 at Los Alamitos on November 23rd. On December 13th he loped away with another 350—this one from Alamitos Bar. Ten days later he waltzed off with the Kindergarten Stakes, same distance—:17.8. Then came the Pacific Coast Quarter Horse Derby trials, in which he defeated Alamitos Bar and four others of the second heat, going the quarter in :21.8.

In the main event, Kenneth Chapman up, Pokey Bar was again first at the wire by a head, Alamitos Bar second by two and a quarter, with Magnolia Bar—all packing 120—grabbing third by a nose. Time was :21.6 with a three-mile tail wind. It was the fastest time ever racked up for the quarter in the history of organized racing under official straightaway conditions. The then existing World's Record was :21.7, established by Vandy's Flash at Los Alamitos in 1960.

Proving this record-smashing time was no fluke, Pokey Bar, on May 5 in the Quarter Horse Championship purse $25,000, trailing so far that I would not have given ten cents for his chances, suddenly stretched himself out and turned loose a burst of blinding speed that put his nose under the wire just ahead of the hard-running Alamitos Bar, with No Butt third by a half—time :21.6. The winner's share of this purse was $13,750.00 which brought Pokey Bar's earnings to a then all-time top total of $146,-548.28, putting him ahead of the next most recent top money winner, Tonto Bars Hank, by $17,647.24, which should have bought Mr. Huntley's flying machine pretty near enough fuel to put him in orbit.

He is still high horse on the latest basis of comparison, the Leading Money-Earning Horses list of 1962, with $162,543.81, and was named Champion Quarter Running Three-Year-Old Colt for that year.

Tonto Bars Hank
(400 yds., 1962 ALB 122f :19.9)

In the heady atmosphere of track competition we should try to understand which elements of greatness carry an individual through the ruck of striving climbers into the light of public acclaim in the world's most grueling test for horses, the so-called Sport of Kings.

The perils of such competition are very real and omnipresent. Their name is legion. In my own small way I have been through this mill as breeder, owner—yes, even as trainer—in the days when short horses first began to clatter their hoofs amid the fanfare of the West's big-time tracks —when Bay Meadows, Inglewood, Centennial, Hialeah, and Tropical Park smashed hard-boot tradition by opening their gates to the scorned quartermilers.

I've known the thrills and the chills, the hopes, joys, and heartaches that beset every owner who picks his silks and pays his fees and follows his horse from the saddling pens. In the blazing sun, in wind and rain, I too have tasted these moments of truth, the sweet and the bitter, the lonely frustrations and that heart-warming eye of the winner's circle camera, and I can say to you sincerely that there is no sport like racing nor one which can more quickly sift the men from the boys.

The lick for early foot is only part of the equipment your horse must take to the tracks if the goal of your efforts is top billing on the straight-aways. He must have tremendous heart, lungs, and bottom, expert management, and, above everything else, the will to win.

This is the story of one that went far.

Before his first retirement—he's back again now—he went 23 times to

135. Pokey Bar, by Three Bars, TB, out of Pokey Vandy, by Vandy.

Photo by Ed Ellinger

136. Tonto Bars Hank, by Tonto Bars Gill out of Hanka, by Hank H.

Photo by Wayne C. Hunt

137. She Kitty, by Robin Reed out of Little Meow, by Tadpole.

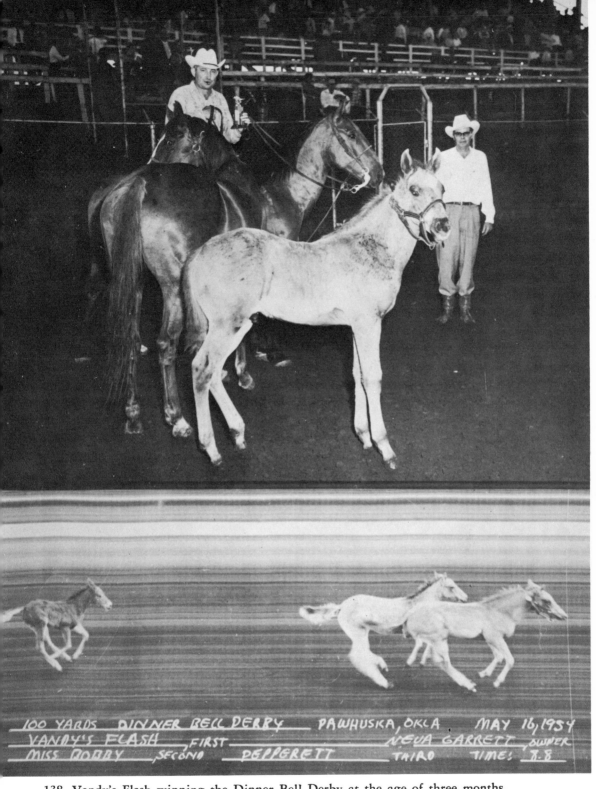

100 YARDS   DINNER BELL DERBY   PAWHUSKA, OKLA   MAY 16, 1954
VANDY'S FLASH   FIRST   NEVA GARRETT   OWNER
MISS BOBBY   SECOND   PEPPERETT   THIRD   TIME: 8.8

138. Vandy's Flash winning the Dinner Bell Derby at the age of three months.

VANDY'S FLASH   JOCKEY EMIL ARMSTRONG, UP.
              THE SHUE FLY STAKE · PURSE $5000.
Winner Eighth Race April 12, 1960.   Los Alamitos Race Course
   Miss Louton (2nd)   350 yds.- 17.5   Pap (3rd)
              NEW WORLD & TRACK RECORD
OWNER: JOHN D. ASKEW   TRAINER: L. G. CULVER

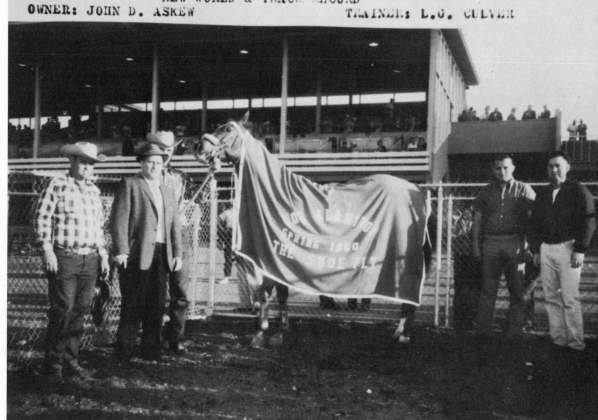

139. Vandy's Flash setting the current World's Record of :17.5 for 350 yards.

140. Kimaleta, a World Record holder, with her owner-trainer O. M. Woodson at Claremore, Oklahoma. She is by Mr. Bar None out of Bonna Lita, by Leo. Her record of :16.7 for 330 yards was made in the Illinois State Fair Futurity of 1962

the post for 14 wins, five seconds, and three thirds. In all but one of these outings he ran in AAA time, the exception in AA. He has taken home from these sprints $129,601. Through 1961 it was the mostest.

We are discussing that 1300 pounds of sorrel lightning, Tonto Bars Hank, a real traveler in anyone's language. His record reads like a fairy tale; only Hank and his backers know the sweat that went into it.

It all got going back in the spring of 1952 when C. G. Whitcomb and son Milo (who own Hank in partnership) bought the mare Hanka (by Hank H out of Hi Baby—double King breeding with Queen H close up) from Jack and Paul Smith of Indiahoma, in the Sooner State.

With mare in tow, they went up to Walter Merrick's, bound for the court of Three Bars. Mr. Whitcomb says:

We thought she was settled when we picked her up, but she failed to produce a colt that next spring, and, as Three Bars had been taken back to Arizona, we bred her to our own good performance horse, Frog W. By him she produced three fine performance horses for us, and when Marion Seward brought Tonto Bars Gill up into this country we took her to his court.

She missed again but was taken back in 1957. Hank was foaled on the 4th of April, 1958. Hanka had won her tier in the trials and finished second in the finals of the Oklahoma Futurity; and was at first owned jointly by Wayne Rossen and myself, but in the summer of 1957 I had purchased Rossen's interest. My son Milo and I owned her when Hank was foaled.

In the fall of 1957 I was kicked and badly injured by a horse, and recovery was so slow I became convinced the days of my activity were over. I arranged to throw in with another party to hold a public dispersal at Grand Island, Nebraska.

Two weeks before this sale a man got in touch with Whitcomb by telephone, offering to buy Hanka, saying he didn't care for the colt's breeding but would give $2000 for the mare and let Whitcomb keep the colt. Since both individuals were already listed, Whitcomb turned him down.

When Hanka and Hank came into the ring they started at $400. When they reached $1550 C. G. got to thinking about this fellow he'd turned down. He announced that if the buyer was not interested in the colt Whitcomb himself would give $900 for Hank and board the mare free till the colt was weaned.

He says:

We never had another bid. They were knocked down at $1550 and the buyer took $900 for Hank. I had two more mares sell the same way, we Whitcombs retaining the colts, one by Jaguar and the other, like Hank, by Tonto Bars Gill.

All three foals did well that summer, and were entered that fall in the All-American with the idea of selling two and putting whichever was left into training. All were given the best of care, growing out well.

Early in 1960 Whitcomb advertised Hank at $10,000, each of the others at $6500. "I put Hank highest because I thought with Tonto Bars on top and King on the bottom he was best bred; also I liked his disposition, size, bone, and the way he was put together."

At this time Whitcomb had $1000 in futurity payments on each of the three. Several persons had expressed interest, but no money changed hands. In March all three were put into training.

Pat Simpson took them to Ruidoso in May. By June he had them pretty well legged up; putting the Jaguar filly and Hank in a schooling race. The filly came in shin-bucked. A week later Hank was off through the mud in his second schooling race, this time against a rather fair three-year-old, again winning.

He started out officially on July 1st. Out of the gate he opened up several lengths of daylight on a pretty good bunch of two-year-olds. At the grandstand he spooked. Paul Jaquez managed to keep him from turning around, straigtened him out, got him going again, and saw him catch and gain on the pair that had passed him, romping in for a win in AA time.

Since Jacquez was committed to another owner, for Hank's second start they put Xavier Torres up; this was for winners of one at 350 yards. Though lugging badly, Hank went on to win in :17.9—a new two-year-old colt record. Says Whitcomb: "After this race a party I'd offered Hank to at $10,000 came rushing over to the barn to see if we'd still make a deal at that price. I said I guessed not."

Hank's third time out was in the Kansas Futurity trials. Torres did not hold him together coming out of the gate, the track cut from under him; he stumbled several jumps before the boy got him straightened. Last to get rolling by one and a half, he caught them all but Lou Tuck's Heavenly Flower, which won by a head, though Hank qualified with third-best time of the trials.

He lugged badly again in the main event, but won in :17.1 (330 yards). "We then," Mr. Whitcomb tells me, "had an offer of $25,000—which we also turned down. His next start was in the Carl Mercer Allowance at 400 yards.

"We put Curt Perner up, and I said if he could ride Hank straight he would set a new record instead of just equaling one. Perner got him out in good shape, he came down pretty straight and won by a length of daylight in :20.2—four-tenths under the record for a first-season colt. Right after this we were offered $40,000."

Forty-eight hours before he was due to take off in the trials for the All-American Hank went off his feed, had a temperature of 105 degrees, and was doctored all day by the track vet. He ate a little next morning, had less temperature and—though plainly not right—was started. A muddy track for a big stout colt.

With Torres back up, the track went out from under him again; the boy let him lug and Rebel Cause beat him by a head, but in such good time that Hank qualified anyway. The Whitcombs were then offered $60,000. "In the finals we put Perner in the irons. He lugged a little, winning by one good length in :20 flat."

His next start was at Albuquerque. "We entered him at 350 yards, which he won (:17.9) on a cupping track, and when the next 440 came along Hank was the only horse willing to go. We moved to Los Alamitos. In his first out there he went the 350 in :17.6, setting a new two-year-old colt and stallion record."

Hank tried next in deep, heavy mud, losing to Rebel Cause by a neck. He grabbed the next 350 handily in :17.7, went on to win the Kindergarten Stakes in :17.7, winding up the year with total earnings of more than $93,000. "Before we left California," Mr. Whitcomb declares, "we were offered $250,000 for him. He had started 12 times, won nine and never was beaten by more than a neck!" It was a wonderful season!

In 1961 bad luck was certainly camped on his doorstep, or so it seemed to his handlers and backers. He was up against all the top aged horses as well as the best of the three-year-olds.

He finished second to Breeze Bar by a head, with the winner setting a new World's Record of :19.9 for the 400 yards, Hank throwing a hind shoe in the final fifty yards. He won his trial in the Derby 440 (:21.9) and, in the finals, fouled up in the gate, was bumped coming out by another late starter, then was cut off.

Perner took him up, went around three horses, driving on to pass all but the hard-flogging Rebel Cause, which, says Whitcomb, "beat Hank by a head in :21.9. Several top horsemen told me they thought it the greatest race Hank had run."

Back at Ruidoso Hank entered the Mr. Bar None Allowance, but was not up to form. "After running out of the money the first and only time thus far," C. G. Whitcomb said, "we scratched, letting the derby and championship go by default."

They took him home for a rest, but two months later hauled him to Los Alamitos, trying to get him in shape for the fall meet. Wieberg was training him now. Perner was away in the Army, so they put William

Strauss aboard. Hank was responding. His first time out was through the mud at 350 yards, which he won by plenty of daylight over top aged horses. His next, at 400, he won by a little bit. Then came the big 440, which he took with ease. These three wins were officially titled the Hard Twist Stakes, the Go Man Go Stakes, and the Autumn Championship, bringing his earnings for the year to $35,738. Well into 1962 he was officially top money-winning Quarter Horse of all time. He was ahead of the heap by at least $8000.

"When we first started running him," C. G. Whitcomb tells me, "Milo saddled him a few times, after which he seemed so gentle and lazy my little granddaughter, just eleven, went to riding him. She had to carry a bat to get him out of a walk. On the track if you hit him more than twice he slows down. The only time he really fires up is when he goes to the saddling paddock and he can see it's going on the record."

At Albuquerque, after coming out of retirement, Tonto Bars Hank (September 16, 1962) in a 400-yarder for "three-year-olds and upwards which have not won two races since June 28," and carrying top weight of 122 pounds, clattered over the route to win by three-quarters over Go Billie Go and Billy Bar Be in the sensational time of :19.9, equaling the World's Record for the distance set by Breeze Bar—packing 117—at Los Alamitos the previous year.

She Kitty
(440 yds., 1962 CEN 118f :19.9)

She Kitty was out of that good track performance mare, Little Meow. She was her dam's fifth foal and first filly; and her daddy was Robin Reed, a track horse by Leo out of Sue Reed by old Joe Reed (P–3). Any way you cut it, she assays considerable concentrated Reed genes and spirit. And on Little Meow's side of the balance she's a double-bred Jack McCue with a deal of Steeldust reaching back through Tadpole, Red Dog, Balleymooney, and Concho Colonel, the cream of Casement breeding.

Little Meow ran in the days of Ed Heller and Hard Twist, when there wasn't much money but plenty of sport and much enthusiasm. Her last big run took place at Littleton, when she shaded the stallion champ Scooter W and other proved veterans in Centennial's first World Championship Quarter.

She Kitty, though small and undeveloped when she made her debut at Raton (June 17, 1961) and first put her hoofs to a straightaway, was first at the wire in AAA time. The track was slow, there was a ten-mile cross wind, yet she did the 350 in :18.3, winning over Count Zero and Dub's

Folly Bars, and seven others. The net value to her owner was $331.73. She took this outing by half a length.

On the 24th, over a sloppy track, she splashed her way again to win, this time in :18.1 over Sugar Bars Hank, Vanna Bar, and others. On July 7th she won at 400 yards—L. Tipton up, Pat Thompson training—in :20.4 (once a World's Record held, I believe, by Hy Dale).

Encouraged by these good works J. and X. Casement put up the $2000 late penalty and sent She Kitty to Ruidoso for a try at the Open Futurity. In a way it proved to be both the most heroic and most tragic point in her two-year-old season. A couple of days before the trials she was definitely "coming down with something." When finally saddled and sent to the track, Tipton had great difficulty getting her warmed up. Yet she won her tier in the fastest time of any trial, making her the logical favorite in the main event.

But, back at the barn, the fet found a temperature of 106 degrees and diagnosed a case of the same virus which had destroyed so many valuable horses in southern New Mexico and Arizona during recent years. In about six days they had the fever partially whipped. The Casements hauled her and a hundred dollars worth of medicine home to the ranch, where a sixty-day complete lay-up put her back on her feet.

At Centennial, over a sloppy track, she again tackled 350, to win in :18.3 over Idle Time and Pepper Lou, with Connie Reba in the beaten field. On October 3rd, in a 330-yard go, she defeated eight challengers in the second division of the Colorado Quarter Horse Futurity trials—time :17.2 on a track labeled fast. On the 7th she won the main event in :17.0, equalling the then-current two-year-old filly record. By this time she was something of a sensation. Six outs, six wins—all in AAA time!

She next started at Los Alamitos in the Thanksgiving Stakes (November 23, 1961), where she went up against Mr. Huntley's Flying Machine, the jet-propelled Pokey Bar, finishing second by three-quarters. The official remarks on this *Chart* state: "If accepted by the AQHA Racing Committee, She Kitty's time of :17.9 will equal the present Two-Year-Old Filly record for 350 yards."

Her next outing was on December 2nd in the Do Good Stakes at 350, which she covered in :18.5 on a sloppy track, hacking $2750 win money from the $5000 purse. Straw Flight finished second by half a length, with Goldseeker, a neck behind, coming up for show.

Straw Flight corralled their next engagement (The Las Ninas) by a scant neck in :18.3, She Kitty was second by another scant neck over Idle Time. The Kitten's share of this one came to $1125. Her final sprint of that year, on December 23rd in The Kindergarten Stakes, was the only time she dropped below third. She came in fifth behind Pokey Bar, Alamitos Bar, Mr. Three Bars, and Rockin' Bar. Time for this 350 was :18.8, and she still collected $630. Her summer sickness at Ruidoso was definitely not yet cured.

She was named Co-Champion Quarter Running Two-Year-Old Filly— ten starts, seven firsts, two seconds, and one fifth, though still in the chips. It was a year of fast times, with records equaled and smashed at several distances.

As a three-year-old she trained well, still under Pat Thompson, and had no excuses until she turned up at Phoenix. All 12 of the races she ran in 1962—even those that she dropped—were run in AAA time, as set out in the chartbooks. Once more she went into action at Raton where (July 1, 1962) she took a 440 in :22.0 (Woven Web's best time). Queenie's Brat copped second (a length behind) and Iron Maiden, by a head, came in to show. The remarks on the chart indicate that, if accepted, She Kitty's time equalled the then-current mare record and the three-year-old filly record.

Two weeks later, in the Invitational Handicap for Three-Year-Olds and Up, she ran third at 400 to Caprideck and Mr. Meyers, receiving $198.26 for show. Time for this go was :20.2 over a track labeled fast. The following week she tangled with Pokey Bar again, coming in second best by three-quarters. Pokey Bar's time for the 400 over a sloppy track was :20.5; Winna Bright grabbed third. This was a Derby trial.

On August 5th, in the Ruidoso Quarter Horse Derby at 400 yards, she was led again by Pokey Bar, who went under the wire a length ahead to win in :20.3 on a fast track. Second money in this event put $6737.50 into the Casement bank account. The Haymaker, three-quarters of a length behind, took the show position.

Pokey Bar in this two-year-old form sometimes had got off to poor starts; he was, however, winning when he hit his first solid AAA; from that time on She Kitty is the only *filly* ever to run lapped on him. (The old champion mare, No Butt, ran lapped on him twice.)

The Kitten's first out, September 15th at Centennial in the Inaugural 350-yard Handicap, was one more time when she couldn't quite make it. In the stretch, a head behind Tonto Ginger, the good colt Diamond Charge (half of an entry) looked to be making a strong bid for the win. At this point She Kitty was running third by a half, a scant head in front of Mr. Meyers (second half of the Askew and Moore entry). Despite everything the Casement filly seemed able to do Tonto Ginger came in first by three-quarters in :17.7. This time, if accepted, would credit Tonto Ginger (by Tonto Bars Gill out of Princess Plaudit by Gold Dusty) with equaling the then-existing mare record. Diamond Charge and She Kitty dead-heated for place, Mr. Meyers picking up third money.

On the 22nd, in the second division of the Derby trials, She Kitty got back in the groove, scampering the 400 yards in :19.9 to equal the World's Record and set a new mare and three-year-old filly record, reaching the wire first by two and three-quarters amid tumultuous applause.

The following week, in the 400-yard Colorado Quarter Horse Derby, she got there first in :20.0, to win by three-quarters over Printer's Devil and Miss Bob's Folly, who was lapped on the Devil until only his horns showed. The Casement take was $4262.50, the mutuel players getting ten cents on the dollar.

Came the 13th of October. At 440 yards in the Colorado Wonderland Handicap, which she won by a length and three-quarters, She Kitty set a new three-year-old filly record by going the route in :21.7—only one-tenth off the current World's Record set by Pokey Bar at Los Alamitos. Tonto Bars Hank seized the place position by a head over Mr. Meyers, who collected third money for Bob Moore. The Kitten's account was swelled by another $3650.

This was her first dash at 440. The *cognoscenti* had prophesied that those last forty yards would kill her. After getting away on top she swerved a little, had to be taken up and straightened, allowing the others to catch her. Yet, when again turned loose, she simply romped away with it. Never again did she seem quite so fit.

They took her to Arizona Downs, where, although sick, she ran three races before being retired. The first, on the 28th, was in the Arizona Quarter Horse Derby, a seven-horse field. Winner was Straw Flight who covered the quarter in :22.2, finishing first by more than a length. Off Base was second by three-quarters, with She Kitty determinedly latching onto third.

On November 4th she ran second to Caprideck, finishing a nose ahead of Straw Flight; next came Tonto Ginger, Vandy's Flash, Rebel Cause, and Mr. Meyers. She ran her last and twelfth dash of the season on the 11th, in the Arizona Downs Quarter Horse Championship, taking third money, three-quarters of a length behind Printer's Devil, who was beaten in this hotly contested go by not more than a neck. Winner here, again, was Caprideck, going the 440 in :22.2, Straw Flight coming up for fourth money, with Off Base and Arizonan trailing.

All in all, she did very well; 12 races in extremely tough company from which she fetched home five firsts, four seconds, and three thirds, earning $18,489.51—total winnings for two years on the straightaways being an acceptable $29,192.06. She was additionally elected Co-Champion Quarter Running Three-Year-Old Filly of 1962.

She holds all alone the three-year-old filly record at 400 and 440 yards and the mare record at 400; also, along with Horse-of-the-Year No Butt, the mare record at 440, and, with Tonto Bars Hank and Breeze Bar, the World's Record at 400 yards.

The latest word has it that she's off to California for a little socializing with Three Bars.

It is with much regret that—because of the extreme difficulty of securing a sufficiency of pertinent information in the time at our disposal—it was found necessary to go to press without biographical data on the following meritorious record-holding individuals: BREEZE BAR, CLABBERTOWN G, SUPER CHARGE and MY TEXAS DANDY JR. These were not passed over lightly; when all else failed their owners were written requesting information which would have obviated this course, but without avail. MADDON'S BRIGHT EYES, MONITA, and TONTA GAL will be found in the section on Outstanding Mares.

Vandy's Flash
(350 yds., 1960 LA 120f :17.5)

The following remarks were winnowed from a 1960 *Quarter Horse Journal* article headed "L. A. Opens":

One more day like Tuesday's Inaugural and the Quarter Horses are going to run out of records to break. Despite the fact that they came up short publicity-wise, opening less than 12 hours after the harness horses' getaway and the same day the Dodgers prepared to defend their pennant, a record week-day turnout of 6,847 went home happy but thirsty.

Though somewhat parched because it was Election Day and nary a bar was open in Orange County, the punters thrilled, chilled and drooled over these phenominal figures—A fantastic :17.5 triumph by Vandy's Flash in the fastest 350-yard burst of speed ever seen anywhere in the $5,000 Shue Fly Inaugural. There was a record-breaking week day opening handle of $423,048. on nine races. The demise of the world's fastest Quarter mare, Miss Louton, by a length and three-quarters in Vandy's Flash's clock-buster.

Two tremendous :17.9 triumphs by Carl Mercer's Aunt Judy and Homer Pettigrew's Miss Petite Bar. And Jockey Danny Canchola winning three races in one day—almost more than he has won in any past Los Alamitos meeting. Coming off an equally sensational :18.0 workout, Vandy's Flash was cooking on the front burner from the start for Jockey Emil Armstrong, returning $9.00 straight for his conquest of Miss Louton as Saul Lasher's Pap closed gamely to salvage the show from Tidy Too, another length down the track.

The only unfortunate thing about this stupendous performance is that the record has no chance of being allowed by the American Quarter Horse

Association because of a stiff tailwind that whisked the horses along throughout the afternoon. But, until the wind dies down and something faster comes along, it'll remain in the memories of everyone as the fastest thing they ever saw since Diamond Mae and Clabber's Win posted track and world records of :17.8.

Miss Louton's only excuse, except that she broke out slightly at the start with Jockey Jay Fishburn, simply was that she was outrun on this occasion, and we sincerely hope her new 19-year-old trainer, Curt Dunlap, doesn't lose his job because he now has failed to live up to his boast that Miss Louton would win all of her starts at this meeting.

Never touching a recognized track as a two-year-old, the nimble and indomitable gelding Vandy's Flash has had an even more meteoric career on the straightaways than his gelded full brother Vannevar—a double-barreled testimonial to the skill and good fortune of his knowledgeable breeder, Dee Garrett of Pawhuska. Racing as a three-year-old during 1957 in the silks of Carl Mercer, this product of the Vandy-Miss Pawhuska courtships won the Ruidoso Quarter Horse Derby, the Albuquerque Quarter Horse Derby, and, for that year's efforts, a delightful $13,398.

1958 saw him shade brother Vannevar with wins in the Ruidoso Quarter Horse Maturity and two other big ones, and piling up an additional $12,688.85 entry on the profit side of the ledger, making him richest gelding among the top money-earners of that season. He came in second to Double Bid in the Ruidoso Quarter Horse Championship, second to Clabber's Win in the Hard Twist and Johnny Dial stakes, and third, but a neck behind the winner, in the Los Alamitos Championship. At the start of his re-markable rise to fame and fortune he ran his first eight starts for Dee Garrett before making his home base at Mercer's Woodland Hills, California establishment. While Vandy's Flash was stabled there, Mercer's trainer was Tom Stevens.

He did a lot of additional running in the colors of John D. Askew of Fayetteville, Arkansas, and was entered by the Askew stables under trainer L. G. Culver in that record-smashing 350 at L. A. Always a horse meriting and getting a great deal of space in the sports columns, Vandy's Flash has many times been described in print as the fastest short horse in America. Following the big April win he was entered on May 7th in the $25,000 Los Alamitos Quarter Horse Championship at 440, a carefully tailored vehicle for three-year-olds and up. Two weeks after the Shue Fly Inaugural he again snatched victory from Miss Louton (by a head) in the Barbra B Stakes, but was disqualified and placed last for interfering. In this L. A. Championship, however, he was on his best behavior. An even-money favorite, he proved once more the top-flight caliber of his sprinting by a one-and-a-quarter-length victory over Triple Lady and Aunt Judy, a pair of the fastest mares in training, by hanging up a new World's Record of :21.7 for the 440, with Tidy Too, Miss Louton, Breeze Bar, First Call, No Butt, Miss Petite Bar, and Bar Flirt in the beaten field! Never far back of the pacesetters, Triple Lady and Tidy Too, he came through in the last few jumps to win going away in his most spectacular fashion, collecting $13,750 for his trouble. This win boosted him to seventh place on the all-time list of Leading Money-Earning Horses, with a total of $48,405.59.

Covering this in his "Down the Straightaway" column (*Western Horseman*), my close friend, the late Leslie Ernenwein, said:

Vandy's Flash, which rewrote the record book at L. A., has proved conclusively two things—He's well named and when he's right he is the fastest Quarter Horse that ever stampeded down a straightaway.

The Flash had given every indication of living up to his name and his reputation when he scored a breathtaking victory on the first day of the meeting. He won the Shue Fly Stakes in :17.5 for 350. Tail wind or no, that's running.

But the $25,000 L. A. Champ was the clincher. As usual, they made him the favorite, and that's how he won—going away, hand ridden—to set a new World's Record of :21.7 for the quarter. All he did was chop one-tenth off the mark of Go Man Go, and when you do that you're flying too close to the ground.

Vandy's Flash broke with his field from the Number Five gate and drifted slightly to the right to run with Triple Lady as Emil Armstrong fought to keep him straight. He collered the Lady 150 yards from the wire and went on to win by a length and a quarter. To look at him, head up and ears pricked, you'd have thought he was taking a leisurely workout. Triple Lady saved the place from Aunt Judy, then came Miss Louton, Breeze Bar, First Call, No Butt, Miss Petite Bar and Bar Flirt.

The victory climaxed a sensational spring campaign for John D. Askew's six-year-old gelding. During the L. A. Meet, Vandy's Flash earned $16,500 in winning three stakes.

As a matter of concrete fact, Vandy's Flash and Tonto Bars Hank cut through the rest of that year's contenders the way Geronimo's Apaches used to go through the lower settlements. As some forgotten observer remarked, "Seemed as though nothing could stand against them when things were right, and precious few could keep up with them when things were going wrong."

And then John Askew sold out. Shortly after this a news item stated: "The seven-year-old gelding Vandy's Flash, recently purchased from John Askew by Robert Grant of Bresa Del Mar [Escondido, California] for a reported $15,000 was named Horse of the Year. The six-man board [AQHA Racing Committee] met January 17 in Denver to select the 1960 champions and review record times set during the past season. Vandy's Flash is the first gelding to receive top honors since the champion naming was started back in 1941 with the selecting of Clabber. During 1960 he started 13 times, winning seven, placing twice and picking up third money once, earning $38,657.16."

After being elected Champion Quarter Running Gelding of 1958, Vandy's Flash in 1959 lost out to Pap. But he came back like Hard Twist in 1960; but this time he was not only named Champion Gelding but became the first, and thus far *only*, gelding ever to be elected World's Champion Quarter Running Horse as well as Horse of the Year. He became, in addition, the first horse ever to win both Los Alamitos Championship Stakes in the same year. Besides this, he copped the Shue Fly Inaugural and the Clabbertown G, finished second in the Pomona Championship and third in the Josie's Bar, hanging up, for even more glory, two new World's Records. He's a stand-out horse any way you care to take him.

Through 1960 Vandy's Flash made 62 starts, 20 of which he won, placing in nine and showing in nine. Considering the competition, he has certainly piled up a record that is powerful hard to beat. About the only way they could beat him in those days was to give him an impost of 130 pounds, by which he lost five races. On the list of Leading Money-Earning Horses, 1949 through 1962, Vandy's Flash stood eighth with total earnings of $84,930.87.

Kimaleta
(330 yds., 1962 SPG 124 :16.7)

About Quarter Horses, O. M. Woodson of Claremore, Oklahoma, has this to say:

When I was eighteen years of age I left home, here in Rogers County, and took employment with H. W. Keeline & Sons at Gillette, Wyoming. I remember my boss, George Keeline, digging at me after I had been on the spread some six months, trying to find out what law I had broken or what charge was against me. Seems that most of the hands he had hired from Oklahoma were running away from something or other. It wasn't that way with me, but I don't think yet I ever really convinced him.

The Keeline operation was large in both acreage and cattle. In summer we used seventy head of horses in the remuda, and they were ridden off the grass—no grain. In winter each cowboy had two grain-fed horses. Being closely associated with horses, I never ceased to marvel at the individualism among them. Some of these horses would look like they could get the job done but couldn't. Some of them didn't look like much but did their work up brown. Up to and including the four years I put in on that ranch I never heard the word "conformation." But don't think the cowboys of that day didn't look them over. That was where I learned what to look for.

That kind of job was the best in the world for learning to read signs. A horse's head, his eyes, his reflexes, action, and disposition. Disposition is one thing that was common to all of them—much of it bad. Let me hasten to add, however, that those which were broken as three-year-olds were generally the most tractable, usable, and the best all-round horses. I rode smooth-mouthed horses that I never could take a rope down on. When I returned to Oklahoma I felt the urge to raise some good horses.

Since I was operating as far south as Alice, Texas, I made the acquaintance of Uncle Ott Adams of Alfred. I might say in passing that it is an opinion of mine that each generation of human critters are just as much obligated to the generations past as a running Quarter Horse is to his ancestors. I am just as much in debt to Ott Adams as he is to Will and Dow Shely.

Uncle Ott has always been adamant against using any blood that is not clean race horse. One shot of dunghill blood and you will get fewer race horses. By "dunghill" I mean horses registered or unregistered, Quarter Horse or Thoroughbred, from whose bloodline sprinters have not consistently been produced.

All breeders, I am sure, play around with theories, so I will tell you mine. I try to keep—and have up to now—my brood-mare blood in bloodlines which show consistency of reproduction. Some might say, "If he does that he needs nothing else." But I do—I need class. For many years I have studied class and can tell you that, while I have not yet mastered it, I have benefited from my efforts in this direction. Class might best be likened to the ceiling of planes. The AAA run where the air is thin. There's plenty of room up there, but, like the Bible says, "Few there be that go in thereat."

In 1943, he tells me, he began to give considerable thought to the many definitions of a Quarter Horse flying about at that time.

I attended horse shows and followed the judges as they placed the horses as they saw them. In all fairness, the judges generally placed the entries as nearly properly as sight and opinion would let them. But the idea kept knocking around in my head that a Quarter Horse was something greater than this.

Many breeders at that time were just breeding good-looking mares to good-looking stallions. I went around to a lot of rodeos, too, and did not find any horses making money in the arena which looked like those at the horse shows—none to speak of, that is.

Here in Oklahoma we are blessed with brush racing. Many rocks have been thrown at brush racing, but a sportsman, be he butcher, baker, or banker, can derive a lot of pleasure and relaxation from this sport. Also, many of the finest sprinters ever to grace the straightaways have come out of the brush.

To illustrate this, one might mention Miss Panama, Hard Twist and Mame Taylor, Little Joe, Jr., Queenie, Chappo S, Clabber, Squaw H, Texas Star, Miss Bank—their name are legion.

Though I will name none, many of our top jockeys and trainers cut their teeth out here in the bushes. Opinions are fluid and many when they are still in the talking stage, but they quickly take on real significance when they're backed with good, hard American dollars.

Two things picked for me the kind of Quarter Horse I wanted to raise. I decided I wanted to raise horses with which I could earn dollars and still have the horses left. I didn't want to have to sell my horse as the horse traders and show-horse people had to do to make any money. It sounded too much like the fable about the goose that layed the golden eggs; I have always felt sorry for that goose. Another thought presented itself to decide me against raising arena horses. I noticed when a cowboy owned a horse he could make a living with he used that horse at the expense of young horses waiting to be tried.

In contrast, new two-year-old colts and fillies were appearing on the tracks each spring. New stars, too. In this I took hope. If I couldn't outrun them this year maybe I could next.

The net result in our breeding operation can be best summed up in the definition of a Quarter Horse I ran across in some book [*Outstanding Modern Quarter Horse Sires*]: "A Quarter Horse is a horse bred to *run* one quarter of a mile or lesser distance superbly well."

Kimaleta was foaled here on the outskirts of Claremore on June the first, of 1960. She was by Mr. Bar None and out of my Leo mare, Bonna Lita. Bonna Lita was out of the Busy Deck (TB) mare Bonnie Goff. Busy Deck, a winner, was by the stake horse Quarter Deck, he by Man O'War. Bonnie Goff's dam was by the Thoroughbred Dagio, he by Ozone. Dagio was a little black stud that was raced on the Arkansas Fair circuit many years ago by the Bolen family of Fayettville. Kimaleta is a dark chestnut with some roan interspersed and some white at the top of the trail.

She is a well-balanced individual with an unusually good back, shoulder, and withers, rather plain about the head. She has a fine disposition and her will, Mr. Woodson says, "is aggressive. She is a mare you enjoy being around. She has been somewhat on the small side all her life, though now she stands 14.2 and might weigh 1000 pounds."

The Woodsons bought Bonnie Goff (Kimaleta's grand dam), curiously enough, scarcely a half-mile from the old home place at the north end of Rogers County. "I showed her to Mr. Charlie Goff, of Chelsea, and when I told him I wanted to raise some good Quarter Horses he said, 'Breed this mare to a good Quarter Horse and you are in business.'"

Mr. Goff raced Quarter Deck and bred Busy Deck, presently selling the latter to Ronald Mason of the Cross J at Nowata. Mason liked the old horse and used him extensively until his death in 1961. Busy Deck contributed generously to the great band of Cross J horses.

Kimaleta's dam, Bonna Lita by Leo, won five matched races and lost two before the trials of the 1952 Oklahoma Futurity. She qualified in the trials by running second to Leo Do by, says Woodson, "six or eight inches." In the main event she ran, with Leo Do, a dead heat for third, lapped on the winning Fanny Leo. N. R. Negraletta ran second by scarcely the length of a good cigar. Time for the 220 was :12.4.

In 1953 Bonna Lita, in foal to Overtime Leo, ran third in the Oklahoma Derby. Mr. Woodson says: "Her first foal, Bozell, was gelded and sold to a rancher who uses him as much as he does a knife and fork. Her second foal was Drifta by Overtime Leo. This one, at this writing, is in the court of Mr. Bar None. She is a fine mare and could run. I matched her ten times as a two-year-old and won them all. In 1957 she won the Consolation Stake at 300 yards in :16.3 under 123 pounds. Also she won the Blue Stem Futurity at Pawhuska. She was eighth on a list of nine qualifiers for the ROM at 300 yards in 1957. It reads like a *Who Was Who*: Vannevar, Clabber Juan, Quick M Silver, Mr. Bar None, Brigand, Easter Rose, Wall Street, Drifta, Sam Bar. Of the nine, she was top weight at 123. At Pawhuska the Blue Stem people would not let us run unless we showed. Well, it just cost five dollars, so we showed. Under Mr. Bill Hedge my mare won their show, so as we went down the road that evening we were not singing the Blues. Drifta had picked up everything loose in Pawhuska that day—two trophies, two blue ribbons, and two checks.

"In 1959 we went back to Pawhuska with Big Lieta and won the Oklahoma Futurity at 300 yards in 16 flat. Incidentally, Big Lieta is a half-sister to Drifta, being by Overtime Leo and out of Lou Jo by Bert. I had the nation's top jock that day—Charles Smith. Big Lieta was Smith's first stakes winner."

Came November of 1961. Woodson engaged Little Joe Ebardt at Claremore to ride Kimaleta some. In a round corral. He says she broke easily, as he finds most of the Bar horses do. In February of 1962 he put Joe on her and had him ride her about thirty minutes a day for three weeks. "Then I started taking her to the track every other day for two more weeks. At the end of this little program I took her to the brush track and galloped through the crowd a few times. The following week we turned three babies in front of the gates and let them work 200 yards, Kimaleta sticking out in front under a light hold all the way.

The following week I put her in the gates with Joe Float, a Register of Merit horse by Vandy Joe and out of Drifta. Joe Float at this time was also a baby; it was his first work from the gates. They broke well and ran straight under light holds, Kimaleta getting there first by a neck, 220 yards.

Up to the trials for the Newkirk Futurity (last part of April) I had given her a total of ten starts, all of which she won and nine of which I collected on. Here in the brush you are lucky if you win ten races and collect nine times. In the Newkirk Futurity trials there were 17 entries; three gates of four and one gate of five. Kimaleta by this time was getting hot away from the latch. She was away first by one-half a side and won in :16.1 by daylight. Joe Float was second and Poncan (full brother to Palleo Pete) was third.

The following week eight finalists went to the post. Again Kimaleta was away first and once more she won in :16.1 with her jockey standing up. She won by daylight. Poncan was second, Joe Float third. Two weeks later the Oklahoma Futurity was up for grabs.

During the meeting the track at Enid had failed to respond to the good care given it. There were 91 entries, come drawing day. In times like these I pay little attention to the horses I am in with. You know and can feel the tenseness of the other jockeys and trainers. This is the hour of business. Every detail is so important. We speak in lower voice, all eyes are watching.

We were in Gate Three. It was a wonderful gateful of colts and fillies. We loaded second and tailboards snapped methodically as other gates were loaded. Very little noise. One colt flounced a little in Gate Four or Five. The jockey said, "No chance, no chance." Then quiet. Then bang—they're off! Kimaleta away first, and then the dust hanging over everything. Ten seconds later I could see them, Charles Waterson down on Kimaleta just shaking his stick a little. I thought she had won it, and when I saw my family move out on the track I knew she had. My! My! what a sweet pony! Jimmie Charge was second, Dynamo Leo third. The following week we were going for the Gold in the finals. We had put away 83 head, but seven still separated us from that pot of shekels.

When you are in the last gateful you wonder what part of it is yours. Any race-horse man who has been there knows his part is from nothing up. As in the Newkirk, Kimaleta had Number Three gate. I remember Montecarlo Bar was in Seven and Mr. Juniper Bar was in Eight. I remembered that N. R. Negraletta, dam of Montecarlo Bar, had outrun Bonna Lita ten years before in this same classic. They were both by Mr. Bar None.

The gate loaded good and then they were away, Kimaleta taking her place once more at the head of the class and remaining there for about 250 yards, at which point Mr. Juniper Bar took over and won decisively by three lengths—330 yards in :17.2 on an off track. Kimaleta ran second, Montecarlo Bar was third, Mr. Yellow Cat fourth, and Sugar Comb fifth. It was a great race and a great day for many, a couple of whom was Yours Truly and Mr. Jeffers—his stallion, Mr. Bar None, had sired the first three in. He was so elated—and properly so—he had all three horses pose in one of his winner's circle pictures.

I felt we had done well; we had put away 89 head of colts and fillies.

We led Kimaleta until they wrote a two-year-old winners preferred at a new track named Midway Downs at Stroud. This is a fine track and they are just waiting for a favorable stroke of fate whereby they may have Quarter Horse meetings with pari-mutuel support. Kimaleta won this race handily, though I consider it one of her poorest of the season.

I next entered her in the Eureka (Kansas) Championship which she won by herself. They treated us fine at Eureka, which makes you wonder if Republicans are such bad people after all.

As I had decided to run Kimaleta in the Illinois State Fair Futurity, I entered her at Turley in a field of three-year-olds and up at 250 yards, $500 a round, winner take all.

The loose footing in her gate let her hind legs go under the tailboard and she was away late by a neck to King Bee Leo, but drove past him at about 75 yards and won from Lady Bar and Linley's Stag in :13.4—that was the day I found out this pony could sickle.

In Illinois the track was so hard I wanted to come home, but we took a roll at it and won our trial in :17.5 under a good hold. Uncle Van ran second and Overtime Bar third. We ran back the next day in front of 7000 people, many of whom were seeing their first Quarter Horse race.

By soaking the track the morning of the Main Event they thought they could give us a sponge to run on, but by post time a horse couldn't make a track that an Injun could see. Kimaleta was quiet in her stall that morning and in the saddling paddock until we were called; then she seemed to sense something big was coming off—I could hardly keep her head away from the grandstand.

We were delayed some behind the gates. I never saw a more eager gate of horses. It must have been those trials the day before that made them so sharp. Kimaleta had Number Six and when they called for Joe Float he flounced and his bridle broke and we went without him.

Kimaleta broke her best, which was good enough, and forty yards out of the gate the horse on her left had plenty of room to go in behind her. I had Otis Craighead on her (124 pounds and that hard track injured her left ankle). In the final strides Mr. Carl Mercer's Uncle Van moved up to Kimaleta's cinch and copped second money. Sandy Bolo (winner of the Michigan Quarter Horse Futurity) was third.

Craighead told me that at about 250 yards the mare ran as if her feet were burning, but I believe it was her ankle. In her second work after I returned home she developed osselet trouble. You could imagine my surprise when they announced her time as :16.7 for the 330 yards.

My! I had never heard of a horse running that fast. Governor Otto Kerner of Illinois presented the trophy, a beautiful walnut plaque shaped like the state, and on the front of it there is metal that looks like gold and into it is cut these words:

Illinois State Fair
FUTURITY WINNER
Open to the World
1962
KIMALETA
Otis Craighead
Jockey

We were some set up, I can tell you. My! My! No one anywhere was ever treated more cordially than we were in Illinois. After returning home I rested Kimaleta and pointed her for the Magic Empire to be run in October. I kept her ankle tight and had her ready for that affair. This was a 400-yarder. We drew into the first heat with Mr. Juniper Bar and even I didn't give her an outside chance of running better than second. The big gelding had won the Kansas Futurity, and outrun horses like Jet Deck.

We had rain, and then the track was dry on top and soft underneath. When they left it was all Kimaleta at 250, it was still Kimaleta at 300, and Kimaleta by plenty at 350. He wasn't there yet and at 400 yards he had not arrived, though his nostrils were on her cinch. She won by half a length, track slow, in :21.6, Mr. Juniper Bar second, and Silent Sal, the Phillips Ranch mare, was third.

If not with your heart, how do you grade a filly like her? She had come back and got the one she had missed in the spring. There were 91 entries and she had put away 90. In the finals, because of a mistake of mine she put herself away. Breaking late, she was wiped out by the mare on her left, being knocked completely off her feet and up on Poncan, making his cause hopeless also. But she is sound again now and will be campaigned some this year, but as long as I own her her heart will be left in her.

Said the editor of the August Chart Book: "The incredible time of :16.7 was posted after Kimaleta won the 330-yard Illinois State Fair Futurity. If accepted [and it was] by the AQHA Racing Committee, this will constitute a new world record (two tenths of a second faster than the current record), a new mare record, and a new two-year-old filly record."

The previous record for this distance (:16.9) was established by Miss Panama in 1948, carrying 121 pounds. It was equaled by Miss Louton in 1959, under 126 pounds.

Out of 10 starts in her maiden season, Kimaleta won eight, placed in one, and was dead last in her final race of 1962. The two Newkirk races were run on an unrecognized track, so she is officially credited with eight starts, six wins, one second, and one run out of the money.

Part VI: Youth Activities

General Information

Although not launched until mid-1961, after most of the major shows had been held and numerous others had completed their plans, Youth Activities events, the most ambitious and soundly conceived of all AQHA projects, got off to a fine start, and with public interest fairly bursting at the seams with vigor and enthusiasm. Ninety trophies were given at shows which incorporated Youth Activities events in the 1961 season. More than one-third of all approved shows in 1962 included such activities. The thought behind all this was that ownership of Quarter Horses among young people was bound to prove helpful and might even create a new era for the breed. No one could have dreamed its reception would, on a nation-wide basis, have proved in this short time so remarkably successful. Of the 808 AQHA approved shows held in 1962 inside the continental United States, Canada, and Hawaii, 312 welcomed boys and girls by including Youth Activities events in their programs.

Fantastic as this may seem, the interest of young people in horsemanship and competitive events did not surprise Garford Wilkinson, one of the guiding spirits in this new departure. He tells me: "Some of our most active show managers foresee the time when youth shows will outnumber adult shows. I may have told you that 111 boys and girls competed in the Golden Spike Quarter Horse Show at Ogden, Utah. We shall permit these young people to compete on unregistered horses for a brief further span, but those who compete for all-around honors must be mounted on registered stock. The last report we saw from the Extension Service of the U. S. Department of Agriculture showed that through 1961 61,811 boys and girls were enrolled in 4-H Light Horse Projects, compared to 37,492 in 1959. On the basis of the thousands of inquiries I have received from state 4-H directors, adult 4-H leaders, and county agriculture leaders in the past year, the increase since 1961 surely has been even more remarkable than that of the 1959–1961 period.

"Our Youth Activities program, of course, is not the same as the Extension Service sponsored projects. All eligible boys and girls may participate in our activities even though they are not enrolled in 4-H, F.F.A., or any other youth program."

The AQHA has enlarged the Youth Activities Program since the last official *Handbook* was published. In 1963, in addition to the All-Around trophy, three new trophies have been provided. Trophies are now given for the best stallion, mare, and gelding at each Youth Activities Events show held in connection with an AQHA approved show for adults. Printed information on this subject is available by writing the American Quarter Horse Association.

"Some shows," Mr. Wilkinson remarks, "which would like to welcome boys and girls cannot yet do so due to a lack of adequate facilities. Several show managers have told me that if they were to provide classes for children, there would not be room or time for adult shows. It would be safe for you to say that the future growth of the Quarter Horse registry is tied closely to the rapidly increasing interest of boys and girls in our breed. Proud parents and grandparents are mounting their little ones on some mighty fine specimens, and this trend will increase as competition increases."

It is believed the inherent love of youth for animals could have no better outlet, no more logical and satisfying object, than a registered Quarter Horse: useful, obedient, companionable, sturdy, thrifty, and long-lived. Here is the ideal lesson for the young owner in sportsmanship, discipline, and responsibility for the health and welfare of a valued dependent. Here, likewise, is an inspiration to the study of practical genetics, the science of breeding, and the engrossing observation of performance in relation to bloodlines. Nor should we minimize the importance of possible substantial profits through the production and sale of offspring, either as individuals of marketable age or as trained and fully developed animals ready for pleasure riding or competition in shows and performance events. Many young people are creating college-education funds through the sale of Quarter Horses they have personally bred.

As remarked earlier, some persons may be astonished to realize there are approximately two hundred Quarter Horse associations now functioning in this country, Canada and Hawaii. Though these are not administratively tied to the AQHA, all of their shows, to be approved, must comply with American Quarter Horse Association rules and regulations. These associations sponsor shows and performance events; many hold annual awards banquets and some have social functions during the year. Members of these associations are real ambassadors of the breed.

Mr. Wilkinson states: "We are proud of the numerous Quarter Horse clinics annually held in various parts of this country and Canada. These clinics—usually held at state universities—are sponsored by local, regional,

Clinics annually held in various parts of the country and Canada. These or state Quarter Horse associations. The last one held in 1962, I believe, was on November 2–3 at the University of Connecticut. The AQHA defrays expenses of one of its representatives to join with college personnel in the conducting of these clinics. Subject matter is varied, including virtually everything of interest, from health problems to training and performance exhibitions."

Convention Address of Mr. C. O. McKerley

Because so much of this subject is so well wrapped up in a speech delivered at the 1962 Convention of the American Quarter Horse Association by Mr. C. O. McKerley (Staff member of Louisiana State Extension Service and Secretary of the Louisiana State Quarter Horse Association), we are presenting it herewith:

I am sure that every person interested in the Quarter Horse breed fully realizes that the future of the breed lies in holding and developing the interest now being shown by our youth. The future of everything that now goes to make up our way of life will be determined in the same manner. But today we are talking about a phase of American life of special interest to our group.

The history of the horse program dates back for many years in Louisiana. In the early 1930's, Mr. C. L. Hill, Animal Husbandry Specialist with the Louisiana Agricultural Extension Service, worked with draft horses and mule producers. Running horses on a brush track has long been a week-end pastime in South Louisiana. Louisiana State University was one of the first colleges to acquire a band of Quarter Horse broodmares.

The first Louisiana State University Quarter Horse Show was held in 1948. Fifty-six horses were exhibited. From this show stemmed two fine Class A shows. They are the L.S.U. National Quarter Horse Show, with 404 entries in 1961, and the Quarter Horse division of the Spring Livestock Show at L.S.U., which had 343 entries in 1962.

In 1953 the Louisiana Quarter Horse Association readily saw the need for a junior division in their show, and two colt classes were offered for 4-H and FFA members. Nine horses were shown that first year. In 1954, seventeen horses were shown. Four classes were offered in 1955, with fourteen horses being shown. In 1956 and 1957 the number of juniors participating remained about the same. Most of these exhibitors came from southwest Louisiana, where the Lake Charles District Show offered classes and premium money from a local level.

The State Quarter Horse Association felt that the growth of the youth program could be greatly stimulated if the project could be guided by the Louisiana State University Agricultural Extension Service. Mr. David Perkins and Mr. Lee Berwick were appointed as a committee to discuss the possibilities with the Director of the Agricultural Extension Service. The Louisiana Quarter Horse Association agreed to sponsor the project by providing funds for the outstanding 4-H or FFA member each year to receive an all-expense-paid trip to the Chicago International Livestock Show under the supervision of the Extension Service.

It was decided by the Extension Service that a horse project would fill a real need, and that its primary objective should be the development of youth into well-rounded citizens.

In 1958 the Extension Service offered a light horse project. Enrollment in this new project grew from 25 4-H members from four counties in 1958 to 2,173 members from 58 of the 64 counties in 1961.

Junior exhibitors were not allowed to compete with adults until 1962. This was due to the different judging dates at the state show, with the same judge making the placings. But now we are going to judge the junior and adult entries at the same time, with the juniors being placed in the open show in their respective age classes at halter. When the open class is completed the juniors will remain and be placed as juniors.

Under this system, junior exhibitors will have an opportunity to receive AQHA points and at the same time to receive recognition within the junior division. We feel that this is absolutely necessary because the progress of a youth program depends primarily on recognition. We also believe that the juniors must be able to receive AQHA points, because many own horses which have the ability to win these points. Another point of concern is that producers will sell better quality horses at a reasonable price to juniors if they are sure that these horses can acquire points.

A new rule was added this year to the effect that if the Champion is declared from an aged class, that animal will not be eligible to continue to compete in the junior division but can compete in the open contest.

Performance classes for juniors are being added to our program also. In the past they have competed with open competition. Classes in reining, roping, cutting, barrel racing, western pleasure, pole bending, showmanship, and horsemanship are offered. These classes will be divided according to the age of the exhibitors with those ten through fourteen years of age as of January 1st comprising one class, and those over fourteen years of age through twenty years comprising another class. Exhibitors who are enrolled in college are ineligible to compete as juniors.

The requirements for the horse project resemble those for other livestock projects. The contestant must own a horse. Registered horses are not required to become a project member, but the importance of a sound, good conformation horse is recommended. The 4-H members must feed, manage, and keep records on their horses throughout the year. And though a registered horse is not required for a horse project, only registered horses may be shown at the district and state shows. These horses must be registered in the 4-H member's name. The 4-H member must own the horse by October 1st prior to the show to be eligible to compete.

In Louisiana we hold five district elimination shows prior to the state show. Animals which do not meet the requirements on condition, conformation, and care are screened and are not allowed to compete at the state show. Premium money is awarded on placings. Performance will not be limited until facilities at the state show present a problem.

Until now we have primarily discussed the process of showing at the district and state shows at which the youth are supervised by the Extension Service. But there are many horse shows held on a local basis throughout the state. New Orleans alone has approximately six hundred horses and holds youth performance classes almost every week-end. Most of these shows do not require the horse to be registered or to be of any particular breed.

There are generally about 18 approved shows held in Louisiana throughout the year. The Louisiana Quarter Horse Association is recommending that these shows use the procedure outlined at the state show for judging youth classes.

We now have come to a very important phase of our horse program. That is, organization and the training of agent leaders. In Louisiana, we use judging and grooming clinics, bulletins, and field days as tools to achieve this goal. We also use films, literature, and other materials furnished by the American Quarter Horse Association. We have made tremendous progress, but education is a slow process. A good educational program takes the united efforts of the Extension Service, the producers, and the breed association.

What lies in the future? In my correspondence with Mr. Charles E. Bell, Jr., of the Federal Extension Service, he clearly points out a rapid upward trend in the horse project on a national basis. Enrollment in this 4-H project increased from 37,492 in 1959 to 61,811 in 1961. Enrollment was reported in fifty states and Puerto Rico.

The nature of the project varies by regions. In the Northeast the greatest interest is in riding clubs, while the Western region seems to emphasize beginning the project with a foal and letting the youth develop along with the animal.

A survey conducted by C. C. O'Mary, Associate Professor, Animal Science Department, Washington State University, showed that the biggest recent change in the 4-H exhibits at livestock shows was the increase in numbers of horses. There was an increase from 2,383 4-H members showing horses in 1950 to 27,052 in 1960. These two sources, along with many others, show a definite rapid increase of interest in horses by youth.

Many Quarter Horse breeders have remarked to me, "We have the breed which can do all the things that the youth programs require. The breed shows at halter, performance, and pleasure, and is versatile in most everything. What can our state and national associations do in the future to encourage youths to use the Quarter Horse?" the breeders ask.

I said earlier that the youth program is greatly increased by recognition. I feel that the American Quarter Horse Association should set up a youth division. This division should carry out youth activities in the same manner as the adult or open divisions. This division should:

1. Classify youth shows, using the same system as the AQHA

2. Set up a youth point system in halter and performance, using the same system as AQHA, except in performance the points would be acquired by the exhibitors in their age classification

3. Provide trophies in halter and performance according to show classification

4. Set up a section in the *Quarter Horse Journal* to recognize the top horses and exhibitors in the nation

5. Assign some personnel to work with the youth program

The state associations should provide recognition and leadership at the state level. They should provide leaders and assist in all educational programs, organize and assist in carrying out approved youth shows. Where funds are needed at the state level, the state association would be responsible to acquire these and aid in promoting the program in general.

I am sure that a combined effort of all organizations mentioned will produce the acceptance desired by the breeders throughout the United States.

Letter from Tarsus

A letter from Garford Wilkinson, who pioneered the youth program as it relates to the American Quarter Horse Association, says under date of May 31, 1963:

I sincerely believe your report of youth activities will be welcomed by most readers, for this program has exploded and there are some who believe the time is not far distant when there will be more youth shows than shows for adults. The first full year for this departure was 1962; 312 of our 875 shows welcomed young people. Of the 668 shows we had approved up to last week in the United States and Canada (for 1963), 339—more than half —have included youth activities. The new *Official Handbook*, dated February 20, 1963, describes our recently expanded Youth Activity program.

I think of Paul's advice to Timothy: "Let no man despise thy youth; but be thou an example of the believers, in word, in conversation, in charity, in spirit, in faith, in purity." I think the time is rapidly approaching when horse traders will be unable to barter an unsound horse, for the young people will be able to guide families in wise selections.

Several states will hold state-wide all-youth shows this summer, and B. F. Phillips, Jr. has arranged for a big-time Youth Clinic at Expectation Stud Farm, Frisco, Texas.

Part VII: Outstanding Modern Mares

Biographical Sketches

Anniversary

Bred by Bert H. Wood, the ROM palomino mare Anniversary (P–15,840) was sired by the 1943 Champion Quarter Running Stallion Joe Reed II, out of Patsy Hug by Bear Hug. Joe Reed II was the most outstanding son of old Joe Reed, P–3, by the record holder Joe Blair (TB), a son of Bonnie Joe. The dam of Joe Reed II was Nellene by Fleeting Time (TB). Nellene was out of the race mare Little Red Nell, who is said to have been sired by Old Billy—which seems hardly likely in view of their ages. Little Red Nell was out of Old Red Nell, also a sprinter, by Texas Chief, alleged to have been the fastest son of Traveler.

The dam of Patsy Hug was the dark-dun Patsy Peavy by Ding Bob (269), whose dam was Mary McCue by Peter McCue. Bear Hug (who sired a large percentage of the Gill Brothers' brood mares) was by Norfleet (by Brettenham, TB) out of the Houseparty Mare by Peter McCue; second dam was Five Dollars by Jim Trammell.

Demonstrably well bred, Anniversary, although she achieved Register of Merit status under the tutelage of Louie Kirk, missed by a considerable margin setting the woods afire when it came to track performance. Her greatest recognition has been acquired as a producer.

Dorothy Wood is authority for the following:

Anniversary was foaled at Benson, Arizona, April 5, 1958, on the anniversary of our marriage. I told my husband we should call her "Marital Bliss" and he said, "Bliss, hell!" So that's what I sent in as a second choice in names. Elmer Hepler, when he heard about it, thought that was pretty funny.

Anniversary was the first offspring of Patsy Hug and Joe Reed II. Then came K Hornet that won the first Pomona Futurity; after which, also by Joe, she dropped Mr. Big while Bill Lamkin was standing Joe over in California.

In her first start [Tucson], Anniversary, coming out of the gate, bucked off her jockey. Our oldest son, Clifford—about eight at the time—was the first to ride her, with his dad keeping hold of the halter shank.

Her first trainer was Louie Kirk; then for a while Jimmy Curry had her.

Anniversary was supposed to be my horse and was registered in my name. One time they ran her as owned by Mr. and Mrs. Bert Wood, so I finally wrote the Association and had her transferred to Bert.

After she came off the tracks we took her to Bart B. S., but she lost this foal at about three months. We then bred her to her sire, Joe Reed II, and got a palomino horse colt. Les Hilton bought this colt and trained him for the MR. ED television series. When the series was cancelled they sold the colt; when it was decided to go on with it again the new owners would not permit them to use the colt. Les told us he was one of the easiest to train he had ever handled. This colt was also in several other TV shows.

Annie's second foal was a dun horse sired by Seco Jimmie (by Seco Joe). He was purchased by Audie Murphy.

Annie's Venture, AAA, came along next, by Depth Charge (TB), and her fourth foal was a filly by Depth Charge which was at her side when the Woods sold Anniversary to Stanfield. This may have been Goldseeker.

At the Stanfield dispersal, held in Tulsa, three of Anniversary's produce, breaking several records, sold for $74,000. Goldseeker, AAA, by Depth Charge, brought $26,000 as a three-year-old; Deep Sorrel, then aged two, was knocked down for $24,000; and Gold Hustler, an untried yearling, fetched another $24,000. Deep Sorrel has since made AAA and is currently the property of Ed Honnen's Quincy Farm, Denver.

Anniversary's seventh foal is Mr. Anniversary, by Clabber Bar, owned—like his dam—by C. W. Mickle's Valley View Ranch at Scottsdale, Arizona, the present home of No Butt.

Ariel Lady

A chestnut mare foaled in 1946, Ariel Lady was bred by Melville Haskell at the Rincon Stock Farm, Tucson, Arizona. Her dam was Lady Albert G (TB) by Ariel out of Dickey Lee by *Omar Khayyam. Her sire, Little Joe, Jr., is about as solidly bred a Quarter Horse as one is likely to find. His father was Joe Bailey (P–4), who was by King (Possum) by Traveler. His dam was Dumpy (2917) by Shorty by Red Devil.

Little Joe, Jr., a sorrel bred by Preston Johnson at Waelder, Texas, foaled in 1937. He was a mighty good-looking horse and favored his Traveler blood. He was twice Grand Champion of the Tucson Livestock Show and stood for several years in Arizona. I knew him well. A good solid AA in the days when that was the highest rating obtainable from track perform-ance, he was a proven sire of Quarter Running and ranch using horses. Through 1948 he had sired 11 starters on recognized tracks, besides a few that were running out in the brush. One of his sprinting sons, Joe Jimmy, defeated the celebrated Miss Panama at Del Rio. Little Joe, Jr. never got the patronage he so richly deserved.

Ariel Lady was raised and campaigned by Mr. Haskell, who has many times expressed the opinion that she was one of the really great mares of the breed. Quality is sometimes rather difficult to recognize, especially when viewed day after day across the nearest fence; but it is one of those attributes which can no longer be questioned as applied to Ariel Lady. She is, as far as I have been able to discover, possibly the all-time greatest pro-ducer of outstanding running Quarter stock the breed has ever known. Double A on the tracks, she outran many a Big Name in her time, estab-lishing a reputation for both determination and early foot. It was not until she was retired to the stud that her astonishing worth became generally apparent.

Her first foal was Spotted Lady, AAA, by Spotted Bull (TB), foaled in 1952. Next came Raza, AAA, again by Spotted Bull. In 1954 she was barren but came on to produce in 1955 another filly, Ariel Beauty, AA, by Spotted Bull (and Beauty gives promise of being a producer, too, being presently the dam of Bobbie Cocoa, AAA, and Pantano Pat, AA). In 1956 Ariel Lady dropped Ariel Bar, AAA, by Lightning Bar, and, in 1957, a full brother, Light Bar, AAA also and co-holder of the three-year-old colt record at 350. The following spring she foaled Ariel Bull, apparently unraced, by Spotted Bull. At about this time she was sold to John Taylor of Chino, California, owner of the good sprinting stallion Dividend, AAA, by Depth Charge (TB). In 1959, by Dividend, Ariel Lady foaled Silent Ariel, AAA, a Cen-tennial track record holder. In 1960, also by Dividend, came a full sister to Silent Ariel; she has made AAA at two. Both these get of Dividend are currently owned by B. F. Phillips, Jr. of Frisco, Texas.

Ariel Lady then was brought to Quincy Farm, Denver, where on March 24, 1963, she foaled a filly by Tonto Bars Gill. Nine foals, one too young to go to the tracks, one unraced, one AA, and six AAA—quite a record, and one which gives every indication of becoming more remarkable.

Ed Honnen, her present owner, purchased Ariel Lady at the John Taylor dispersal in 1959 with her Dividend filly foal at side, and bred back to Dividend. Now, with a horseman's optimism, Mr. Honnen has returned Ariel Lady to the court of Dividend for the 1963 season.

She is currently at the top of the list of Leading Dams of Register of Merit Qualifiers.

141. Anniversary, by Joe Reed II out of Patsy Hug, by Bear Hug. C. W. Mickle holding.

142. Ariel Lady, by Little Joe, Jr. out of Lady Albert G., by Ariel, TB. Betty Bowdle is up. Charlie Hall, Rincon Stock Farm trainer, is holding.

143. Blackwell's Tick Tac (at right), with her yearling foal Gold Note.

144. Bright Eyes, heavy with last foal. She was put to sleep in June of the year picture was taken.

145. Bright Eyes, taken in 1951, just after she equalled World's Record in the mud.

146. Bunny's Bar Maid running in the Kansas Futurity at Ruidoso Downs.

Blackwell's Tick Tac

Twelfth on the list of Leading Dams of Register of Merit Qualifiers (1945 through 1962) is Blackwell's Tick Tac (P–5802). She was bred by Lou Kirk (Gallup, New Mexico) and foaled in 1935. Her sire was Jack Dempsey (by Big Boy); her dam was Miss Dock Harrington by Jack. Jack Dempsey's dam was Oklahoma Queen (by A. D. Reed out of Brunks Queen). Miss Doc Harrington's dam was Ribbon (by Last Chance out of Juanita).

Tick Tac was raised by John Alonzo on the Indian Reservation west of Albuquerque. About 1945, Lewis Blackwell (that great trader) bought a gelding called Revenue (later registered as Revenue Barnes) at El Paso from a Mr. Jim Shirley who had been running him at Albuquerque that fall. Shirley was then racing the gelding at El Paso; he has run against such good ones as Shue Fly (who beat him by scarcely a head). It turns out that Revenue Barns was Tick Tac's first foal, sired by a little horse named Teddy.

While the Blackwells had the gelding at the New Mexico State Fair, John Alonzo came by and told how he had traded the horse for an old iron wash pot and a few scrawny chickens. Mrs. Blackwell says:

After the meet we went out to the Reservation and traded Revenue back to John for a half-interest in Tick Tac and another Jack Dempsey mare named Red Wing, and bought their filly foals (Miss Revenue and Pueblo Belle), both by the same little horse called Teddy. John seemed very interested in building up his stock of horses. We, too, had become interested in a breeding program, which was the main point behind the half-interest deal. We were to take the two mares and breed them to a good stallion and share the foals with Alonzo.

A few months later John needed some money to buy a piece of land and so he sold us his half interest in Tick Tac and the others. Still later we bought Revenue again. We kept Tick Tac from then on until her death in 1953.

She had had three foals when we got her; Revenue Barnes, a horse called Income, and the filly named Miss Revenue that we bought and match raced until she was injured. Miss Revenue is now in the brood-mare band of Lou Tuck, to whom we sold Custus Rastus, at Littleton, Colorado.

Tick Tac had six live foals for us and all of them could run. Her first for us, by a Thoroughbred horse named Brown Cabin (a son of the famous Cabin Camp), was a horse colt we called Tuffy. The morning he was foaled another mare attempted to take him away from Tick Tac and in the excitement they ran him through a fence. He was such a tough little customer he came through the ordeal with nothing worse than a few scratches. One spring meet at Tucson we raced Tuffy. He was two years old and did real good for us. We sold him the following summer to Marion

Seward. He has told us that while he owned him he ran him 27 times and won 24. Sometimes he raced him twice the same day.

Tick Tac's fifth foal (1948) was a filly by Hard Twist which the Blackwells named Legal Tender Bee. She made AAA and is now in the mare band of Charles Works, Vancouver, Washington. Mr. Works bred her to Ricky Taylor (a horse strong in Dempsey blood), and from this mating came the AAA Mr. Terrific.

Currency Bee, by Hard Twist (1949), was Tick Tac's sixth foal. He also made AAA and, as a four- or five-year-old was that year fifth on the list of Leading Money Earners.

Cold Cash, by Hard Twist (1950) made AAA.

Gold Note, by Custus Rastus (TB, 1951), was Tick Tac's eighth foal; she too made AAA on the tracks.

Tick Tac's ninth (1952), again by Hard Twist, lived only a few hours.

In 1953 her last foal, according to Lucille Blackwell, was "called Determine because he was so determined to live. He was prematurely foaled, Tick Tack dying the day following his birth. He was so weak he walked down on his hocks when he got up, but on a prescribed formula began to strengthen and walk more up on his legs. Even now, however, he has one back leg that's a little crooked. For that reason he was not accepted for registration by the AQHA inspector. As a youngster Determine was raised in a trap with Ricky Taylor and another horse colt. Many a time, looking out the window at them, I have watched them get boogered over something and take off up the hill to the back of the pasture. Determine was always the last to get started but was invariably leading by the time they pulled up."

Tick Tac one year was the Association's leading dam of AAA and AA foals. Another year she stood second only to Do Good. She had, by this time, been dead several years.

Bright Eyes
(250 yds., 1950 RIL 120 :13.4; 220 yds., 1950 RIL 125 :12.1)

In the words of Melville Haskell, at that time head of the since-absorbed American Quarter Racing Association, "In a class by herself at the top of the list, and the horse to beat in any race that includes her, is C. L. Maddon's Bright Eyes." In the June, 1950, *Quarter Horse Journal*, Mr. Haskell wrote: "Outstanding champion of the quarter tracks in 1949, she had won a matched race from Tidy Step at the Agua Caliente Track in Tiajuana, Mexico, early in the year and had equalled the [then] World's Record of

:12.1 for 220 yards in a warm-up race at Tucson. On the second day of the trials she came out in the 250 yard Speed Stakes to help warm up several horses entered to run against her later on in the Championship Quarter. This she managed to do quite effectively by winning in :13.4 and equalling the World's Record for the distance. Bert Wood's Little Sister W finished second a length and a quarter behind her and Ray Seeley's Tidy Step, winner of the 440 yard Stakes at Bay Meadows last fall, was three-fourths of a length farther back. Bright Eyes took command almost immediately after leaving the gate, was driven hard for the first sixteenth and won under a hand ride from there on in."

Said Leslie Ernenwein (June, 1950): "World's Champion Quarter Horse is her official title now, but back in 1948 at Albuquerque a man peered through his binoculars and expressed it more pungently when he cried— 'Bright Eyes by herself!' " In 1954 Ernie said: "I suppose there have been other two-year-old fillies making their first start who've looked just as pretty, but she is the one I've never forgotten. When she came hightailing down that straightaway to win by three lengths [New Mexico Futurity Trials of 1948] I understood what the Bard meant about the 'poetry of motion.' She had it. She did that quarter in :22.6. There were skeptics at the track that day who called her victory a fluke. They predicted it would be different when the chips were down in the big Futurity. Well, it was— but not much. You could see the ground break from under Bright Eyes when she scat-catted out of the gate and went down on her knees. Even so, she overtook the field and forged to the front within 200 yards and won by almost a length in the exact time of that first race. Fluke, my eye. This filly had been touched with the magic wand of greatness."

Montague Rockingham, writing in the *Texas Livestock Journal*, December, 1951, declared: "When J. E. Madden's brown colt Plaudit (by Himyar) defeated the thought-to-be-invincible Lieber Karl and won the Run for the Roses in 1898, little did he dream that half a century later one of Plaudit's descendants would be crowned Queen of the Quarter Tracks."

In the *Quarter Horse Journal* of November, 1952, F. Curt Keen told of her final race: "On August 29 Bright Eyes went to the post with a top field of sprinters at Albuquerque to try her luck in the Open Championship. She broke so hard from the gate [coming out] she tore the muscles of her right hind leg, ripping the tendon off her stifle joint and fracturing the bone. The game mare, undoubtedly in great pain, finished the 440 dash second only to the winner, Dalhart Princess, who ran the course in :22.4, Bright Eyes lapped on her by half a length. When the race was over she could hardly walk."

C. L. Maddon's Bright Eyes, though she didn't look it, weighed 1120 and stood a fraction over 15 hands. Bay she was, with a pale blue right eye, blazed face and three white socks. She was foaled May 12, 1946, at Maddon's barn outside Albuquerque. Her sire was Gold Mount (by Brush Mount by Chimney Sweep (TB), by Broomstick), her dam was Plaudett by King Plaudit, Thoroughbred son of Plaudit, the Kentucky Derby winner. Breeder of Bright Eyes is J. W. Shoemaker, Watrous, New Mexico.

She started 25 times during her career, garnering 18 firsts, five seconds, and was never worse than fifth; in a low purse era her earnings exceeded $16,500. She finished as a AAA at five of the seven official distances and succumbed, the mother of four, on June 29, 1958.

She dropped her first foal in 1954, Bright Bar by Three Bars (TB). He started five times, won three, was once second, and once out of the money. In his second and third outings he was taking a virus and ran with a 103 degree temperature. He won his Futurity trial easily in :22.5 and went on to win the main event at the same pace, eight years after his dam had won it in :22.6. These five races qualified him as AAA and he was retired to stud where, says Maddon, he gives every indication of becoming a good sire.

Bright Eyes proved barren in 1955 but the following spring produced Bright Red, a sorrel colt by Leo. He didn't get to the races because in his second year they had Bright Eyes in a sling trying to keep her alive. In 1957 she dropped Me Bright (AAA) a bay filly by Leo. The old mare's final foal, also a filly and likewise by Leo, because of a bad accident had to be put to sleep. Bright Eyes had begun to go stiffly lame sometime before she had this foal and, in trying to turn, would frequently fall. "We kept her in a sling when she had this foal," Maddon says, "and she raised this baby to three months of age. The foal had a tiny navel rupture we were going to have fixed, but she tore herself terribly while tied and we were forced to destroy her. It was hard to have to put Bright Eyes to sleep and then have to do the same thing with her foal."

Bright Eyes won the New Mexico Futurity in 1948 and the Championship in 1949 and 1951, and all the speed stakes at Tucson in 1950. Bar Bright won the Futurity in 1956; Me Bright won it in 1959; Bar Bright, a granddaughter, won it in 1960.

Van A. Smelker, Jr. said, shortly after her death, "Through the years good horses come and go, but only a few carve a niche in the memories of horsemen. Bright Eyes is one of these special cases that will remain a legend and be talked about for years wherever horsemen gather."

In 1951 Bright Eyes co-held, with Monita, the coveted title World's Champion Quarter Running Horse, and they each co-held the additional title of Champion Quarter Running Mare for that same season; Bright

Eyes by herself had been named Champion Quarter Running Mare for 1940 and 1950.

She was a great mare and a game one.

Bunny's Bar Maid

In October of 1961 Renee Smelker led off her monthly racing column in *Hoofs & Horns* by saying: "The All-American Futurity at Ruidoso was preceded by a number of headline-making events, but the race itself produced the biggest shocker of the season when Hugh Huntley's Pokey Bar shaded the sensational Bunny's Bar Maid and eight other entrants by a length and a half."

It was, sure enough, a major upset in the calculations of almost everybody concerned. Prior to the race the winner had gone practically unmentioned; all the prerace ballyhoo and spotlights revolved around the fabulous Bar Maid, Golden Note, and the ill-fated Faila Tabu. The reporter contingent were all in a hubbub over the latter, and sports writers were mostly blowing the bugles for either the Bunny or Golden Note; no one—but no one—was giving any attention to Mr. Huntley's flying machine. All the smart money was down on the Spencer Childers entry, and with mighty good reason.

Let's take a careful look at her career.

Childers and his Mrs. had got into the Quarter Horse business in 1942; Spencer's hobby up to this point being calf roping and steer-team roping. They'd also been showing a few horses at halter. When they discovered, that the type of horse which won championships generally wasn't too handy at anything else, they turned to the breeding of performance horses, Spencer says.

As his business began taking more of his leisure, Mr. Childers decided their production of horses exceeded his requirements for roping stock. Casting about for additional ways of using these offspring, he was happy to note the performance-type horse was not necessarily confined to the rodeo arena.

"The turning point in the quality level of our racing stock," Mr. Childers declared, "began in 1956 when Walt Culbertson, at that time training for us, decided to retire and sell his great mare Black Easter Bunny. She had run 109 races, never started in any race graded lower than AAA, co-held and still co-holds the mare record at 300 yards and was, I believe, the all-time high money-winning mare with $42,000 in her bankroll, all picked up in runs whose total purse money was $5000 or less. Needless to say, this mare was not easy to come by, even with prices far lower than now. I finally offered my wife the choice of a new mink coat or Black Easter Bunny for Christmas. She did not hesitate a moment."

In the first two years of her brood-mare career Easter Bunny was sent to the court of Three Bars, the first product of this mating being Childers' AAA stallion Bunny's Bar Boy. The second was Bunny's Bar Maid, or "Pretty Maid"—this being Mrs. Childers name for her. The Bar Boy was foaled on their Fresno ranch; before his sister appeared 25 head were moved back to a ranch Spencer had purchased near Lone Jack, Missouri, some 35 miles from Kansas City. "This," he says, "was in aid of putting our horse operation a little nearer my business. A year later we made the same trek again in the opposite direction, returning all our horses to the West Coast."

Mrs. Childers has always been completely devoted to their horses, spending a great deal of her time with them, usually being up before dawn. She personally handles the mixing of feeds for the brood mares and foals, morning and night. During the foaling season she is out in the pastures once an hour when the mares are close up, acting as midwife. She found the transition from California climate to the snow and below-zero cold of Missouri a little hard to take, which is the reason all the stock went back to the coast.

The fabulous Bar Maid was foaled May 27, 1959, in a warm barn on the crest of a cold hill near Lone Jack. Childers was away in New York and, as he tells it, "When I returned two days later, Florence proudly took me out to see the new arrival. Even at this age it was easy to see something different had been added. I told Mrs. Spencer: 'Florence, I believe this is the one we've been shooting for.'"

When the rest of the youngsters would be running and playing in the pasture Bunny's Bar Maid, still as a rock, would eye them disdainfully. After they had finished, she would then take off and put on a show that was something to see.

Scarcely caught up and only halter broke, the Bar Maid came along much faster in her training than anyone could have expected. She was running in world's record time at Los Alamitos ninety days after her training commenced, and before she was twenty-two months old. In her first outing on a recognized track she breezed home in 18 seconds flat, four and a half lengths in front of the good mare Triple Tiny. "From that time on," says Childers, "she has pretty well ruled the roost around here. But" said he, thoughtfully, "if we had it all to do over, I think we'd have waited another three or four months before putting her into training."

Good horses have good mothers and Childers is a breeder who believes this. One of his ads in a livestock journal reads: "Great Horses Have Great

Dams—*an interesting proof of the prepotency of speed blood.* Above these words was a picture of Black Easter Bunny winning at 440 over Pokey Vandy and Palleo Pete (June 2, 1956). The advertisement goes on to point out: "Pokey Vandy second and Palleo Pete third were the dams and sire respectively of the first three horses in the 1961 All-American Futurity at Ruidoso. Other horses in this photo-finish include Vanetta Dee, Dividend, and Rocket Bar."

Bunny's Bar Maid is co-holder of the two-year-old filly record at 350 yards—:17.9. Her first season earnings of more than $72,000 included wins in the Juvenile Championship at Los Alamitos and the Kansas Futurity, and a second to Pokey Bar in the All-American.

R. L. and Barbara Rufus, Bar Maid's trainers, tell me: "She was the greatest race horse we ever had anything to do with. Along with her natural running ability was her great heart and competitive spirit. She was a wonderful horse to take care of; she always ate well and had regular periods for napping. She welcomed attention and admiration. She had a great deal of pride and knew dang well she was someone important.

"It was exactly sixty days from the first day we took her to the track that she had her first run. The day she stepped on the track for the first time at Fresno (where we do our winter training) she evidenced this intense spirit of competition." "I accompanied her on my pony horse," said Rufus, "as I do all the colts to get them started and, although she didn't understand what we were up to, she would never let the pony even get lapped on her—she just wouldn't let him. She did everything right all through her training; her :18.6 was the fastest qualifying race at Los Alamitos during the 1961 spring meet."

Four trials were run for that year's All-American—a 400-yard go. It had, as usual, been raining; the track was slow. Golden Note (by Palleo Pete) won her seventh of eight starts, first division, by a length and a quarter in :20.7; Pokey Bar upped his winning streak to four out of six by a comfortable daylight margin, second division, in a modest :20.8; Bunny's Bar Maid came up for a lion's share of the publicity by a remarkable two-and-one-half length win in the third heat, timed at :20.6 after being badly left at the gate. Faila Tabu's death reduced the fourth division to an eight-horse field, from which Art Bar (by Lightning Bar) emerged victor in :20.9.

Scarcely anyone figured the Bar Maid for anything less than a narrow win when they went to the post for the main event. Through six previous starts no horse had been lapped on her when she crossed the beam, and that trial seemed the clincher. The crowd bet her into the ground. No one doubted she would win; all the speculation revolved around the $64 question of which horse would barrel in for second.

Like a greased pig, Pokey Bar streaked from gate Number One, taking an early lead, which he maintained past the camera and straight into the winner's circle. The time he hung up was :20.1—a new two-year-old record. This kind of thing is what makes horse races; if there were no surprises there'd be mighty few viewers; but not all those fans went home singing praises.

Bunny's Bar Maid is consistent; she ran just as good a race as she had in the trial, only this time it didn't get the job done.

R. L. Rufus tells me: "From the first time we worked her she suffered suspensory trouble; she was always run in elastic bandages to give her extra support. Her first race was won in :18.0—victor by four and one-half lengths, the greatest distance any horse had ever got in front of a field at Los Alamitos. She cut a tenth off of that in her second race, sailing in first by two lengths over Mr. Three Bars and Art Bar."

Her third was the Juvenile Championship. She and Bar Mike bumped leaving the gate, Golden Note going to the front by one full length. Pulling herself together the Bar Maid overtook and outran the Burr brothers' bundle by that same distance—time :17.8, Mr. Three Bars finishing third.

"We then hauled her to Ruidoso," said Rufus, "where she became a victim of the virus; she cut a hind leg for good measure. For some time she ran a temperature of 104 degrees and we constantly battled the infection which had developed in her leg. It began to seem that we would not be able to start her in the Kansas Futurity trials."

Through it all she continued to put away the groceries, keeping up her strength. From the time she ran (May 8th) in the West Coast Juvenile until the 28th of July, she was galloped maybe fourteen times and worked twice in preparation for the Kansas Futurity. "She couldn't have been very ready," Rufus confided, "yet she ran the fastest trial (:17.9), defeating Little Bits Bull by one and a half lengths, Miss Hijo coming in for the show. Bunny's Bar Maid won the Futurity by one and a half lengths in :18.1, fighting a head wind. Connie Reba placed and, again, Miss Hijo took third money."

The Bar Maid next started in the third division of the All-American trials, which was run in the mud. Spraddled in the gate, she stumbled badly when she broke, going almost to her knees. Recovering, she came on, driving, to win the trial by two and a half lengths—400 yards in :20.6, beating Leona Dee and Three Chicks. Her odds on this go were one to nine.

"Coming out of the gate she pulled a ligament in one hind ankle; this, added to her suspensory trouble, bothered her to the extent that she never again ran in her old free and easy style," said Rufus. "Before she had been like water flowing. Probably her greatest race was the run she put up in the

All-American finals, finishing second to Pokey Bar and, with all of her troubles, coming in ahead of that fast-stepping Golden Note. After the race it was discovered she had burned her heel in back and speedy-cut in front. She was beaten one and a half lengths."

Back to California for the Pomona Futurity. In the trials the colt John L. Taylor rammed into her at the start, driving her sideways and popping a splint. In this heat Alamitos Bar beat her by half a length in :17.9. On Futurity Day she had only one sound leg left, yet ran second to Golden Note (17.8) beaten only by a neck. "Her final race as a two-year-old," said Mr. Childers, "was the Thanksgiving Handicap at Los Alamitos. I guess too much had been knocked out of her; she didn't even extend herself. She ran fourth, beaten one and a half by Pokey Bar, She Kitty, and Straw Flight. At least they were all great sprinters. We took her home to rest up at Fresno."

She was back in training on February 11th and appeared at the Vessels track a month later. Her qualifying race was the fastest work of the 1962 spring meet, and there were a lot of cheering fans when she scampered the 350 in :18.0. She looked as good as ever.

Entered for the Inaugural, overeager to run, she went through the gate prematurely, hurting her back. The vet prescribed a three-month vacation. Since that would keep her out of two derbys she had already been nominated for, and leave only the late fall to run in, Mr. Childers decided to retire her. She was bred to Go Man Go and has foaled a fine looking filly.

Do Good

A brown mare foaled in 1938, Do Good was bred by Jim Harkey of Carlsbad, New Mexico. She was by St. Louis (by Eck Davis, TB) out of Little Flossie by Duggan; second dam Old Floridene by Harmon Baker (by Peter McCue).

I have been unable to discover that she was ever raced; although she may have been. At the Vessels Ranch on a cloudy day (December 15, 1963) I took the snapshot of her which illustrates this discussion. On the Leading Dams of Register of Merit Qualifiers list (1962) she was fourth among dams with four or more AAA produce, and second among dams of six or more qualifiers. She has a remarkable record in the stud, and Chief Johnson once said to me, "She is *the* foundation mare of the Vessels Ranch running-horse program."

She has produced, in the following order, Bay Girl Close (15,141), bay mare, in 1942 by Big Joe; Senor Bill (14,556), brown horse, 1943, by Chi-

147. Do Good, the foundation mare of the Vessels Ranch running horse program.

148. Eagle Call, by Red Eagle out of Ruth Landolt, TB.

Photo by John H. Williamson

149. Hula Girl P., by Ed Echols out of Leilani, by Parker's Chicaro.

150. Lena Horn, by Dock (he by Zantanon) out of Julie W, by Joe Hancock.
The photo shows her at 20 years.

151. Little Meow, by Tadpole out of Jackie McCue, by Jack McCue.

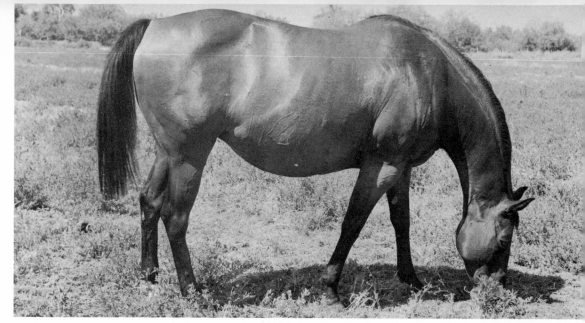

152. Miss Bank at the age of 16.

Snw Baby-120# Hyglo-120# Lucky Manners-125# B. Seven-125#

Squaw H-125# Billy Harris-125# Miss Bank-129#

Oct. 4, 1947 New Worlds Record For 1/4 mile in .22. Fla.

153. Miss Bank setting a new World's Record of :22.0 for the quarter at Albuquerque. The record, which was not accepted by the AQHA, was set on October 4, 1947.

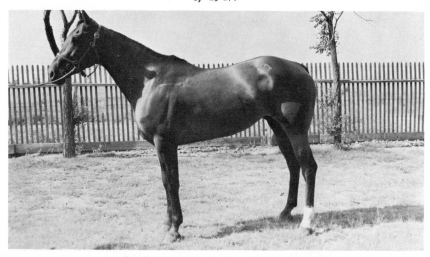

154. Miss Panama after being retired.

155. Garrett's Miss Pawhuska at 15 years.

156. No Butt, Kenneth Chapman up.

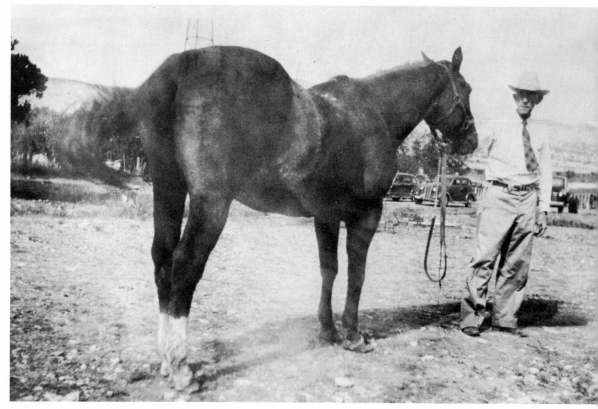

157. Celebrated Panzarita (747), taken when an old mare.

caro Bill. Senor Bill, AAA, started 65 times for nine firsts, 17 seconds, 14 thirds, and $997.72, plus eight halter points.

After skipping two years she produced in 1946 the bay horse Clabber II, by Clabber. This stallion, a noted sire, achieved AAA in track performance, and from 28 starts got seven wins, eight seconds, and three thirds, earning $2,649.50 in a low-pay period.

Next foal dropped was Clabber Shu V (18,133) a bay mare, 1947, by Clabber; this mare went to AA, started 28 times for eight firsts, five seconds and a third, banking $3,100.50.

The following spring Do Good foaled Charro Bill V (18,132), a bay horse by Chicaro Bill. He achieved AA, made 78 starts, won 11 times, placed 11 times, was third 12 times, and earned $7,012.25.

In 1950 Do Good produced the celebrated Chicado V (29,689), a brown mare by Chicaro Bill (P–1,297). Chicado V made six starts, with three wins, one second and one third, banking $5,215. In December, 1952, she was named Quarter Running Horse of the month. In the write-up accompanying this honor, Van A. Smelker, Jr., of the AQHA Racing Division, said, among other things:

A most remarkable first start was established by Chicado V, a full sister to Senor Bill. Starting late in her two-year-old year, on September 27, 1952, her first outing was in an open two-year-old race against some of the top colts and fillies in training, including Cee Bars, Tucson Gangway, Dandy Duchess and Diamond Tiara. Breaking like an experienced horse, Chicado V flashed the 350 yards in :18.1 to set a new two-year-old world's record, breaking the old mark of :18.3 previously held by Stardeck F. This time also established a new track record at Pomona. This is, of course, the fastest time a two-year-old has ever run this distance. Only one horse, Woven Web (Miss Princess), has bettered :18.1 and four others have equalled this time, those being Chappo S, Miss Bank, Question's Gold and Stymie. In her second and last outing to date she was entered in a handicap for two-year-olds and was given second top weight of 122 pounds, high impost of 125 being given to Bardella who was chosen Quarter Running Horse of the Month for April, 1952. This 330-yard event was featured at Bay Meadows race track and was composed of 12 top two-year-olds representing an honor roll of sires and dams. Convincing everybody that her first race was not a fluke, Chicado V ran the distance under an excellent ride by Jockey M. Volske in :17.2, to equal the fastest time set by two-year-olds this year. Putting a fraction of daylight between herself and Bardella is a feat well accomplished. The fast time recorded equals the track record held jointly by Monita, Dolly Mack and M. T. Pockets.

It was also mentioned in this citation that her sire, Chicaro Bill (a bay horse of 1931 by Chicaro, TB), had sired 16 head to qualify for the Register of Merit and that her full brother, Señor Bill, was present co-holder of the 350-yard stallion record, was a former holder of the same record at 330, and had once held the 350-yard three-year-old record. That Chacado V's dam, Do Good, was currently third on the list of dams who had had produce qualify for ROM, and that her owner, Frank Vessels, Sr., was tied for sixth place on the list of leading breeders of Register of Merit qualifiers. Chicado V is the dam of War Chick, AAA.

In 1951 Do Good foaled the bay mare Ram Bam by War Bam (TB).

The following spring the celebrated matron dropped Do Good Bam, AA. Do Good Bam made 10 starts, with one first, two seconds, no thirds, and earned $1417.50. She is the dam of winners Alamitos Bar, AAA, and Good Van, AA.

Do Win (56,429), 1953, by Direct Win (TB) was Do Good's AAA next. A bay gelding, he made 190 starts, achieving 24 firsts, 26 seconds, and 27 thirds, plus $32,780.80.

Do Good proved barren in 1954, but the following season produced Do More Good (53,351), a bay mare, by Lee Moore; she started nine times and collected $87.50.

Do Direct Good (112,182), a brown gelding, was foaled in 1956 by Direct Win (TB); he made 88 starts, with five firsts, six seconds, and seven thirds, banking $3937.50.

Do Van came along in 1957 by Vandy; made 11 starts, with no wins, and earned $292. Do Good's last foal, her thirteenth, was Do Chick (118,-771), by Triple Chick (by Three Bars, TB, out of Chicado V). Do Chick, a brown AAA gelding, 1958, made ten starts, garnering three wins and $1225.67.

Eagle Call

Foaled in 1944, Eagle Call was bred, trained, and raced while a young mare by her original owner, G. H. Harrison of Houston. She was sired by Red Eagle out of Ruth Landolt (TB).

Red Eagle (P–375) was by Jiggs, a good son of Uncle Jimmie Gray. His dam was the Sorrel Gretymeyer Mare by Pug (by Little Joker). Eagle Call's mother, Ruth Landolt (TB) was by Midway, third in the Kentucky Derby, later exported to South America, where, I am informed, he was a successful sire. Midway was by Ballot, a son of *Voter. Ruth Landolt's dam was My Della by My Play (full brother to Man O' War) and out of Della Robbia by *McGee. Eagle Call was foaled at a private stable on Broadview Drive, where she was reared in a 29-acre paddock just a few blocks from the Houston International Airport.

Mr. Harrison tells me his object in breeding Ruth Landolt to Red Eagle was to breed a type of Quarter Horse that would outperform the local half-breeds competing in short races in the Houston area. He says: "Eagle Call was run in some thirty or more matched races, winning at least half of them. She ran second her first outing with a four-horse field, winning next start in a matched race. Her most colorful race was won over Miss Beatrice, a high-class filly that had won several races prior to this match, including a win over Eagle Call in an earlier match. Eagle Call's win was at Arrowhead Park before a capacity crowd at Houston's most famous racing plant."

Eagle Call's dam was bred in Kentucky by the gentleman who is currently president of Churchill Downs. Mr. Harrison says: "Whether she raced in his colors is speculative, but she did race at Epson Downs, Houston, and Galveston Downs, Galveston, in the days of Thoroughbred racing in Texas."

Mr. Lester Goodson, Eagle Call's present owner, says: "I have trained and raced the following foals from Eagle Call—Bull Eagle, AAA, by Bull's Eye (by Joe Reed II); Eagle Flight, AAA, by Bull's Eye; Buddy Bull, AAA, by Bull's Eye; Sonny Bull, A, by Bull's Eye; Eagle Top, AAA, by Top Deck (TB); Eagle Deck, AA, by Top Deck; Go Eagle Go, AAA, by Go Man Go. Five AAA's, one AA, and one straight A."

On the Leading Dams of Register of Merit Qualifiers list, 1945 through 1962, Eagle Call—though listed alphabetically in fourth place—in the number of AAA qualifiers is actually as high as any mare shown.

Mr. Goodson further states: "I am now breaking and training a young stallion by Three Bars (TB) out of Eagle Call. We call him Eagle's Bar Man. Eagle Call is now in foal to Three Bars, and will have foaled before this reaches print."

89'er

At Jess Hankins' ranch at Rocksprings, Texas, in April of 1944, the bay filly was born which is now called 89'er. She was sired by Mr. Hankins' great stallion King (P–234, by Zantanon, the Mexican Man O' War, which Ott Adams bred at Alice, Texas). Her dam was a registered Quarter mare named High Glee whose sire was My Pardner (417, bred by Ed Echols of Tucson) by Uncle Jimmy Grey (by Bonnie Joe, TB). My Pardner's dam was Mollie Echols by Brown Billy by Pancho. High Glee's dam was Dogie Mare by Dogie Beasley out of Cora Bell Mangum. Which is pretty straight Quarter Horse breeding.

Bud Warren, Perry, Oklahoma, bought 89'er before she was named and has had her ever since. Most horses represent a cash outlay, but this mare has earned her keep many times over. She helped Bud become one of the nation's top breeders. In 1962 she led the list of Dams of Racing Register of Merit Qualifiers, and here is how it all came about.

As near as we can discover, she dropped her first foal in 1949—Mr. 89'er (AA) by Leo. The next year came Miss Sabre (AA) by Leo, and the following season she produced Whimper (35,322), her first AAA, by Leo. In 1952 she foaled Leo Bob, AAA, by Leo, and the next season came up with 89'er's Boy (AA) from Leo, and in 1954 the same combination produced Sooner Leo (a straight A). In 1955 she produced Mora Leo (AA) by Leo; and then they changed the combination by breeding her to Sugar Bars (by Three Bars, TB), from which union came Niner (AA) in 1956. Either she rested in 1957 and 1958 or proved barren. In 1959 she came out with Strip Runner (AAA) by Croton Oil (Bud's replacement sire, by Leo).

In her younger days, according to Mr. Warren, she won several matched races before being returned to the task of raising young'uns. AQHA records reveal she started twice on a recognized track. At Tulsa, in 1947, when she was three, she won a 220-yard go and finished second in another.

Later information shows her to be the dam of 14 foals, of which 11 started and the nine above noted achieved Register of Merit status. Some of them could do other things. Leo Bob, for instance, was Reserve Champion at the 1962 Tri-State Fair, held at Amarillo. Two years prior to this Leo Bob and his get placed first at Amarillo in a get-of-sire halter class.

During her career on the tracks Miss Sabre made 35 starts, winning five, placing in five, and finishing third in four others. Sooner Leo, apparently the poorest of her starters, ran five times and placed once. Perhaps with more starts he'd have made a better showing. One foal not mentioned above is Leo Niner (also by Leo); he came out of the gates three times to capture one third.

Hula Girl

In her youth, and even today it seems to me, this sorrel daughter of Ed Echols (by Zantanon) out of Leilani by Parker's Chicaro (by Chicaro Bill) looked more like a show mare than like something produced to burn up a track. Actually, she was well along in cutting-horse training, being shown between times, when the jibes of bystanders changed Pollard's whole program. As Mark Herra tells the story, Art Pollard was leading her from the ring of an Arizona show where she'd just been named Grand Champion when patronizing questions and half-concealed grins decided Pollard to find out if she *could* do anything besides look pretty.

He hired a local boy, Cal Johnson, to get her legged up. Cal didn't know anything about track competition or how to ready a nag for the sprints. He just pitched in. With considerable enthusiasm if not much savvy, he chucked her into a race and collected place money; this was in January, 1950. Two weeks later Hula Girl equaled the three-year-old filly record for 350, going the route in :18.5.

Pollard, changing trainers, put Gordon Cooper in charge of her outings. Cooper insisted she be nominated for the Arizona Derby. Pollard looked his surprise, knowing she'd be up against Silhouette and Ed Heller; but he gave Cooper the nod. When the race came off there was plenty of sweat on the backs of all concerned. In the final jump Silhouette (by Piggin String, TB) dead heated Hula Girl for the win, Ed Heller coming in half a length behind. Time was :22.7—no short horse derby had been run in faster time. Billy Gabbert, the Heller jockey, said afterward with understandable exaggeration: "At the eight pole that Hula was so far in front, if all motion had stopped I couldn't of got off Heller and hit her with a rock!"

A lot of eyes popped, for here was a halter mare outrunning the best sprinters stabled at Rillito. One man who wasn't surprised, however, was old Charlie Araujo, Quarter Horse judge and AQHA inspector from Coalinga, who remarked with a dry grin that Hula Girl was bred to do anything.

Sent to the breeding pen, Hula Girl first, in 1952, dropped War Chant (AAA) by Three Bars (TB). This colt was sold to John Mawson of Los Angeles at six weeks of age. As a two-year-old he distinguished himself by running off with the PCQHA Open Futurity at Pomona.

Arizonan (AAA) was produced by Hula Girl in 1953—his sire was Spotted Bull (TB). On the way to becoming Champion Quarter Running Gelding of 1955, this colt managed to set a couple of two-year-old records, negotiating the 350 in :17.9 and the full quarter in :22.1. To date he has earned in excess of $27,000.

Defiance, full brother to Arizonan, came along the following year to make AA. Severely injured by barbed wire, he was thought for some time to be unable to get to the tracks.

In 1955 the Pollard show-mare-turned-sprinter found Hula Baby (by Lightning Bar, one of the more brilliant sons of Three Bars, TB). This filly was purchased by Hoss Inman as a yearling. She went AAA under the Inman colors in 1957 and topped the Denver sale in 1958, purchased by G. B. Howell of Seagoville, Texas. In 1962 a match race for a considerable amount of cash money was arranged between Inman and Howell; the winning Howell entry—you've guessed it!—was the two-year-old daughter of Hula Baby by Leo San.

In 1956 Hula Girl produced Little Leilani. This one looked like a real go-getter and sold as a yearling to Jack Clifford of Kelseyville, California. Her race training was begun at Bay Meadows in the spring of 1958. Clifford was primed to go all the way with this filly, but she died of colic before she was started.

The mare was barren in 1957, but in 1958 she did very well indeed, producing Sonoitan (AAA) by Spotted Bull (TB). Extremely well conformed, this was the one, says Pollard, he'd been waiting for. Losing the Southwestern Futurity by a scant two inches, he went on in 1960 to score several impressive wins, defeating such good ones as Bar End, Tough Bar, Dynago Miss, Bar Clabber, Miss Vanity, Miss War Bar, Hoodwink, and others of similar caliber.

Savage Son was Hula Girl's contribution for 1959. By Depth Charge (TB), he never got to the tracks. When still a short yearling he received a brain injury that disrupted his equilibrium. He was bought and by a Minneapolis group syndicated for stud service, now standing in Minnesota.

Hula Girl, bred to Lightning Bar, came up in 1960 with Hula Bars—hard luck again. Pollard has called him the finest Lightning Bar colt, for looks, he'd ever seen. He was featured on the cover of the October (1960) *The Stockman Magazine*. Then tragedy struck in the form of a virus and Hula Bars was no more. An offer of $25,000 had been refused for the untried colt.

In 1961 Hula Girl was barren again. She was courted but failed to settle. In 1962 she foaled Pueblo Girl (by Old Pueblo, a currently fashionable Thoroughbred stallion), and not a few consider this the most promising of all her nine offspring. Mr. and Mrs. Herbert J. Alves are the proud owners. She will remain at Sonoita Stallion Manor for schooling and training and make her debut on the tracks in 1964.

In April of 1963 Hula Girl foaled to the courtship of the good Thoroughbred sprinter, El Kentuck, presently standing at the Pollard establishment. Art says: "Had it not been my good fortune to acquire Hula Girl at the beginning of my modest operation I seriously doubt that I would be producing race horses today. She was pretty much the pathfinder."

Lena Horn

A black mare foaled in 1943, Lena Horn was bred by Charles Whitehorn of Pawhuska, Oklahoma. She was sired by Dock (2172) out of Julie W, a daughter of Joe Hancock (P–455). This Traveler–Peter McCue cross has frequently been the springboard not only for paragons of the straightaway but for some unusually prepotent breeders. Lena Horn was bred in speed-crammed bloodlines. With the blood of the sprinting McCues close up, through Joe Hancock, she got more early foot from Dock, her sire, whose own sire was the celebrated Zantanon, unquestionably the greatest sprint horse ever sired by the redoubtable Little Joe—which Ott Adams considered to be Traveler's most distinguished son.

Dock was bred by M. Benavides Volpe, the Laredo ranchman who fetched Zantanon back out of Mexico. Dock's dam was Pluma by Valentino, his maternal grandmother Jabalina by Strait Horse—names to conjure with. Zantanon, according to Volpe, could go 300 yards in :15.8 from a walking start. Mr. Volpe, in fact, insists he could do better than this; he has said Zantanon was the fastest and smartest breaking horse he has ever seen—and he has seen quite a passle and bred many, too.

A great heritage, and Lena Horn has passed a good share of it on.

She has produced Leolena (P–25,488), 1949, by Leo. This was her first Leo foal; as a filly Leolena set a new two-year-old record at Albuquerque in 1951—300 yards in :16.2; she retired AAA and is now owned by C. W. Mickle, Valley View Ranch, Scottsdale, Arizona.

She presented Bud Warren with Handicap (P–29,187), a bay stallion now doing stud service elsewhere, in 1951. Handicap, unraced, was by Leo.

Lalani Leo, AAA by Leo, was foaled on the Bud Warren spread at Perry, Oklahoma, and sold in 1959 to Sonny and Sissy Walker, Skull Valley, Arizona, for $18,400. As a youngster this mare equaled the world's filly record, I am told, at Ruidoso.

Leo Horn, by Leo in 1953, is a solid AAA campaigner owned by Ed Maloof, Las Vegas, New Mexico. A sorrel horse (P–42,194).

Leovada, a well-known stallion currently in service, was foaled in 1954; he is a bay and was sired by Leo. He ran and is rated AA.

Leo Tip Tap (P–55,614), also at stud duty, is a chestnut horse foaled in 1955. Leo was his daddy, too.

Lena Horn dropped Salad Oil (P–112,216), by Croton Oil, in 1959. This sorrel mare, AAA on the tracks, is being kept by the Warrens for use as a brood mare. She has been bred to Sugar Bars and is being successfully shown at halter.

Cabin Fever, by Leo, is a two-year-old (Lena's foal of 1961) and will be started, Mr. Warren reports, later on this season

Lena Horn will foal this year (1963) by Sugar Bars, P–42,606, by Three Bars (TB). She appears on the list of Leading Dams of Register of Merit Qualifiers.

Little Meow

Milo Burlingame once said to me, "Peter McCue, in my opinion, was the greatest short-race horse in the history of the world, and he was also the finest breeder." At least with the latter part of that opinion a good many persons have agreed wholeheartedly, and not a few still do. Those who believe the McCue blood has thinned or been hopelessly lost with the demise of the last of Peter's mighty sons simply don't know what they are talking about. The blood may be mixed with other genes now, but it is still producing some mighty fine runners, and Little Meow was one of them.

Sired by Tadpole, a cow-working sprinter, she was foaled in a Casement pasture April 6, 1947, has a wire-cut nose, stands 14.3 and, on the distaff side, has a close-up concentration of the best capabilities one has been led to expect in horses double-bred to the Peter McCue tradition. Her dam was Jackie McCue by Jack McCue (by Peter McCue). Jackie was out of Sparkie by Spark Plug (by Jack McCue)—straight running blood. All of Little Meow's topline sires were bred by Casements, clear on back to Concho Colonel, which Dan Casement bought from Billy Anson of Cristobal, Texas, in 1911. Meow's sire, Tadpole, was a son of Red Dog (P–55) out of Mae West (P–56) by Coke T, a Roberds' horse by Brown Dick. There was plenty of run on this side, too.

At the impressionable age of one week Little Meow was left an orphan when her mama was struck down by lightning. They put the little filly on a big Suffolk work mare which had recently foaled, and the orphan flourished like a green bay tree until she ran into a wire fence, badly gashing both nostrils. Jack's wife Xenia sewed her back together; about the only evidence now left of the experience, aside from the scar, is the habit she acquired of lapping up water as a cat laps milk. Says Jack, "A very slow and aggravating habit."

It did not impair her memory. Fresh home from the track at Littleton several years later, she was turned into a corral where the children were splicing a new orphan on old Slumbum, the Suffolk work mare. Meow nickered greetings, sidled over to her old foster mama, nosed the colt aside, and promptly went to nursing.

Jack Casement began to get to work on Meow in June of her two-year-old year and ran into the sort of opposition one might expect of a critter brought up on a nurse mare and spoiled rotten by children. At considerable trouble and expense the Rocky Mountain Quarter Horse Association had arranged a pari-mutuel race meet at Kremmling, Colorado, in mid-July of 1949. It was the first real short horse meet ever held in the state and naturally the Casements hoped to get a showing for Little Meow. They'd had her down to a doings in Nebraska over the Fourth, but she'd appeared too young and green for sour apples; so they fetched her over to Kremmling four or five days ahead of the meet, and with the appreciated help of Cotton Merritt and

Billy Gabbert (who had the top two-year-old, Ed Heller, there), Jack was able to give her considerable work—several times each morning out of the gate with a good horse. This might not be the most orthodox training but, with the old relay and Roman champion Floyd Murphy in the irons, she ran second to another Triangle Bar filly first time out, after bucking some fifty or sixty yards. She won her second start handily. Until the middle of August they hauled her around to the county fairs, where she did very well for the Casements, then on to the State Fair at Pueblo for the Rocky Mountain Futurity.

Since Murphy was obligated to someone else they put a neighbor boy, Chuck Deming, on her for this go; he topped the scales at 138 but brought Little Meow home on top in the trials and in the Futurity, too.

The next year they ran her again at Kremmling. Tommy Chavez won a championship race on her at Cheyenne Frontier Days, and from there she was trucked to Centennial where she was turned over to a Thoroughbred trainer, Whiz Gilchrist of the El Peco Stables, who put Kennedy on her to win a 440 go against older horses. She also won Centennial's first so-called World Championship Quarter; the great Scooter W (Champion Quarter Running Horse Stallion of 1948) was in the beaten field. Shortly thereafter she was retired to the stud.

She was first taken to Leo, but before she could settle Leo was injured and had to be temporarily taken out of service; so they brought her home and bred her to Ambrose, a local horse Cotton Merritt thought a lot of. The foal of this mating was named Little Turtle; at the track he played second fiddle to Alfaretta (also in the Casement stable) but proved reliable and hard-knocking, securing his ROM and afterward going on to make a crack barrel and rope horse.

Meow's next foal (by Little Joe the Wrangler) was called Hairless Joe, which went off to rodeoing. Her third was by Leo, another horse colt; they call him Lonsum Polecat. He showed considerable promise, except in the mud, and most of his races were run on wet ground. But he stayed in the money against a good class of horses, solidly ROM.

The fourth foal dropped by Little Meow was by Leo's good son, Robin Reed. Old Tom Cat they called him; Pat Thompson hauled him to Ruidoso and got a win first rattle out of the gates. He then collected a virus and was laid up for most of the season. Next spring a trailer hitch broke loose while he was being hauled to Pat Thompson's to resume his training. The trailer went upside down in a deep borrow ditch. They cut Old Tom Cat out. He was sore but not cut up too much—not enough to keep him from going AAA and later on becoming an AQHA Champion. That year, at the Denver National, he came out on top in a very tough show.

Little Meow's fifth was a Robin Reed filly which they named She Kitty. Small and undeveloped when she came to the tracks, at Raton she opened up a lot of eyes when she won her first out in AAA time. Her charts tell an astonishing story; she has run with the best—was part of the 1962 triple threat—and in 22 starts was never rated less than AAA. Her 1961 two-year-old form shows 10 starts, seven firsts and two seconds; in 1962 she came out 12 times against frontline competition, grabbing five firsts, four seconds, three thirds, and earned $18,489.51, bringing her two-year earnings up to $29,192.06. She was named Co-Champion Three-Year-Old Quarter Running Filly of 1962. A stakes winner, she holds two three-year-old filly records, the mare record at 400 yards, co-holds with No Butt the mare record at 440 (:21.7), and co-holds with Breeze Bar the world's record at 400 (:19.9). Leroy Tipton rode She Kitty in all of her outings.

Little Meow, after these foals, skipped a year, but now has a classy un-raced Three Bars colt known as Whammy Cat.

At five, Little Meow was Champion at the Colorado State Fair, at the Kansas State Fair, at Nebraska's biggest Quarter Horse show at Burwell, at the Wyoming State Fair, and, winding up this phase of her competitive career, at Denver's National Western. *The Blood Horse*, published at Lexington, Kentucky, carried her photograph and a write-up in its September 17, 1955, edition.

Miss Bank

Though her records have all been lowered in subsequent years, about the finest tribute that can be paid this mare is to point out that she, of them all, is the only member of this sprinting breed to have the distinction of holding at one time or another, every World Record across the Quarter Horse board. Equally fantastic, she ran in excess of three hundred official races over a period of eleven years; approximately 85 per cent of these outings she won, and no one has kept track of the matched sprints she ran. She was bred on the Ross Perner ranch, Sierra Blanca, Texas, and was foaled in June of 1940. Mr. Plunk Fields, a Lower Rio Grande Valley rancher, invited to pick out for himself one of a large crop of Perner yearlings, after much study chose this bay filly. Perner then said if Fields cared to unload her he could have fifty dollars and pick out another. Fields just grinned and drove off with Miss Bank.

Her dam, Apron Strings, had been used as a polo mount; cool-headed, smart, dependable, and extra well reined. The sire of Miss Bank, Captains Courageous, never entered a horse show or worked a cow; he was a Thoroughbred Remount Stallion.

Named by a subsequent owner, Mr. Leon Gillespie of El Paso, she was christened Miss Bank when, at Alamagordo, she ran against one of George Orr's track scorchers. When race-course officials inquired what she was called, Gillespie just shrugged. "Well," he was told, "you can't run her here without you give her a name." One of Gillespie's business enterprises was conducted under the sobriquet of The Old Bank Club; suddenly inspired, he said with a chuckle, "Just call her Miss Bank," and that was what they did. Going 350 yards, she sailed home first by half a length.

So far as I know she was never unsound in her whole career. Longer than tall, she is a solid bay, very rugged and handsome, though showing her Thoroughbred blood unmistakably. She is fine boned and breedy, has a powerful forearm, stifle, and gaskin and, for her time, had speed to spare. Many trainers have spoken highly of her fine disposition, and she always ran as though determined to win.

As an example of her ruggedness, several years ago Roy Rice (of Fabens, Texas) matched a horse at her for a race to be run over a course of 350 yards at El Paso's old Sheriff's Posse Corral. Miss Bank was the victor by a quarter of a length, but Rice wasn't satisfied. Three-quarters of an hour later they ran it over again, Miss Bank winning this go by daylight. In less than an hour after the second run Rice insisted on doing it again. In each of these sprints Miss Bank whipped Rice's horse by a successively wider margin. These races were run for $50 apiece.

Bank's sire, Captains Courageous, was by Stimulus.

"At the turn of the fifties"—Art Pollard of the Sonoita Stallion Manor speaking—"I purchased Miss Bank from Jim Derrick of Carlsbad. The price was seventy-five hundred, which at the time was probably a new high for brood mares. She failed to reproduce herself while in the brood. She mothered five foals, the swiftest probably being Fantasy, which made AAA her first official time out." Injuries hampered the performances of Lightning Bank and Bankette; notwithstanding this, C W. Mickle of Scottsdale, Arizona, paid $41,000 for Bankette at public auction. Manor Orphan will be in track competition in 1963.

A second generation not too infrequently makes a more vigorous showing, than the one before it as witness Bankette's fine son Rebel Cause (by Top Deck), named Co-Champion Quarter Running Three-Year-Old Colt for 1961.

Miss Bank died of acute colic at the age of twenty. Her like may never be seen again.

Miss Panama

Deep in the heart of the South Texas cow country, in a region known also for fine running horses, there are still a number of short-horse men, and none more respected than Anton Jahn, the former jockey. Back in 1942 he bought Ace of Diamonds, then twenty years old, to help his mare Dixie find a couple or three foals that, by his figuring, ought to hang up a mark. Not all his neighbors laughed at this notion, but there were admittedly a number of scoffers. For years old Ace had been the half-starved partner of a colored man's mule, the pair of them used for pulling his plow. But Jahn remembered that in his youth this sorry old horse had been unbeatable for 300 yards

Now the *Stud Book* tells us Ace of Diamonds was by Cotton-Eyed Joe, a son of Peter McCue out of Hattie W, but *The Quarter Horse* for June of 1949 claims on the testimony of Shorty Saski, the man who raised and raced him, that old Ace was by Johnny (by Cotton-Eyed Joe) out of a daughter of Karnes City Jim. However that may be, in the following spring Dixie came up with a little brown filly, which her next owner, Bob Chudej, when she was two years old rechristened Miss Panama—and she did hang up a mark they're still shooting at. Down at Del Rio on April 30, 1948, defeating Pep, Bo-El, and Johanna, she ran the 330 in :16.9, and in all the years since it has only once been equaled.

Where did she get this blinding speed—from Johnny? Cotton-Eyed Joe? Karnes City Jim? Did it come from Dixie's side of the fence? Or was this just another instance of the remarkable prepotency known to be inheritable from Peter McCue?

Breeders began going around in circles; several smart-money gents beat a path to Jahn's door, and old Ace, rediscovered, had his moment in the sun. Jahn had already duplicated the formula, producing a full brother to this latest speedball; this product of his establishment was called Skiddoo and one of Jahn's neighbors, Ed Hajek, had some Little Dick mares and let old Ace court one of them, getting the respected Miss South St. Mary's. Skiddoo was all right and Hajek's filly proved a running fool, but neither of them (nor anything subsequently) quite came up to the Panama level.

She had flash and bloom and speed to burn. Local breeders finally settled most of the credit on Little Dick. He was the product of a mating engineered by a Negro, Wilson Sulden, who had raised and trained short horses for a number of white men. Sulden bred an old race mare named Flora (by Pilgrim) to Sleepy Dick (by Little Rondo) in 1910, producing Little Dick, the most noted race horse and begetter of race horses in all of Lavaca County. But all the hows and the whys of it notwithstanding, nobody succeeded in getting another Panama; she stands by herself, uniquely alone.

She got her early training from Anton Jahn and Willie Shelton of Halletsville, mostly in a sandy stretch of Jahn's horse pasture. He admits he had some trouble getting her used to the chute. The story is told that Jahn's little boy did most of the feeding and taking care of her; there was real love between them and she followed him around like a dog. When he tired of this he would take her to the horse lot and whisper, "Go to sleep"; and Panama (whom they called Scooter then) would actually lie down and go to sleep!

A brown in color, Miss Panama weighed at the height of her fame about 1000 pounds; she has a tuft of gray hair on her forehead and a white left hind ankle. She is exceptionally well made and has a proud carriage without blemish; she is very fond of small fry. After she hit her stride in 1948 she was practically unbeatable at 330 yards. She won four straight that spring at Tucson and Del Rio, all of them at better than the previous world mark. She won the Speed Championship at Tucson by a length and a half; she then dropped her own World's Record to :16.9 on the opening day of the Del Rio meet, finishing one and a half lengths ahead of Pep, the previous record holder. Then she won two more, defeating Stella Moore, Miss Bank, Mae West, Joe Jimmie, and others. Prior to an injury later in the season she took most of the other greats in her stride—Pelican, Badger's Gray Lady, Miss Steamship, Blondy L, Hard Twist, Tonta Gal, Bay Annie, Miss South St. Mary's, B Day, Leota W, Hyglo, and so forth. At the top of her career she campaigned under the colors of Lewis Blackwell. Even after retirement she set another world record at the Blackwell sale when Peter Licavoli of the Grace Ranch, Tucson, bid her in for $9800, a new high for Quarter mares sold at public auction.

While under Grace Ranch ownership Miss Panama produced two Register of Merit qualifiers—Panama Twist (by Hard Twist) and Panama Devil (by Devil Red, TB).

Early spring, 1955, found this great mare in the hands of Art Pollard (currently of Sonoita, Arizona), who had purchased her from Hoss Inman of Lamar, Colorado); Pollard bred her to Lightning Bar (by Three Bars, TB) and got Pana Bar, Champion Running Two-Year-Old Colt of 1958. In two seasons of racing this colt earned in excess of $12,000.

The year 1957 saw the birth of Panama Ace (by Spotted Bull, TB), who was named Champion Running Two-Year-Old Colt of 1959 after finishing second by half a length to Galobar in the first All-American. He earned over $28,000.

Tommy Dean, now a successful trainer, jockeyed Miss Panama to a number of her more spectacular performances, and has this to say: "Panama was the fastest horse I ever knew for three hundred yards, and could run a Quarter with the best, too, as she did in winning the World's Championship Quarter at Tucson. No better mare ever lived."

It is believed she is now in foal again. She was sold in the latter part of

1962 to R. L. French, Jr., owner of the Anacacho Ranch in south Texas, which is currently the home of Panama Ace.

Miss Pawhuska

Out of six official starts on recognized Quarter Tracks Dee Garrett's great mare (discovered by him before Bud Warren found Leo) won all six. Dee owned her before she ever set foot on a track. Her first outing was in one of the trials for the Oklahoma Futurity, which has been won seven times by daughters of Leo. Miss Pawhuska won her heat on August 27th, 1948, and went on to win the second running of this famed Futurity. The track was no better than good, competition was extra special, and tension quite noticeably was in the air. The start was delayed by Tidy M, who had to be taken from the gates and resaddled. While this was going on, with the management and everyone else in a swivet, the whole field had to be unloaded and walked. But at last everything was in readiness, the gates were sprung and the field was off. Breaking from the far outside, and pressed the whole distance, Miss Pawhuska was in front by a nose when, neck and neck, she and Savannah G (by Question Mark) crossed the finish line. Lapped and scarcely three feet behind came the out-thrust jaws of Red River Pride. A bare two lengths difference separated the winner from the last of the also-rans. Time for the 220 was :12.7.

Her last race was as a three-year-old and was also staged at Enid, a matched affair against the young and highly regarded stallion Bob K K, then owned by Art Beall, Horse Editor of *The Ranchman*. Miss Pawhuska got there fust with the mostest.

Bedded down with the brood mares, Dee Garrett's great filly proved even more of a sensation, coming up with a World's Champion Quarter Running Horse, a pair of Champion Quarter Running Geldings, and one three-time winner of the coveted mare title. No other mare in history has equaled this performance.

Her first foal, Vandy's Betty (1951, by Vandy) was a AAA mare who went to J. V. A. Carter, where she produced Van Deck, AAA, and Van Moon.

In 1952 Miss Pawhuska foaled Vanetta Dee, AAA and one of the all-time greats of the Quarter Tracks, Vandy again being the proud daddy. Vanetta Dee won the Nebraska Quarter Horse Trials and Futurity of 1954. She was Champion Quarter Running Three-Year-Old Filly of 1955. In 1956, 1957, and 1958 she was named Champion Quarter Running Mare. She retired as richest mare in Quarter racing history, with earnings of $82,376 plus a

Howell trailer. In six and a half years of track performance she was completely out of the money in but eight races. Match that if you can! She made 94 official starts, was first 31 times, placed 20 times, and showed 16 times. Her first foal (1961) was by Pana Bar; she has a 1963 colt by Go Man Go and is now bred to Top Deck.

Vannevar was third to come from Miss Pawhuska (1953, by Vandy). This colt, gelded, went AAA and was named Champion Quarter Running Gelding for 1956 and 1957, holds two gelding records, and has already earned $39,946.79.

Her foal in 1954 was Vandy's Flash, AAA, once again by Vandy. In 1958 he was named Champion Quarter Running Gelding. He grabbed this kudo again in 1960 and went on that year to be named World's Champion Quarter Running Horse, the first gelding to receive this highest award since the naming of Champions was inaugurated in 1941. He holds the gelding record at 440 (:21.7), co-holds the gelding 400 yard mark (:20.1) and holds the gelding record at 350 (:17.5). Through 1961 he had earned $81,108.87 and is currently the property of the Bresa Del Mar Ranch at Escondida, California

In 1955 Miss Pawhuska foaled Vansarita (by Vandy), which went into the stud unraced. She foaled by Clabbar Bar in 1961 a sorrel colt called Vanzi Bar and died when the youngster was only forty days old. He was bottle raised

Miss Vanity, AAA, came in 1958 (by Vandy) and was sold to John Askew. She made her high rating in her very first start and was the first of her mother's foals to go into AAA her first season.

In 1961, by Vandy, Miss Pawhuska at age fifteen dropped Vansarita Too, already entered for the All-American of 1963.

Garrett's Vandy, from the same combination, came along in 1962, the first horse colt since Flash, and the Garretts say they are planning on keeping him as a stallion—one which they hope will follow in Vandy's hoofprints.

On February 10, 1963, Miss Pawhuska foaled another sorrel colt. Mrs. Garrett thinks he looks like Vandy's Flash and is endeavoring to reserve for him the name of Flashie Vandy.

Miss Pawhuska, certainly one of the finest producers of the breed, was herself bred by Bill Rowe of Carlsbad. The Garretts got her from Earl Jackson as a yearling and later purchased her mother from him, and raised two foals from the dam before she died; these foals were Miss Vandy and Vanessa Dee. Miss Pawhuska was sired by Leo out of Jenny Dee by Jimmie Allred. Jenny Dee (16,818) was bred by Helen Michaelis, of Eagle Pass, and her dam was Big Bay Mare. Jimmie Allred (P-281) was a bay horse foaled in 1931, bred by Horace Wilson of Fort Worth; his sire was Dan by Old Joe Bailey by Eureka by Shelby; his dam was Alice McGill by Little Hickory Bill by Hickory Bill by Peter McCue.

Monita
(250 yds., 1949 DR 107 :13.4)

By Joe Moore out of Goodwin's Juanita by Priory (TB), the chestnut mare Monita was bred by J. F. Goodwin of George West, Texas, and foaled in 1947. She was campaigned extensively by Lewis Blackwell and in 1953 co-held the World's Record at 440 yards (:22.0), which she equaled at Centennial Park as a four-year-old in 1951 under 121 pounds; a AAA mare, she also held in 1953 the following track records: Bay Meadows 1951, 330–125–:17.2f; Del Rio 1950, 300–110–:15.9f and 1949, 250–107–:13.4f: She has, in addition, held at various times several other records, including the World's Record at 250 yards, set at Del Rio in 1949, which has twice been equaled but never lowered.

In 1955 (at eight years of age) she still co-held the World's Record at 440 yards (:22.0) with Pokey Vandy and Woven Web; also the 250 with Bright Eyes and Super Charge, as well as several track records. She was a hard-knocking campaigner who ran, year in and year out, with the best.

It was in her first race (2177), October 21, 1949, at Del Rio, that smashed the existing 250-yard World's Record and set up the mark of :13.4, which still stood in 1963, defeating Martini Girl, Black Ace, and Jimmie Dee, and winning $900. In a matched race with Johanna (by Little Joe, Jr.) at Del Rio the following year (October 26th) Monita chalked up :15.9 for 300 yards and picked up $3000 for the win, establishing a new track and three-year-old record. In an invitational handicap for all ages at Bay Meadows on March 31, 1951, she ran the 330 in :17.3, defeating Savannah G, Clabbertown G, Clabber's Lady V, Little V, Grey Question, Lee Moore, Little Smoke Echols, Red Gown L, and Ed Heller, collecting $635. In a handicap for all ages at Centennial (August 31, 1951) she grabbed $4370, going the 440 in :22.0 and defeating Bright Eyes, War Star, Leota W, Raindrop, Blob Jr., Diamond Bob, Bonnie Bert I, Dutch S, Minerva, and Dalhart Princess. She was named World's Champion Quarter Running Horse and Champion Mare of 1951.

On February 2, 1952, she picked up another $1475 at Sportsman's Park in the Winter Quarter Horse Championship Stakes, going 295 yards in a reported :15.6, defeating War Star, River Flyer, Black Easter Bunny, Tonto Bars Gill, and Little Sizzler. In the Raton Quarter Horse Handicap Prep she gained $519.90 by sprinting 400 yards in a reported but unaccepted time of :20.6. In the Bright Eyes at Raton she grabbed another $476.97, going 250 yards in :13.5, defeating several headliners including Martini Girl and Miss Meyers. In the Barbra B Handicap at Centennial, August 29, 1953, she banked $715.05 and another win by traveling 400 yards in :20.4. In the Shu Fly at Albuquerque, on September 27th, she picked up $1494.24 going 300 yards in :15.9, shellacking another batch of 11 top sprinters.

In the William V. O'Conner Allowance at Los Alamitos, on May 1, 1954, she ran off with $990 more, defeating Chudej's Black Gold, Nug Bar, Wall Street, Barjo, Rocky Bobby, Vinegar Bend, and Clovis Champ by going the quarter mile in :22.3.

The above are among her more spectacular performances. She made 89 starts, winning 30, placing in nine, and taking third money in 11. On the list of Leading Money-Earning Horses, 1949 through 1962, Monita stands twenty-third with $49,143.53.

Retired to the stud in 1956, she produced in 1957, by Leo Tag, the sorrel Della's Queen (96,028), AAA, which in 14 starts corraled two firsts, a second, and three thirds, banking $1424.95. She missed in 1958 but the following spring dropped, by Vandy, the chestnut colt Fly Man Fly (three starts, no wins). In 1960 Monita foaled a chestnut filly, Flyita, by Jet Flight.

No Butt

This is the profile of a latter-day Cinderella, the kudos in print of an eight-year-old mare that, sans the advantages of fashionable parentage, has consistently confounded the prognostications of the pundits and, fetching home the brass rings against the stiffest competition any Quarter mare ever was thrown at, has finally emerged triumphant as 1962 Horse of the Year, World's Champion Quarter Running Horse, Champion Aged Mare, and Champion Quarter Running Mare—an achievement tracing solely to merit.

Nobody ever gave No Butt anything.

In any short list from the distaff side of individuals whose accomplishments stick like burrs to one's thinking No Butt stands out like a lighthouse of encouragement to those hardy souls whose faith in grass-roots Quarter blood has withstood the arguments for constantly touted Thoroughbred genes.

Her dam, Red Bottom (P–12,994) was by Barney Owens (P–2202) by Jack McCue by Peter McCue. Her sire is Joe Less (P–2992—sire of 3 AAAs) by Joe Moore (P–1856) out of June (1713 by Universe, TB). Joe Moore's daddy was Little Joe by Traveler. Yet No Butt, running third, was lapped on the mighty Pokey Bar in the Los Alamitos Quarter Horse Championship stakes (May 5, 1962) when Pokey Bar ran the 440 in the World Record time of :21.6, defeating Alamitos Bar by a nose, with No Butt latching onto third-place money by that nose and a half.

In Vol. XIV, No. 1 (Page 10A) of the *Quarter Running Horse Chart Book*, you will find the following: "No Butt in 1961 made all of her 15 starts in stake and feature events. Running with some of the best Quarter Horses in training, No Butt won the Redwood City, Belmont, Freeway and the Clabbertown G. She was a second-place finisher in the George Washington and the Pomona Championship. She collected thirds in the Santa Cruz, Vallejo and the Go Man Go. Her total money winnings for 1961 were $10,575."

She won four—no other horse in competition did that. Yet the year-end emoluments somehow passed her by.

Said Guy Purinton, at that time still her owner:

No Butt was foaled on my Rafter P horse ranch near Tipton, California. Guy Corpe of Sacramento owed me a small training bill and asked me to take the mare Red Bottom for the bill. I was not particularly impressed with her breeding and felt sure she was a cull or he would not let her go for so small an obligation.

I told him I didn't want the mare. Three days later he showed up at my place with her, fetching her over in a truck. She was a very ordinary-looking bay mare, and plenty spooky. Nothing would do but I take her for the bill.

I got part cash, and settled off this training bill in the best deal I ever made in my life. I later offered the mare to Ralph Bell for $200 while she was still carrying No Butt. When she foaled I hadn't sold her.

When No Butt was two my trainer and I were looking for colts to break for the track; I didn't give her a thought. Earl Laughlin, the trainer, considering her, kept arguing in favor of giving her a chance. I finally gave in and, with five others, she was broke and put into training.

She was a great favorite of Guy's daughter, Jo Anne, who was five. Guy still figured they were wasting their time. But Earl said, "Time is all that rascal needs." His faith was unshakeable. The other youngsters outworked her but Earl kept saying, "Give her time—she's a *race horse*."

She was not a large filly but was beautifully balanced, with as good a shoulder as anything they had. In her first go she was small and pretty green but managed to run fourth with some good colts at Pleasanton. Ed

Burke, Los Alamitos' Racing Secretary, asked why they were carrying her, but Earl was bound she was a winner, that all she needed was a little more time. When they started her at Fresno, Earl told Purinton, "Bet your money today." No Butt, being eased up, won by five (:18.5 for 350). Purinton said without much enthusiasm, "She did not set any woods afire as a two-year-old."

By the time she was three she had filled out considerably, and now began to show what she could do. She went AAA+ and has been there ever since. Through January, 1962, she had run 44 times in AAA and had been named 1958 Champion Quarter Running Three-Year-Old Filly.

A good many horsemen thought she should have been named Champion Mare in 1961. She won a cool $2000 more and started four times less than at least one other who was honored. Not only did she outrun First Call but the sensational Vanetta Dee, Go Man Go, Triple Lady, Vandy's Flash, Clabber's Win, Table Tennis, Clabber Bar, Easter Maiden, Alamitos Bar, Quick M Silver, and others too numerous to mention here, including the top three of that season, Pap, Breeze Bar, and First Call. But you can't win them all.

Through 1961 No Butt had been co-holder with Woven Web (TB) and First Call of the Mare Record at 350 (:17.8) and has at various times set or equaled a number of other records. During the meet at Los Alamitos she did the 350 in :17.7, establishing a new mare record at that distance.

She has never pulled up sore, and has run equally well under several trainers and jockeys; her disposition is above reproach. Guy's daughter, now ten, could take her fresh from the track and do anything with her.

About three years ago, fed up with racing, Purinton decided to sell off his horses. He says: "We had a very poor sale at Artesia and I had to bring many of the horses home. We had all hated to see No Butt and several of the other good mares go; they had been great favorites with all of us. I think the two happiest people in the world were my wife and daughter when I called to say I was bringing some of them back. When I drove into the yard with the van I saw a great banner Jo Anne had rigged up: *Welcome home, No Butt, and Daddy Too!*"

It was Guy's opinion that No Butt was the fastest horse in the world at 300 yards and possibly 350; he would have liked to run her against First Call at 350 for the title and some money, but it never came off.

He sold her, sound as a dollar, to Charles Mickle of Valley View Ranch, Scottsdale, Arizona, for $35,000 in August. She has earned in excess of $63,680, and is fourteenth on the Leading Money-Earning Horses list, 1949 through 1962.

Panzarita

"In her youth, Panzarita (747) was a picture horse, splendidly conformed, a gallant chestnut filly who came honestly and logically by her astounding speed and stamina. Bred by J. Frank Norfleet, she was foaled in 1931 at Hale Center, Texas. She was sired by Spark Plug out of the great broodmare Five Dollars by Jim Trammell. A superb individual, she was not only many times first at the wire but, after retirement, proved to be one of the finest producing matrons of the breed. On her race record alone she is entitled to the profound respect of all knowledgeable horsemen; in combination with her record as a matron she comes pretty nearly being in a class by herself."

The above was written for *The Quarter Horse Journal*, Vol. II, No. 1, October, 1949. Raymond Hollingsworth, then Secretary of the AQHA, and the writer dug up most of the information you will find in this account. Panzarita was the result of Frank Norfleet's almost uncanny knowledge of horses. He bred Five Dollars to Spark Plug because, regardless of sires, all her previous foals had been outstanding, and he considered Spark Plug "the only stud as good as Five Dollars of all the sires she was bred to."

Spark Plug was a large stallion, weighing 1350 and standing 15 hands. A chestnut sorrel with white markings. Many horsemen of note have called Jack McCue and John Wilkens the greatest sons of Peter McCue. On the score of Jack McCue's achievements there can be no question, and Spark Plug was possibly his most distinguished get. Curley Daugherty once told me: "I have always considered Spark Plug's dam to be even greater than his sire. Her name was Silver; she was a daughter of Chickasha Bob. Old Man Stead of Tulia, Texas, raised Spark Plug. Excepting only his daughter Panzarita, he was the fastest-breaking horse I ever saw. He sired fast horses and more top roping stock than any other stallion of his time."

His mother, too, was very fast at the getaway, and could go on out to three-eighths of a mile. "I recall one day," declared Mr. Daugherty, "when she ran and *won* three races, one at 220, one at 440, and the last at 660. I consider that a real test of stamina."

Panzarita's dam, Five Dollars, was a bay standing 14.3 and weighing about 1150. She was distinguished by exceptionally heavy gaskins and stifles, and is held to have been the best mare Frank Norfleet ever owned—which is high praise indeed. She was never raced, being kept exclusively for breeding, but her full brother, Bartender, set quite a few track records in Mexico, I am informed. Though no records are available, it seems rather likely Jim Trammell, her sire, was bred by Thomas Trammell of Sweetwater.

In 1948, during a period of considerable correspondence with Mose Newman of that area, I became convinced that both the Newman and Trammell families at about the turn of the century were associated with fast horses and bred not a few. These were wholehearted believers in the value of good blood. Both families were convinced that right type Thoroughbred blood could be used in the improvement of Quarter stock, but there was never any Newman-Trammell horse-breeding outfit. Mose Newman declared in a letter to me: "My people moved into the Sweetwater country and settled there in 1879 from central Texas and brought with them a small herd of cattle, a few horses of the Quarterbred type, and bred these horses of this type from time to time until about 1900. During this period we matched a good many races of one-quarter of a mile and less. At about 1900 we got out of Quarter Horses and embarked on the business of producing Thoroughbreds."

The house of Newman was composed of the father, James F. Newman, and three sons—A. T. "Cap" Newman, H. S. "Auti" Newman, and Mose Newman. "Mr. Thomas Trammell," Mose informed me, "passed away about 1918; he was a resident of Sweetwater from about 1883 and owned the 9R Ranch located some fifty miles west of town, where he ran a few Quarter Horses, producing several nice ones. The principal stallion used by Mr. Trammell was Barney Owens, a horse that he acquired in Missouri, perhaps about 1890. We were never associated with Mr. Trammell in the breeding of horses. We were interested with him in the ranching business in New Mexico, ending about 1905. Mr. Trammell's first wife was my father's sister—this is perhaps how the names came to be so closely related from the early days."

Over a period of two years I corresponded with many breeders on the subject of the horse, Jim Trammell; my efforts in this direction were implemented by Raymond Hollingsworth, who has established the identity of the dam. Jim Trammell, for twenty years chief stallion for the Norfleets, was a beautiful, rich, dark sorrell with three or four little black or dark spots across the hips and a small white strip in his face. He had small, alert ears, a very balanced, whole-bodied way of going, extreme maneuverability, and looked the very picture of a race horse according to those who knew him best. A letter, dated 1949, from Mr. Hollingsworth states:

"I went to Plainview and talked to Mr. Norfleet and also Shorty Warren. They told me Jim Trammell was sired by the original Barney Owens out of a race mare brought in here to run against some of the Trammell stock, and they dealt for the mare and bred her to Barney Owens and got Jim Trammell."

Curly Daugherty told me: "Jim Trammell ran in the Hart Camp pasture just south of us for many years. My dad got two colts by him and everyone around here liked him very much. He was by old Barney Owens."

Raymond Hollingsworth unearthed from the AQHA files a letter from J. Frank Norfleet, dated 1945, which says in part: "Jim Trammell, his sire Barney Owens. The dam of Jim Trammell was a very classy mare called the A. P. Bush mare from Kentucky. I kept Jim Trammell for many years, sold all his horse colts to Captain Fitzgerald, head of the New York Jockey Club and Piedmont Polo Park."

Bob Norfleet, in a letter to me under date of April 4, 1948, said: "We and the XIT Syndicate wanted some young studs and went to Sweetwater and bought five. We took one and the XITs took the rest; one of theirs they kept on the Yellow House division and he was called School Boy. The one we kept was Jim Trammell. He was as good as anybody's horse and we didn't care anything about papers; we were told he was by Barney Owens. He was lightning fast and would take you right into a bunch of mustangs, of which there were plenty around at that time, and put you where you could rope any one you wanted; we roped lots of them on Jim Trammell. I think we got him in 1895 or 1896. He was very old when we sold him to a man at Portales, New Mexico, and did not live long after."

Barney Owens was the sire of Dan Tucker, the father of Peter McCue.

"Jim Trammell's get," said Bob Norfleet, were fast and had plenty of sense, making good cow and race horses that did not have to be babied. Many of them we sold into the East as polo stock. I recall one time I rode one of Jim's colts a hundred miles without stopping and made it in twelve hours."

Frank Norfleet named Five Dollars' foal Panzarita because, he said, she would be the kind of windburner the Newmans had raised in Pan Zareta, the Thoroughbred mare which whipped Joe Blair at Ciudad Juarez and established a World's Record for five-eighths that has stood for forty-seven years. Mr. Norfleet, in this prediction, came as close to the target as a man can get; Panzarita set the fans of the short tracks crazy.

A chestnut sorrell weighing 1150 in normal condition, she was 14.3, with a red mane and tail, a wide streak in her face, and white stockings on both hind legs. W. B. Warren has told us: "She could run just about as fast as horses run when she wanted to, but she was spoiled rotten and lots of times she would buck instead. One time, at Panhandle, I started her at three-eighths, packing bronc buster's weight of 150 pounds. There were eight horses in this go. During the whole first eighth she had her mind set on bucking; then she started to run. I can't think how fast she must have gone—she passed every horse except Dick Dilling and Cabin Camp. These three finished just a head or a nose apart, Cabin Camp, Dick Dilling and Panzarita. You might as well say they had one-eighth the start of her. Cabin Camp and Dick Dilling were *race* horses. Ed Deal owned Cabin and Dick Dilling belonged to Bob Burris, and this pair were out for blood.

"I really think when everything was right Panzarita could run the quarter in twenty-two flat. I have worked out some real good horses and I don't think I have ever worked a faster one. If I could have got her at the right time she would have been known from coast to coast, but she had been messed up before I ever got her. Also her feet had been ruined. You had to catch everything just right to tell what she could do—but she had speed and plenty of it."

Curly Daugherty has told me she was a very good cow horse. "She was level headed, very agreeable to ride and showed a lot of cow sense. When racing, I have seen her start in a bunch of the best racing horses and she would go away out in front in a way that made it seem the others were backing up. She showed more early speed than any horse I ever saw. She was very good in the herd when working a roundup. She was smart and quiet and would not scare the cattle. When you got ready to cut one out she was always ready. Quick moving and quick thinking—that was Panzarita."

Charles Hepler wrote: "We bought Panzarita from Curley Daugherty in 1948. She foaled Jim Dandy that year. He won the Fort Worth show from a list of 32 entries as a two-year-old and was sold to August A. Busch of the St. Louis Brewing Company for $3000. She has raised us six or seven good foals and we still have most of them and they are not for sale." [This letter is dated 1949; I think it likely Charley meant to say they had bought the mare in 1938, because these dates don't gee with Association produce records, which we will get to in a moment.] "When we purchased Panzarita from Mr. Daugherty," Charley goes on to say, "he contracted for the third foal, which turned out to be the filly, Panzarita Daugherty, that was named Grand Champion at Amarillo and Pampa."

According to the AQHA Performance Division's produce records, Panzarita (747) foaled the following produce:

Panzarita Velvet (81,867), a sorrel mare, 1936, by Chubby

Jim Dandy (826), bay horse, 1937, by Chubby

Pansy's Pride (6,891), bay mare, 1941, by Band Time (TB)

Panzarita Daugherty (2,121), bay mare, 1942, by Little Joe the Wrangler (by Joe Hancock). [This foal, in due course, became the dam of Mr. Hancock, ROM and halter point winner, Mr. Sparkplug, Champion gelding, Mayflower Daugherty, halter point winner, Hill's Poco Bay, 40 halter points, Showdown Jr., 11 halter points, and Poco Wrangler, 25 halter points and 4½ performance points.]

Tough Company (2,696), bay horse, 1943, by Chicaro Bill

Panzarita Hep (24,292), bay mare, 1947, by War Chief (by Joe Hancock)

Panita Lass (27,994), bay mare, 1948, by Little Joe the Wrangler

Chris Hep (24,288), chestnut mare, 1950, by Natches

Pandy Time (Appx.), bay mare (aged), by Band Time (TB).

Queenie

Champion Quarter Running Mare (1944–45) and World's Champion Quarter Running Horse of the 1945–46 season, Queenie, known in the days of her greatest glory as the "Club-Footed Queen of the Quarter," was foaled at Rayne, Louisiana, in the spring of 1939. Her breeder was Martin J. Richard. She was sired by Flying Bob (standing then in Abbeville), probably the most illustrious son of Chicaro (TB), out of Sister, who was by a Mr. Weekly's horse (a son of Old D. J., who could run a mile like nobody's business, and could burn the grass right off the quarter track).

Flying Bob, first registered as a Thoroughbred under the name of Royal Bob, was later declared to have been out of the Quarter mare Zeringue's Belle (by Old D. J.). Although Flying Bob was too old at the time of his discovery to be campaigned on recognized Quarter tracks, he was given a special citation for the season 1944–45 when his good son Dee Dee was Champion Quarter Running Stallion and Queenie (our heroine) was named Champion Quarter Running Mare. The Performance Department of the AQHA said of Queenie (*Quarter Horse Journal*, December 1958): "She deserves special recognition for her accomplishments since she raced with a right hind foot so badly deformed it must have hurt her with each race."

Sister, Queenie's mama, was considered a mighty fast sprinter in her neck of the woods. Her races were run over a course of four arpans— roughly 768 feet. Her average time for this distance when at her best was :13.2—this didn't leave much leisure for daisy picking. Her jump was measured at 22 feet. In spite of her club foot, Martin Richard began working Queenie at two. Racing her occasionally, he kept her in training a full two years, then quietly took her into Southeast Texas and, when the time was ripe, ran her at a top-flight horse and took everything but the owner's eyeteeth. The late George Orr, of El Paso, was so impressed with the club-foot's performance that he bought her and Effie and several of their kin.

Space does not permit a description of Queenie's many and spectacular track performances; suffice it to say that while in the ownership of J. Rukin

158. Queenie, by Flying Bob out of Sister, by a son of Old D. J.

159. For courage and drive: Shue Fly.

160. Stella Moore on her 16th birthday being fitted for new plates.

161. Tonta Gal, by Clabber out of Peggy Cooper, by Doc, a son of Possum.

162. Vanetta Dee and colt by Go Man Go (1963).

Jelks (Tucson) she dropped her first foal, Little Queeny (20,552) by Piggin String (TB)—the year was 1948. She achieved AA.

The following spring she produced Queen O' Clubs J (29,440) by the same sire. This foal also went to AA and later became the dam of Royal Bar, recently purchased by Bob Burnquist of California for $75,000.

Queenie then got down to business in grim earnest, producing in 1950 the stallion Rukin String (35,722, by Piggin String) who went into AAA and became Champion Quarter Running Two-Year-Old Colt of 1952, set several records, and was retired to the breeding pen.

Queenie's next was another product of Piggin String's court, Gunny Sack (42,856), AAA on the track. In 1952 Queenie produced Joe Queen, AAA, (P–36,183) by Joe Reed II (the Champion Quarter Running Stallion of 1943). "Joe Queen," Art Pollard says, "displayed as much if not more heart and desire to run than any of the old mare's amazing group of offspring." It is a known fact Joe Queen never raced sound, but this did not keep him from winning his division of the RMQHA's Futurity Trials at Centennial, going the 330 in the excellent time of :17.2 and winning by half a length over Crazy and Ridge Butler. Leo Bob won the main event, with Joe Queen second. The next year, in the Rocky Mountain Quarter Horse Association World's Championship Dash, Joe Queen really caught fire, going the quarter mile in :22.3, whipping Bull Eagle, Ridge Butler, Vanetta Dee, Miss Myrna Bar, Rukin String, Bardella, and Miss Nellie Snip in this order. He is presently at stud in California where a $100,000 offer for him was recently refused.

In 1953 Queenie produced Edam Taylor (P–40,655) by Tailor Made C— who unfortunately died following surgery as a two-year-old. At the time of his death he was being conditioned at the newly opened Las Vegas Race Course.

Queenie's Girl was the foal next brought into the world. This brown mare (P–45,893), by Tailor Made C, was started three times as a two-year-old, finishing third to Kid Sid and Bull Bar first out. She next whipped Pap (World's Champion Quarter Running Horse of 1961 and Champion Gelding), Dark Intruder, Catch Bird, Gold Nita, Brown Lace, and others. A stifle injury prevented Queenie's Girl from realizing her full potential. She was retired after her third race.

Bond Issue (103,728) came along in 1955. This one was sired by Buy-meabond (TB). Following several good races this bay colt went AAA. And then came Alliance (91,388) by Alumnus (TB), in 1956. A bay colt, also, Alliance went to AA. Apparently Queenie in the following year was barren.

In 1958 Miss Queenie (111,348) came along for another AAA. Her daddy was Depth Charge (TB), and she is currently the property of Clarence Scharbauer of Midland, Texas.

I doubt if any mare in the history of the breed has achieved the equal of this astonishing produce record. She has had seven owners of record, as follows: Martin Richard of Rayne, Louisiana (her breeder), George Orr of El Paso, J. Rulkin Jelks of Tucson, Bert Wood of Tucson, Bill Horton of Buffalo, Wyoming, Audie Murphy of North Hollywood, and Art Pollard of Sonoita, Arizona, who still has her.

Art says Queenie was twenty-one years old when he got her. "Everything known to man and nature has been applied in an all-out effort to settle her these past several seasons, but to no avail. It is believed she could conceivably be settled and she is currently bred to El Kentuck (TB)." Although twenty-four years old as of 1963, she is alert and in excellent flesh, and Mr. Pollard assures us "this tremendous little old lady will want for nothing throughout her remaining years."

If she never brings home another foal her record should stand for a considerable while; 10 foals, nine of them in the Register of Merit, five of them AAA.

Shue Fly

Champions may come and swiftly go, faster times may be established, but deep in the hearts of most short-horse fans there will always be one set-apart place kept bright with memories of a chestnut mare whose flying hoofs and unbounded courage made track history for more than eight years.

We are speaking, of course, of the Hepler brothers' celebrated Shue Fly.

The editor of the 1947 *Year Book* of the now-defunct American Quarter Racing Association never spoke more accurately than when he said: "No defeat can ever take away the glory that Shue Fly won during her many years of competition on the Quarter Tracks. Running against the top short horses of America, she beat every horse that ever defeated her on a recognized track right up until her last great race. She had the heart and proud courage of a true champion, and won most of her races the hard way—coming from behind in a dazzling burst of speed to catch her competition at the wire."

She may perhaps have lacked the smoothness which has characterized some of the other great sprinting mares, but this was more than offset by her power and never flinching determination. To us who have seen her go to the post, head high and proud of carriage, and have watched her overcome poor starts and tremendous margins to win by merest inches at the wire, her place is assured and secure forever. When she was right there was nothing quite like her.

In the minds of those who esteemed this old mare, background and bloodlines were just a pair of words. She was a Quarter mare. It mattered little which horse sired her or which dam gave her birth. Performance, in this breed, was always the prime objective—and she had that. But in the years since she has been retired to the stud, pedigree with breeders has tended to become something of a sacred cow. Was she sired by Cowboy (P–12) and out of Lady Luck, or is she indeed—as some stories have it—the daughter of Erskine Dale (TB) and Nancy M?

The Heplers were satisfied she was bred as stated; they spent no little time and money looking into this matter. The *Stud Book* shows her to be by Cowboy (P–12) out of Lady Luck by Booger Red. Cowboy was by Yellow Jacket by Little Rondo by Lock's Rondo. Cowboy's dam was Roan Lady by Stalks by John Wilkens by Peter McCue.

It has been said she never packed a rider before she was three; that right after she was broken she ran second to Question Mark in a half-mile race at Trinidad. At Durango, Colorado, in August of 1940 she was entered by Abe Salazar in a 440 go on a half-mile oval under the name of Spanish Girl. Joe Tom (then owned by the Heplers) drew post position Number One. Mamie Taylor (dam of Hard Twist) got away in the lead by a neck, a lead she held as they went into the turn. They were sure enough burning the grass up when Joe Tom widened out, slammed into Mamie, knocking her off stride into Spanish Girl, who went snorting into the outside rail. Finding considerable clear ground straight in front of his nose, another horse, Al Hardin's Play Boy, came in on the rail to win.

Beyond three-eighths, Shue Fly was never outstanding, yet she held a track record of :40.0 for three and a half furlongs and a one-time World's Record of :22.3 for the quarter.

The Hepler brothers, ranching in the hills of southern New Mexico, had been regaled with many a tale of this flying filly in the days when old Bob Burris was match-racing her; but to these the Heplers paid little attention until, at Deming, one fine afternoon in 1940, they had a close-up view of what she could do.

Burris was wearing a pretty long face. He'd been campaigning Shue Fly from three-eighths up to half a mile and let it be known that running this quarter was far from being what she was best at. The competition was a crackerjack field of veteran quarter-milers—Cyclone, Sparky, Joe Tom, and a Burns Blanton mare from the wastes of Arizona. Entrance fee was $200, cash on the barrelhead. Burris put up an awful display, appearing extremely loath to part with his money, but finally coughed up. Shue Fly won without wetting a hair. The Heplers considered each other without comment.

They made it a point to watch future performances. Each one bit deeper. Much studying convinced them that, while she obviously ran with the idea of winning, she had no intention of reducing competition by trying to bury it in the dust she flung up. She gave them all a good run for the shekels, many of the best finishing near enough to get their owners to figuring that next time they'd do it. Was this cultivated or mere happenstance? Were these victories in inches cleverly stage managed or was it just a matter of uncontrollable luck?

The Hepler boys lost a lot of sleep trying to make up their minds.

They were real he-coons from the Bitter Creek valley; they'd been running a string on brush tracks for years—it was plain common knowledge Brother Roy had been raised on mare's milk. But not even Elmer could get a line on that Burris cyclone.

On the 7th of December, 1941, Shue Fly made her first run at Tucson. This was a matched quarter against the "Iron Horse" Clabber on the old Hacienda Moltacqua track. A horse justly famous for the terrific power with which he broke from a gate, he was the current World's Champion Quarter Running Horse and Stallion Champ.

The mare got off slow; a good length of daylight was between them at the eighth pole. Then, suddenly, all that daylight was gone and she was lapped on him, driving hard for the wire. She flattened more and went barreling past, going under the wire a length on top to hang up a time of :22.6—a record in those days, and one that remained unbroken until Queenie (March 31, 1946) lowered it by a tenth.

On December 21st Shue Fly unwound in an overnight race at three-eighths, again breaking slowly but four lengths ahead at the quarter and winning, pulling up, in :36.0.

The following year she was back at Tucson for the Speed Trials, starting first in a quarter-mile free-for-all under 125 pounds, winning easily in :22.8 over Clabber and Don Manners. Then came the race that convinced the Heplers. It was run on a Wednesday (February 18, 1942) and was called The World's Championship Quarter, carrying a thousand-dollar purse. Four horses were entered—Shue Fly, Clabber, Joe Tom, and Nobodies Friend (the King Ranch entry), the greatest sprinters of that season. Each of those four was in there to win. In the crowd were people from 14 states. In the words of the *Year Book*, most of the betting was on second place; no horse in the race was conceded a chance to outrun the mare unless she fell down.

Which is just what she did!

Burris was standing just back of the gate and, when it flew open, he snatched off his hat and gave Shue Fly a wallop. The startled mare over-jumped and went to her knees. The whole crowd gasped. "Gawd a'mighty!" one fellow shouted when it seemed as though the jockey would fly over her head. But Hank Laswell held on, the mare staggered up and got going again, a long seven lengths behind the last of the field. Every gal out there —and most of the guys—jumped onto their feet to shout encouragement.

The noise was terrific. "*Come on, Shue Fly! Come on, Shue Fly!*" Over and over like the words of a chant—and Shue Fly came. Out from behind she sailed, foretop flying, a flashing sunlit sorrel streak that brought a shine to appreciative eyes. You'd have sworn she was too far back to catch the pack. She not only caught them but came through on the rail, passing Nobodies Friend, which had run straight and clear, to win by a nose, equaling her record of the year before. It was the most hair-raising finish of any race we can remember. That delirious crowd nearly wrecked the place, everyone trying to outshout his neighbor. Shue Fly had done it— and had won going away!

In the midst of all this racket and excitement, Bob Burris clawed through to the Heplers to yell: "Boys, will you give me three thousand for her?" You ought to have seen Elmer snatch out his pen.

From that day on she was the darling of the Quarter tracks, a veteran campaigner on the world's toughest circuit. Quoting *The Short Horses*: "It has been reported that Shue Fly won a quarter race at Albuquerque during the fall meeting of 1942 in twenty-one and four-fifths seconds from a regulation score and flagged start. This seems more than likely consider-ing her time, twice repeated, at Moltacqua from a flat-footed start."

Quoting from the 1944 *Year Book of the American Quarter Racing Asso-ciation*: "She runs smoothly and, though not exceptionally fast out of the gate, can turn on a dazzling burst of sheer speed when it is needed. We have seen her move a flying one-eighth in well under ten seconds. She seems to know where the finish line is and usually makes her move in time so that her nose is out in front at that important point. We believe she would look just as good at 550 yards as she does at one quarter and con-sider her a dangerous mare at three-eighths."

She was foaled in 1937, ran her first race in 1940 and was retired from the tracks in 1948 and bred. "Unfortunately," Lelah (Mrs. Elmer) Hepler tells me, "most of Shue Fly's foals died at birth or at the age of a few months except for those listed here. Little Fly, a sorrel mare by Little Joe the Wrangler (by Joe Hancock), foaled in 1949; Watch Him Fly, a sorrel gelding by Aldeva (TB) foaled in 1956; La Mosquita, foaled in 1957 by Little Request (TB); Royal Charge (AAA) by Depth Charge (TB), foaled in 1958; and Baby Shue Fly by Johnny Dial. All of them went to the track and won races, La Mosquita and Royal Charge making the best records. La Mosquita is being bred this year to Johnny Dial, World's Champion Quarter Running Horse and Champion Stallion of 1952."

Shue Fly died March 25, 1963.

Stella Moore

Though she holds no records at the present time, during her long career on the tracks this daughter of Joe Moore (by Little Joe by Traveler) was a real free-wheeling sensation. Her owner, Q. I. Roberts, challenged any Thoroughbred in the world to beat her at the quarter. In a letter dated December 22, 1948 he wrote: "Have been wanting to write you for the past several weeks, but have held off, expecting I would have some interesting news, but it just has not broken. For three weeks we have been right on the verge of matching Stella against one of Fred Hooper's stakes-winning Thoroughbreds. We had a conference with him last Friday, and it now looks as though we will run against either Olympia, Ocean Drive, Education, or Sylly Gyp for $15,000 a side over a course of one-quarter mile. Mr. Hooper said he very definitely wanted to run it and would try and arrange to do so at Hialeah about the middle of January."

On January 7th, Mr. Roberts wrote to say: "Everything happened so quick that I just did not have time to let you know. We discovered on January 1st that we were going to run and had to haul her 350 miles to run the afternoon of the 5th. After we arrived she had only two days' rest and went off her feed."

Here is the account, as put together from the AQRA files. Stella left Palatka, Florida, at 9:00 A.M. on the morning of Sunday, January 2, 1949, and did not reach her stall at Tropical Park before 9:00 P.M. that evening. She ran the race at 3:00 P.M. the following Wednesday afternoon, without benefit of any work on the track, an entirely new one to her. She was schooled at the gates Tuesday morning and had a gallop. Mr. Roberts and Odey Benoit, her trainer, were so confident of victory that they disdainfully shrugged away any possible difference these circumstances might be expected to make.

The chutes were placed 6 ft., 3 in. back of the starting pole—not sufficiently close, however, that the gates would start the clock when they opened. When the clock actually started the horses were very nearly a complete length out of the gates. Olympia had been loaded in No. 4 and Stella in No. 7. This placed Stella directly in the center of the 70-foot track.

They broke very nearly even, though Trevino (on Stella) came out with a tight right rein as though for some reason he had not been quite ready. The track was heavy and cupped badly. At about 250 yards the mare appeared to strike a soft spot and veered to the right, drifting across the track to the grandstand railing. Olympia passed and, by 360 yards, had gained a length. At this point the mare put on a very determined drive and slowly closed, to be beaten at the quarter pole by a head. Jockeys, sitting on benches at the finish line, declared that Stella went ahead of the horse just after they crossed the quarter.

If such was the fact, it becomes obvious the 30 feet wasted by the mare when Trevino allowed her to drift to the outside rail cost her the race. It was clocked in :22.6 by teletime.

This description is given, not to alibi the mare or take credit from Olympia's fine dash, but to show some of the circumstances that, combined, may well explain why a mare that had run 60 feet to the second time after time failed to live up this time to the expectations of her backers.

She was bred by Ott Adams at Alice, Texas. One of the outstanding sprinters of the 1948 season, she was sired by Joe Moore out of Canova by Chicaro's Bill. In discussing Stella with me, Mr. Adams declared: "Canova's dam was the Tom O'Connor mare by Big Jim. O'Connor said they could rope any deer on her right out on the prarie. She also foaled Adam, the good Quarter Horse owned by B. L. Smith of Junction. Canova has never been in training or raced but has proved a wonderful breeder. She produced both Stella Moore and Bill Roberts. Chicaro's Bill was out of Verna Grace (Fair Chance) by Little Joe, which gives Stella two crosses to Little Joe. Verna Grace was a great little race mare who was trained and run by Johnnie Armstrong along with the celebrated Lady of the Lake."

Mr. Adams said later: "Chicaro's Bill sired Canova, who produced Stella Moore—this cross of Traveler blood with Chicaro blood has proved itself to be of the finest and produces race horses of top quality. Stella Moore should never have been raced with Miss Princess until she was four; she was too young to race 440 yards against the world's greatest quarter-miler —however, she outran Miss Princess [Woven Web, TB] to within a few yards of the finish."

No mean accomplishment for a filly barely three years old at the time. At this time Stella held the three-year-old record at 330 yards. The Association had had quite a time deciding who should be given top billing— Leota W (by Leo), Stella Moore (by Joe Moore), or Miss Pinkie (by Blob) —all of which had the same time when corrected according to the grading and qualification standard of the American Quarter Racing Association. Van Smelker, Secretary-Treasurer of the Association, hinted that a race including all three might settle things nicely. In the end the kudos went to Stella; she was named Champion Three-Year-Old of 1948, and Champion Quarter Running Mare of 1952. She was retired at Tucson in the spring of 1954 and bred to the Stan Snediger Thoroughbred, Be Sure Now.

From this mating came Segura Miguel, who proved to be a very solid AA, winning in September of 1957 the Ruidoso Southwestern Futurity ($22,700), the largest purse won by a Quarter Horse up to that time. Bred back, Stella failed to settle and was again bred to Be Sure Now (TB), producing in 1957 a filly that died the day she was foaled. She was bred then to Leo and foaled the beautiful filly Betrayed, which was put into training by Walter Merrick. She consistently pulled up sore from her works and went unraced. She is now at the ranch of Ray Lewis (Del City, Texas) with a fine stud colt at side.

Stella missed again in 1959 and was brought back to Florida and bred to Sheila's Reward (TB), producing Stella Reward in 1960; this filly was entered in the 1962 Ruidoso Open Quarter Horse Futurity, but did not start.

Bred back, after foaling, Stella in 1961 dropped another fine-looking filly, which they've called Sheila Moore. That year they took Stella to a Florida Thoroughbred—Feast—and got a horse colt.

At two and three, Stella was never able to race with others of her age but was forced to compete with the fastest short horses of her time.

Tonta Gal
(220 yds., 1946 RIL 120 :12.1)

In the early years of organized Quarter Racing the female of the species appeared definitely to have the real corner on speed; all top records were consistently held by fillies or mares. In 1946 a fast stepper named Tonta Gal hung up a record in the 220 slot that still stands unbeaten. Bred by Chester Cooper of Roosevelt, Arizona, she was foaled in 1943, and stacks up to have been one of the greatest. She was by Clabber out of Peggy Cooper by Doc, a son of Possum; second dam by Blue Eyes by Possum (Nat Gardner, who knew him, has said that Blue Eyes wouldn't run worth a damn, and pretty near broke Uncle Mabry). Possum, however, was a real bolt of lightning.

Van Hastings, late of Ashurst, Arizona, told me:

He ran two races in Texas; one at the San Antonio Fair as a two-year-old, being easily the winner, and one at Kyle, Texas. At Kyle he was matched against Yellow Jacket, one of the fastest short horses of that day. This was

a real "betting" race, as both horses had many backers. It got around later
that the Kyle bank was several thousand dollars short the next morning.
Possum won without wetting a hair. I have seen most of the best race
horses from his day to this, and I do not believe he could have been outrun
by any of them, including Miss Princess (Woven Web).

He had one of the fastest getaways I ever saw. From an 18-foot score,
I believe he could have done the 440 in :21.5. I have seen his full brother,
Little Joe, run several races; he was certainly a good one, but he didn't
have what Possum had. I think Possum took more after Traveler, and
Little Joe more after his dam (Jenny by Sykes Rondo). In Texas I had
more to do with Possum than anyone; I was the first to put a saddle on him.

In discussing her 1946 campaign the *Quarter Running Horse Year Book*
(1947) had this to say of Tonta Gal:

She moved up to rate close behind the leaders and was very hard to
beat at the shorter distances. She started 12 times—won six, was once second, four times third, and only once unplaced. At Rillito she set a new
World's Record for 220 yards when she broke on top of a good field of
horses and won *easily* in :12.1 (Chart 398 shows Flicka, Wampus Kitty,
Danger Boy H, Lue Kirk, and Anneta in the beaten field). Later on in
the season she won, at 330 yards, from Bay Annie, Prissy, and Flicka in
:17.6 on a good track (Chart 453), and then equalled the [then] World's
Record for 350 yards at Winkelman, Arizona, in a special matched race
against Prissy, supervised and timed by officials appointed by this Association (Chart 474). That she ran a full quarter is evidenced by her excellent
performance in the Championship Stakes at Rillito when she ran second
to Hard Twist, beaten only a head (Chart 498).

Tonta Gal is a big mare with a tremendous amount of power and proves
that Thoroughbred blood close up is not always an attribute of a Quarter
Running Horse. It is interesting to note that her pedigree shows three
crosses to Possum, one in the third generation and two in the fourth, and
that the only Thoroughbred names appearing are those of *Porte Drapeau
and Uncle Jimmy Gray, both in the third generation.

Tonta Gal, as a crowd getter, had few peers. She always gave the best
that was in her whenever it was needed to fetch home the bacon. She
always ran against the best at any track, and is the dam of Tonto Bars
Gill and Bar Tonto (by Three Bars); Peligal and Tonto Basin (by the
1947 Champion Quarter Running Stallion, Pelican); Desecho, Mr. Desecho,
and Tonta Lass (by Glass Truckle); and of Tonto Hug (by Bear Hug).
All but two of these offspring—and Mr. Desecho at this writing is still
under age—have qualified for the Register of Merit. Tonta Lass, for instance, was one of ten finalists at the first All-American Futurity. Tonto
Bars Gill has been on the Leading Sires lists for several years, third from
top in the Leading Sires of Winners list for 1961, tying with Top Deck for

second most winners; one of his great sons, Tonto Bars Hank, topped the list of Leading Money Earners (1949 through 1961) was chosen Co-Champion Quarter Running Three-Year-Old Colt (1961) and his owners C. G. and Milo Whitcomb, so I am told, have turned down $250,000 for him. Bar Tonto, another of Tonta Gal's sons, is currently leading sire for the Gill Cattle Company.

In 1948, when so many of our breeders were sending their best mares to Thoroughbred stallions, I tried to point out that not *all* Thoroughbred blood can be successfully crossed on Quarter stock; this has of late been rather generally accepted, I think. In *Champions of the Quarter Tracks* (Coward–McCann, 1950) I suggested that progeny of the so-called American Families—or speed lines—is demonstrably better suited to the production of outstanding quarter-mile performance than the blood of most other Thoroughbreds.

Running in 1960 as two-year-olds, were more AAA than AA youngsters; 15 per cent of these starters qualified in AAA as against 13 per cent in AA. Of 68 half-bred starters, through three-year-old performance, 35, or 51 per cent, were graded AAA, while 15, or 22 per cent, got no higher than AA. A 50-head total out of 68 starters went into the Register of Merit.

Thoroughbred sires that have been proven by progeny appear to possess to a high degree the ability to transmit early speed, as indicated by the fact that of this 1958 crop roughly three-quarters of the starters sired by these stallions went into ROM. On the other hand, half-breds by Thoroughbreds other than those included in the current Top Ten, apparently did not affect the percentages at all. Here again I would suggest that breeders take a good long look at the mothers of these youngsters.

There's no substitute for a good mother and Tonta Gal, by any standard, will have to be placed in the very front row.

Vanetta Dee

Second from the top on the 1959 list of Leading Money Earners, Vanetta Dee, in a John D. Askew advertisement, had the following written of her: "During her six-season career, plus 1959 (through August), she has earned $78,925.25. In 87 races, she has been completely out of the money in only seven." In the list of Leading Money-Earning Horses, 1949–62, she stands ninth with $84,930.87. She was elected Champion Quarter Running Mare for three years straight (1956, 1957, and 1958); in 1955 she was named Champion Quarter Running Three-Year-Old Filly by the Racing Committee of the American Quarter Horse Association.

She was bred by Dee Garrett, Pawhuska, Oklahoma, foaled in 1952;

sired by Vandy, she was out of Miss Pawhuska by Leo. Miss Pawhuska was the second winner of the Oklahoma Futurity (1948), and is the dam also of such additional headliners as Vannevar, Vandy's Flash, Miss Vanity, and Vandy's Betty, full brothers and sisters to Vanetta Dee.

In 1954, as a two-year-old, she started twice, won twice (including the Nebraska Quarter Horse Futurity, banking $520.

In 1955 she made 23 starts, winning eight, placing in five, and showing in four others, while earning $11,430. She won the following stakes and features: The Fullerton and the Clabbertown G at Los Alamitos, Lotus Room Handicap and three other handicaps at Centennial; allowances at Pomona and Bay Meadows. She placed in the Gold Bar and the Hard Twist at Los Alamitos, an Allowance at Centennial, and the Pomona Handicap Race. She showed in the Newport-Balboa at Los Alamitos.

1956 saw her start in 18 outings, winning six, placing in one, showing in four, and banking $14,763.50. She won the Johnny Dial at Los Alamitos, the Bay Meadows Invitational, the Northern California Burlingame, and an allowance. Placed in the Lincoln Birthday Allowance at Bay Meadows. Showed in the Burlingame (February), the Bay Meadows, the Gold Bar and Clabbertown G at Los Alamitos.

In 1957, of 18 starts she won four, placed in eight, and showed in three, earning $16,478.70. Won the Bay Meadows New Year Handicap, an allowance at Los Alamitos, the Bright Eyes at Ruidoso, the Au Revoir Handicap at Centennial. Placed in Handicap San Francisco (Bay Meadows), Pomona Quarter Horse Championship and two allowances, the Ruidoso Handicap, the Gold Bar (Los Alamitos), and, at the same track, the Autumn Championship and the Clabbertown G. Showed in the Johnny Dial, the Shue Fly, and the Hard Twist Stakes (Los Alamitos).

In 1958, her peak year in earnings, she made 21 starts, winning five, placing in four, and showing five times, while banking $26,997.04. She won three handicaps at Bay Meadows, an allowance at Ruidoso, and the Quarter Horse Championship. She placed in the Autumn Championship at Los Alamitos, a handicap at Pomona, and the Inaugural and a handicap at the Bay Meadows Spring Meet. Took third money in the Barbara B and the Miss Princess at Los Alamitos, the Inaugural (Fall Meet) at Bay Meadows, the Pomona Quarter Horse Championship, and the Ruidoso Wonderlad Stakes.

In 1959, her final year of track performance, she started in 12, won six, placed in two, and earned $12,187.92 and a Howell Trailer. At Los Alamitos she won the Shue Fly and the Miss Princess, two allowances at Ruidoso, trials and finals of the Howell Trailer Handicap at Pawhuska; and placed at Los Alamitos in the Marathon, and at Ruidoso in the Quarter Horse Championship.

She was retired at Pawhuska in August of 1959. From a total of 94 starts she had 31 wins, placed 20 times, showed 16, was completely out of the money in but eight races, and retired the richest mare in Quarter racing history—and, as of 1963, she still is.

In the stud, she has produced, April 15, 1961, the sorrel filly Vanetta Bar, by Pana Bar (Lightning Bar–Miss Panama); February 27, 1962, the sorrel colt, Unnamed, by Go Man Go (Top Deck, TB,–Lightfoot Sis).

Part VIII: Outstanding Modern Sires

Biographical Sketches

Leo

A majority of our greatest Quarter Horse stallions have been little, or at best but moderately, appreciated when they were available for stud service. This was true of Tiger, Sykes Rondo, Lock's Rondo, Cold Deck, Traveler, Yellow Jacket, Question Mark, and Joe Reed II, to name just a few.

In the process of gathering data for this book I drove more than a hundred and seventy miles to talk with a horse-racing rancher who I thought might have some unpublished pictures of Traveler. He didn't. But at one point in our conversation I asked him which of the Gardners had owned Traveler in Texas, and what top horses he got while the Gardner family had him. To which B. A. Gardner replied: "Uncle John Gardner, my grandfather's brother, owned Traveler. Grandpa Alec Gardner was the one who first owned him. For a long time Granddad would not breed his best mares to Traveler—he had other stallions which he reckoned were better."

For quite some time this was also the case with Leo; only in the last eight or nine years have breeders come to admit his worth. A chestnut sorrel, he was foaled at Cameron, Texas, in 1940, bred by J. W. House, and sold for a handful of dollars at a very tender age. Following a few impromptu trials in back-country sprints he showed up at Pawhuska, Oklahoma, the property of John W. Tillman. A search through the early *Year Books* of the American Quarter Racing Association revealed that he was mentioned in the "Not Registered" section of the 1945 *Year Book* as a Celebrated American Quarter Running Horse owned by E. M. Salinas of Eagle Pass, Texas, with the following record: *Eagle Pass '44 300 catch :165f.*—this in a day when Little Joe, Jr. (whose time for the distance was :16.4f) was considered one of the finest horses on the short tracks.

Tillman ran Leo principally at Pawhuska, where he established a track record (300 yards in :16.0) which stood for several years. Mr. Tillman states: "I bought him from Lester Manning at Gatesville, Texas, as a two-

399

year-old. He was an extremely fast colt that spring, racing with and defeating such good sprinters as Red Sails, Johnny Barnes, Good Eye, and Cyclone. These were all in their prime when he met and defeated them. I do not know of a poor foal sired by him. In my opinion [and Mr. Tillman told me this in 1950] he is probably the best sire brought to Oklahoma in a good many years. When I owned him he could run the eighth in :12.1 on the track here at Pawhuska, and when he was ready there were not over five or six horses that could outrun him up to 300 yards. He has always had a wonderful disposition, is easily handled, was a perfect gate horse, and had the heart and ability to come from behind and outrun good horses."

Leo defeated Cyclone, a very highly regarded horse, at Pawhuska, going 220 yards in :12.0 for a purse of $3600 when he was three years old. Blondy Meyers, trainer of Cyclone, said he didn't believe any horse living could have outrun Leo that day. The then current record for 220 on a recognized track was :13.0, set (and still held) by Clabber in 1937. It was not until 1946 that Tonta Gal (a chestnut four-year-old by Clabber) set the current World's Record of :12.1 for an eighth, under 120 pounds. And in all the years since this record was established only two others have managed to equal it—My Texas Dandy, Jr. in 1947 at Eagle Pass, under 115 pounds, and Maddon's Bright Eyes at Rillito in 1950, carrying 125.

Leo is said to have won 20 out of 22 matched races. Three years after defeating Cyclone he very nearly had both front legs cut off in a trailer accident. Taken out of stud service, and with this handicap, he ran his last race at Tulsa in 1947, where he was whipped by a head by Little Joe (not Traveler's son) at 375 yards.

For some time Leo was owned by Gene Moore of the Rocking M Ranch at Fairfax, Oklahoma, who says: "Leo is a good sire because he has the ability to mark his colts in conformation and style very similar to himself, and his bloodlines contain some of the fastest blood known to the American turf."

Bill Morgan of Pawhuska trained Leo during most of his racing career. He first did stud service in 1943, being bred at that time to but very few mares. Somewhat later, bred to the Thoroughbred mare Squaw Baby (by Centimeter), he got the sorrel Leo II, which won several match races and some purse competition.

In 1945 the Quarter mare Swamp Angel by Grano de Oro (he by Traveler's son, Little Joe, out of the celebrated Della Moore—dam also of Joe Reed P–3 and Joe Moore) produced the track-burning bay Leota W by Leo. She was Co-Champion Two-Year-Old of 1947 and missed being named Champion Three-Year-Old Filly in 1948 only by a whisker. An-

163. Leo at 23 years of age. Mrs. Warren at halter.

Photo by Orren Mixer

164. Little Fanny.

165. Three Bars, TB, taken in the '40's at Douglas, Arizona.

166. Vandy, age 20, taken February, 1963.

167. Vandy, from an oil painting made shortly after he was retired from racing.

168. Tonto Bars Gill as he looks today.

Photo by Darol Dickinson

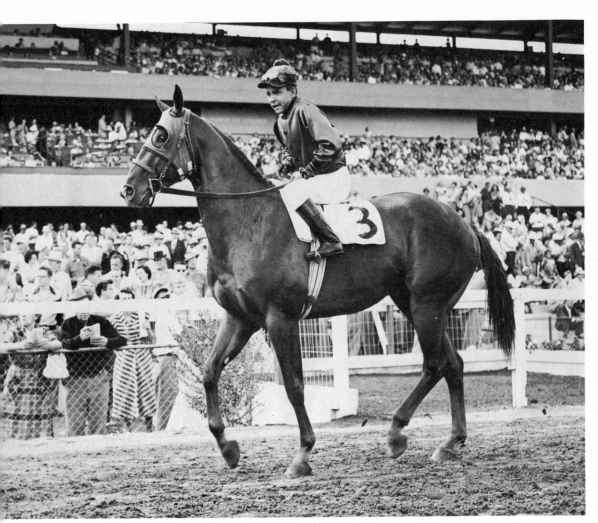

169. Tonto Bars Gill at Centennial, 1952.

170. Moon Deck, by Top Deck out of Moonlight Night, by Peace Pipe, TB.

Photo by Western Livestock Journal

other of Leo's get in 1945—also bred by Bud Warren—was the good mare Flit, retired to stud with a AA rating.

Until Mr. Warren acquired him Leo was bred but lightly and almost entirely to cowhorse mares. After Leota W and Flit began kicking up the dust on recognized straightaways a number of breeders began more thoroughly to assess his abilities, with the result that in 1950 Bud Warren had to turn away 33 registered mares.

By 1951, Leo's get had won four out of five renewals of the Oklahoma Futurity. Leota W took the first of these juvenile classics in 1947. In 1948 it was won by Garrett's Miss Pawhuska. In 1950 Leola, also bred by Mr. Warren, corralled this epic and went on to become the first Quarter Horse to win three futurities (capturing the Colorado and Wyoming classics, also). The fourth of Leo's get to run off with the Enid epic was Mona Leta, setting a new two-year-old record by going the 220 in :12.2, to win by two open lengths over Lady Fairfax (by Leo) and Might Do (by Can-Do), with five others in the beaten field. Not satisfied with this, Mona Leta went on to win the Colorado Futurity at Centennial by two open lengths, going 330 yards in :17.0, lowering another record for two-year-olds, and bettering the best time made at this distance by any horse on the short tracks during 1950. In her division of the trials two other Leo youngsters, Robin Reed and Leolita, came in second and third.

This same year another Warren-bred filly by Leo—Leolena—set a new two-year-old filly record at Albuquerque by going 300 yards in :16.2 to win by two lengths over Hi Maria and Chudej's Black Gold, both consistent performers well up in the money. Robin Reed, by Leo, finished third in Colorado's Rocky Mountain Futurity. In the Kansas Futurity, run at Meade, the third division of the trials was won by Leolita, who went on to win the main event over Running Iron (by Piggin String, TB) and Leolena, with Dwight's Leona (by Leo) finishing fourth. In the Nebraska Futurity at Burwell, the first division of the trials was grabbed by Kanzo (by Can-Do), with Dwight's Leona a close second. In the finals Kanzo scored again, almost nipped at the wire by Dwight's Leona, which was beaten by scarcely a neck.

Almost all Leo's forebears have been sprint runners, many of them famous. Sired by Joe Reed II out of Little Fanny by Joe Reed (P–3), Leo is a full brother to Bert Wood's Little Sister W (AAA). Through November, 1951, Leo had sired more futurity winners than any other sire of Quarter Horses and stood third on the *Thoroughbred Record's* list of Leading Quarter Horse Sires. The Quarter Running Horse Chart Book for August of 1951 shows Leo as a recognized AA horse. (The AAA rating had not been established during Leo's track competition; if it had been,

I believe he could have qualified.) In my personal opinion he is the great-est sire of Quarter Horses currently available at stud. Certainly Three Bars (TB) has outdone him, but the latter has had the help of the very best mares obtainable.

One of Leo's finest sons, and very possibly his greatest, is Palleo Pete, Champion Quarter Running Stallion of 1954. This comparatively young stallion appears to have inherited all his sire's best qualities, plus the capacity and ability to pass them along.

Leo is one of the greatest brood-mare sires of the breed. The celebrated get of many other leading sires have had Leo daughters for their dams. Leo combines in blood and genes some of the finest speed lines in the annals of American racing.

On the 1962 Leading Sires of Winners list he stands thirteenth among those with most wins, and eighth among those with most winners. On the Leading Sires of Register of Merit Qualifiers list (1945 through 1962) he stands second only to Three Bars. He stands at the top of the Leading Maternal Grandsires of Register of Merit Qualifiers list. On the Leading Sires of Money Earners list Leo stands fourth.

Three Bars (TB)

Since the days of the imported Janus, perhaps no other horse in the turbulent history of straightaway performance has become so towering a legend as Three Bars while still around to be bred to. Certainly no other stallion within my memory has made such a name or so deep an impres-sion not only on the whole shifting fabric of Quarter Racing but on the nation's breeders, big and small. So vast an institution has Three Bars become in the pip-squeak span of a single decade that he can ignore every criticism leveled against him and, like Liberace, laugh all the way to the bank.

Several times I've tried to point out the extremely high percentage of top mares he has courted. Not for a moment do I believe that Three Bars achieved such tremendous renown all by himself or strictly on his own obvious merits. Not all of his get have been pacesetters; not all which have tried have managed to latch onto ROM ratings; but on the basis of the latest figures available, no other stallion presently in sight has even come close to catching up with his record.

I had a chance years ago to breed a running mare to Three Bars for $300. I got to thinking of a few of his get that went up like rockets and came down the same way. I took the mare to Red Man, feeling pretty smug about the fine colt she dropped. He looked like a corker, but no one, alas, has ever heard of him since.

Which reminds me of a story that has had some circulation. The mighty Three Bars once sold for $300, and the buyer was subsequently so little pleased that he gave the horse away to get him off his hands. According to Len Tracy of the *Thoroughbred Record*, Jack Goode, a trainer at the old Association Track at Lexington, and two other enterprising gents, Ned Brent, who still breeds an occasional stakes winner, and Bill Talbert of Lexington, back in 1939 pooled their resources and bought Myrtle Dee by Luke McLuke (already in foal to Percentage) from Mr. J. W. Parrish of Midway, Kentucky.

"The colt obviously had some speed," young Goode told Len Tracy, "but whenever he turned it on he would come back to the barn with the muscle of a hind leg restricted and the flesh all around it feeling colder than frog legs. I tried everything, but couldn't overcome the difficulty. We finally sold him to Beckham Stivers for $300, to be paid if Three Bars ever managed to win."

Says Len Tracy:

Seems that Mr. Stivers had no better luck with the horse, and finally gave him to Vernon Cloud "free gratis." Somehow Cloud cured the malady or it wore itself out. The colt raced in '44 as a four-year-old. In the name of Mrs. Cloud he won three of his four starts. He did not race in '45, but the following year garnered eight victories and three seconds from 17 starts, earning $16,940. At seven he placed once and earned $550 in six starts, and was retired the next year to the stud. . . . As a Thoroughbred sire, Three Bars got the winners of 116 races and over $110,000 in six crops to race.

"Three Bars won $20,140 racing and earned I don't know how much at stud," declared Jack Goode. "My partners and I each got $100 out of him after putting in considerable money in training and feed. But we used to laugh about it with Beckham Stivers because he put in $300 and training expenses on the horse and got absolutely nothing out, because when Three Bars won it was for somebody else."

I would imagine that Three Bars and his present owner, Sidney H. Vail of Oakdale, California, have had some quiet chuckles themselves over the turn of events. In a recent letter Sid Vail said to me: "It might be interesting to note that I bought Three Bars in 1945 for $10,000, which is the exact amount of his stud fee today."

It would be difficult to estimate how much of the long green Mr. Vail has got out of the old horse to date, but it would probably keep a lot of us in clover for quite a while. According to the latest computations of the

American Quarter Horse Association, Three Bars has sired 348 registered Quarter Horse foals; 258 of these have started, of which 176 have qualified for the Register of Merit and 116 are rated AAA. He is the Leading Sire of ROM Qualifiers. His 258 starters have totaled cumulative earnings of$1,825,521.52. Now hold your hat, because that ain't all! His closest competitor in this field (Top Deck) reveals get earnings of but $569,060.62 —very nice, to be sure, but scarcely more than half. And, in addition to this, Three Bars tops the Leading Sires of Winners list for 1962; and has topped these lists for several years now and is currently second on the list of Leading Brood-mare Sires. Leo, who tops this list, has for many seasons been perhaps his closest or most consistent competitor throughout the whole stud picture on an over-all basis, if such a horse can really be said to have had a close competitor.

"Among his 116 AAA get," declares his owner, "I wouldn't attempt to say which are the best ones, but among the latter would probably be Pokey Bar, Tonto Bars Gill, Alamitos Bar, Lightning Bar, Triple Chick, Gold Bar, Bardella, Little Chloe, Miss Myrna Bar, and Miss Bar Leo."

I'm a little more brash than Sid, I guess. To this list I would add Mister Bar None, Sugar Bars, Bar Depth, Royal Bar, Bunny's Bar Maid, and Josie's Bar for certain. And there are others, too, which ought to be in this great company but which at the moment, I can't lay names to. But Breeze Bar is surely one; he still co-holds the World's Record at 400 yards—no mean accomplishment in this day and age. Of grand-get, I think, my nod would go first to Tonto Bars Hank (the breed's top money winner, 1949 through 1961), with Kimaleta and Mr. Juniper Bar loping right at his heels.

In the breeding pen, for prepotency and over-all class of offsprings, of all Three Bars' sons I would have to put Tonto Bars Gill at the top of the column; I don't know whether he's the eldest, but for my money he has shown not only great gains but the greatest accomplishments. He was himself a first-rate sprinter and his class shows up in quite a number of his get. Remember his whirlwind daughter, Miss Mow-Em-Down Louton?

And there is Galobar, winner of the first All-American at Ruidoso. Hugh Huntley says of this gallant sorrel: "Josephine R when we purchased her had already produced Josie's Bar by Three Bars, and she was a world's champion. For this and other reasons we thought it best to breed the mare back to him, and Galobar was the result of this mating. We have continued to breed her back to Three Bars and have had Bar Raider, a stallion sold to Lloyd Jones of Perry [Oklahoma]; Barphine, a filly killed accidentally before she got to the tracks; and Romabar, a AAA filly. I believe Josephine R has had six AAA foals to race.

"Galobar did not have a very long track career. She won two races at

Ruidoso before winning the first running of the All-American, Sept. 7, 1959. After this she was entered in a futurity at Pomona, but seemed sick after she was on the grounds. The vets could not diagnose her trouble, so we brought her home. We then discovered a broken exhaust pipe on the van, and she had been gassed by the fumes. Our vet doctored her and, thinking her fully recovered, we took her to Los Alamitos the following year. She won one race, but it seemed to take too much out of her; the best course seemed to retire her to the brood-mare band, and this is what we did. Last spring she foaled a nice horse colt by our stallion, Depth Charge, now entered in the All-American for 1964. A recent write-up in a local paper states: 'For an oddity, three offspring of Three Bars, the old Thoroughbred sprint favorite, finished one-two-three in the sixth race as Nolton Pattio got Hugh Huntley's Big Bar home at $8.70, a couple of jumps ahead of E. J. Chapman's Lux Bar and A. B. Green's Gray Bar in :18.3—which wasn't exactly "Bar-rowed" time.'"

Then there's Sugar Bars, the very good son of Three Bars out of Frontera Sugar, currently standing at the Bud Warren establishment at Perry, Oklahoma. In 1962 this horse was third-best sire of winners at track performance in the nation. Through 1962 he has sired 85 starters, of which 34 earned Register of Merit ratings and 24 were AAA. Sugar has sired four AQHA Champions: Bars Bailey, at show and working classes; Sugaree Bars, at show and racing; Otoe, at show and racing—and Otoe has the distinction of being the only *two-year-old* who has made the AAA Racing Register of Merit and also qualified for the title of AQHA Champion—and Connie Reba, at show and racing. Connie Reba equaled the world record for mares in 1962 (Los Alamitos, 350 in :17.8) and set a new record for three-year-old fillies; being awarded in 1961 the Roll of Honor certificate for scoring highest number of points in racing. Sugar Bars is as respected a begetter of Quarter conformation as he is for horses of great speed and working ability.

About everyone, I suppose, knows that Pokey Bar (Three Bars' jet-propelled son out of the Champion Quarter Running Mare Pokey Vandy) is the world's record holder at 440 yards (:21.6) and, through 1962, was at the top of the Leading Money Winners list (1949–1962), replacing Tonto Bars Hank last year, and, for this prowess, named Champion Quarter Running Three-Year-Old Colt of 1962. He was also the winner of the 1961 All-American Futurity and, until the recent appearance of Jet Deck, considered on the basis of demonstrated performance, to be the fastest quarter-miler in breed history.

And then there is Mr. Bar None, brilliant from wherever one stands. This son of Three Bars out of that racing Murl L by Moca Burnett, was so powerful a track contender he very richly earned his title of Champion Quarter Running Two-Year-Old Colt of 1957, going on to be named World's Champion Quarter Running Horse and Champion Stallion of 1958, and he is still twelfth on the list of Leading Money Earners (1949 through 1962). He is twelfth on the 1962 Leading Sires of Winners list, with 13 winners of 37 races. Among Leading Sires of Money Earners (1949 through 1962) he is thirty-fourth, though he has been at the trade so short a while that about all he has had is one crop of 25 starters from 45 registered foals to put their shekels to work for him. In 1962 this first crop to race included such fine representatives as Mr. Juniper Bar, named Champion Quarter Running Two-Year-Old Gelding, Kimaleta, World's Record holder at 330 yards; and such sterling AAA contenders as Montecarlo Bar, Beaumont Bar, Buck's Bar None, Hank H. Bars, My Bar None, Running J Bar, and so on.

In the list of top stallions sired by Three Bars one would have to include the late Pollard sire, Lightning Bar who was felled by death's touch in the early years of what seemed likely to be a remarkable career. In five years at stud his get put him sixth on the 1962 Leading Sires of Winners list; from 43 starters he got 24 winners of 55 races. Seventy-nine starters through 1962 put him seventh on the Leading Sires of Money Earners list (1949 through 1962) with total earnings of $298,033.39. He sired, among others, Pana Bar, Champion Quarter Running Two-Year-Old Colt of 1958; Lightning Belle, which earned $54,000 in 12 starts; Cactus Comet, a AAA AQHA Champion; Doc Bar, an AQHA Champion; and such AAA stalwarts as Manor Born, Dick Killian, Heads Or Tails.

As a sire, a running horse, and a points-earning cutting horse, Three Bars' son Bar Bob must be mentioned. A AAA AQHA Champion out of a daughter of Leo, he is the first Quarter Horse in some two hundred thousand to merit these four coveted honors: AQHA Champion Stallion, AAA track performance, Register of Merit in Cutting, and first in nation for 1961 Get of Sire.

Another son who has been for some time in the sire line is Barred, out of the good mare Ready by Red Joe of Arizona, currently sixteenth among sires of Register of Merit Qualifiers (1949 through 1962), and fifteenth among Leading Sires of Money Earners for the same period—and this from only 69 starters. He has sired 30 ROM get, 11 of them AAA.

Bunny's Bar Maid by Three Bars out of Black Easter Bunny (by Hysition TB) stands eleventh on the all-time list of Leading Money-Earning Horses.

Bar Tonto by Three Bars out of Tonta Gal by Clabber is senior stallion for the Gill Brothers at Tucson.

Another AAA AQHA Champion son of Three Bars is Mr. Three Bars out of Burke's Gayle by Leo Tag. Nor can one forget Triple Chick, currently standing at the Vessels Ranch. He is by Three Bars out of the great brood mare Chicado V; he has had 15 starters in the past two years, of which nine are Register of Merit and five are AAA.

I guess everyone recalls that Miss Myrna Bar; and Little Choe was named Champion Quarter Running Two-Year-Old Filly of 1962. She dang near set the tracks afire!

Bob's Folly was another great sprinting son of Three Bars; he was out of Hot Heels by Midnight Jr. and, in his day, set a couple of World's Records before being retired to the stud. Through Dec. 31, 1962 he had 54 starters from 188 registered foals; 23 or more went ROM and 18 AAA.

Seco Bars, a grandson by Copper Bars out of a daughter of Depth Charge, was the sixteenth speed horse to become a AAA AQHA Champion.

Royal Bar (by Three Bars out of Queen O' Clubs J—a daughter of Queenie and Piggin String) recently changed hands for $75,000 after a strenuous career on the tracks. Clabber Bar (Three Bars out of Peggy N by Clabber), following his AAA stint on the straightaways, sold for $85,000; and Bar Depth, twenty-second among money makers, is a Three Bars tornado (out of Seco Midnight by Depth Charge) that quit the Goodson feed and stables for a cool $100,000.

Fifteen of Three Bars' get are sprinkled through the all-time list of 50 Leading Money Earners; according to the AQHA's 1962 figures, these are: Pokey Bar, topping the list with $162,543.81; Bunny's Bar Maid, eleventh ($72,288.96); Mr. Bar None, twelfth ($72,124.89); Galobar, thirteenth ($68,282.65); Triple Lady, fifteenth ($61,931.00); Alamitos Bar, seventeenth ($58,036.50); Little Chloe, twenty-first ($53,571.26); Bar Depth, twenty-second ($51,540.92); Rocket Bar, twenty-fifth ($47,480.24); First Call, thirty-seventh ($37,534.47); Bardella, thirty-eighth ($36,845); Bob's Folly, fortieth ($35,519.73); Mr. Three Bars, forty-third ($34,746.09); Missile Bar, forty-fourth ($34,452.10); Breeze Bar, forty-sixth ($33,642-.25); and Miss Bar Leo, forty-seventh ($32,745.84).

One could go on with this name dropping indefinitely—but you can't get them all into the space of one short sketch. We have included those that come most easily to mind. Josie's Bar, by the way, fetched $28,000 at public auction in a brood-mare sale.

Summing up: Three Bars unquestionably is the most fashionable sire of short-distance sprinters to come our way in more than two hundred years; no other stallion since the AQHA was organized has got within shouting distance of his fantastic record in the stud. Looking back over his accomplishments and the continuing performance of horses carrying his blood, I would not care to bet that he will not reign supreme forever.

Vandy

Foaled on the Dave Ware ranch near Bartlesville, Oklahoma, on April 15, 1943, he was named "Bambi" after the protagonist of a much-talked-about movie. The sorrel youngster, always gamboling about the yard, became a great pet, and when they got his papers, the Wares were somewhat put out to find him registered under the name of Vandy.

Mr. Ware had owned Joe Blair and still had around the place what some persons consider to have been Joe's finest daughter, Jean Ann Blair. Ware is believed to have kept her in the hope that before he got out of the business she could find him a colt that would really go places. This hunch proved to be correct.

Fred Koontz, of Tulsa, a long-time breeder of Thoroughbred horses, had a grandson of Phalaris named Sweeping Light out of a mare by Sweep. A son of this stallion, Going Light, also owned by Mr. Koontz, was readied for the tracks by Claude Hart of Pawhuska. This colt was astonishingly fast but was such a hard runner he sored up in the shoulders whenever worked. After two years of trying they took him out of training. Hart bought the horse, but while he was looking around for some mares he remembered the Blair mare that Ware had. He and Jean Ann's owner got together on the subject, Hart pointing out that Tryster was the daddy of the young nonstarter's dam. Ware knew, of course, that Tryster's sire was the famed Peter Pan, that good son of Commando, best son of Domino. He did not have to be told how well the Leamingtons and Dominos nicked; this had been proved in the case of Joe Reed II. A deal was arranged, and the match produced Vandy. The new colt went to the post in the spring of 1945.

With scarcely 18 days of training he went into the Open Futurity at Pawhuska, finishing third, barely beaten in a photo finish after being carried to the outside two different times. It was his only outing at two. Ware was disappointed. He took the colt home and sold him that Fall. Tom Gray bought Vandy and his dam in a package deal for $2750. With Connie Brown for his trainer, Vandy broke like a bolt of blue lightning.

They ran him against all comers, on official tracks and out where the hoot owls fly without lanterns. Lap-and-tap and from behind closed gates, it was all one to Vandy. Starting 22 times he won 19, ran second twice, and came in fourth for the other one. He ran a first and second lapped on Miss Princess at Del Rio; he took two at Raton, in the first setting a Track Record and then lowering it in the second. At Albuquerque the altitude bothered him, yet he came in second to Barbra B when, on September 30th, she set the Association Record for three-year-olds. The Chart Book, commenting on Barbra B's form that season, summed up: "She won seven out of her eight starts, defeating such horses as *Vandy, Señor Bill, Flicka, Tonta Gal, Hard Twist, Pumpkin, Miss Bank* and * *Fair Truckle.*" In his final race, a 330 at Eagle Pass, Vandy broke down right out of the gates, but recovered and went on to win by half a length. I have been told he made it back to the winner's circle, but so great was his pain that it took quite a while to return him to his stall. He had always been a very hard breaker; several winner's photos show a snapped girth. At Woodward, I am reliably informed, it was decided to run Vandy around the turn for six furlongs. This was a purse race; he had never been up against a turn before. The gates flew open, he came out hell-a-whoopin', blew the turn, careened through the paddock gate and, still heating his axles, blurred between track and grandstand to reach the wire first—and find himself disqualified.

During 1946 he was continually in transit, moving from track to track, never home, competing against the best in the field. They ran him at anyone who'd give him a race. If a man had a horse that was bent for three furlongs Brown would pile the tack on My Question; if 220 was mentioned Lady Gray got saddled; and if 300 was asked for they would put Vandy into it.

Vandy runs now in a two-acre paddock. He's a horse that likes attention, and he generally gets his share.

Dee Garrett bought him from Connie Brown in November of 1949. Gray had given him to the trainer right after he broke down at Del Rio. He was not put into regular stud service until 1950; prior to this he had bred but five mares (test shots). Garrett says: "I had gone to Eagle Pass in the fall of '49 hoping to find a young stallion, some well-bred Quarter Horse with several good dashes of sprinting Thoroughbred blood. I had not actually been looking for a Thoroughbred, though I was certainly hunting for a sire of speed. It was at Eagle Pass that I saw Vandy's first colts run. Lady Vandy, then seventeen months old, went the 220 under one hundred pounds in an astonishing :12.2—that was good enough for me."

Practically everyone who has handled Vandy has had something to say about his grand disposition. Garrett says: "My grandchildren thought nothing of playing around him or holding him and, now that they are older, they act as official guides for anyone wanting to go look at our horses." Dee gave $4500 for him; it was probably the best buy he'll ever make.

The only really top mare Vandy has had is the Leo mare, Miss Pawhuska. From her he got Vandy's Betty, AAA (1951), a mare who went to

J. V. A. Carter, where she produced Van Deck, AAA, and Van Moon; Vanetta Dee, AAA, one of the all-time greats of the Quarter Tracks, winner of the Nebraska Quarter Horse Trials and Futurity of 1954, Champion Quarter Running Three-Year-Old Filly of 1955, Champion Quarter Running Mare in 1956, 1957, and 1958, and richest mare upon retirement in quarter racing history with earnings of $82,376 plus a Howell Trailer (she made 94 official starts and ran out of the money only eight times); Vannevar, AAA, named Champion Quarter Running Gelding for 1956 and 1957, holds two Gelding Records and has earned thus far $39,946.79; Vandy's Flash (1954), also AAA and likewise gelded, Champion Quarter Running Gelding for 1958 and again in 1960, and that year named World's Champion Quarter Running Horse, the first gelding to receive this highest award since championships were inaugurated in 1941, holds Gelding Record at 440 (:21.7), co-holds the Gelding 400-yard mark (:20.1), is holder of the Gelding Record at 350 (:17.5), and through 1961 earned $81,108.87; Vansarita, which went into the stud unraced; Miss Vanity, AAA; Vansarita Too (entered for the All-American of 1963); Garrett's Vandy, a 1962 stud colt his owner is planning to ready for a replacement; and the brand-spanking-new Flashie Vandy (name applied for). This, admittedly, is a winning combination—how many others have come up with such a nick?

Vandy, in my opinion, is as good a sire as Three Bars. If I were breeding Quarter stock today, I would search out and buy a Quarter mare bred as nearly like Miss Pawhuska as possible and permanently board her at the Dee Garrett establishment.

Out of halfway good mares Vandy gets horses which quickly learn what to do when they get to the track; he breeds a fine disposition, a competitive spirit and a tremendous capacity for early foot—*velocity* is the word I would put above his stall.

As I see it, the difference between the stud performance of Three Bars and Vandy has been mainly a matter of opportunity. Anyone is entitled to a guess on this subject. It is my notion that Vandy, with the same kind and number of mares that went to Three Bars, would come up with a similar record.

Through 1962, AQHA statistics show him with 231 registered foals and 128 starters, of which 78 have gone into the racing Register of Merit, 38 of them with AAA ratings. He is close to the top on all applicable Leading Sires lists.

Tonto Bars Gill

It has often been said by people whose pronouncements deservedly carried weight that good horses have good mothers. T.B.G. had one of the finest—Tonta Gal, bred by Chester Cooper at Roosevelt, Arizona. She started at four in 1946 with very moderate success in the colors of Joe Bassett (of Payson). Purchased by Roy Gill of the Gill Cattle Company, she was described in the AQRA's 1947 *Quarter Running Horse Year Book* as having "moved up to rate close behind the leaders" and "very hard to beat at the shorter distances." Starting 12 times that year, she won six, was once second, four times third, and only once unplaced. "At Rillito she set a new World's Record for 220 yards when she broke on top of a good field of horses and won easily in :12.1 (Chart 398)." Later in the season she won at 330 yards from Bay Annie, Prissy, and Flicka in :17.6 on a track scarcely good, then equaled the World's Record for 350 at Winkelman in a special matched race against the celebrated Prissy (by Colonel Clyde). The above 220 yards is still a World's Record. Melville Haskell has called Tonta Gal "a big mare with a tremendous amount of power." She was sired by the World's Champion Clabber out of Peggie Cooper by Doc (by Possum by Traveler). Her second dam was by Blue Eyes (by Possum by Traveler).

Tonto Bars Gill was sired by Three Bars (TB) and, as nearly as I can discover, is far and away his best son up till now, both on the track and in the stud.

T.B.G. made his first start at Phoenix (according to information prepared by the Performance Division of the AQHA) on December 22, 1951. Because it was hand timed this outing was not officially recognized. In his next outing he ran second to Slap Out at 350 yards; his third start, a win, was not recognized because of hand timing (the reported time was :18.4 for 350 yards). The condition of the track was not mentioned.

He ran 24 races in 1952; seven of these he won, in five he placed, in one he showed, in five he was fourth, and in the remaining six he ran unplaced. In all, he started 34 times; 16 of these were run in AAA time and were officially so rated; five of these 34 starts, because of hand timing, were not accepted by the AQHA. He defeated such sterling performers as Chudej's Black Gold, Currency Bee, Monita, River Flyer, Black Easter Bunny, Little Egypt, Parker's Trouble, Tidy Step, Barjo, Hy Dale, Sahuaro, Silhouette, Little Sister W, Tonto Lad, Barbara L, Little Nip, Hygro Jr., Dalhart Princess, Robin Reed, Ed Heller, Sheelgo, Leola, Clabber's Lady V, Blob Jr., Clabbertown G, Chappo S, Lorane's Vandy, Question's Gold, and Miss Ruby.

Tonto Bars Gill in 1952 was co-holder—with Bright Eyes, Blob Jr., and Mona Leta—of the three-year-old record for 440 yards (:22.2g); co-holder, with Hy Dale, of the same record at 400 yards (:20.5f); and co-holder, with Slow Motion and Stella Moore, of a like record at 330 yards (:17.2f). He also co-held that year, with Blob Jr., the stallion record at 440 (:22.2g). And I am told he was Champion Quarter Running Three-Year-Old Colt that same year. Injured off track in his fourth year, he was retired and purchased by Marion Seward (Wray, Colorado) in 1956 for a reported price of $5500. Seward bought T.B.G. from Mrs. F. R. Glover of Bloomfield, Colorado, along with one of his daughters, for whom he paid $1000. This was the filly, Miss Louton, who subsequently raced to fame and a considerable bank account under the bright orange-and-black colors of Mr. Seward, to be named Co-Champion Quarter Running Mare and Co-Champion Three-Year-Old Filly of 1959. She was out of a mare (Miss Lou Dandy) by My Texas Dandy, and was foaled in 1956. She was trained by Pat Simpson.

Old stud cards describing the service of Tonto Bars Gill show him standing in 1953 in Tucson at a fee of $250; in 1956 at Wray, Colorado, for $150. (At that time it was stated: "He still holds the three-year-old colt record for 440 yards—:22.2f; his bloodlines combine the famous sire Three Bars with the World's Record holder Tonta Gal, whose record went into the books in 1946, equaled twice but never broken: this is the oldest record of any type now held by Quarter Running Horses.") That same year Seward advertised that T.B.G. had thus far had but six foals. "Of his three 1954 foals the two that raced qualified for Register of Merit. Miss Tontalue who raced in 1956 won five races, plus the honor of being declared Grand Champion Mare at the Yuma Colorado Fair. He will be represented in 1957 by Tonto Junior, his only 1955 foal." In 1958 Tonto Junior won the Kansas Derby and Seward advertised T.B.G. at $500, and had this to say: "This Great Sire's Star Studded Get includes—Miss Louton, one of only two two-year-olds by Tonto Bars Gill—the other, Tonto Flax. Seven wins in nine starts, one second, out of the money only once; wins included Ruidoso Quarter Horse Futurity, RMQHA Futurity and the Raton Quarter Horse Nursery Handicap."

Then T.B.G. again changed hands. His present owner, Charles Loughridge (of Santa Fe), tells me: "In 1960 I bought Tonto Bars Gill for $75,000 from M. Seward. Until my purchase, T.B.G. stood at Seward's Ranch for $500. In 1960, his last season there, he had 82 registered foals; I do not know how many mares were bred. In 1961 the fee was $750; he stood at my ranch (the Haigler Ranch) at Haigler, Nebraska. Far fewer mares were bred—there should be about 30 foals. In the fall of 1961 we moved him to the Charlie Horse Ranch (mine) at Pena Blanca, New Mexico, and stood him at a fee—refund, or return—of $2000. Sixty-eight mares were bred to him and, as far as I know, 59 are in foal—such mares as

Mona Leta, AAA, by Leo; Ariel Lady, AAA, producer of seven ROM, by Little Joe, Jr.; Amber's Star, AAA, by Top Deck; On I Go, AA, by Be Sure Now (TB); Dixie Dee—appendix—set Track Record at Sunland in winter of '61; Bella St. Shade, AAA, by Bob Shade; Miss Bartender (dam of Senor George) by Bartender; Hanka, a solid ROM and dam by T.B.G. of the celebrated big money-earning Tonto Bars Hank, Champion Quarter Running Stallion and Champion Quarter Running Two-Year-Old Colt of 1960, Co-Holder (with She Kitty and Breeze Bar) of the World's Record at 400 yards and, with Breeze Bar, the stallion record at the same distance (:19.9), the three-year-old colt record at 400 yards, and the two-year-old colt record at 350 yards.

"Hanka is by Hank H. Other mares worth mentioning which are currently in foal to Tonto Bars Gill are: Miss Lou Dandy (dam of Miss Louton) by My Texas Dandy; Cue Chick, AAA, by Red Chick W; Patsy Chick, AAA, by Red Chick W; Ima You (dam of Ima Pixie) by Revenue (one of the sires discussed in *Outstanding Modern Quarter Horse Sires*); Miss Sahuaro (dam of Sahuaro Miss, AAA) by Pelican (Champion Quarter Running Stallion of 1947); Wagon It (producer of two ROM) by Wagon N; Hy It, AAA, by Float Hy; Ariel Gazelle, AAA, by Ariel (TB); Abby Lane, AA, by Custus Rastus (TB); Bow String, AA, by Piggin String (TB, and Co-Champion Quarter Running Stallion of 1943–44); Dreamalong, AAA, by Gray Dream; Kitten's Ida Red, AAA, by Joe Less (sire of No Butt, World's Champion Quarter Running Mare of 1962); Sissy Babe, AA, by Texas Dandy; and eight of Hugh Bennett's mares, including Miss Whiskers and April Girl."

Mr. Loughridge also states: "The first year that more than one or two proven running mares were bred to him was 1961. In 1963 29 Register of Merit mares, or producers of ROM, were bred. To me his record of the past few years—considering the kind of mares he had—is astonishing. He is a beautiful horse, has a wonderful temperament—quite easy to handle and manage. We ride him regularly, though he is pretty much retired, due to that injured shoulder, on the 100-acre ranch that we built from the bottom, with him in mind. It is not the fanciest place, but it is practical and built entirely for the handling of brood mares. T.B.G. is the only stallion we use. We do have two teasers, and are slowly collecting mares of the type we think are justified."

Some of Tonto Bars Gill's better get are Tonto Bars Hank, Miss Louton, Tonto Ginger, Tonto's Time, Tonto Junior, Miss Tontalou, Sahuaro Miss, and Miss Twig—these are all AAA. Boulder Bars is also AAA, and Tonto Polly was on the 1961 Honor Roll of Working Cowhorses. Some of his get have shown.

His 1961 record reveals 32 ROM get, foal earnings in excess of $270,000, second to Three Bars (TB) in number of winners, third (after Three Bars and Direct Win, TB) in number of two-year-old ROM get, and third to Three Bars and Top Deck (TB) in number of wins by foals.

The 1962 Leading Sires lists show him credited with 342 registered foals, 135 starters, 52 enrolled in the ROM, and 25 that have made AAA.

LEADING SIRES OF 1962 RACE WINNERS (Top Five)

	Winners	Starters		Wins	Starters
Three Bars (TB)	38	57	Three Bars (TB)	86	57
TONTO BARS GILL	34	77	TONTO BARS GILL	69	77
SUGAR BARS	25	45	Little Request (TB)	57	31
LIGHTNING BAR	24	43	Direct Win (TB)	56	37
VANDY	24	42	SUGAR BARS	56	45

Moon Deck

Bred by J. B. Ferguson at Wharton, Texas, this dark-brown stallion (P–163,343) without star or other markings was foaled in 1950. His sire was the Thoroughbred Top Deck, currently second on the Leading Sires of Money Earners list (1949 through 1962) with 122 starters with cumulative earnings of $569,060.62. Top Deck is a son of Equestrian, whose sire was Equipoise; Top Deck's dam was River Boat by Chicaro. Moon Deck was out of the good mare Moonlight Night, a half-bred by Peace Pipe (TB) out of Mae by Henry (by Dewey). Moonlight Night, a 1200-pound sorrel, was run in many matched races and beaten by only half a length by Shue Fly.

Moon Deck was himself a successful race horse. He first started at Del Rio (Texas) as a two-year-old and won at three-eighths in :34.4. He was the first horse to set the 549-yard record at Los Alamitos, which he later broke. In the list of Leading Money-Earning Horses of 1955 he stood sixth, with $8353. He started 13 times that year, winning three, was second in two, and was two times third, against top competition.

In the Los Alamitos Quarter Horse Championship (May 7, 1955) at 440 yards, he came in first by one and one-half lengths, defeating Scoop Bam, Ridge Butler, Miss Myrna Bar, Clabber Juan, Miss Meyers, Spotted Lady, Miss Pitapat, Palleo Pete, and Flicka Hyloah—practically an all-star cast. The time, with four-tenths deducted for grading purposes, was :22.6 on a heavy track. At Ruidoso (July 3, 1955) in the Quarter Horse Championship he came in third behind Gold Bar and Maroon, with Brigand,

Monita, Mr. Scott, and Barjo in the beaten field; the winning time (:22.6) equaled the track record co-held by Maroon.

As a matter of fact, he ran well at any distance from 350 to 549 yards; and, on the track or off, he is a stallion well known for his equable disposition.

He is the sire of Miss Jet Deck, co-holder of the two-year-old filly record at 350 yards (:17.9); Miss Moon Bar, co-holder of the same record at 400 yards (:20.2); Caprideck (400 yards under 127 pounds in :20.0, which, if allowed, constitutes a new gelding record), elected the 1962 Champion Quarter Running Gelding; and, last but far from least, the 1962 Champion Quarter Running Stallion and Champion Two-Year-Old Colt Jet Deck. One might almost call this the Moon Deck Year.

Jet Deck in 15 starts failed only once to grade AAA. In his first year on the straightaway he achieved a very outstanding record of 11 wins, one second, and two thirds in 15 outings. His total earnings for 1962 were $138,341.91—a new two-year-old record and one which made him all-time high money winner for a given year in Quarter Racing up to that time.

Jet Deck was bred by W. H. Carter of Clovis, California; Moon Deck, Jet's sire, is owned by James V. A. Carter and holds court at Clovis. He was trained and managed by Wilbur Stuchal of Atlanta, Kansas, and stood up well under the pressure of a season of stiff competition.

A bay, Jet Deck was foaled in 1960, stands 15.1 and weighs 1050 with shoes on. He was the stand-out track sensation of 1962, running off with five feature events. In the Juvenile Championship at Arizona Downs he covered the 400 yards under 120 pounds in :20.3; at Los Alamitos, in the Los Alamitos Futurity, he went 350 yards under 118 in :17.7; in addition he won the Pacific Coast Quarter Horse Association Futurity, the Los Alamitos Juvenile Championship, and the Kindergarten Stakes. The new two-year-old colt record which he set in the Kindergarten was 400 yards under 120 in :20.0.

He is out of the AAA Miss Night Bar by Barred (AAA) out of Belle of Midnight by Midnight Jr. (whose dam was Salty by Billy the Tough). Jet Deck is owned by J. B. Chambers of Denver. Jay says: "Jet Deck first started at Bay Meadows on February 17, 1962. He was recommended to me by Jockey Charles Smith and my trainer, Wilbur Stuchal, on account of his bloodlines and appearance."

Still in fine fettle and going like a prairie fire, in The Inaugural (4th Running) at Bay Meadows, January 5, 1963, he came in second by a neck to Western Stables' Tiny Charger, who went the 350 in :17:99, Pacific Bars finishing third, one neck behind.

On April 17th I received the following note from J. B. Chambers: "Jet

171. The four-legged rocket: Jet Deck. Charles Smith up.

Photo by Jack Stribling

172. Ready to run: Palleo Pete (taken 1957).

173. Little Request, TB, by Requested out of Little Wichita, by *Royal Ford.

174. Mr. Bar None, by Three Bars out of Murl L., by Moco Burnett.

175. Johnny Dial, age 14.

176. Go Man Go, by Top Deck out of Lightfoot Sis, by Very Wise, TB.

177. Depth Charge, TB.

Photo by Ed Ellinger

178. Rillito Race Track as it looked in the days when the greats of the Quarter Horse breeding pens flew down its three furlongs straightaway.

Photo by Karl Johnson

179. The 1963 Southwestern Futurity at Rillito Park.

Deck is back at Los Alamitos. On Opening Day he won the 350-yard Shue Fly Stakes in :17.9 but through bad luck was disqualified. It was a real tough break as he did not start the trouble. Last Saturday in the PCQHA Derby Trials, there were two heats of seven horses each. Scooper Chick won the first division in 22 flat for the quarter mile. Jet Deck, in the second heat, covered the same course to win in :21.7—one-tenth off the World Record. Tiny Charger, second, was back three-quarters and Moolah Bar was third. Jet will run in the Derby itself next Saturday for approximately $25,000 (he has now earned more than $140,000)."

On Sunday, April 21st, Mr. Chambers wrote: "Jet Deck was bumped badly coming out of the gate by Bar Depth which was in the No. 9 position. However, Jet Deck came on to win in :21.9, paying $2.60, $2.40, $2.20. Moolah Bar was second, Chudej's Rhoda showed. This boosts Jet Deck's total earnings to $152,504—this is still $10,039 short of Pokey Bar's all-time high."

But Jet Deck was not to remain in second place long. By winning the Los Alamitos 1963 Spring Championship, he topped the former all-time Leading Money Earners high (until then held by Pokey Bar at $162,543.-81) with total earnings to date of $166,254.00. In the same race, J. B. Chambers' sensational colt established, if it is accepted by the AQHA Racing Committee, a new World's Record for the quarter mile, winning by two and one-half lengths over Straw Flight in a hell-tearing :21.5!

A real four-legged rocket.

Moon Deck is currently standing in Clovis, California, at a fee of $2000. He is also the sire of Miss Bar Moon (AAA), and Top Moon (AAA), winner of the Pacific Coast Quarter Racing Association Futurity at Pomona, 350 yards in :17.9.

1962 LEADING SIRES OF WINNERS
Sires in CAPITAL LETTERS are ROM Qualifiers

Sires	Wins	Winners	Starters
Three Bars (TB), Ch. 40 by Percentage	86	38	57
TONTO BARS GILL, Ch. 49 by Three Bars (TB)	69	34	77
Little Request (TB), Cr. 50 by Requested	57	23	31
Direct Win (TB), Ch. 47 by With Regards	56	23	37
SUGAR BARS, Ch. 51 by Three Bars (TB)	56	25	45
LIGHTNING BAR, Ch. 51 by Three Bars (TB)	55	24	43
VANDY, Ch. 43 by Going Light (TB)	43	24	42
Top Deck (TB), Br. 45 by Equestrian	42	14	23
MOON DECK, Blk. 50 by Top Deck (TB)	41	10	12
TINKY POO, Br. 49 by Wayward Irving	40	11	13

BOB'S FOLLY, Blk. 53 by Three Bars (TB)	39	15	34
MR. BAR NONE, Ch. 55 by Three Bars (TB)	37	13	28
LEO, Ch. 40 by JOE REED II	33	19	39
CHUDEJ'S BLACK GOLD, 49 by Depth Charge (TB)	32	10	16
Jackstraw (TB), Ch. 42 by Silver Horde	32	6	12
Triple Chick, Br. 55 by Three Bars (TB)	31	11	17
BARRED, Ch. 46 by Three Bars (TB)	27	10	15
MR. 89'ER, Ch. 49 by LEO	27	13	19
PALLEO PETE, Pal. 52 by LEO	26	11	27
Bold Gallant (TB), B. 45 by Questionnaire	25	11	14
PARKER'S TROUBLE, Ch. 49 by ED ECHOLS	25	14	29
GO MAN GO, Ro. 53 by Top Deck (TB)	23	7	11
JOHNNY DIAL, Br. 48 by Depth Charge (TB)	22	11	16
DIVIDEND, Ch. 51 by Depth Charge (TB)	21	9	20
ROBIN REED, Ch. 49 by LEO	21	9	25

MOST WINNERS

	Winners	Wins	Starters
Three Bars (TB), Ch. 40 by Percentage	38	86	57
TONTO BARS GILL, Ch. 49 by Three Bars (TB)	34	69	77
SUGAR BARS, Ch. 51 by Three Bars (TB)	25	56	45
LIGHTNING BAR, Ch. 51 by Three Bars (TB)	24	55	43
VANDY, Ch. 43 by Going Light (TB)	24	43	42
Direct Win (TB), Ch. 47 by With Regards	23	56	37
Little Request (TB), Ch. 50 by Requested	23	57	31
LEO, Ch. 40 by JOE REED II	19	33	39
BOB'S FOLLY, Blk. 53 by Three Bars (TB)	15	39	34
PARKER'S TROUBLE, Ch. 49 by ED ECHOLS	14	25	29
Top Deck (TB), Br. 45 by Equestrian	14	42	23
MR. BAR NONE, Ch. 55 by Three Bars (TB)	13	37	28
MR. 89'ER, Ch. 49 by LEO	13	27	19
Bold Gallant (TB), B. 45 by Questionnaire	11	25	14
JOHNNY DIAL, Br. 48 by Depth Charge (TB)	11	22	16
PALLEO PETE, Pal. 52 by LEO	11	26	27
TINKY POO, Br. 49 by Wayward Irving	11	40	13
Triple Chick, Br. 55 by Three Bars (TB)	11	31	17
BARRED, Ch. 46 by Three Bars (TB)	10	27	15
CHUDEJ'S BLACK GOLD, 49 by Depth Charge (TB)	10	32	16
CLABBER II, B. 46 by CLABBER	10	19	18
LEO TAG, Ch. 49 by LEO	10	14	23
MOON DECK, Blk. 50 by Top Deck (TB)	10	41	12
NUG BAR, Ch. 50 by Three Bars (TB)	10	18	17

LEADING MONEY-EARNING HORSES OF 1962

	Starts	Win	Place	Show	Earnings
JET DECK, B. 60 by MOON DECK	15	11	1	2	$138,341.91
HUSTLING MAN, S. 60 by GO MAN GO	17	7	2	3	105,122.33
TINY CHARGER, B. 60 by Depth Charge, (TB)	13	4	5	3	58,561.84
MR. JUNIPER BAR, Br. 60 by MR. BAR NONE	11	3	7	0	56,196.91
LIGHTNING BELLE, S. 60 by LIGHTNING BAR	12	3	7	0	54,434.37
LITTLE CHLOE, S. 60 by Three Bars (TB)	7	5	1	0	53,571.26
BAR DEPTH, Blk. 60 by Three Bars (TB)	18	4	4	1	51,540.92
POKEY BAR, S. 59 by Three Bars (TB)	8	6	1	1	41,846.53
MISS BAR LEO, S. 60 by Three Bars (TB)	17	10	1	1	32,745.84
TOP MOON, Blk. 60 by MOON DECK	20	7	7	3	30,698.07
GO EAGLE GO, S. 60 by GO MAN GO	17	5	4	2	29,680.81
ALAMITOS BAR, B. 59 by Three Bars (TB)	9	4	4	0	28,645.00
GOODWIN GIRL, B. 60 by Lapara Joe	13	4	5	2	27,727.72
MOOLAH BAR, Ro. 60 by Moolah Bux (TB)	16	5	1	3	27,354.65
FLY STRAW, Ch. 58 by Jackstraw (TB)	25	10	3	4	25,311.88

LEADING MONEY-EARNING HORSES, 1949 through 1962

POKEY BAR, S. 59 by Three Bars (TB)	$162,543.81
JET DECK, B. 60 by MOON DECK	138,341.91
TONTO BARS HANK, S. 58 by TONTO BARS GILL	133,918.37
HUSTLING MAN, S. 60 by GO MAN GO	105,122.33
PAP, S. g. 54 by PAPITAS	90,931.36
GO MAN GO, Ro. 53 by Top Deck (TB)	86,151.32
REBEL CAUSE, B. 58 by Top Deck (TB)	85,586.40
VANDY'S FLASH, S. g. 54 by VANDY	84,930.87
VANETTA DEE, Ch. m. 52 by VANDY	81,855.67
MISS LOUTON, Ch. m. 56 by TONTO BARS GILL	74,718.56
BUNNY'S BAR MAID, Br. m. 59 by Three Bars (TB)	72,288.96
MR. BAR NONE, Ch. 55 by Three Bars (TB)	72,124.89
GALOBAR, Ch. m. 57 by Three Bars (TB)	68,282.65
NO BUTT, B. m. 55 by Joe Less	63,688.45
TRIPLE LADY, Pal. m. 56 by Three Bars (TB)	61,931.00
TINY CHARGER, B. 60 by Depth Charge (TB)	58,561.84
ALAMITOS BAR, B. 59 by Three Bars (TB)	58,036.50
AUNT JUDY, S. m. 57 by VANDY	56,215.17
MR. JUNIPER BAR, Br. g. 60 by MR. BAR NONE	56,196.91
LIGHTNING BELLE, S. f. 60 by LIGHTNING BAR	54,434.37
LITTLE CHLOE, S. f. 60 by Three Bars (TB)	53,571.26

BAR DEPTH, Blk. 60 by Three Bars (TB)	51,540.92
MONITA, Ch. m. 47 by Joe Moore	49,143.53
TIDY TOO, Ch. m. 56 by LEE MOORE	48,694.12
ROCKET BAR, Ch. g. 52 by Three Bars (TB)	47,480.24
GOLDEN NOTE, Pal. m. 59	47,479.41
CLABBER'S WIN, Ch. 54 by Direct Win (TB)	44,742.46

LEADING SIRES OF REGISTER OF MERIT QUALIFIERS—
1945 through 1962

Immediately following name of sire, figure with letter "F" is number of registered foals; figure after letter "S" is number of starters. First column is of sires with 23 or more qualifiers; second column is of sires of 11 or more AAA get.

	Qualified		*AAA*
Three Bars (TB) F-348, S-258	176	Three Bars (TB) F-348, S-258	116
LEO F- 473, S-292	156	LEO F-473, S-292	58
VANDY F-231, S-128	78	Top Deck (TB) F-161, S-122	41
Top Deck (TB) F-161, S-122	72	VANDY F-231, S-128	38
JOE REED II F-238, S-153	66	LIGHTNING BAR F-155, S-79	35
Depth Charge (TB) F-90, S-78	53	Depth Charge (TB) F-90, S-78	30
TONTO BARS GILL F- 342, S-135	52	Little Request (TB) F-81, S-38	27
PIGGIN STRING (TB) F-90, S-85	51	TONTO BARS GILL F-342, S-135	25
LIGHTNING BAR F-155, S-79	49	Direct Win (TB) F-142, S-69	24
TEXAS DANDY F-165, S-87	44	SUGAR BARS F-314, S-85	24
HARD TWIST F-154, S-82	42	SPOTTED BULL (TB) F-46, S-78	20
CLABBER II F-142, S-80	41	BOB'S FOLLY F-188, S-54	18
Direct Win (TB) F-142, S-69	37	CLABBER II F-142, S-80	17
Flying Bob F-76, S-62	37	PIGGIN STRING (TB) F-90, S-85	16
Little Request (TB) F-81, S-38	35	MOON DECK F-40, S-20	15
BARRED F-200, S-69	34	BARRED F-200, S-69	14
My Texas Dandy F-128, S-68	34	Custus Rastus (TB) F-88, S-47	14
SUGAR BARS F-314, S-85	34	Be Sure Now (TB) F-28, 8-28	14
SPOTTED BULL (TB) F-46, S-78	31	HARD TWIST F-154, S-82	13
War Bam (TB) F-48, S-39	29	SUPER CHARGE F-165, S-35	12
Custus Rustus (TB) F-88, S-47	27	GO MAN GO F-95, S-17	12
CLABBER F-81, S-59	26	TEXAS DANDY F-165, S-87	11
BOB'S FOLLY F-188, S-54	25	War Bam (TB) F-48, S-39	11
Question Mark F-218, S-64	25	ROBIN REED F-142, S-51	11
ED ECHOLS F-233, S-47	24	TINKY POO F-91, S-37	11
DEE DEE F-168, S-56	23	PALLEO PETE F-95, S-37	11
LITTLE JOE, JR. F-163, S-38	23	BULL'S EYE F-98, S-36	11
RED CHICK W F-126, S-55	23	Triple Chick F-57, S-17	11

Palleo Pete

Bred by Fred Swalley and foaled at Ponca City, Oklahoma, April 30, 1952, this first and only palomino ever to become a World's Champion Quarter Running Stallion in the entire history of organized Quarter Racing is an individual of much solid merit and a great deal of what might be called front-page personality. He has sprinting blood on both sides of his pedigree and will get, when bred to sprinting mares, some extremely high-class runners, as he has proved.

Unquestionably Leo's greatest son, he is out of Osage Star Lady, one of the short-horse tribe's finest brood mares. Swalley says: "We bought Pete's dam after a great deal of patient searching. *Her* dam, Sodey May, was by the Alred Dun, a son of Yellow Wolf (one of the best sons of Gonzales Joe Bailey, P–4); Sodey May was out of a Palmer Thoroughbred mare." The sire of Palleo Pete's dam (Osage Star Lady) was Osage Star (P–704) by Oklahoma Star (P–6) by Dennis Reed (TB). Osage Star's dam was Quarter Lady (P–511) by Quarter Deck (TB), a stakes-winning son of Man O'War.

Now let us take a quick look at some of the bloodlines coming down to Pete through the mares in Leo's pedigree. The dam of Joe Reed (P–3) was the celebrated sprint queen Della Moore by Dedier (Old D.J., a famous Louisiana sprinting sire whose chief importance in the stud stemmed directly from the caliber and transmitting capacity of his daughters). The dam of Joe Reed II (1943 World's Champion Quarter Running Stallion) was Nellene by Fleeting Time (TB), out of the running mare Little Red Nell, who is said to have been by Old Billy; dam of Little Red Nell was Old Red Nell, the track-burning daughter of Texas Chief, probably the fastest son of Traveler. The dam of Leo (himself a celebrated match-race horse) was Little Fanny, who was pastured for more than ten years at the Bert Wood stud, not too far west of my ranchhouse windows.

Little Fanny (P–1572) was bred by the noted breeder J. W. House at Cameron, Texas; she was foaled May 9, 1937, a bay with black points and star on forehead. She has no record of racing that I have been able to discover, but she was well made. She was by Joe Reed (P–3) and a fine producer. In addition to Leo, she produced Bill Reed (who ran many matched races and was hand timed at Austin in :21.0 at 220), Ashwood (has official records with AQHA), Tic Tac Sims (used entirely as a roping horse), Tucson A (official records with AQHA), Little Sister W (AAA), Merry Time (official records), Gusdusted (official records), Firebrand Reed (AA), and possibly another one or two.

Little Fanny was out of Fannie Ashwell (by Ashwell, TB). Fannie Ashwell's dam was Fannie Richardson, who, in her time, had a tremendous reputation, and *her* dam was Sister Fanny by Whistle Jacket; all four of these mares had track performance records and were highly considered.

The dam of Palleo Pete, also a famous producer, was a roping mare who raced a little, too; she ran four matched races and didn't lose one.

As a two-year-old Palleo Pete made 16 starts, although only six were officially recognized by the Performance Division of the American Quarter Horse Association. His first start under AQHA supervision was on July 14th in a division of the Kansas Futurity trials at Centennial. "By this time," says Fred Swalley, "he was widely enough known that they just about bet him into the ground. It was a 330 go and he won his trial easily in :17.4, by four or five lengths. On the following day he won the Kansas Futurity under a good hold."

At Enid, a knee which had been troubling him ever since a 220-yard purse race on the Pawhuska track, which he had copped in :12.2, began to really act up. Mr. Swalley declares: "I guess folks got used to seeing us bathing his knees; we doctored them all summer, even sitting beside him on a bucket, the Mrs. on one side and I on the other, soaking those knees with hot Epsom Salts water. He loved to be fussed over."

He won his division of the Oklahoma Futurity trials over Miss Adelita and Bucket Baby—this was the only time any individual ever ran lapped on Pete when the track was dry. In thirteen of the fifteen races he won, he was ahead at the finish by from one to five lengths of open daylight. His two world records were set with Jimmy Hardinbrook in the stirrups, riding easy, just coasting along. At Denver he had two lengths of light, and later, at Albuquerque, in the Winner-Take-All, he had one open length, running easily under a hold. Swalley says: "We weren't out to set records, only to win."

It is hard to tell what Pete might have done if they'd ever got down to really running for the works; I think it likely he had the ability to hang up a record that might still be on the books. But back to Enid and his only "official" defeat—the Oklahoma Futurity—when, as Renee Smelker told it, "two other Leos, Miss Adelita and Bobbie Leo, skimmed over a muddy course to take first and second."

At Centennial, in the Imperial Hotel Purse on August 25th he hung up a new Two-Year-Old Record for 350 yards (:18.1) which stood for four years. Hardinbrook told us: "He could have gone a lot faster than that."

Pete's bad knee had put him into a limp again. Fred and Doc Johnson did their best to get him in shape for the Stallion Stakes, but to no avail. They took him home to rest up a little for the Albuquerque meet. Afraid to take any chances, they never really worked him until they got to Albuquerque the week of the big Winner-Take-All. A quarter-mile go, it was the biggest and most widely advertised juvenile event of the season.

Diamond Mae had been hauled in for this one, and Fred was having a rough time, about as badly worried over the competition as he was over Pete's knee. Pete, thus far, had never gone the full quarter, and Diamond Mae had an awesome reputation. It was a ten-horse field, with Miss Mackey and Pete carrying 120 pounds, the rest 115. Barbara Tex had gate No. 1; then Roaming, Bobbie Leo, Buddy Leo, Mackey Jimmey, Bella St. Mary; then Pete in No. 7 with Diamond Mae right alongside in No. 8, and, beyond her, Bonnie Bow and Miss Mackey.

The gates flew open and Pete went to the front—not by much but still in front; and the farther they went the faster Pete moved, finishing first by one length of daylight, in :22.3, over Bobbie Leo, Diamond Mae, and Buddy Leo, in that order. Another two-year-old record and his last outing for the year. Officially he had started only six times, but since five of these were victories in important features and in his one non-win he had managed to pull in third, it was a record no other stallion contender could match and he was named Champion Two-Year-Old Colt and Champion Quarter Running Stallion of 1954.

Gene Cummins bought Palleo Pete from Gomer Evans in March of 1956. It was too late in the year to advertise him at stud, and so Cummins decided to put him back in training. He had a badly cut front hoof that was hard to keep a shoe on; in this comeback one of his best races was the Championship Quarter at Bay Meadows. Here is the way they finished: Black Easter Bunny first by a head, Pokey Vandy second by a nose, Palleo Pete third by a head, Dr. Rand V fourth by a neck, Barica fifth by a head, Blob's Boy sixth by a neck, Dividend seventh by one length, Rocket Bar eighth, Little Hot Shot ninth by one and a half, and Vanetta Dee. Time :22.5 against a head wind.

Pete's first crop of foals came in 1958—seven registered get. All went to the track, all raced; 3 AAA, 3 AA, and one A. Each season he has bred more mares; in 1962 he bred 76 at $500. Among his better-known get are Golden Note, Co-Champion Quarter Running Two-Year-Old Filly of 1961; Mr. Palleo (AAA); Palleo's Note (AAA); Tom Duggan (AAA). They are good in other fields of performance, also. Vern Smith (Idaho) has a matched pair of fillies—Lola Payola and Goode Two Shoes—which are making a name in cutter racing. Bill Jackson (Ontario) has a top roping horse on steers or calves. Bill Hoskins (Norco) says Palleo's Paul is making good at bulldogging. Chuck Taliaferro (trainer) declares Pete's colts learn to run quickly and win early. Jim Sharp (trainer) says: "They're sensible and good doers at the track, so they run more often."

The 1962 Leading Sires of Winners list shows him with 27 starters, of which 11 were AAA winners of 26 races; 10 of the others qualified in AA He is also on the Leading Sires of Money Earners and Leading Sires of Register of Merit Qualifiers lists.

Little Request (TB)

The stakes-winning Thoroughbred, Little Request, foaled in Kentucky (1950), was bred by Charles Nuckles & Son and sold as a yearling in the Keenland Sales for $20,500, and proved to be one of the fastest juveniles to perform in the West. In 32 starts he stayed on top to the half in 22; in 19 of these 22 his time was never worse than :22.2 (tenths) for the quarter. He won the Haggin Stakes and the Starlet Stakes, and set a Track Record at Hollywood Park—five furlongs in :58.2 (1952). As a two-year-old he won $40,875 before injuring a foot, ran some at three and four years, bringing his total earnings to $51,275. Also, at Hollywood Park he ran five and one-half furlongs in 1:03⅘—just one-fifth off the track record held by Colonel Mac. He has defeated such horses as Decorated, Chanlea, Fleet Khal, Deanza, Refresher, and Ali's Gem.

Requested, the sire of Little Request, won $116,595. His 13 wins include the Youthful, Tremont, East View, and Wakefield Stakes; the Babylon Handicap; the Cowdin, Flamingo, and Wood Memorial Stakes. The dam of Little Request, Little Wichita, was winner of five. Little Wichita's dam, Little Visitor, was winner of 22 and earned $38,512. Little Wichita was by *Royal Ford (by Swynford out of *Royal Yoke). In 1951 Glenn Turpin (at that time manager of the Three D's Stock Farm) told me: "The late W. T. Waggoner imported Royal Ford from England and paid a very handsome sum to get him. He was at stud at the Three D Farm near Arlington, Texas, and sired some very good colts. The best and most widely known of his get probably was Heel Fly. He was sold to T. P. Morgan, San Antonio, Texas, with other horses, about 1938."

Little Request's second dam (or maternal grandmother) was by Sweep (who was by Ben Brush out of Pink Domino); this grandmother's dam was Margaret Hastings by Hastings.

Requested's dam, Fair Perdita, was by Eternal, who was out of Hazel Burk and sired by Sweep.

In April, 1956, Little Request stood, at $300, on the Rolling Hills property of Mr. Gordon Shultz; an advertisement of this date reads in part: "But race track performance, as a factor in selecting a stallion, becomes secondary when his first colts are foaled. The produce are the best guide in the selection of a stallion for breeding purposes."

Truer words were never spoken. So let us now consider the few crops Little Request has sent to the straightaways. His first crop reached the tracks in 1958. Two youngsters were started. Fame Gold Quest won his second start at Bay Meadows on March 3rd. The other colt, First Request, ran second to Field Boy at Turf Paradise. Both turned out to be winners. From his second crop to race (the year was 1959), Little Request was represented by eight starters; seven of these achieved AAA ratings. The standout filly of this crop was Lip Request, winner of five out of nine starts, including the Cal-Bred Stakes and Kindergarten Stakes, both run at Los Alamitos. As a three-year-old, she came back to win the Johnny Dial Stakes, and a total of $28,260. She was out of Miss Lipstick, herself a star of the Quarter tracks and a daughter of Clabber. One of the better colts from this crop was El Diablito, winner of the Pacific Coast Quarter Racing Association Futurity at Pomona. El Diablito was out of Dawn Reed by Joe Reed II and ran consistently in AAA time. A later winner of the Cal-Bred Stakes was Silver Beau, a gray colt by Little Request out of Miss Teal. He also won, at this same meet, the Los Ninos Stakes.

The best of a good bunch of 1960 foals was Flicka's Request. Out of Flicka Hyloa, this colt won an allowance race at Los Alamitos in the very good time of :17.8 and sold, at the California Mid-Winter Sale (Pomona), for $18,000, going to Raymond Guthrie, Prineville, Oregon. Another 1960 foal, Time Request (out of Lady Me by Joe Reed II), won the Juvenile Championship at Bay Meadows, June 18, 1962.

Other good AAA foals by Little Request include Cocktail Susie, Off Base, Fame Goldquest, La Mosquita (out of Shue Fly), and El Chiquito.

Little Request is currently owned by Robert H. Grant of Bresa Del Mar Ranch, Escondido, California, whose foreman tells me: "A lot of credit for Little Request's success as a sire of running Quarter Horses should be given Henry Moreno. It was Mr. Moreno who gave this stallion his first chance. He purchased Little Request in 1954 and owned him until January of 1963 when we acquired him."

Stan has been most helpful in assembling background material for this survey. He did not tell me what the Grants paid for this horse, but a piece I clipped from the *Western Livestock Journal* reveals the price to have been $115,000.

Mr. Moreno says:

Little Request weighs 1200 pounds and stands 15.2½ hands; B. F. Whittiker bred the sire. One of Mr. Nuckles, Sr.'s last requests before he died was that the colt be named "Little Request."

He was handled by Tony Dias as a reining horse and, while working very well, was never shown. He also worked cattle and had a lot in him.

Ross Brinson, a former Quarter Horse man, better known as trainer of Clabber, Lucky, Band Play, Wayward Boy, Colonel Clyde, and Driftwood, picked Little Request on conformation and bought him at the Keenland Sales on behalf of Mr. Joe Palmisano of Phoenix, Arizona.

Ross was his trainer when Little Request won his major races, winning two stakes at Hollywood Park. While at this meet he established new track records at five and five and one-half furlongs; he was declared Two-Year-Old Champion of the West Coast. Mr. Brinson informs me that Mr. Palmisano turned down $150,000 for him at that time. He also said he had seen some of the fastest sprint Thoroughbreds and believes this horse to have been the fastest-breaking Thoroughbred he'd ever trained. This colt was so highly regarded there was even a prospective match race cooked up between him and Bardella, the Champion Two-Year-Old Quarter Running Horse Filly of that year. This race did not materialize because Little Request had a commitment in the East to run in the Belmont Futurity, in which he led for the first five-eighths before being overhauled by Native Dancer in, I believe, world-record time.

Little Request was first started at Golden Gate and was five lengths in front his first time out. He was running so fast he didn't make the turn and finished third on the outside fence. Johnny Longden then requested to ride him; he won his next out by eight lengths, Longden going on to ride him in his stakes victories.

I have long been a student of bloodlines and conformation and my family has been in the Quarter Horse business for quite a while. I kept up with this horse while he was racing. He had so much speed I thought he might cross well with Quarter mares. I saw him race and was going to try and breed a mare to him. Meanwhile he suffered some injuries and was laid up at Dave McClintock's place in Anaheim. Through Dave I bought him from R. H. McDaniel, who owned him at that time.

In 1958 Little Request was standing at Hoss Inman's Flying I Ranch just outside Lamar, Colorado, at $300, where he was at service through April of that year, which saw the first of his colts make their debut on the straightaways. In 1961, standing at Bresa Del Mar, his fee was increased to $500; in 1962 his service was advertised at $750 and remained at this figure during 1963.

Other AAA winners by Little Request are Ipana's Request, Joe Quest, Our Request, Vicki's Request, Vickie Fay, Whistling Wind, Anna Request, Dandy's Request, Fleet Pat, and Anson Request—and I may have missed a few. Among his AA get are Little Devine, Little Drift, Mamie's Request, Little Capri, Barquest, Squaw Quest, Royal Request, First Request, Requesting, and Ring A Bell.

According to current statistics Little Request has sired 81 registered foals, including 38 starters, 35 qualified for Register of Merit, and 27 with AAA rating. Percentagewise, this is a pretty hard record to beat.

Joe Palmisano lost Little Request by dropping him into a race from which, I am told, he was claimed by R. H. McDaniel.

On the 1962 Leading Sires of Winners list Little Request stands third, with 57 wins from 23 winners out of 31 starters; he is led only by Tonto Bars Gill and Three Bars (TB), both of which had more starters. Among Leading Sires of Register of Merit Qualifiers (1945 through 1962) Little Request stands fifteenth. He's a pretty hard horse to overlook.

Mr. Bar None

Last year I went over to Ruidoso specifically to see and talk with Oscar Jeffers, Jr., the horseless carriage salesman who gave up his trade to take on the full-time chore of raising sprinters and conditioning them for AAA track performance, a pastime in which he's become quite proficient. "June," as all his friends call him, is the gentleman who produced Mr. Bar None. He started with a calico pony and twenty acres of Oklahoma grass, away back in the days when he fancied himself to be a calf-roping whingding.

I found him easy to talk to, even easier to like. He's a man with a lot of savvy and one who is able to laugh at his mistakes. It became increasingly evident he hasn't made many. He allows he didn't actually become acquainted with Quarter Horses until he swapped a top roping horse for a weanling filly named, of all things, N. R. Negraletta. His friends thought June had gone off his rocker, but the laugh was on them when, as a two-year-old, she went loping off with the Texas Futurity.

When the filly moved on to other and bigger gains, Jeffers, really hooked, began planning toward the day when he might breed her. He had his ears wide open. In 1954 he bought a mare named Murl L from Byrne James over at Raymondsville. By Moco Burnett (he by Texas Jack, a grandson of Peter McCue), she was out of Daybreak I by Little Hickory (another grandson of Peter McCue). And Moco's dam was by Joe Hancock, still another grandson of the estimable Peter. These are the kind of Quarter Horse bloodlines that come replete with built-in run.

By this time Mr. Jeffers had listened to a great deal of gas concerning the loudly touted advantages of judicious admixtures of Thoroughbred genes. But June was no fool. He took Murl L to the court of Three Bars, the most fashionable Thoroughbred between two oceans, and the following spring found Jeffers the owner of a chestnut colt he did not have to teach how to make like a rocket. Either June or his Mrs. must have known straight off they'd come up with a winner. They called him Mr. Bar None and sat back with confidence to wait for the jackpot.

The short-horse fraternity had spent three long years trying to dislodge

Go Man Go from his nest of coveted kudos atop the quarter pole, and it was beginning to look like a pretty hopeless task. It took the Jeffers colt to do it, and he did old June up proud. In his two-year-old form he was elected Champion Two-Year-Old Colt of 1957, when he girded his loins and really turned loose, being named in 1958 World's Champion Quarter Running Horse, Champion Stallion, and Champion Three-Year-Old Quarter Running Colt.

In two years of racing he made 35 starts, grabbing 22 firsts, 10 seconds, one third, and three fifths. He retired a champ and retired *sound*. Can anyone wonder that Oscar June Jeffers, now with a horse establishment numbering 450 acres, named this spread the Mr. Bar None Ranch!

Ten wins and eight seconds from 18 outings was the Bar None record during his initial track season. Renee Smelker very ably summed the whole thing up when she wrote in "Quarter Running Stallion Champions," (*Hoofs & Horns*, April through August, 1962): "Mr. Bar None had been campaigned hard for two full seasons when he went to Los Alamitos for the 1958 fall meeting. He had started 33 times . . . all but a few of his outings having been with the keenest of company. He had done everything that could be asked of a three-year-old—matching strides with the older stars and outrunning most of them at one time or another—and his breeder-owner-trainer, Oscar Jeffers, Jr., vowed he would retire the honest colt at the end of the Los Alamitos meeting. He'd finished fifth in his first two ventures, the Hard Twist and Clabbertown G, then rested for two weeks before tackling the stellar field invited into the Autumn Championship. No more fitting conclusion to a sparkling career could be wished for than his performance in the Championship. He won the $25,000 feature by three-quarters of a length over Vanetta Dee, Double Bid, Clabber's Win, Go Man Go, Dividend, Vandy's Flash and Clabber Bar."

In the stud he has been astonishingly successful, time, age and competition considered. At $1000 he stood in 1961 at Wagoner, Oklahoma, to outside mares, live foal guaranteed. In 1962 some results were noted from his first crop to race. His get came in one, two, three at the sixteenth running of the Oklahoma Futurity at Enid (purse $9200, net value to the winner $4600. Mr. Juniper Bar took it by two and one-half lengths, Kimaleta second by a head, Montecarlo Bar third by three-quarters. Time for the 330 was :17.2.

Mr. Juniper Bar, out of Red Juniper by Red Man (a sprinting son of Joe Hancock), has proved himself a stellar performer, being elected Champion Quarter Running Two-Year-Old Gelding of 1962, winning seven out of 11 starts, and three times placing. Kimaleta, out of Bonna Lita by Leo (best known son of Joe Reed II), currently holds all by herself the World's

Record at 330 (:16.7 under 124 pounds), established as a two-year-old in 1962. Other worthy get to Mr. Bar None's credit are Montecarlo Bar (AAA), Beaumont Bar (AAA), Buck's Bar None (AAA), Hank H. Bars (AAA), My Bar None (AAA), Running J. Bar (AAA); and the recent stakes winners (through March, 1963) Mr. Streaky Bar and Gates Bars, winners respectively ofthe Columbus Futurity and Live Oak Derby; Bar None Gates (AA), Canplay Bar (AA), Gates Bars (AA), Mr. Minnie Bars (AA), and Woody Bar (AA). And, except for the two stakes winners above noted, these are all from his first crop to reach the tracks—foals of 1960, 45 registered, 25 starters.

Mr. Bar None stands twelfth on the 1962 Leading Sires of Winners list with 13 winners of 37 races. He was at that time credited with 13 ROM qualifiers, eight of them AAA. He also appears as the twelfth name on the list of Leading Money-Earning Horses, 1949 through 1962. His son, Mr. Juniper Bar, stands nineteenth on the same list; among Leading Money-Earning Horses of 1962 Mr. Juniper Bar stands fourth, and was named Champion Quarter Running Two-Year-Old Gelding for the year.

Johnny Dial

A brown horse foaled July 1, 1948, Johnny Dial racked up the fastest time recorded by any stallion running during the first eleven years of organized Quarter Racing. A spectacular competitor, he was always the horse the rest had to beat. He had a heart that was bigger than all outdoors.

Few jockeys could ride him. Disposition had nothing to do with this; he got away so quick and with such a bone-jarring leap they simply could not stay with him. Part of this trouble, Ray Boland thinks, grew out of the fact that "in the gate he generally seemed half asleep." "He was very calm, not easily rattled," this Hepler neighbor declares. "Many's the time I've watched him stand there and yawn. But quick as those gates moved he'd be off like a bat out of Carlsbad. He always broke with a terrific burst of speed; he could not have moved faster had he been jet propelled."

During the years he was campaigned on the straightaways—1950 through 1953—Johnny Dial smashed the records of such outstanding sprint kings as Brigand and Tonto Bars Gill, outrunning not only the justly celebrated Barbara L (by Patriotic, TB), but such hard-knocking paragons as Black Easter Bunny, Clabbertown G, Miss Ruby, Tonta Lad, Aunt Amie, Mona Leta, Chappo S, Little Egypt, Dolly Mack, Dalhart Princess, Billy Van Dorn, Miss Tacubaya, Grey Question, Ed Heller, F. L. Kingbee, Barker's Pride, Legal Tender B, Monita, Stalking Gal, and a host of others of top-string caliber.

On September 23, 1950, he made his first official start in a trial for the New Mexico Futurity at Albuquerque, winning by one length—440 yards in :23.0 on a track described as good. Out of his first nine races he chalked up three wins, three seconds, one third, and was twice out of the chips. The last race of his third year, run through a flogging rain, was the California Quarter Horse Championship at 440, which he lost by three-quarters of a length in :23.0 to Black Easter Bunny, Johnny Dial banking $1000 for the place position. He was elected World's Champion Quarter Running Horse and Champion Stallion for 1952—the third stallion in thirteen years to attain this double honor. He ran five more races, coming out of the 1953 season with three wins and one place. As a race horse he was an unqualified and highly scintillating success. That year he topped the Leading Money Earners list. From 27 starts he won 14, placed six times, showed twice, and was but five times out of the money, running against the best of his day. He was the darling of the sport writers, a horse that brought forth their most treasured superlatives.

He was bred by Charles E. Hepler, Pinon, New Mexico. He was sired by Depth Charge (TB) out of Black Annie by Rodney, a son of Old D. J. Indeed, Black Annie, reputed to have been one of the greatest match-race mares ever to come out of Louisiana, was a double-bred Old D.J., this great foundation sire of modern Quarter Horses being her paternal grandsire and, additionally, the sire of her second dam. Black Annie is said to have run 30 races, never once being headed.

Through 1961 Johnny Dial had only 29 starters; 17 were winners, 19 Register of Merit qualifiers, and 10 AAA. On the 1962 Leading Sires of Winners list he stood fifteenth with 11 winners of 22 races from 16 starters. No other son of Depth Charge, to my knowledge, has approached Johnny Dial in performance. Some part of this edge must have come from his dam, Black Annie, whose worth has never been adequately acknowledged. Out of eight starters, foals of 1960, six qualified for the Register of Merit.

Until recently Johnny Dial was owned by the L. K. Newells of Sky Farm, Miami, Oklahoma. Mrs. Newell told me: "In addition to Johnny's grand conformation he has a truly marvelous disposition—calm, never flurried, good-natured as the day is long. In the last race Johnny ran he packed 132 pounds—and won. It has been confidently asserted he could be led to the post with a piece of twine."

Ray Boland told me over the 'phone: "Johnny's racing career really got started at Carlsbad, his first actual race being the Carlsbad Futurity, in which he beat the great mare Hy Dale (a former World's Record holder at 400 yards) by a head. He was only nineteen months old when he did it.

Any of the Stauss boys will tell you about him. When Johnny set the world Stallion Record at Bay Meadows he drew the No. 3 gate. There was some discussion between trainer Bill Grounds and Felix Durroseau (booked to ride him) about the track being plowed so deep along the inside there. Felix told Bill: 'Just pray that gate comes all the way open, and hold onto your hair!' And R. D. Hay has told me he never rode Johnny that he did not have the feeling he was on a winner."

The *Quarter Horse Journal* for April, 1963, carried the following spot news announcement: "Johnny Dial, the World Champion Quarter Running Horse for 1952, recently sold to Ed Honnen, owner of Quincy Farms, Denver."

Go Man Go

(440 yds., 1958 RUI 119 :21.8)

Bred by J. B. Ferguson of Wharton, Texas, Go Man Go was foaled in 1953. He was sired by Top Deck out of Lightfoot Sis by Very Wise (TB). Top Deck, a Thoroughbred, was by Equestrian (by Equipoise). Very Wise was a son of Wise Counsellor. Lightfoot Sis was out of Clear Track by Dun Horse out of Ella. The demonstrated performance of Go Man Go is of the very finest; no other stallion has ever been named World's Champion Quarter Running Horse three years in a row (1955, 1956, 1957). Evidence now on the ground appears to indicate a good possibility that he may also prove phenomenal in the stud.

In his hard-knocking career on the tracks he held many records, some of them were world's records. He was purchased by Frank Vessels and William H. Peckham for $125,000, at that time an all-time high price for a Quarter Horse.

He won the Pacific Coast Quarter Horse Association Futurity, September 24, 1953, going 330 yards in :17.2; the Clabbertown G in 1956, 1957, and 1958; the Los Alamitos Autumn Championship, December 21, 1957, going 440 yards in 22 seconds flat.

His first crop to go to the tracks, a very small one, were foals of 1958; from this the following achieved Register of Merit status: Go Billy Go (AAA); Angie Miss (AAA); Dynago Miss (AAA); Mr. Meyers (AAA); Polly Jane (AAA); Ima Lady Gay (AAA); and Go Dolly (AA). He has subsequently Hustling Man, AAA, winner of the 1962 All-American Futurity; Go Eagle Go, AAA; Christy Go, AAA; Go Lad Go, AAA; and Go Buddy Go, AA.

The following undated chart includes his record through his first three seasons.

Age	Starts	1st	2nd	3rd	AAA	AA	A	Earnings
2	10	9	1	0	9	1	0	$16,122
3	13	10	0	0	13	0	0	29,431
4	8	5	3	0	7	0	0	26,822
Total	31	24	4	0	29	1	0	72,373

Information passed along by Chief Johnson, of the Vessels Ranch, indicates total earnings of $93,862.

April issue of the Chartbook, 1955, when Go Man Go had had but four outings as a two-year-old, named him Horse of the Month, and said in part: "On three successive week-ends, the aptly named colt had breezed to the same number of wins, leaving all challengers a good margin of daylight at the wire. In his third start, he stepped off the 350-yard course in :18.2, just one-tenth of a second off the two-year-old colt record. Palleo Pete set the mark of :18.1 at Centennial last fall, late in his two-year-old career. In this race Go Man Go was home by a length and one-quarter in front of Clab-Win, a good Grade AA filly that had never been out of the money in five starts, with two wins to her credit.

"Although there are many differences of opinion as to the outstanding campaigner of the Los Alamitos meeting, there is little question as to the superiority displayed by this roan Top Deck colt in his age class. He has shown the ability to run in any kind of going and has evidenced Grade AAA ability in three of his four starts. Barring any of the unforeseen mishaps that are the constant plague of the race horse, Go Man Go shows enough speed to carry him through many successful seasons."

The Chartbook editor further stated: "His sire, Top Deck (TB), has, in two short years, become one of the leading sires of speed. Of sixteen qualifiers through 1954, all but two have run in Grade AA or AAA time. During the recent Los Alamitos meet his get were among the leading stake and feature event winners. Ridge Butler, a three-year-old son, captured the $20,000 PCQHRA Derby, and Moon Deck—a five-year-old son—won the coveted $10,000 Quarter Horse Championship. Other winners sired by Top Deck at this meeting were Mackay Boy, Skipdeck, Maydeck, Skippy's Baby and Black Dale. Top Deck's eight winning starters accumulated a total of fifteen wins."

The dam of Go Man Go, Lightfoot Sis by Very Wise (TB) has produced at least three other qualifiers for the Register of Merit. These are Bo Cue Blanc (AA) by Captains Courageous (sire of Miss Bank), Tee Beau (AA) by Babe Ruth, and the mare Miss Mackay, by Top Deck.

Go Man Go was the first two-year-old ever to become a world's champion. He was Champion Quarter Running Two-Year-Old Colt of 1956, Champion Quarter Running Three-Year-Old Colt of 1957; he is a former holder of the world and stallion records at 440 yards, a former co-holder of the world and stallion records at 350 yards and co-holder of several colt records, all of which have now been lowered. His stallion and world's record at 440 was :21.8—and there is no time to pick many posies at that speed. He held at one time the distinction of having won more money than any other individual in the history of Quarter Racing and is currently sixth on that list with a bank account of $86,151.32. In 1960 he stood at Gosselin Farm at a fee of $500. In 1963, at $2500, he stood at Vessels Ranch.

With 95 registered foals and rather newly in the stud, through 1962 he had but 17 starters, of which 12 qualified in AAA. I believe we can expect to hear a great deal more of him.

Depth Charge (TB)

Historically this stallion has been a producer of early speed; many of his two-year-old Thoroughbreds have been exceptionally fast, which led (as one of his owners, Mr. Gordon W. Shultz, has pointed out) to his being bred to Quarter mares.

A brown horse foaled in 1941, standing 15.3 and weighing 1370, **Depth Charge**, among Thoroughbreds, was Leading Sire of two-year-old winners in 1953; having out 23, second largest number since 1916. His Stakes Winners include Dark Charger, third-highest-weighted filly on Experimental Handicap—114 pounds—with three wins at three years, including the Miss Maryland Stakes, and seconds in Bahamas and Jasmine Stakes; Free Stride, El Encino Handicap, one mile and one-quarter in 2:00.4; Haunted, Cinderella Stakes, second in Hollywood Lassie Stakes; Spanish Charge, Duncan F. Kenner Stakes, third in Hialeah Juvenile Stakes; Encantadora, 11 wins, Silver Stakes, World Record for five furlongs—:57.; Baloma, Fair Grounds Debutante Stakes, equaling track record; Queen Margie, Hialeah Juvenile, Singing Tower Stakes at two, winner at 3 1956; Reticule, Futurity Special, second in Fair Grounds Debutante Stakes. Others placing in stakes include Marga, Depth O, Street Scene, Writer and Fleet Charge.

Depth Charge is a son of the great Bold Venture, winner of the Kentucky Derby and Preakness Stakes, unbeaten at three years and the only Kentucky Derby winner to sire more than one Derby winner. Bold Venture is the sire of Assault, winner of $675,470, Triple Crown, Horse of the Year in 1946; Middleground, winner of the Kentucky Derby, Hopeful, and

Belmont Stakes; and stakes winners Marcador, On Your Own, Incline, Woven Web, Pleasure Fund, Mild Retort, and Re-Torta.

Depth Charge's dam, Quickly, is also the dam of Count Fleet and Count Speed. She was the winner of 32 races, including Durham Plate, Barrie Plate, H. J. McIntire Memorial and Queensway Handicaps; and was third in the Long Beach Handicap. She was the dam of four winners, including Depth Charge; Count Fleet (16 wins, $250,300, the Kentucky Derby, Preakness, Belmont, Wood Memorial, Withers, Wakefield, Champagne Stakes—in world-record time for two-year-olds—Pimlico Futurity); and Count Speed (nine wins including Midway Handicap, and world's record for one and one-sixteenth miles (1:41).

Quickly's dam, Stephanie, was a winner at two years, the dam of six winners, including Quickly; Crout au Pot (35 wins, including Arlington Inaugural, Bryan and O'Hara Memorial Handicaps); Silver Spear II (Union Jack and Clearwell Stakes and Durban Summer Handicap); Poesy (winner four seasons and dam of stakes winner I Appeal); Great Haste (26 wins and placed in stakes); County Clare (Atlantic City Turf Cup, Boardwalk, Longfellow (first division), Magic City Handicaps, 11 wins, $137,450); Discernment (three wins at two and three years); Stepwisely (produced the stakes winner Bolero, 16 wins, $156,450, world records for six and seven furlongs, San Carlos, San Jose, Pacific, Preview, A. B. Spreckles Handicaps, Del Mar Derby).

Depth Charge has been on the Leading Sires of (Quarter Horse) Money Winners for a number of years; in 1955, for instance, he was eighth on this list, behind Three Bars (TB), Top Deck (TB), Leo, Vandy, Joe Reed II, War Bam (TB), and Hard Twist; in 1957 he was sixth, behind Three Bars, Leo, Top Deck, Joe Reed II, and Vandy; in 1959 he was seventh, behind Three Bars, Leo, Top Deck, Vandy, Joe Reed II, and Clabber II; in 1961 he was fifth, behind Three Bars, Top Deck, Vandy, and Leo.

He has been the sire of such spectacular sprinters as Johnny Dial, World's Champion Quarter Running Horse and Champion Stallion for 1952; Super Charge, Champion Quarter Running Two-Year-Old Colt for 1953; Brigand; That's My Boy; Dividend; Three Deep; and David Cox—to name those which come most easily to mind.

On the Leading Sires of ROM Qualifiers, 1945 through 1961, he stood seventh, behind Three Bars (TB), Leo, Top Deck, Vandy, Joe Reed II, and Piggin String (TB), and was followed by such sterling sires as Texas Dandy, Hard Twist, Clabber II, Flying Bob, My Texas Dandy, Barred, and Tonto Bars Gill.

Through 1962 Depth Charge has sired 90 registered foals, 78 of which have started, 53 of which have qualified, and 30 of which have achieved AAA rating.

He was purchased by Hugh Huntley because "we thought," Mr. Huntley said, "he was a top horse to cross with the right kind of Quarter mares. I bought a half interest in him from Audie Murphy in 1959, then bought the other half interest from Gordon Shultz toward the end of 1960."

Top Deck (TB)

A brown horse with irregular blaze extending into both nostrils and over upper lip, Top Deck was foaled on the King Ranch, April 28, 1945. From the Thoroughbred view he was bred in the purple, and was obviously the result of a carefully engineered attempt to produce a superior running horse. Celebrated names abound in his pedigree. His sire was Equestrian, and on top male line he goes straight to Domino through six generations. Equestrian's sire was Equipoise by Pennant (by Peter Pan by Commando). Ben Brush appears twice in Equestrian's fifth generation; Man O' War was the sire of his dam.

Top Deck's dam, River Boat, was out of Last Boat by *Sir Gallahad III. River Boat's sire was Chicaro by *Chicle out of Lady Hamburg II. In River Boat's sixth generation, Domino (through Commando) appears once and Ben Brush (through Broomstick) twice.

Top Deck, officially, was unraced; he was, however, run against time on the King Ranch by Earnest Lane (of Odom, Texas); this was before Bob Kleberg, Jr. got into the habit of shipping his prospects into the East. Mr. Lane has said he timed Top Deck at 220 yards "in :11.2 for a very fast start." He asked Mr. Kleberg to let him keep the horse at the ranch, as he thought he could break the Quarter Horse people. However, Mr. J. B. Ferguson has told me that after making the deal with Mr. Kleberg and the King Ranch, Lane moved the horse to his place at Odom where he came up lame after being worked several times. It was at this time that Mr. Lane began breeding him to outside mares. Mr. Ferguson says: "I bred one of my fastest mares named Skippy F to him and got his very first foal, Stardeck F, foaled in 1948. She won the Texas Futurity and ran on an associated track.

"We purchased Top Deck from Mr. Lane in 1954. The horse had a wonderful disposition, and at the time we purchased him he had a bog spavin on his left hind leg. We have continued to breed this stallion from time to time to a limited number of mares. Because of the unknown quality of his get, we were unable to get the top mares to breed to him because most of the breeders were inclined to breed to Three Bars, Depth Charge, and others, and they failed to recognize the fine breeding in this individual. I think there will be no question after the results of 1962. A grandson, by Go Man Go, named Hustling Man won well over $100,000 in futurities and other races. Another grandson, by Moon Deck, named Jet Deck won the large races at Los Alamitos plus the big futurities, winning in 1962 $138,341.91. I do not think this record of produce from one sire will be equaled in several generations, having reached approximately $250,000 in one season."

Top Deck, at Odom, Texas, under E. H. Lane's management, was standing at $300 "if mare is left thirty days or longer," or at $200 "if mare is bred and taken away." He stood in 1962 at $1000—"live foal guaranteed."

Top Deck is the sire of such outstanding sprinters as Go Man Go, World's Champion Quarter Running Horse for 1955, 1956, and 1957; Moon Deck, AAA and sire of Jet Deck, the 1962 Champion Quarter Running Stallion and Champion Quarter Running Two-Year-Old Colt; Mr. Mackay, AAA; Rebel Cause, AAA and 1961 Co-Champion Quarter Running Three-Year-Old Colt, and 1962 Champion Aged Stallion; Antler's Trade, AAA; and Ridge Butler, AAA, Champion Quarter Running Three-Year-Old Colt and top money-earning horse of 1955, which recently sold to Adams & Fenton for a reported price of $77,000.

According to the American Quarter Horse Association's published figures for 1962, Top Deck stands fourth on the list of Leading Sires of Register of Merit Qualifiers among sires of 23 or more, and third on the same list among sires with 11 or more AAA get. He stands second on the all-time Leading Sires of Money Earners list. He has sired 161 registered foals, 122 of which have started; from these he has gotten 72 qualifiers, 38 with AAA rating.

Index

447